The Eucharist in Medieval Can[illegible] Law

Thomas M. Izbicki presents a new examination of the relationship between the adoration of the sacrament and canon law from the twelfth to fifteenth centuries. The medieval Church believed Christ's glorified body was present in the Eucharist, the most central of the seven sacraments, and the Real Presence became explained as transubstantiation by university-trained theologians. Expressions of this belief included the drama of the elevated host and chalice, as well as processions with a host in an elaborate monstrance on the feast of Corpus Christi. These affirmations of doctrine were governed by canon law and promulgated by popes and councils; and liturgical regulations were enforced by popes, bishops, archdeacons, and inquisitors. Drawing on canon law collections and commentaries, synodal enactments, legal manuals, and books about ecclesiastical offices, Izbicki presents the first systematic analysis of the Church's teaching about the regulation of the practice of the Eucharist.

Thomas M. Izbicki is interim Associate University Librarian for Collection Development at University Libraries, Rutgers University. His publications focus on Pius II, Juan de Torquemada OP, Nicholas of Cusa, and the sacraments in canon law. His most recent book is *Religion, Power, and Resistance from the Eleventh to the Sixteenth Centuries: Playing the Heresy Card* (ed. Karen Bollermann, Thomas M. Izbicki, and Cary J. Niederman).

Elevation of the Host, attributed to Niccolò di ser Sozzo, Siena, mid-fourteenth century (New York, Columbia University, Barnard College Library, MS 1, p. 189).

The Eucharist in Medieval Canon Law

Thomas M. Izbicki
Rutgers University

CAMBRIDGE
UNIVERSITY PRESS

University Printing House, Cambridge CB2 8BS, United Kingdom

One Liberty Plaza, 20th Floor, New York, NY 10006, USA

477 Williamstown Road, Port Melbourne, VIC 3207, Australia

314-321, 3rd Floor, Plot 3, Splendor Forum, Jasola District Centre, New Delhi - 110025, India

79 Anson Road, #06-04/06, Singapore 079906

Cambridge University Press is part of the University of Cambridge.

It furthers the University's mission by disseminating knowledge in the pursuit of education, learning and research at the highest international levels of excellence.

www.cambridge.org
Information on this title: www.cambridge.org/9781107561809

First published 2015
First paperback edition 2020

A catalogue record for this publication is available from the British Library

Library of Congress Cataloging in Publication data
Izbicki, Thomas M.
The Eucharist in medieval canon law / Thomas M. Izbicki, Rutgers University.
pages cm
Includes bibliographical references and index.
ISBN 978-1-107-12441-7
1. Lord's Supper – History – Middle Ages, 600–1500.
2. Canon law – History – To 1500 – Sources. I. Title.
KBR3085.I99 2015
264′.36–dc23

2015016412

ISBN 978-1-107-12441-7 Hardback
ISBN 978-1-107-56180-9 Paperback

For my daughters Julie and Amelia.

Contents

Preface

> We ordain (statuimus) the sacrament of the Altar to be borne to the sick with due reverence, the priest having upon him at the least a surplice with a stole and light borne before him in a lantern with a bell, that the people may be stirred up to due reverence, which must be informed by the priest's wisdom, to kneel down, and the least humble to pray unto and honour the same, wheresoever it happen the king of Glory hidden in bread to be borne.[1]

> The substance of the mass consists in the words *This is my body* and *This is my blood* etc., which only a priest says.
>
> Baldus de Ubaldis[2]

This book began with a medieval manuscript in Baltimore. Manuscript 14 of the John Work Garrett Library of Johns Hopkins University contains a handwritten insert with a painted picture of the Dijon bleeding host, then housed at the Chartreuse of Champmol in Burgundy, accompanied by a brief text in French and two more in Latin. This find led to a conference paper and then to an article.[3] Research on the Dijon host led the author to the canon law pertaining to the Eucharist. Much has been written by scholars on medieval canon law, but comparatively little has been concerned with sacraments other than penance and matrimony. The Eucharist proved to be worthy of detailed study, also taking into account related evidence not just from theology but also from art, liturgy, and devotional practices. The writers on liturgy were especially useful. One, Lothair of Segni, was an architect of the canon law as Pope Innocent III. Others, Sicard of Cremona and Guillelmus Durantis Senior, themselves were canon lawyers.

[1] *Lyndwood's Provinciale: The Text of the Canons Therein Contained, Reprinted from the Translation Made in 1534*, ed. J. V. Bullard and H. Chalmer Bell (London, 1929), 104.

[2] *Ad tres priores libros decretalium commentaria* (Lyon, 1585; Aalen, 1970), fol. 282ra.

[3] Thomas M. Izbicki, "The Bleeding Host of Dijon: Its Place in the History of Eucharistic Devotion," in *Saluting Aron Gurevich: Essays in History, Literature and Other Related Subjects*, ed. Yelena Mazour-Matusevich and Alexandra S. Korros (Leiden, 2010), 227–246.

The focus of the book is the discipline of the Eucharist, including enactments about sacramental practice, interpretation of those texts, diffusion of their instructions to clergy and laity, and their enforcement. Attention also is given to parochial practice where useful evidence exists. Among the questions addressed are: How did medieval canon law take account of belief in the Real Presence of Christ in the Eucharist, especially in the twelfth and thirteenth centuries, when the language of transubstantiation was becoming common? Did the subtle theology of the Schools get filtered down to parish priest and, through him, to the men and women of the individual parish? What did the authorities think the parish priest, who might be uneducated himself, needed to know? What did bishops want their subordinates to teach as doctrine, and at what level of sophistication? What practices were approved or disapproved on the basis of belief in Christ's corporeal presence? Answers to these questions explain what resources a parish needed in order to celebrate mass, give communion, reserve the Eucharist for the sick, carry viaticum to sickbeds, and (eventually) venerate the consecrated host in processions on the feast of Corpus Christi. They also determined what a good priest was expected to do and for what failings a bad priest could be punished, usually by an archdeacon.

In all cases, canon law functioned as a form of disciplinary theology. Sacramental theology was to be affirmed by correct practices, including the gestures and prayers of the laity. This theology was developed over several centuries, beginning with the Carolingian age, when Paschasius Radbertus wrote about a very literal presence of Christ in the sacrament. This theology became a matter of controversy and then of dogma from the eleventh century onward. The implications of this belief in the Real Presence were explained eventually in terms of Aristotelian ideas of the physical universe. Theological doctrine and Aristotle were made to fit together, often with great subtlety, including a sense that the material universe might serve as a medium for the divine presence.[4] This emphasis, in turn, must be seen as directly related to the increasing attention to Christ's humanity evident at least from the twelfth century onward, not just in theology but in widespread devotions. Imitation of Christ, a concept with patristic roots, entered into ideas of priesthood and polity, just as it did into devotional theology.[5] These developments were parallel to a

[4] For a brief survey, see Gary Macy, *Treasures from the Storehouse: Medieval Religion and the Eucharist* (Collegeville, Minn., 1999). On materiality, see from different viewpoints Marilyn McCord Adams, *Some Later Medieval Theologies of the Eucharist: Thomas Aquinas, Giles of Rome, Duns Scotus and William of Ockham* (Oxford, 2012); Caroline Walker Bynum, *Christian Materiality: An Essay on Religion in Late Medieval Europe* (Boston, 2011).

[5] Giles Constable, "The Ideal of the Imitation of Christ," in Constable, *Three Studies in Medieval Religious and Social Thought* (Cambridge, 1995), 145–248. This development, in turn, allowed the identification of the pope as Vicar of Christ, Jesus's representative on

desire for theological reassurance and practical succor similar to beliefs about the utility of relics, together with a fear that magical acts could be worked using stolen hosts.[6] Dependence on such physical signs could be seen by some theologians and prelates as undermining reliance on faith, even leaving aside the frauds of some keepers of "wonder hosts" and other supposed relics. Nonetheless, belief in the benefits of the Eucharistic presence extended to ideas of spiritual communion by sight and a conviction that outrages committed on consecrated hosts might be requited with divine vengeance.[7]

A sixteenth-century version of Lyndwood's *Provinciale*, translating a statute of John Peccham, archbishop of Canterbury, described viaticum processions as bearing "the king of Glory hidden in bread."[8] In such language, both clergy and laity affirmed the corporeal presence of the Lord in the consecrated host; but how the former taught the latter to honor that miraculous presence is an important part of this inquiry. In addition, there were challenges of inspecting and authenticating or disproving supposed sacramental miracles of the sort mentioned earlier. Wonder hosts that bled or manifested human flesh, often in the form of a child, might be regulated to prevent some clergy from defrauding the laity and to discourage substituting "miraculous" objects for true faith. Nonetheless, host cults like that at Wilsnack met a need for reassurance among many of the faithful that ideas of invisible presence might not provide.[9]

The available sources for medieval Eucharistic theology and sacramental practice are many and varied. The most important source material of this project has remained, however, the canon law broadly construed.[10] The major normative texts, conciliar, papal, and patristic, of earlier periods were included in collections of canons. These eventually were represented in the

earth, see Michele Maccarrone, *Vicarius Christi: Storia del titolo papale* (Romae, 1952). The implication for the priest as Christ's representative will be addressed in Chapter 1 of this book.

6 G. J. C. Snoek, *Medieval Piety from Relics to the Eucharist: A Process of Mutual Interaction* (Leiden, 1995).

7 Miri Rubin, *Gentile Tales: The Narrative Assault on Late Medieval Jews* (New Haven, Conn., 1999).

8 *Lyndwood's Provinciale*, 104; Lyndwood, *Provinciale seu Constitutiones*, 249, "ut populus ad reverentiam debitam excitetur, qui ad prosterendum se, vel ad adorandum saltem humiliter informetur Sacerdotali prudentia, ubicunque Regem Gloriae sub panis latibulo evenerit deportari."

9 Morimichi Watanabe, "The German Church Shortly before the Reformation: Nicolaus Cusanus and the Veneration of the Bleeding Hosts at Wilsnack," in *Reform and Renewal in the Middle Ages and the Renaissance: Studies in Honor of Louis Pascoe, S.J.*, ed. Thomas M. Izbicki and Christopher M. Bellitto (Leiden, 2000), 208–223.

10 For a general introduction to the topic, see James A. Brundage, *Medieval Canon Law* (London, 1995).

Decretum or *Concord of Discordant Canons* of Gratian. Beginning in the mid-twelfth century, this was the textbook of the faculties of canon law in the new-born universities. These canons were commented at length by professors, and their students carried the law to the far corners of Europe. New conciliar canons and papal letters were added to the mix, eventually in collections authorized by the papacy. Most important were the decrees of the Fourth Lateran Council (1215). These conciliar decrees and the growing body of papal decretals were taught in the classroom and commented in written works, some of which eventually were printed. The inquiry, however, could not remain at the level of doctrine. Legal norms propounded at the highest levels were filtered down to the local level through local councils and synods. The Lateran norms for pastoral care, in particular, were implemented by local councils and synods during the thirteenth and early fourteenth centuries.[11] New enactments, like those implementing the feast of Corpus Christi on the local level, were issued throughout Europe well into the sixteenth century.

The messages of popes, bishops, and academic canonists must be assessed in the light of the realities experienced by local priests and the laity. These norms were transmitted by synods and enforced by bishops and archdeacons, especially through visitations.[12] Additional guidance was provided in manuals for pastors, confessors, and inquisitors.[13] All of these must be consulted to show how norms were not just received but enforced down to the parish level, even in the face of dissent. Excerpts from some of these sources have been offered in translation. These are the author's own unless otherwise indicated. An additional problem is presented by changes in writings about the learned law. Late medieval and early modern canonists often were uninterested in the sacraments or simply repeated what their predecessors had said verbatim. Only after the Reformation challenged the system of seven sacraments did a new form of liturgical regulation appear. The decrees of the Council of Trent reaffirmed the sacraments, and Tridentine reforms were adopted locally as far from Rome as Mexico and Peru. These decrees and the decisions of the post-Tridentine Roman curia, especially the Congregation of Rites, made the medieval texts less relevant to teaching and pastoral care. That form of sacramental discipline remained largely intact until the Second Vatican Council introduced liturgical renewal leading to changes in rites and paraliturgical practices.

[11] On synodal statutes as a genre, see Odette Pontal, *Les statuts synodaux* (Turnhout, 1975).

[12] Noël Coulet, *Les visites pastorals* (Turnhout, 1977).

[13] Antoine Dondaine, "Le manuel de l'Inquisiteur," *Archivum Fratrum Praedicatorum* 17 (1947), 280–312; Pierre Michaud-Quantin, *Sommes de casuistique et manuels de confession au Moyen Age (XII–XVI siècles)* (Louvain, 1962).

Note that the quantity of the material exceeds the possibility of exploring every issue in detail. Some matters, like the mass as sacrifice and the fraction of the host before communion, although important, receive relatively little attention. Others, like the regulations for vessels, vestments, and altar linens, are all but omitted. Even penance for loss of a host, found in one of the penitentials, has been omitted as tangential to the main argument.[14] It has not been possible, moreover, to examine every bit of surviving evidence about the celebration of the mass. Thus the author was not able to review many of the defects that might be found in the celebration of the mass by a negligent priest, and less is said about the failings of priest and parish in caring for the church and its furnishings. The interested researcher can find these matters treated in the same sources employed by the author.

This book could not have been written without the help of many other persons. Elizabeth Friend-Smith of Cambridge University Press guided this project from its inception. Outside readers provided useful recommendations for the development of the manuscript. Thomas Turley; Gary Macy; Ian Levy; Gerald Christianson; Chris Brennan; Joachim Stieber; Mary Sommar; Anders Winroth; Ryan Greenwood; and my wife, Margaret Schaus, have played roles in this project. Several libraries have provided access to rare texts or made loans of books and articles relevant to this project. These include the libraries of Rutgers University, the University of Pennsylvania, Princeton University, Johns Hopkins University, Bryn Mawr College, and the New Brunswick Theological Seminary. Manuscript books were consulted at the Vatican Film Library of St. Louis University, and the digital facsimile of the commentary of Paulus de Liazariis was provided by the Special Collections Department of the Hessburgh Library, University of Notre Dame. Nonetheless, responsibility for this project remains entirely mine.

[14] *Medieval Handbooks of Penance: A Translation of the Principal "libri poenitentiales" and Selections from Related Documents*, ed. John T. McNeill and Helena M. Gamer (New York, 1938), 111, 114, 253, 275.

Citations to texts of canon law

All texts from the *Corpus Iuris Canonici* are cited from this edition: *Corpus Iuris Canonici*, ed. Emil Friedberg, 2 vols. (Leipzig, 1879; Graz, 1959).

The *Decretum* of Gratian

The Distinctions (*Distinctiones*) are cited in this form: Distinction and chapter (e.g., D.40 c.6).

The Cases (*Causae*) are cited in this form: Case, question, and chapter (e.g., C.24 q.1 c.6).

The *Tract on the Consecration of a Church* (*Tractatus de consecratione ecclesiae*) is cited in this form: Distinction and chapter (e.g., De cons. D.2 c.8).

The Decretal collections are cited by book, title, and chapter

Decretals of Gregory IX or Liber extra (e.g., X 5.38.12).

The *Liber sextus* of Boniface VIII (e.g., VI. 1.1.1).

The Constitutions of Clement V, Constitutiones clementinae or Clementines (e.g., Clem. 1.3.5).

The Ordinary Gloss [Glossa ordinaria] to a collection is cited in this form:

Ordinary Gloss at [text]. The individual glossed word or phrase in the text is indicated, where necessary, by v. [*verbum* or word] (e.g., Ordinary Gloss at D.40 c.6 v. Nisi).

The *Quinque Compilationes Antiquae*, the most important compilations of decretals before the *Liber extra*, are cited by collection, book, title, and chapter

For example, c. *Firmiter credimus* in *Compilatio quarta* is cited as 4 Comp. 1.1.1.

Note on commentators

Decretists

A Decretist was a commentator on Gratian's *Concordantia discordantium canonum* or *Decretum*, the fundamental textbook of canon law in the twelfth- and early thirteenth-century universities. These canonists composed glosses on the texts and occasionally wrote systematic treatments of the *Decretum*, usually called *summae*. Among the earliest of these writers were Paucapalea, Rufinus, and Stephen of Tournai. Later, toward the turn of the thirteenth century, Simon of Bisignano, Sicard of Cremona, and Huguccio of Pisa distinguished themselves. The work of the Decretists culminated in the Ordinary Gloss on the *Decretum*, composed by Johannes Teutonicus and later updated by Bartholomew of Brescia. The canonists concentrated thereafter on the decretals of the popes.

Decretalists

A Decretalist was a commentator on the official letters or decretals of the popes, especially those issued in the late twelfth and thirteenth centuries. These were collected at first by individual doctors but eventually by the papacy. The most important of these collections, the *Decretals of Gregory IX* or *Liber extra* (1234), became the main textbook of canon law, displacing Gratian's *Decretum*. The Ordinary Gloss on the *Gregorian Decretals* was composed by Bernard of Parma in the mid-thirteenth century. Among the most influential Decretalists were, in the thirteenth century, Pope Innocent IV, Geoffrey of Trani, Henricus de Segusio (Hostiensis), and, in the early fourteenth century, Johannes Andreae. They composed *summae* and commentaries that dominated the study of canon law later.

Canonists and collections

Anselm of Lucca (d. 1086) – Anselm succeeded his uncle as bishop of Lucca, when the latter became Pope Alexander II (r. 1061–1073). Anselm was a strong supporter of the Gregorian Reform. His collection of canons both supported reform and assembled important texts related to the sacraments.

Antoninus of Florence (d. 1459) – Antoninus, a Dominican of the Observant movement, was made archbishop of Florence in 1446. His works designed for pastoral care include a monumental *Summa moralis* and three manuals for parish priests and friars serving as confessors, each of which was written in Italian or translated from the Latin. Both theology and canon law supported his advice on pastoral care.

Antonius de Butrio (d. 1408) – Antonius taught Francesco Zabarella and commented on the *Gregorian Decretals*. His commentary primarily reflects received opinion on sacramental practice. Antonius also was involved, until his death, in unsuccessful efforts to end the Great Western Schism (1378–1417).

Astesanus (d. c. 1330) – Astesanus, a canonist from Asti in northern Italy, became a Franciscan. His *Summa Astesana* was a massive guide for confessors and others engaged in pastoral care, expounding legal and theological norms for their instruction.

Bartholomew of Brescia (d. 1258) – Bartholomew taught canon law at Bologna and revised the Ordinary Gloss of Johannes Teutonicus on Gratian's *Decretum*. This updated version of the glossed *Decretum*, with references to the *Gregorian Decretals*, was the most widely read after it appeared.

Bartholomew of Exeter (d. 1184) – Bartholomew, a canonist, was bishop of Exeter from 1161 to his death. The penitential he prepared for his diocese made extensive use of older texts, representing ideas of pastoral care preceding those evolved at the University of Paris and legislated by the Fourth Lateran Council (1215).

Bernard Gui (d. 1331) – Gui, a Dominican, served as an inquisitor in the south of France between 1307 and 1323. His writings included the

Practica inquisitionis hereticae pravitatis (*Practice of Investigating Heretical Depravity*). This manual included discussions of errors about the sacraments and formulas for renouncing those errors.

Bernard of Parma (d. 1266) – Bernard studied and taught at Bologna. William Durant the Elder was among his students. His commentary on the *Gregorian Decretals* became the Ordinary Gloss, read by all later canonists.

Burchard of Worms (d. 1025) – Burchard, a German noble, became bishop of Worms in 1000. He is best known for his *Decretum*, an influential collection of canon law texts including several related to the sacraments. Book 19, On Penance, became known as the Corrector; and it included evidence for abuses in past Eucharistic practice.

Collection in Seventy-Four Titles – The *Collection in Seventy-Four Titles* or *Diversorum sententiae patrum* was an early collection supporting the Gregorian Reform. It is believed to have been a source for the collection of Anselm of Lucca, but is offers little of the material Anselm included in his books about the sacraments.

Compilatio prima, or *Breviarium extravagantium* (c. 1190) – Bernard of Pavia compiled this collection containing older canons together with later papal texts. Also included are the canons of the Third Lateran Council (1179), held by Pope Alexander III.

Compilatio quarta (c. 1216) – The collection contains the later decretals of Innocent III. It also includes the canons of the Fourth Lateran Council.

Compilatio quinta (c. 1226) – Honorius III ordered creation of this collection, which includes his decretal *Sane*, authorizing the elevation of the host.

Compilatio tertia (c.1210) – This collection was compiled by Peter of Benevento on the instructions of Innocent III. It contains the decretals from the early years of Innocent III's pontificate. The most influential commentary on this compilation was composed by Johannes Teutonicus.

Decretales Pseudo-Isidorianae or *False Decretals* – This collection combined genuine with forged texts, many supporting the papacy. It was composed c. 830 during the Carolingian period. Some of the oldest texts concerning the discipline of ecclesiastical rites appear in it.

Deusdedit (d. 1097/1100) – Deusdedit, a Benedictine, was made a cardinal by Pope Gregory VII (r. 1073–1085). His collection of canons was another to support the Gregorian Reform. Like the *Collection in Seventy-Four Titles*, it is more concerned with simony than with sacramental practice.

Francesco Zabarella (d. 1417) – Zabarella taught canon law until, as a teacher in Padua, he became involved in politics. The Pisan pope John

XXIII made him a cardinal in 1410, and he participated in the Councils of Pisa (1409) and Constance (1414 to his death). Among his writings were a commentary on the *Gregorian Decretals* and a *consilium* on resolving the Great Western Schism (1378–1417).

Geoffrey of Trani (d. 1245) – Geoffrey had a career teaching law before undertaking a career in the Roman curia. He died as a cardinal at the First Council of Lyon. His most influential work was a *summa* on the titles of the *Gregorian Decretals*.

Gratian – The *Concordia discordantium canonum* is traditionally attributed to Gratian of Bologna, described as a Bolognese monk, with an estimated date of 1130. The collection actually was created in multiple stages over several years. The final version included the *Tractatus de consecratione ecclesiae*, an exposition of the canon law of the sacraments.

Guido de Monte Rocherii or de Monte Rochen (c. 1331) – Guido was a priest in Teruel in the Crown of Aragon. His *Handbook for Curates* was grounded in both theology and law. It was widely diffused both in manuscripts and print, which made it one of the most important of medieval pastoral manuals.

Henricus de Segusio (Hostiensis) (d. 1270/1271) – Henricus de Segusio both studied and taught law before serving King Henry III of England. He then entered the Roman curia, becoming cardinal bishop of Ostia in 1261. His chief writings were a *summa* on the titles of the *Gregorian Decretals* and a commentary on that collection, the latter including extensive discussions of sacramental discipline.

Huguccio of Pisa (d. 1210) – After a career in canon law, Huguccio became bishop of Ferrara in 1190. His massive *summa* on the *Decretum* showed considerable creativity. His ideas on the Eucharist included an argument that the water in the chalice became Christ's phlegm, which was rejected by Innocent III.

Innocent III, pope (r. 1198–1216) – Lothar of Segni, a Paris-trained theologian, wrote on the sacraments before his election to the papacy. As pope, Innocent was the source of many influential decretals, including the decretal *Cum Marthae*, focused on the Real Presence in the Eucharist. His Fourth Lateran Council (1215) issued several canons concerned with the sacraments and pastoral care, including one requiring confession and communion at Eastertide, the Easter Duty that remains an expectation for all Roman Catholics.

Innocent IV, pope (r. 1243–1254) – Sinibaldo Fieschi, a canonist, became a cardinal in 1227 and pope in 1243. He convened the First Council of Lyon (1245), which both tried to depose the Emperor Frederick II and issued decrees later included in the *Liber sextus* of Boniface VIII. His *Apparatus in quinque libros decretalium* was one of the most influential commentaries on the *Liber extra*, although it paid minimal attention to the mass and the Eucharist.

Ivo of Chartres (d. 1115) – Ivo became bishop of Chartres in 1190 and held that see until his death. Ivo supported reform and took a serious interest in sacramental theology and practice. His *Decretum*, an extensive canonistic collection, begins with a preface discussing the methodology for the interpretation of the canons.

Johannes Andreae (d. 1348) – This Bolognese canonist remained a layman, married with children. His writings on canon law included an extensive commentary on the *Gregorian Decretals*, summarizing previous teachings, and the Ordinary Gloss on the *Constitutions of Clement V*.

Johannes Teutonicus (d. 1245) – Johannes studied canon law at Bologna and later taught there. He compiled the Ordinary Gloss on Gratian's *Decretum*. Johannes also commented on the canons of the Fourth Lateran Council and *Compilatio tertia*.

John of Acton (d. 1350) – An Oxford-trained canon lawyer, John held ecclesiastical positions in the diocese of Lincoln. His commentary on the constitutions of the legates Otto and Ottobono was widely distributed within the ecclesiastical province of Canterbury.

John of Burough or Johannes de Burgo – John of Burough, a Cambridge-educated theologian, was the chancellor of the university. He composed the manual, *Pupilla oculi* (*c.* 1385), a revision of William of Pagula's *Occulus sacerdotis*. His manual brought Scholastic theology, as well as canon law, to the instruction of pastors in their duties.

John of Erfurt – This Franciscan composed a manual for confessors that comprised among others expositions of the things every priest should know, including in sacramental practice. The text was composed in the late thirteenth century and revised c. 1302.

John of Freiburg (d. 1314) – John, a Dominican friar, composed a revision of Raymond of Peñafort's *Summa de casibus conscientiae*. His revisions brought the theology of Thomas Aquinas into its instructions to pastors and confessors. An alphabetical version, the *Summa Pisanella*, was prepared by Bartholomew of San Concordio of Pisa.

Juan de Torquemada (d. 1458) – Torquemada, a Dominican theologian, was promoted to the cardinalate because he defended Pope Eugenius IV (1431–1447) at the Council of Basel (1431–1449). His commentary on Gratian's *Decretum* defended the papacy. Its exposition of the *Tractatus de consecratione* included a rare critique of Hussite Eucharistic errors in a work of canon law.

Nicholas de Tudeschis (Panormitanus) (d. 1445) – Tudeschi, a Benedictine monk, studied canon law with Francesco Zabarella. He pursued a career teaching and composing legal works, including a massive commentary on the *Gregorian Decretals*. Nicholas later served Pope Eugenius IV as an envoy to the Council of Basel; and then he represented Alphonso V of Aragon in the same assembly, being named a cardinal by the antipope Felix V.

Nicholas Eimeric (d. 1399) – Nicholas, a Dominican, served as an inquisitor in the territories of the Crown of Aragon. His controversial actions, including attacks on the Eucharistic beliefs of the local Franciscans, led to two periods of enforced exile. Nicholas's *Directorium Inquisitorum* (c. 1377) attacked both condemned heresies and witchcraft. It was widely circulated and was republished with extensive additions by Francisco Peña in 1578.

Nicholas of Ausimo or Osimo (d. 1453) – Nicholas, a Franciscan Observant, had studied law in Bologna. He brought his background in theology and law to a supplement to the *Summa Pisanella*, a revision of the *summa* by John of Freiburg.

Nicholas of Cusa (d. 1464) – Cusanus, a German, studied canon law at the University of Padua and rose to the cardinalate. As papal legate in Germany (1450–1452) and bishop of Brixen (1450–1464), he promoted reforms in pastoral practice. His attack on the bleeding host cult at Wilsnack was not supported by Pope Nicholas V (r. 1447–1455).

Otto, cardinal legate (d. 1250/1251) – Otto appeared in England as a papal legate in 1237. His legatine constitutions were important to the English church and were coupled in transmission with those of Cardinal Ottobono. Among their focal points were matters of liturgy and the sacraments.

Ottobono, cardinal legate, briefly Pope Adrian V (d. 1276) – Ottobono was a nephew of Pope Innocent IV, who made him a cardinal in 1251. He was papal legate in England from 1265 to 1268, attempting to mediate between King Henry III (r. 1215–1272) and Simon de Montfort. His legatine constitutions and those of Cardinal Otto were glossed by John of Acton.

Panormia – This widely diffused collection of canon law was created in the late eleventh or early twelfth century. It once was attributed to Ivo of Chartres, but that attribution has been discarded. It contains extensive excerpts from theological discussions of the Real Presence in the Eucharist.

Paucapalea – Paucapalea, a twelfth-century canonist (c. 1140), is believed to have been the first commentator on Gratian's *Decretum*. His brief glosses on the *Tractatus de consecratione* were the earliest comments on the sacramental teachings in that section of the *Decretum*.

Paulus de Liazariis (d. 1356) – Paulus, a student of Johannes Andreae, wrote an extensive commentary on the *Constitutions of Clement V*.

Raymond of Peñafort (d. 1275) – Raymond, a canonist and Dominican friar, compiled the *Liber extra* or *Gregorian Decretals* for Pope Gregory IX (r. 1227–1241). The collection, arranged in five books on judges, judgment, the clergy, marriage, and crimes, was subdivided into topical titles containing the canons of the Fourth Lateran Council (1215) and major papal decretals, especially those of Innocent III. Raymond also composed a *Summa de casibus conscientiae,* an influential guide for hearing confessions and providing pastoral care.

Regino of Prüm (d. 915) – Regino, a Benedictine monk, became abbot of Prüm and then of Saint Martin's, Trier. His book *De ecclesiasticis disciplinis* combined questions about discipline and rites to be put to parish priests with canons supporting those rules of behavior. This work was employed by Burchard of Worms when compiling his *Decretum.*

Rufinus (d. 1192) – Rufinus taught canon law in Bologna in the twelfth century. Stephen of Tournai was among his pupils. Rufinus's *summa* on the *Decretum* (c. 1160) was widely influential.

Sicard of Cremona (d. 1215) – Sicard studied canon law and eventually became bishop of Cremona (1185). His commentary on Gratian's *Decretum* drew heavily on the work of Simon of Bisignano. His *Mitralis* was an extensive discussion of liturgical offices.

Simon of Bisignano – Simon taught canon law in Bologna in the 1170s. He wrote a commentary on the *Decretum* of Gratian; however, little is known otherwise.

Stephen of Tournai (d. 1203) – A pupil of Rufinus in Bologna, Stephen later became bishop of Tournai. The commentary *Fecit Moyses tabernaculum* on the *Tractatus de consecratione* was later attached to Stephen's *summa* on the *Decretum.*

Thomas of Chobham (d. 1233 / 1236) – Thomas studied in Paris under Peter the Chanter. He served in the diocese of Salisbury and composed a *Summa de poenitentia,* which gave practical advice to priests grounded in canon law.

William Durant the Elder (d. 1296) – William, a Frenchman, studied canon law under Bernard of Parma in Bologna. He served the papacy, becoming bishop of Mende in 1286. William wrote on legal procedure and composed an extensive exposition of the liturgy drawing on the works of Innocent III and Sicard of Cremona.

William Lyndwood (d. 1446) – William Lyndwood, who had studied canon law at Cambridge and Oxford, served both Church and Crown. He became a bishop in 1442. His *Provinciale* collected the canon law of the province of Canterbury, arranged on the lines of the *Gregorian Decretals* and glossed.

William of Pagula (d. 1332) – Although William of Pagula had a doctorate in canon law from Oxford University, he spent his remaining years as a parish priest. William's most important work was the *Occulus sacerdotis* or *Priest's Eye*. This manual instructed priests in the essentials of sacramental theology and the discipline expected in the performance of pastoral duties.

Abbreviations

Constitutiones Concilii Quarti Lateranensis	*Constitutiones Concilii Quarti Lateranensis una cum commentariis glossatorum*, ed. Antonio García García (Città del Vaticano: Biblioteca Apostolica Vaticana, 1981).
Corpus Iuris Canonici	*Corpus Iuris Canonici*, ed. Emil Friedberg, 2 vols. (Leipzig: Tauchnitz, 1879; Graz: Akademische Druck- u. Verlagsanstalt, 1959).
Councils & Synods	*Councils & Synods with Other Documents Relating to the English Church*, 2 vols. in 4, vol. 1, ed. Dorothy Whitelock, Martin Brett, and Christopher N. L. Brooke (Oxford: Clarendon Press, 1981); vol. 2, ed. F. M. Powicke and C. R. Cheney (Oxford: Clarendon Press, 1964).
Decrees of the Ecumenical Councils	*Decrees of the Ecumenical Councils*, ed. Norman P. Tanner, 2 vols. (Washington, D.C.: Georgetown University Press, 1990).
Handbook for Curates	Guido de Monte Rocherii, *Handbook for Curates*, trans. Anne T. Thayer (Washington, D.C.: Catholic University of America Press, 2011).
Hinschius	*Decretales Pseudo-Isidorianae et capitula Angilramni*, ed. Paul Hinschius (Leipzig: Tauchnitz, 1863; Aalen: Scientia Verlag, 1963).
Lyndwood, *Provinciale seu Constitutiones*	William Lyndwood, *Provinciale (seu Constitvtiones Angliæ) continens constitutiones provinciales quatuordecim*

archiepiscoporum Cantuariensium, viz. á Stephano Langtono ad Henricum Chichleium (Oxford, 1679; Farnborough: Gregg, 1968).

Mansi — *Sacrorum Conciliorum nova et amplissima collectio*, ed. Giovan Domenico Mansi et al., 53 vols. (Paris: H. Welter, 1901–1927; Graz: Akademische Druck- u. Verlangsanstalt, 1961).

Pastors and the Care of Souls — *Pastors and the Care of Souls in Medieval England*, ed. John Shinners and William J. Dohar (Notre Dame, Ind.: University of Notre Dame Press, 1998).

PL — Migne's *Patrologia Latina* accessed via the *Patrologia Latina Database*.

Das Sendhandbuch des Regino von Prüm — Regino of Prüm, *Das Sendhandbuch des Regino von Prüm*, ed. F. W. H. Wasserschleben and Wilfried Hartmann (Darmstadt: Wissenschaftliche Buchgesellschaft, 2004).

Repertorium poenitentiariae Germanicum — *Repertorium poenitentiariae Germanicum: Verzeichnis der in den Supplikenregistern der Pönitentiarie Kirchen, und Orte des Deutschen Reiches*, 8 vols. (Tübingen: Niemeyer, 1996–2012).

Synodicon Hispanum — *Synodicon Hispanum*, ed. Antonio Garcia y Garcia and Francisco Cantelar Rodriguez, 11 vols. (Madrid: Biblioteca de Autores Cristianos, 1981–2013).

Introduction: the sacraments in medieval canon law

The twelfth century saw theologians define the sacraments proper apart from other rituals. These rites were supposed to be effective signs, leading the believer to salvation and the conferral of grace by God. The sacraments were identified eventually as seven in number: baptism, confirmation, penance, the Eucharist, holy orders, matrimony, and extreme unction. Some, especially baptism, were shared by all Christians, beginning with infancy. Matrimony was the sacrament only the laity was expected to experience, whereas holy orders defined the priesthood, including the episcopate, as the most important ecclesiastical office. Only priests properly ordained could consecrate the Eucharist or absolve sinners, and only bishops could ordain new priests. Baptism and confirmation, as well as holy orders, were sacraments that could not be repeated. The others, even extreme unction, could be repeated as needed. Penance and reception of the Eucharist were linked, with the one preceding the other at least once a year.[1]

The formulation of a systematic idea of seven sacraments was contemporary with the creation of a widely diffused body of canon law taught to generations of students. The most important book in this development was the *Decretum* or *Concordantia discordantium canonum* of Gratian. That collection took shape beginning in the early twelfth century (to c. 1130), and it became the first textbook of canon law in the newly born medieval universities. Gratian tried to bring harmony to more than a millennium of authoritative texts that often did not exactly agree with one another on issues of law and ritual. When the *Decretum* attained its vulgate form, it had three major parts: the *Distinctiones*, a treatise on law; the *Causae*, a set of hypothetical cases, including a tract on penance; and a tract on sacramental law, the *Tractatus de consecratione ecclesiae*. The *Causae* seem to have been the core of the collection in its earliest form. The *De consecratione* probably

[1] This scheme is not found in *Hugonis de Sancto Victore De sacramentis Christiane fidei*, ed. Rainer Berndt (Münster, 2008). It is, however, found in book IV of the *Sentences* of Peter Lombard; see *Magistri Petri Lombardi Parisiensis episcopi Sententiae in IV libris distinctae*, 3rd ed., 2 vols. in 3 (Grottaferrata, 1971–1981) and *The Sentences*, 4: *The Doctrine of Signs*, trans. Giulio Silano (Toronto, 2010).

was added later, part of the second major version of the collection. The last changes made included the insertion of additional texts later canonists thought too important to omit, the *paleae* or "chaff." The *De consecratione*, divided into five distinctions, focused on churches and the central rites performed in them: the Eucharist, the focus of Western sacramental theology, and baptism, the gateway to the other sacraments.[2]

The *De consecratione* exposed students of canon law to such theological concepts as the Real Presence of Christ in the consecrated Eucharistic elements, bread and watered wine. It also reflected the concern of the Gregorian reformers with simony, the buying and selling of spiritual gifts and rites, as well as their opposition to clerical concubinage and advocacy of papal primacy. Other portions of the *Decretum* dealt with marriage, penance, and the proper conduct of the clergy in all aspects of their calling.[3] Gratian also selected canons that set forth the requirements for ordination and the election of bishops. In part these Distinctions 59–61 required a gradual ascent of worthy persons through minor and major orders toward the episcopate. Partially, too, they were intended to prevent the elevation of unworthy persons to bishoprics and the intervention of lay authorities in episcopal elections. Not even the emperor was to intervene except to give his assent, at least according to some texts, while others admitted some imperial role in choosing a pope (D. 62 and 63).

Previously, the law governing sacred rites had occupied only a modest place in collections of canon law, and the Eucharist was mentioned only occasionally.[4] An increased treatment of sacramental issues, however, can

[2] The most influential recent book on the complicated evolution of the *Decretum* is Anders Winroth, *The Making of Gratian's Decretum* (Cambridge, 2000). For a brief sketch of Gratian's method and sources, see Peter Landau, "Gratian and the *Decretum Gratiani*," in *The History of Medieval Canon Law in the Classical Period, 1140–1234: From Gratian to the Decretals of Pope Gregory IX*, ed. Wilfried Hartmann and Kenneth Pennington (Washington, D.C., 2008), 22–54. For an argument that the *De consecratione* is part of Gratian's original project, see John Van Engen, "Observations on *De consecratione*," in *Proceedings of the Sixth International Congress of Medieval Canon Law, Berkeley, California, 28 July–2 August 1980*, ed. Stephan Kuttner and Kenneth Pennington (Vatican City, 1985), 309–320.

[3] For Gratian's ideas about the sacraments, see Stanley Chodorow, *Christian Political Theory and Church Politics in the Mid-Twelfth Century. The Ecclesiology of Gratian's Decretum* (Berkeley, 1972), 9–13, 90–95, 113–114; Onyoo Elizabeth Kim, *Law and Criminality in the Middle Ages* (Cheltenham, 2006), 77–128. On the simony issue, including doubts whether the crime vitiated ordination, see Kathleen G. Cushing, *Reform and the Papacy in the Eleventh Century. Spirituality and Social Change* (Manchester, 2005), 95–99, 118, 122. On marriage, see *Marriage Canons from the Decretum of Gratian and the Decretals, Sext, Clementines and Extravagantes*, trans. John T. Noonan, Jr., ed. Augustine Thompson, http://faculty.cua.edu/Pennington/Canon%20Law/marriagelaw.htm, accessed on June 27, 2012.

[4] For example, only scattered references appear in *Decretales pseudo-Isidorianae et capitula Angilramni*, ed. Paul Hinschius (Leipzig: Tauchnitz, 1863; Aalen: Scientia Verlag, 1963).

be traced at least to the work of Regino of Prüm, *Libri duo de synodalibus causis et disciplinis ecclesiasticis*, which he composed in the tenth century for use in pastoral practice. Regino composed his collection with inquiries made by a bishop or his delegate to parish priests during a synod. The opening questions were concerned with the church and its equipment, including the quality of the chalice and paten used in the mass. These and the corporal on which the host would rest at mass were to be kept clean. The questions that followed those on the church were focused on the priest's life and ministry. These questions focused not just on clerical concubinage and other disciplinary issues but also on the performance of rites. The priest was to answer, among other things, how he celebrated mass, at what hour, how he baptized, whether infants died unbaptized, how consecrated hosts were retained for viaticum, and how the sick received anointing and communion.[5] The priest was expected to know certain exorcisms and blessings by memory or from written texts, and he was to know how to sing. Among the books the pastor was to have was a penitential for hearing confessions.[6] All of these requirements were backed with texts from older sources, including the *Theodosian Code*, Carolingian capitularies, canons of councils, papal letters, and penitentials.[7]

The most important treatment of ritual law before the Gregorian reform was the *Decretum* of Burchard of Worms, a collection partly based on Regino's text.[8] Burchard also brought into the collection of canons the tradition of *Libri poenitentiales*, assigning fixed penances for particular offenses, including misuse of the Eucharist for magical purposes and vomiting up the host. A version of this material was added to Burchard's *Decretum* as the Corrector, which was intended to guide priests in dealing with penitent sinners.[9]

The Gregorian reform had brought the issue of simony to the fore along with efforts to impose celibacy on the clergy. This was part of an effort to bring values once restricted to the monastery into the public and private spheres of Western Christendom.[10] The reformers relied on canon law to buttress their efforts to eradicate these ills. The collections from this

5 *Das Sendhandbuch des Regino von Prüm*, 24–39.

6 *Das Sendhandbuch des Regino von Prüm*, 35–38.

7 *Das Sendhandbuch des Regino von Prüm*, 4–7.

8 Greta Austin, *Shaping Canon Law Around the Year 1000: The Decretum of Burchard of Worms* (Farnham, 2009), 224–227.

9 *Medieval Handbooks of Penance: A Translation of the Principal "libri poenitentiales" and Selections from Related Documents*, ed. John T. McNeill and Helena M. Gamer (New York, 1938; New York, 1990), 111, 275. Dropping the host also was punished; see *Medieval Handbooks of Penance*, 278.

10 Gerd Tellenbach, *Church, State and Christian Society at the Time of the Investiture Contest*, trans. R. F. Bennett (Oxford, 1940; Toronto, 1991).

period vary in their attention to the sacraments. For example, Deusdedit gave them no coherent exposition.[11] The *Collection in 74 Titles* added to its texts about simony; another group focused on ordination of clergy, who was to or was not to be ordained. It also gave attention to baptism and confirmation.[12] Anselm of Lucca, however, assembled a whole book in his collection concerned with the sacraments. The book treated the Eucharist and the mass, as well as baptism and confirmation, with a strong emphasis on baptism. Anselm affirmed, by including a text of Augustine of Hippo, that the sacraments effected salvation even if their minister was not a good person.[13] This book followed a long one on the election, consecration, and powers of bishops with minimal references to the priesthood.[14] Anselm also included a book on matrimony that opened with an affirmation of the contractual nature of a marital union.[15] The collection ended with a brief book on penance and a single canon about the anointing of the sick.[16] The sacraments also received detailed attention in the collections associated with Ivo of Chartres, who had a serious interest in Eucharistic theology.[17]

The teaching of canon law at the universities was accompanied by the development of commentaries on Gratian's collection: At first little attention was paid to the *De consecratione*. Some Decretists ignored the texts on the Eucharist and baptism, and others merely glossed them in passing. Only with Rufinus in Italy and the canonists of Cologne would the canon law of the sacraments be developed at length. The Eucharist attained pride of place in the law of the sacraments, as it did in theology and devotional practice. Priestly monopoly on the Eucharist via ordination was affirmed.[18] Eventually transubstantiation became the accepted terminology for explaining the Real Presence of Christ in the Eucharist as effected by the priest's words of consecration. This term was variously

[11] *Die Kanonessammlung des Kardinals Deusdedit*, ed. Victor Wolf von Glanvell (Paderborn, 1905; Aalen, 1967).

[12] *The Collection in Seventy-Four Titles: A Canon Law Manual of the Gregorian Reform*, trans. John Gilchrist (Toronto, 1980), 129–157, 160–162, 193–197. On ordinations by heretics, see *Collection in Seventy-Four Titles*, 197.

[13] Anselm of Lucca, *Collectio canonum una cum collectione minore*, ed. Friedrich Thaner (Innsbruck, 1906–1915; Aalen, 1965), 459–480. Kathleen G. Cushing, *Papacy and Law in the Gregorian Revolution: the Canonistic Work of Anselm of Lucca* (Oxford, 1998).

[14] Anselm of Lucca, *Collectio canonum*, 265–356.

[15] Anselm of Lucca, *Collectio canonum*, 483–506. Megan McLaughlin, *Sex, Gender, and Episcopal Authority in an Age of Reform, 1000–1122* (Cambridge, 2010), 16–49.

[16] Anselm of Lucca, *Collectio canonum*, 511–516.

[17] Christof Rolker, *Canon Law and the Letters of Ivo of Chartres* (Cambridge, 2010), 107–121 esp. 107 no. 113.

[18] Ian Christopher Levy, "The Eucharist and Canon Law in the High Middle Ages," in *A Companion to the Eucharist in the Middle Ages*, ed. Levy, Gary Macy, and Kristen Van Ausdall (Leiden, 2012), 399–445.

understood, but more spiritual interpretations of the sacrament had little impact on the law. Discussions of communion included a different emphasis, one on membership in the Church shown by receiving communion in one's own parish.[19] Baptism remained the means of membership in the Church and the essential gateway to the other sacraments. Priests were supposed to baptize except in an emergency, and bishops were to confirm the recently baptized.[20] Matrimony eventually became part of the sacramental system with consent of the couple emphasized over consummation as the crucial element in the making of a valid marriage.[21]

The canon law of the sacraments continued evolving while the Decretists interpreted Gratian's collected texts. The papacy held four general councils at the Lateran, which legislated for the Western Church on topics ranging from the Trinity to simony to the color of clerical street clothes. The most important of these councils for sacramental issues and clerical discipline was Innocent III's Fourth Lateran Council (1215). The Lateran canons circulated as a group even before being included in systematic collections of canon law. Mostly importantly, they were included in the *Decretals of Gregory IX* or *Liber extra*, edited by the Dominican friar Raymond of Peñafort and addressed by Pope Gregory to Europe's universities in 1234. Thereafter they were the subject of university lectures, and synodal decrees implemented them across all of Europe.[22]

The Lateran canon *Firmiter credimus* (c. 1), which accepted the doctrine of the Trinity taught by Peter Lombard as dogma, included a section about the sacraments. It affirmed the ordained priest's monopoly of the power to consecrate the Eucharist. Also reaffirmed was the saving power of baptism for both children and adult converts.[23] The council accepted the validity of sacramental rites in different languages (c. 9), especially in the Eastern lands acquired during the Crusades. Greek priests, however, were not to rebaptize those that Latin clergy had baptized, nor were they to cleanse altars that the Latin priests supposedly defiled with Eucharists

19 Gary Macy, "The Dogma of Transubstantiation in the Middle Ages," *Journal of Ecclesiastical History* 45 (1884), 11–51.

20 Thomas M. Izbicki, "Baptism, Confirmation and the Eucharist," in *The Cambridge Companion to Medieval Canon Law*, ed. Anders Winroth and John Wei (forthcoming).

21 *Marriage Litigation in Medieval England*, ed. Richard H. Helmholz (London, 1974).

22 *Constitutiones Concilii quarti Lateranensis una cum Commentariis glossatorum*, ed. Antonio García García (Città del Vaticano, 1981). On the impact of Lateran IV, see García García, "The Fourth Lateran Council and the Canonists," in *The History of Medieval Canon Law in the Classical Period, 1140–1234*, 367–378.

23 *Decrees of the Ecumenical Councils*, 1.230–231.

using unleavened rather than leavened bread (c. 4).[24] The mass was supposed to be celebrated rightly everywhere using appropriate vessels, vestments, and church furnishings (c. 19). The reserved Eucharist for communion of the sick and the holy oils used in baptism and anointing were to be locked up to prevent their theft for use in magical practices (c. 20).[25] Most important for the daily practice of religion in parishes was the decree *Omnis utriusque sexus* (c. 21) in which the faithful were required to confess their sins to their own priest before receiving communion once a year at Easter time. This Easter Duty became a crucial part of pastoral care. A good confession was supposed to purify the believer, who might fear damnation from receiving in a state of sin, before the entire congregation received consecrated hosts in an act of parochial solidarity. The text became a bone of contention almost immediately. Friars skilled as confessors were resented by parish priests for ministering to their parishioners, and revenues in the forms of offerings and bequests were lost when devout lay persons chose burial at a church of a mendicant order. This led to arguments over whether the pope could license friars to intrude into pastoral care.[26] The Lateran Council also simplified the rules governing marriage, allowing for easier identification of degrees of relationship that truly impeded matrimony. The council, however, emphasized public celebration of nuptials before a priest and penalization of unions contracted secretly.[27]

General councils said little more about the sacraments until the Council of Vienne met in 1311–1312, issuing decrees that later were incorporated into the *Constitutions of Clement V, Constitutiones Clementinae* or *Clementines*. That assembly (c. 1) reaffirmed baptism of infants, saying it was probable that they too, like adults, received an infusion of sanctifying grace in the rite (Clem. 1.1.1 § 3). The council (c. 31) also forbade religious (mostly meaning friars) administering of the sacraments to parishioners without permission of a parish priest except where law or a papal privilege permitted it.

[24] *Decrees of the Ecumenical Councils*, 1.239, 235–236.

[25] *Decrees of the Ecumenical Councils*, 1.243, 244. On the fear of profanation, see Thomas M. Izbicki, "*Temeraria manus*. Custody of the Eucharist in Medieval Canon Law," in *Proceedings of the Thirteenth International Congress of Medieval Canon Law. Esztergom, 3–8 August*, ed. Péter Erdö and Szabolcs Anzelm Szuromi (Città del Vaticano, 2010), 539–552.

[26] *Decrees of the Ecumenical Councils*, 1.245. R. N. Swanson, *Religion and Devotion in Europe, c. 1215–c. 1515* (Cambridge, 1995), 26, 33. On the mendicant–secular controversy and its theoretical implications, see Decima Douie, *The Conflict Between the Seculars and the Mendicants at the University of Paris in the Thirteenth Century* (London 1954); Yves Congar, "Aspects ecclésiologiques de la querelle entre mendiants et séculiers dans la second moitié du XIIe siècle et au dèbut du XIVe,"*Archives d'histoire doctrinale et Littéraire du Moyen Âge* 28 (1961), 35–151.

[27] *Decrees of the Ecumenical Councils*, 1.257–258.

That decree too found its way into the *Clementines* in a section on privileges (Clem. 5.7.1). A decree attributed to the council but probably added to the *Clementines* afterward insisted that baptism had to occur at fonts in churches, not in private homes, except in an emergency (Clem. 3.15.un.). The only other important conciliar decrees on the sacraments before the Reformation theologians challenged medieval sacramental theology and rites were the decrees of union with Eastern Churches issued by the Council of Florence (1438–1445). That assembly affirmed using either leavened or unleavened bread in the Eucharist, as well as the seven sacraments in general.[28]

Another and more common source of canon law was the decretal letters of the popes of the twelfth and thirteenth centuries. Beginning in the twelfth century, bishops, judges, and other clerics dispatched queries about the law to the popes. Their replies provided clarifications or interpretations of matters of law. These decretals were supplemented on occasion with constitutions intended to provide guidance to the entire Church. These texts were collected, unofficially at first and then officially, until Gregory IX issued his collection. The most important decretals, concerned with the sacraments, were issued by the popes of the early thirteenth century. These found their way into *Compilatio tertia*, *Compilatio quarta*, and *Compilatio quinta* before most were incorporated into the *Liber extra*. Thereafter, additional decretals and constitutions were included in the *Liber Sextus* of Boniface VIII, the *Clementines*, the *Extravagantes of John XXII*, and various other collections of *extravagantes* or additional decrees of the late medieval pontiffs. In the *Extra*, decretals about sacramental matters were added under the titles "On the Celebration of Masses, the Sacrament of the Eucharist and Divine Offices" (*De celebratione missarum, et sacramento eucharistiae et divinis officiis* = X 3.41), "On Baptism and its Effect" (*De baptismo et eius effectu* = X 3.42), and "On the Custody of the Eucharist, Chrism and Other Sacraments" (*De custodia eucharistiae, chrismatis et aliorum sacramentorum* = X 3.44).[29]

Some decretals focused on the Eucharist. Innocent III's *Cum Marthae* (3 Comp. 3.33.5 = X 3.41.6) provided proofs that the words of consecration used in the canon of the mass were accepted from Christ by the apostles and their successors. He also said the water in the chalice

[28] *Decrees of the Ecumenical Councils*, 1.527 (Greeks), 541 (Armenians), 590 (Maronites).

[29] *Canones Sammlungen*, ed. Emil Friedberg (Leipzig, 1897; Graz, 1958); *Quinque Compilationes Antiquae nec non Collectio canonum Lipsiensis*, ed. Friedberg (Leipzig, 1882; Graz, 1956). Innocent III authorized *Compilatio tertia*, and Honorius III authorized *Compilatio quinta*. Titles on the mass and baptism appear in the *Compilatio Romana*; see *Die Dekretalsammlung des Bernardus Compostellanus antiquus*, ed. Heinrich Singer (Wien, 1914), 84–85.

probably was transmuted (*transmutari*) together with the wine, representing the unity of the faithful with the Father through the Christ.[30] Honorius III declared that Latin priests were not to use leavened bread like the Greeks did (5 Comp. 3.24.6 = X 3.41.14). He also approved the practice of elevating the host, requiring the faithful to bow their heads in adoration (5 Comp. 3.24.1 = X 3.41.10).[31] Later popes had little to say about the Eucharist, except that Clement V extended the feast of Corpus Christi to the entire Church (Clem. 3.16.1). That canon repeated the original decree of Pope Urban IV from 1264 authorizing the celebration of the feast, which seems not to have been widely heeded.[32]

A few important decretals addressed baptism and confirmation. Alexander III restated the formula for infant baptism and issued a form for conditional baptism when the validity of the rite was uncertain (2 Comp. 5.19.1 = X 3.42.1; 2 Comp. 5.19.2 = X 3.42.2). Innocent III said both water and the right words were required for the sacrament (3 Comp. 3.34.3 = X 3.42.5), and he condemned the belief that infant baptism did not forgive original sin. Innocent also said that infants would grow up in the faith free from the inherited stain of original sin. Adults had to consent to their own baptisms. Non-Christians could not be compelled to convert, but feigning acceptance of the baptismal character obligated acceptance of the faith itself (3 Comp. 3.34.1 = X 3.42.3).[33] Other decretals, most of them issued by Innocent III, were concerned with the right practices of anointing and laying on hands in ordinations (2 Comp. 1.11.un. = X 1.15.un.) and with the rite for ordaining subdeacons (2 Comp. 1.12.un. = X 1.16.1).

There were several decretals concerned with espousal and marriage, making up book IV of the *Gregorian Decretals*. The complications of marital politics of wealthy or politically important families included betrothing even the very young but not always following through with a marriage when another alliance became desirable.[34] Consequently, the popes issued many decretals regulating espousal (X 4.1), especially

[30] Charles de Miramon, "Innocent III, Huguccio de Ferrare et Hubert de Pirovano: Droit canonique, théologie et philosophie à Bologne dans les années 1180," in *Medieval Church Law and the Origins of the Western Legal Tradition: A Tribute to Kenneth Pennington*, ed. Wolfgang P. Müller and Mary E. Sommar (Washington, D.C., 2006), 320–346.

[31] Miri Rubin, *Corpus Christ. The Eucharist in Late Medieval Culture* (Cambridge, 1991), 54–72; G. J. C. Snoek, *Medieval Piety from Relics to the Eucharist. A Process of Mutual Interaction* (Leiden, 1995), 47–48, 55.

[32] Barbara R. Walters, Vincent J. Corrigan and Peter T. Ricketts, *The Feast of Corpus Christi* (University Park, Pa., 2006).

[33] Innocent denied anyone could baptize himself, even when in danger of death; see 3 Comp. 3.42.2 (= X 3.42.4).

[34] Christiane Klapisch-Zuber, *Women, Family and Ritual in Renaissance Italy*, trans. Lydia G. Cochrane (Chicago, 1985), 231–241.

betrothal of very young children (X 4.2). Along with these concerns, which were tied to the consensual theory of matrimony, there remained the many impediments to proceeding with the sacrament, based on god-parent relationships (X 4.11), adoption (X 4.12), consanguinity or blood relationship, and affinity or sexual ties, marital or extramarital, with members of the proposed spouse's family (X 4.13 & 14). With all these concerns about licit marriage were rules on legitimizing illegitimate children (X 4.17),[35] also laws about dissolution of marriages on technical grounds (X 4.19).

The promulgation of the *Gregorian Decretals* to the universities opened the way to a fresh discussion of the canon law of the sacraments. The Decretalists of the thirteenth century were creative thinkers about all aspects of the canon law, including the canons governing the sacraments. Of these writers, those most concerned with the sacraments included Johannes Teutonicus, who glossed *Compilatio tertia* and composed the Ordinary Gloss on the *Decretum*, and Bernard of Parma, who compiled the Ordinary Gloss on the *Extra*. Godfrey of Trani and Henricus de Segusio (Hostiensis) wrote commentaries on the titles of the *Extra*, and Hostiensis did an extensive commentary on that entire compilation.[36] Later commentaries became addenda to the major writings of these Decretalists, and some canonists ceased commenting on those titles of the *Gregorian Decretals* that were concerned with dogma and sacramental practice. The last canonist to add anything substantive on the sacramental canons was Johannes Andreae in the early fourteenth century.[37]

The provisions of the canon law about the sacraments, especially new canons, had to be put into practice through local councils and synods. The canon law provided legal language for papal legates, archbishops, and bishops to employ. For example, even before the Fourth Lateran Council met, the canon law and sacramental theology taught in Paris affected the English church. The 1175 Council of Westminster used texts from the *De consecratione* when prohibiting communion by intinction and requiring use of a chalice of gold or silver, not tin, at the mass.[38] The *Decretum* also was reflected in one of the canons issued by Hubert Walter, archbishop of Canterbury, in 1200 requiring that the mass be read from a

35 John Russell, *The "Sanatio in radice" before the Council of Trent* (Roma, 1964).

36 Innocent IV did not write much on the sacraments. For the other early Decretalists, see Kenneth Pennington, "The Decretalists 1190–1234," in *The History of Medieval Canon Law in the Classical Period*, 211–245; James A. Brundage, *Medieval Canon Law* (London, 1995), 56–58.

37 Johannes Andreae is considered the last major canonist of the classical period; see Brundage, *Medieval Canon Law*, 58–59.

38 *Councils & Synods*, 1 pt. 2, 990.

legible missal. Gratian's influence also was reflected in the phrasing of the canon governing baptism and confirmation, saying the rite could be repeated if there was doubt it had been rightly administered.[39]

The many synods held across Europe during the century following the Fourth Lateran Council issued decrees, the level of detail varying, to implement the council's disciplinary agenda. Some of these local enactments reused passages from the *Gregorian Decretals* with minimal differences of wording, while other councils paraphrased or summarized the Lateran canons.[40] Another source for the wording of decrees about the sacraments was synodal legislation from Paris, where many churchmen had studied. Particularly influential were the statutes of Odo of Sully, bishop of Paris (1198–1208), and his successors. His decrees influenced ecclesiastical legislation not just in France but in England and Germany.[41] The Lateran canons and the Paris statutes combined as the major influences on synodal enactments about the sacraments, producing a coherent body of pastoral law across Europe from England to Bohemia and Moravia.[42] These decrees affected pastoral practice through reading of them at synods and their inclusion in visitation instructions given to archdeacons.[43]

The Parisian synodal constitutions required that baptism be administered reverently by priests to both infants and adults with no more than three godparents, two of the same sex as the candidate, attending each person who received the sacrament. The constitutions accepted baptism by lay persons in emergencies, but the priest was to inquire whether the right form of words had been used. The baptismal font was to be kept locked up against the use of blessed water in magic, and the holy oils too were to be kept secure.[44] Odo of Sully and his successors issued regulations requiring priests to remind the faithful about the need to have their children confirmed by the bishop, the only minister of the sacrament,

39 *Councils & Synods*, 1 pt. 2, 1060–1062.

40 Pontal, Odette, *Les statuts synodaux* (Turnhout, 1975), 86; *Les sermons et la visite pastorale de Federico Visconti archevêque de Pise (1253–1277)*, ed. Nicole Bériou, Isabelle le Masne de Chermont, Pascale Bourgain, and Marina Innocenti (Roma, 2001), 1080. For example, the Lateran decree on clerical costume was enacted at the local level with small changes; see Thomas M. Izbicki, "Forbidden Colors in the Regulation of Clerical Dress from the Fourth Lateran Council (1215) to the Time of Nicholas of Cusa (d. 1464)," *Medieval Clothing and Textiles* 1 (2005), 105–114.

41 *Les statuts synodaux Français du XIII*^e^ *siècle*, ed. Odette Pontal, 5 vols. (Paris, 1971–2001), 1.51–93; C. R. Cheney, *English Synodalia* (London, 1968), 19, 21, 25, 34, 55–57, 82–84; Paul B. Pixton, *The German Episcopacy and the Implementation of the Decrees of the Fourth Lateran Council, 1216–1245: Watchmen on the Tower* (Leiden, 1995), 83–85.

42 For example, a decree from Ferrara urged observing a uniformity of rite (*ritum unifiormitatem*) in Mansi 25.903.

43 *Les statuts synodaux français du XIII*^e^ *siècle*, 4.6 Table 1.

44 *Les statuts synodaux français du XIII*^e^ *siècle*, 1.54–57.

following baptism.[45] These statutes gave particular attention to the Eucharist, including celebration of the mass, reservation of the sacrament, and providing viaticum for the sick.[46] Additional synodal precepts from Paris supplemented Odo's instructions about the mass, requiring reverence for the elevated host.[47]

How the Lateran decrees and the Paris statutes influenced local enactments is most easily studied in England. These texts entered English canon law via local councils and synods that employed them as models. One conduit of this influence was the statutes of Salisbury issued by Bishop Richard Poore by 1219, who reenacted them when he moved to the see of Durham. The Salisbury statutes were widely imitated. They included an affirmation of the Lateran decree about the Trinity, followed by one requiring priests to teach their congregations the Creed, *Pater noster* and *Ave Maria*. Poore wanted children taught by priests because their parents often were negligent.[48] The Salisbury statutes affirmed the seven sacraments with baptism as the gateway to the rest. Confirmation by the bishop armed the believer against the devil, and the Eucharist united him or her with Christ.[49] Poore issued a detailed instruction about baptism that included a text from the Paris constitutions explaining how the faith of the godparents, two of the three of the same sex as the child, could suffice for those too young to consent to the sacrament. The formula for baptism was reaffirmed, as was the ability of any lay person to baptize in an emergency.[50] Poore permitted use of French or English in place of Latin as long as the form of words was correct.[51] What he said about securing the holy oils was derived directly from Lateran IV.[52] Poore required priests to exhort the faithful to have their children receive the sacrament of confirmation. He added that sponsoring a child for confirmation, like being a godparent, created the marital impediment of spiritual relationship.[53]

Following the *Decretum* and *Firmiter credimus*, Poore affirmed the sole power of the priest to consecrate the Eucharist. The mass was to be read from a correct copy of the Sarum use, and the faithful were to kneel reverently when the consecrated host was elevated.[54] The pastor was to instruct his flock that that they were not to receive communion unworthily.[55] Poore urged that the faithful confess and receive

[45] *Les statuts synodaux français du XIIIe siècle*, 156–59.
[46] *Les statuts synodaux français du XIIIe siècle*, 1.58–61, 80–81.
[47] *Les statuts synodaux français du XIIIe siècle*, 1.82–83.
[48] *Councils & Synods*, 2, pt. 1, 57, 61. [49] *Councils & Synods*, 2, pt. 1, 65.
[50] *Councils & Synods*, 2, pt. 1, 67–68. [51] *Councils & Synods*, 2, pt. 1, 69.
[52] *Councils & Synods*, 2, pt. 1, 68. [53] *Councils & Synods*, 2, pt. 1, 71.
[54] *Councils & Synods*, 2, pt. 1, 79. [55] *Councils & Synods*, 2, pt. 1, 77–79.

communion three times a year unless enjoined by the priest to abstain. He added, following *Omnis utriusque sexus*, that this should occur at least once a year.[56] Poore's decrees covered the sacrament of penance in terms derived from the statutes of Paris. These included a requirement that the confessor stay in plain sight but out of earshot, especially when hearing the confessions of women. Likewise, they affirmed the Church's prohibition against confessors revealing secrets learned when interrogating penitents, the "seal of confession."[57]

These same statutes repeated much of what Lateran IV and the Paris statutes said about matrimony, including the right form to be used in the sacrament and the impediments to licit marriages. Poore also warned against clandestine marriages and the use of magic in the marital context, which might be blamed on the husband's impotence.[58] Rounding out his treatment of the sacraments, the bishop ordered teaching the faithful about extreme unction, including that the rite could be repeated as necessary.[59] However, Poore said little about ordination as such, although he addressed the need to have parochial vicars when the incumbent of a cure was a religious house or an absentee priest.[60] At least one thirteenth-century council, following a few years after Poore issued his statutes for Salisbury, treated all of the sacraments in order from baptism through confirmation, the Eucharist, penance, extreme unction, and matrimony to ordination, including exclusion of simoniacs from reception of holy orders.[61]

In the fifteenth century, many of the enactments for the province of Canterbury, including those modeled on Poore's statutes, were incorporated into the *Provinciale* of William Lyndwood to guide the actions of bishops, archdeacons, and priests.[62] By the late thirteenth century, enforcement of such regulations usually fell to the local archdeacon.[63] The care of the sacraments and the means of their administration was part of the "visitation of things" (*visitatio rerum*).[64] For, in England there have been many examples of how statutes were enforced by archdeacons, who

56 *Councils & Synods*, 2, pt. 1, 72–73. 57 *Councils & Synods*, 2, pt. 1, 71–75.
58 *Councils & Synods*, 2, pt. 1, 86–90. 59 *Councils & Synods*, 2, pt. 1, 90–91.
60 *Councils & Synods*, 2, pt. 1, 96. 61 *Councils & Synods*, 2, pt. 1, 140–148.
62 William Lyndwood, *Lyndwood's Provinciale: The Text of the Canons Therein Contained, Reprinted from the Translation Made in 1534*, ed. J. V. Bullard and H. Chalmer Bell (London, 1929), 3, 94–103, 105–106.
63 Visitation brought authoritative norms to the parish, but it also used the testimony of local elites; see Ian Forrest, "The Transformation of Visitation in Thirteenth-Century England," *Past & Present* no. 221 (November 2013), 3–38; Geneviève Hoëttick-Gadbois, "Les marguilliers, 'chevilles ouvrieres' de la vie paroissiale d'apres les visites archidiaconales de Josas, 1458–1470," *Revue d'Histoire de l'Eglise de France*, 92, 228 (2006): 25–46.
64 *Visitatio rerum* was supposed to accompany inquiry into the conduct of the clergy and laity (*visitatio hominum*); see Noël Coulet, *Les visites pastorals* (Turnhout, 1977), 30–31.

sought to discover whether parishes even had the necessary equipment to support the administration of the sacraments. They also were supposed to inquire whether the Eucharist and holy oils, as well as baptismal water and other holy things, were kept safe.[65] A manual for archdeacons from northern France assigned these men to visit not just parishes but non-exempt monasteries.These instructions concerned "visiting" the priest and the parishioners, the church, manse and priory, sacramental practice and the sins that might be committed by any Christian. The archdeacon was to correct and instruct, even teach, the clergy and faithful. One major concern of the author was to prevent archdeacons exacting too much in procurations, their upkeep during a visitation.[66]

The wide spread of similar ideas and practices is shown by the statutes for the diocese of Olomouc in Moravia issued during the fourteenth and fifteenth centuries. The statutes said baptism should be conferred within a month, and only the children of princes were exempt from baptism at the parish church. This rule bound all parents outside cases of necessity, when place and minister yielded to the priority of saving souls.[67] The diocesan statutes of 1461 threatened to fine priests who did not possess a correct order for baptism. Priests were to teach their flocks how to perform an emergency baptism, but they were to investigate whether the rite was done correctly. The priest was to remind the faithful to have children confirmed by the bishop, and the marriage impediment created by sponsoring a confirmand was to be emphasized during preparation for the rite.[68] By 1318 the faithful of Moravia were told to confess and receive three times in a year, or at least at Eastertide as the Lateran Council required. Viaticum processions and sickbed communions were regulated.[69] These statutes offered indulgences to those who knelt at the sight of the procession or followed after it reverently, reciting the *Pater noster* and *Ave Maria*. Indulgences also were offered to those who venerated the elevated host.[70] By 1349 the feast of Corpus Christi had entered the diocesan calendar.[71] At the other end of Christendom and almost two centuries later, the Spanish diocese of Mondoñedo was still

[65] English statutes routinely required archdeacons to look at books, vestments, and liturgical objects; see *Councils & Synods*, 2, pt. 1, 28, 148, 379. For examples of English visitations, see *Pastors and the Care of Souls*, 146, 220, 227, 293, 297–298, 300.

[66] Elizabeth Kay Todd, "*Libellus pastoralis de cura et officio archidiaconi*: A Thirteenth-Century Handbook for Archdeacons; a Critical Edition and Introduction," PhD Dissertation, Ohio State University, 1993.

[67] *Synody a statuta Olomoucké diecéze období středověku*, ed. Pavel Krafl (Praha, 2003), 140.

[68] Krafl, *Synody a statuta Olomoucké diecéze období středověku*, 221–223.

[69] Krafl, *Synody a statuta Olomoucké diecéze období středověku*, 131–132.

[70] Krafl, *Synody a statuta Olomoucké diecéze období středověku*, 162–164.

[71] Krafl, *Synody a statuta Olomoucké diecéze období středověku*, 152.

giving instructions in 1534 for visitors to take especial care about "the sacrament of the altar" (*Sacramento del altar*) and all the other sacraments.[72]

Importing Latin canon law into culturally Greek lands in the period of the Crusades added a challenge for the makers of synodal legislation. Thus the Latin statutes for Cyprus, made after the Sack of Constantinople and the Fourth Lateran Council, required imposing the council's norms on a frequently resentful population.[73] A provincial council forbade Greeks and Latins to insult one another, but it described anyone who did not accept all seven sacraments as a heretic.[74] The Cyprus statutes included a restatement of the decree *Omnis utriusque sexus* with its requirement that the faithful perform the Easter duty of confession and communion.[75] Eucharistic practices were particularly divisive, because the Greeks thought the Latins Judaized by using leavened bread, while the Latins thought the Greeks stubbornly disobedient. The statutes required veneration of the host, made of unleavened bread, when it was elevated or when it was carried to the sick. Greek prelates and priests were supposed to admonish their lay folk to show reverence to the host when in a church used by the Latins or when they saw it being carried.[76] The Latins wanted the Greeks to admit that the Eucharist was valid if celebrated according to either rite.[77] Eventually observance of the feast of Corpus Christi, with the carrying of a consecrated host through the streets, was decreed for Cyprus.[78]

The laity was to be taught how to baptize in a case of necessity, and they were to be admonished to have their children confirmed by the bishop.[79] Confirmation by the bishop according to Latin practice was enjoined, while a warning was issued against excessive anointing of children being baptized by priests or recently baptized by lay persons.[80] Confirmation in the Roman church, probably because it was administered by a Latin bishop claiming local superiority, bound a person of Greek origin to attend Latin masses weekly and receive the sacraments "in the way of the Latins" except in a case of necessity. Violation of this command could lead to excommunication.[81]

[72] *Synodicon Hispanum*, 1.67.
[73] Christopher Schabel, "Martyrs and Heretics. Intolerance of Intolerance: The Execution of Thirteen Greek Monks in Cyprus in 1231," in Schabel, *Greeks, Latins, and the Church in Early Frankish Cyprus*, Variorum Reprints (Farnham, 2010), III, 1–33.
[74] *Synodicum Nicosiense and Other Documents of the Latin Church of Cyprus 1196–1373* (Nicosia, 2001), ed. Christopher Schabel, 122–123.
[75] *Synodicum Nicosiense*, 94–95. [76] *Synodicum Nicosiense*, 98–101.
[77] *Synodicum Nicosiense*, 124–127. [78] *Synodicum Nicosiense*, 222–223.
[79] *Synodicum Nicosiense*, 98–99, 122–125. [80] *Synodicum Nicosiense*, 124–125.
[81] *Synodicum Nicosiense*, 154–155.

These precepts of universal and local canon law were complex enough for churchmen to produce a stream of manuals to guide the simple priest in his work of pastoral care, whether through guides for confessors or more general books for curates.[82] A few examples must suffice. Thomas of Chobham's *Summa confessorum* discussed the sacraments with an eye toward pastoral care based on both universal canon law and local statutes. Most of these rules are found in the section "Things a Priest Should Necessarily Know" (*Que sacerdos debeat necessario scire*). Chobham's ideas on the sacraments in general were traditional, emphasizing the exterior sign with interior effects. All seven were instituted in the New Testament or, in the case of marriage, made more effective by the Church.[83] The priest had to know the form of baptism for his own acts and teach the laity how to baptize in an emergency. The baptismal formula could be said in any language, not just in Latin. The rite also required water and the intention of baptizing. It was to be offered at Easter and Pentecost apart from cases of necessity, where children were under a threat of death before one of those feasts. Godparents were obligated to teach the faith to their godchildren, for whom they stood as sureties. The godparents incurred the impediment of spiritual kinship for themselves, their children, and their godchildren.[84] Confirmation was not as necessary for salvation as baptism was, but it strengthened the believer. Adults who failed to seek confirmation sinned, as did parents who failed to have their children confirmed. Confessors were to ask about this and instruct parents to take their offspring to the bishop. Confirmation sponsors too incurred the impediment of spiritual kinship.[85]

Chobham thought that what a priest needed to know about the Eucharist was greatest on account of the presence of the body and blood of Christ. A man, the priest, could bring about Christ's presence in a way that an angel could not do.[86] The priest needed the right materials, the words approved by the Church, his ordination, and the intention to consecrate the materials present on the corporal. After the words of consecration had been said, the body and blood were present, although the accidents of bread and wine remained. Although they seemed separate, there was blood with the body and body with the blood.[87] Chobham warned against

[82] Pierre Michaud-Quantin, Sommes *de casuistique et manuels de confession au moyen âge* (Louvain, 1962); Leonard E. Boyle, *Pastoral Care, Clerical Education, and Canon Law, 1200–1400* (London, 1981).

[83] *Thomae de Chobham summa confessorum*, ed. F. Broomfield (Louvain, 1968), 88–91.

[84] *Thomae de Chobham summa confessorum*, 91–99.

[85] *Thomae de Chobham summa confessorum*, 167–174, 193–195.

[86] *Thomae de Chobham summa confessorum*, 99–100.

[87] *Thomae de Chobham summa confessorum*, 100–103, 104, 121–123.

giving communion to small children who might reject it, and it was not to be given to impenitent sinners. Lay persons were to receive communion at least once a year, and those who failed to do so could be excommunicated.[88] Those condemned to death were to be permitted confession and communion, but they were not to hold hosts in their mouths when being hanged. Priests to whose churches the bodies of repentant criminals were carried after execution sinned if they denied the deceased a Christian burial.[89]

Perhaps the most influential of the *Summae confessorum* was that composed by Raymond of Peñafort. It was written by a Dominican with an eye toward fellow friars serving as confessors. His *Summa* discussed the administration of the sacrament of penance at length; and it included an entire book on marriage, a crucial subject for dealing with penitents. It also gave attention to ordination, including indications of who should or should not be ordained. Raymond's *Summa* treated fewer sacraments than Chobham had, but it treated those in greater depth. Consequently it was widely circulated throughout Western Europe, influencing pastoral practice.[90]

Similar messages can be found in the *Manipulus curatorum* of Guido de Monte Rocherii, one of the most widely circulated manuals. The *Manipulus* discussed all seven sacraments, although penance was treated at greater length apart from the others. It discussed the form of the sacrament of baptism, its matter, and the proper minister. Guido defended baptism of children, but he doubted the desirability of the forced baptism of the children of Jews, who might naturally follow their parents back into Judaism, vitiating the practical effect of the rite.[91] Confirmation was treated briefly, affirming its spiritual value and its administration by the bishop.[92] Guido offered an extensive exposition of the Eucharist and interpreted the mass for his readers, giving symbolic interpretations of various actions. Guido addressed defects in the mass at length, but he said nothing about the elevation of the consecrated elements in his exposition of the canon. The transformed bread and wine were present on the altar; but the *Manipulus* affirmed, as orthodox writers usually did, the unity of Christ under those visible signs.[93]

88 *Thomae de Chobham summa confessorum*, 103, 104–107.
89 *Thomae de Chobham summa confessorum*, 128–129.
90 *Summa Sancti Raymundi de Peniafort . . .* (Roma, 1603; Farnborough, 1967); Raymond of Peñafort, *Summa on Marriage*, trans. Pierre Payer (Toronto, 2005).
91 Guido of Monte Rochen, *Handbook for Curates*, 15–35.
92 Guido of Monte Rochen, *Handbook for Curates*, 35–43.
93 Guido of Monte Rochen, *Handbook for Curates*, 43–108.

Writing in the vernacular, John Mirk emphasized the priest's duty to teach his flock. He gave the formula for baptism in both Latin and English and reminded the priest that the character could not be imposed twice. Baptism was to be administered at Easter or Pentecost except in a case of necessity, when even the midwife or the parents could perform the rite. Godparents were to teach the child the *Pater noster, Ave Maria,* and Creed. Godparents could not sponsor a child for confirmation by the bishop, and both godparents and confirmation sponsors incurred the impediment of spiritual kinship.[94] Mirk gave the simple priest brief instructions for the mass in which he affirmed the Real Presence, saying the faithful were to learn to honor the host by kneeling and saying the *Pater noster* or another prayer when bells called attention to the elevation. Communion was to be received at Easter, but communicants were to get a drink of wine and water to cleanse the mouth after receiving. The faithful were offered both spiritual and practical benefits for honoring the sacrament.[95] Mirk's *Instructions* required secure reservation of the host and threatened the priest with penalties for various possible failings in the celebration of the mass.[96]

Sacramental theology penetrated beyond these pastoral manuals. Conduct literature reflected the belief in the Real Presence. Thus both the *Enseignemenz a Phelippe* and the *Enseignement a Ysabel* advised being attentive at mass, as well as saying prayers, aloud or silently. These instructions especially urged being "quieter and more attentive" while "the body of our Lord is present at the mass."[97] *How the Good Wife Taught Her Daughter* promised that the daughter would "fare best on the day When you have seen God," almost certainly at the elevation of the host. The daughter also was taught to say her prayers at church, instead of chattering "to friends or acquaintances."[98]

Worries about errors concerning the sacraments were evident in the later Middle Ages, making their way into manuals for inquisitors and the

94 John Mirk, *Instructions for Parish Priests*, ed. Edward Peacock, 2nd ed. (London, 1902; Woodbridge, 1996), viii, 3–6, 17–21. Mirk based his work on the *Oculus sacerdotis*, as did the author of *Sacerdos parochialis*; see Niamh Pattwell, "Canons and Catechisms: The Austin Canons of South-East England and *Sacerdos parochialis*," in *After Arundel: Religious Writing in Fifteenth-Century England*, ed. Vincent Gillespie and Kantik Ghosh (Turnhout, 2011), 381–393 at 391–392.

95 Mirk, *Instructions for Parish Priests*, 8–10, 57, including the text of the prayer "Ihesu, lord, welcome thou be." Mirk gave instructions for communion of the sick in danger of death at *Instructions*, 57–58.

96 Mirk, *Instructions for Parish Priests*, 58–59.

97 *Medieval Conduct Literature: An Anthology of Vernacular Guides to Behaviour for Youths, with English Translations*, ed. Mark D. Johnston (Toronto, 2009), 8–9, 19.

98 *Medieval Conduct Literature*, 288–289.

conduct of trials. Baptism and confirmation usually aroused no focused dissent outside Languedoc, where the Cathars were accused of rejecting all seven sacraments.[99] However, Eucharistic heresy and magical practices using sacred things were widely feared in the later Middle Ages. The Dominican inquisitor Bernard Gui, writing in the early fourteenth century, reported that the Modern Manichees (Cathars) rejected the sacrament of the Eucharist, warning that they substituted their "blessed bread" for the Eucharist as a counter-sacrament.[100] The Cathars also were accused of despising matrimony. Gui said they replaced sacramental marriage between a man and a woman with marriage between the soul and God.[101] The Waldensians were reported to dismiss consecration of the Eucharist by a sinful priest, undermining the reliability of ordination; but they supposedly permitted any "good" person, women included, to consecrate. According to Gui, the Waldensians used verbal tricks to avoid affirming transubstantiation and received Easter communion only as a means of avoiding suspicion of heresy.[102] Nicholas Eimeric, another Dominican inquisitor, writing later in the same century, had much the same thing to say about the Cathars and Waldensians. Eimeric, however, failed in an accusation that Aragonese Franciscans too fell into sacramental heresy by saying, among other things, that the Real Presence departed from a dropped host.[103]

Inquisitors' records from the late thirteenth and early fourteenth centuries included inquiries about eating the "blessed bread" of the heretics instead of receiving communion. More than one deposition before the tribunal of Toulouse also said the heretics rejected the consecrated host as "mere bread," not the body of Christ at all, a baked item instead of a sacrament.[104] Many of the same opinions can be found in the inquisitorial register of Jacques Fournier, bishop of Pamiers, which also records mocking of the elevated host by heretics.[105]

[99] Bernard Gui, *Manuel de l'inquisietur*, ed. Guillaume Mollat, 2 vols. (Paris, 1964), 1.12.

[100] Gui, *Manuel de l'inquisietur*, 1.12–13, 24–25; Gui, *The Inquisitor's Guide: A Medieval Manual on Heretics*, trans. Janet Shirley (Welwyn Garden City, 2006), 36, 44–45.

[101] Gui, *Manuel de l'inquisietur*, 1.14.

[102] Gui, *Manuel de l'inquisietur*, 1.42–45, 72–73, 80–81; Gui, *The Inquisitor's Guide*, 54–55, 65–66, 75.

[103] Nicholas Eimeric, *Directorium inquisitorum*, ed. Francisco Peña (Rome, 1587), 273–274, 278–279. Gary Macy, "Nicolas Eymeric and the Condemnation of Orthodoxy," in *The Devil, Heresy and Witchcraft in the Middle Ages: Essays in Honor of Jeffrey B. Russell*, ed. Alberto Ferreiro (Leiden, 1998), 369–381.

[104] *Inquisitors and Heretics in Thirteenth-Century Languedoc: Edition and Translation of Toulouse Inquisition Depositions, 1273–1282*, ed. Peter Biller, Caterina Bruschi, and Shelagh Sneddon (Leiden, 2011), 301, 347, 415.

[105] *Regestre d'inquisition de Jacques Fournier (éveque de Pamiers) 1318–1325*, ed. Jean Duvernay, 3 vols. (Paris, 1978), 1.355.

Another whole category of errors listed by Gui was the effort to use the consecrated host and holy oils for magical purposes.[106] There was nothing new in this, as the canonists' care for protecting the reserved Eucharist, holy oils, and even baptismal water shows; and tales of host desecration focused on either witches or Jews.[107] Inquisitors can be found asking about theft of hosts or holy water for sacrilegious rites.[108] Ultimately, these fears of misuse of the sacraments and renunciation of the faith, tied to fears about impotence even within sacramental marriage, found their way into the *Malleus maleficarum*, the best-known manual for witch hunting.[109]

Later sacramental heresies focused on the Eucharist, especially after the outbreak of the Great Western Schism in 1378. John Wyclif rejected the doctrine of transubstantiation, consequently denouncing the adoration of the elevated host as idolatrous.[110] John Hus was suspected of embracing Wyclif's errors. In a 1411 letter to Pope John XXIII, Hus had to deny saying the material substance of the host, bread, remained after consecration; and he also denied saying the host was the body of Christ when it was elevated but not when the priest replaced it on the corporal.[111] The Church authorities responded to these perceiving challenges with condemnation. In May of 1415 the Council of Constance condemned Wyclif's ideas about the Eucharist and the priesthood.[112] One month later, the council sentenced John Hus to death, partially for resisting condemnation of Wyclif's teachings.[113] In May of 1416 Jerome of Prague was condemned even though he claimed acceptance of transubstantiation.[114] Pope Martin V, elected at Constance to end the Great Western Schism, issued bulls, addressed to all bishops and inquisitors everywhere, promulgating articles for the interrogation of suspected followers of Wyclif and Hus. Inquisitors were to ask whether the accused believed Christ, not bread and wine, was on the altar once the words of consecration had been said.[115]

[106] Gui, *Manuel de l'inquisietur*, vol. 2, 22–23, 52–53. See also Gui, *The Inquisitor's Guide*, 153, 167–168.

[107] *The Occult in Medieval Europe*, ed. P. G. Maxwell-Stuart (Basingstoke, 2005), 75–76, 89; Miri Rubin, *Gentile Tales: The Narrative Assault on Late Medieval Jews* (New Haven, Conn., 1999).

[108] *The Occult in Medieval Europe*, 126–127.

[109] *The Malleus maleficarum*, trans. P. G. Maxwell-Stuart (Manchester, 2007), 125–126, 146–147.

[110] Ian Christopher Levy, *John Wyclif: Scriptural Logic, Real Presence, and the Parameters of Orthodoxy* (Milwaukee, 2003), 239–245.

[111] *The Letters of John Hus*, trans. Matthew Spinka (Manchester, 1972), 54 Letter 18.

[112] *Decrees of the Ecumenical Councils*, 1.411.

[113] *Decrees of the Ecumenical Councils*, 1.422.

[114] *Decrees of the Ecumenical Councils*, 1.434.

[115] Mansi 27.1204–1215 at 1212.

Many in Bohemia revolted after the execution of Hus. This Hussite movement demanded communion under both species for the laity (Utraquism). The chalice became the symbol of their revolt. The movement divided and fought internally over issues of religious practice, but it survived in some form down to the Reformation.[116] The Lollards, who looked to Wyclif as their founder, suffered persecution including for holding unorthodox opinions on Eucharistic theology and practice. They suffered penalties ranging from compulsory reception of communion to burning by the secular arm. Nonetheless, their dissident beliefs survived down to the time of the English Reformation, when new theologies of the sacraments appeared. The Eucharist and the priesthood remained central in these controversies, and Rome responded to Protestant dissent by reaffirming its rites and dogmas at the Council of Trent.[117]

This was the larger background in theory and common practice for prelates, pastors, and teaching canonists as they worked out the full details of Eucharistic practice in the later Middle Ages. These teachings and practices will be discussed in the following chapters. The initial focus will be on the belief in the Real Presence and the coming of the Presence in the mass (minister, materials, and words). The following chapters will address communion of the well in church and the sick at home, including protection for the reserved sacrament from magical uses. The book concludes with the feast of Corpus Christi, belief in wonder hosts, and (in brief) Reformation challenges to medieval Eucharistic theologies and practices.

[116] Frederick G. Heymann, *John Žižka and the Hussite Revolution* (Princeton, 1950).

[117] Shannon McSeffrey, *Gender and Heresy: Women and Men in Lollard Communities, 1420–1530* (Philadelphia, 1995), 49–50.; John A. F. Thomson, *The Later Lollards 1414–1520* (Oxford, 1965), 246–247.

1 The Real Presence of Christ, the minister, and the materials of the Sacrament

The Real Presence and the language of transubstantiation

The idea that Christ was present in the Eucharist, the Real Presence, was not new in the twelfth century when Gratian's *Decretum* was taking shape. The collections of canons, from Carolingian times onward, included texts that touched on the Eucharist; but that sacrament was not given close attention apart from purely disciplinary enactments until the time of Ivo of Chartres (d. 1115). Following the work of Ivo and Gratian, the Real Presence was given more attention, including in commentaries by canonists. By the end of the twelfth century the idea of transubstantiation, transformation of the species into Christ's body and blood or the substitution of the elements with the substantial divine presence, while their accidents remained visible, had entered the canon law. This was reflected, in turn, in the canonists' treatment of the minister, materials, and form of the Eucharist, together with the right practices surrounding the mass, communion, and reservation of the sacrament for comforting the sick and dying.[1] These essentials were present whether in a rural parish or at the papal court.[2] Moreover, anyone who might "presume to think, or to teach, concerning the sacrament of the body and blood of our Lord Jesus Christ" different than what the Church taught could be regarded as a heretic.[3]

The earlier collections of canons included extracts from the works of the Fathers, as well as conciliar decrees and papal texts, genuine and

[1] Thomas of Chobham added "intention" to this list; see *Thomae de Chobham summa confessorum*, ed. F. Broomfield (Louvain, 1968), 100.

[2] Note the discussion of Holy Thursday in Agostino Patrizzi, *Caeremoniale Romanum* (Paris, 1689; Ridgewood, N.J., 1965), fol. LXXXXVIIII^{v}, and the mass of the presanctified, at fol. C^{v}–CIII^{r}, both of which added ceremony to the basic rite celebrated anywhere.

[3] See a translation of the decretal *Ad abolendam* of Lucius III (X 5.7.9) in *Heresy and Authority in Medieval Europe: Documents in Translation*, ed. Edward Peters (Philadelphia, 1980), 171. An earlier decree of the Second Lateran Council, which condemned those who rejected the sacraments, did not enter the canon law; see *Decrees of the Ecumenical Councils*, 1.202.

forged. The Latin patristic texts showed two different trends in interpreting the biblical texts on the Last Supper and the reception of communion. Ambrose of Milan preferred a more literal idea of Christ's presence, while Augustine of Hippo opted for a more spiritual interpretation, emphasizing faith and charity. He also emphasized the role of the priest, in union with the Church, and the cultivation of charity among the faithful, compared to the Donatists' supposed lack of charity.[4] By Carolingian times, some idea of the Real Presence was widely accepted, but emphases differed. Writing to instruct young monks, Paschasius Radbertus identified the Eucharistic presence with the flesh and blood born of Mary, an Ambrosian theology of the sacrament. Writers like Ratramnus of Corbie preferred a more spiritual, Augustinian interpretation.[5] Paschasius and those who followed him did not present their doctrine in a dogmatic context. This became a matter of contention in the eleventh century. Berengar of Tours taught a very spiritual approach to the Real Presence, while Lanfranc of Bec and others argued for a more corporeal interpretation of the presence, even identifying the Eucharistic body with the flesh born of the Virgin Mary. Berengar was forced to recant his teachings twice. The earlier oath, imposed by Cardinal Humbert of Silva Candida, was very literal minded but allowed for the possibility that some of the materials remained after consecration. The text found its way into the canon law as the chapter *Ego Berengarius* in the *Decretum*.[6] Even Lanfranc, however, admitted the sacramental sacrifice was bloodless to avoid horrifying the faithful.[7]

The Eucharistic occupied only a modest place in early collections of canon law, with almost no attention to the Real Presence or the theology of the priesthood. Regino of Prüm (d. 915) composed his book with an eye toward the review of pastoral practice during diocesan synods. Regino posed several questions to priests about the celebration of the mass, but

4 Joseph Wawrykow, "The Heritage of the Late Empire: Influential Theology," in *A Companion to the Eucharist in the Middle Ages*, ed. Ian Levy, Gary Macy, and Kristen Van Ausdall (Leiden, 2012), 59–91 at 67–80.

5 Gary Macy, *Theologies of the Eucharist in the Early Scholastic Period* (Cambridge, 1984), 35–53. An idea of change can be found in Amalar of Merz, *On the Liturgy*, ed. Eric Knibbs, 2 vols. (Cambridge, Mass.: Harvard University Press, 2014), 2.126–127.

6 Gary Macy, "The Theological Fate of Berengar's Oath of 1059: Interpreting a Blunder Become Tradition," in Macy, *Treasures from the Storehouse: Medieval Religion and the Eucharist* (Collegeville, Minn., 1999), 20–35. For the more intellectual Paschasian arguments against Berengar than Humbert's, see Lanfranc, Archbishop of Canterbury, *On the Body and Blood of the Lord*; Guitmund of Aversa, *On the Truth of the Body and Blood of Christ in the Eucharist*, trans. Mark G. Vaillancourt. (Washington, D.C., 2009). Berengar's spiritual approach was not new, as Aelfric's letter for Bishop Wulfsige, among others, shows; see *Councils & Synods* 1/1.223.

7 Lanfranc, *On the Body and Blood of the Lord*; Guitmund, *On the Truth of the Body and Blood of Christ in the Eucharist*, 5.

these questions did not include inquiries about belief in the Real Presence. The closest was one asking whether the priest consumed the body and blood of the Lord "with fear and reverence" (*cum timore et reverentia*) after mass.[8] Similarly, the canons in book I of Regino's collection addressed the discipline of the mass, communion, and viaticum; but the Real Presence received little attention. A canon from a Council of Reims only warned against letting women take the "sacred body of Christ" (*sacrum corpus Christi*) to the sick.[9] A canon from the False Decretals attributed to "Clement" required consuming the offerings made at the altar that were not used in the liturgy, but it warned against mixing those offerings with daily food.[10]

Reform movements gave only limited attention to the Real Presence before the twelfth century. Burchard of Worms (d. 1025) gave detailed instructions for the discipline of the sacraments in his *Decretum*.[11] Book V was devoted to the Eucharist. One canon, derived from the Pseudo-Isidorean collection and attributed to "Pope Alexander," said the Passion of Christ was to be mixed (*miscenda*) with the offerings made at the mass.[12] Another text, combining material attributed to Cyprian, Ambrose, and Hilary, referred to the Eucharist as "the medicine of the body of the Lord" (*medicina corporis Domini*). Being separated from Christ's body was alienation from salvation.[13] Nowhere, however, did Burchard include a text attempting to explain the presence of Christ. Similarly, although Anselm of Lucca (d. 1086) was one of the Gregorian reformers who devoted an entire book of his collection to the sacraments, he too did not address the Real Presence directly. Quotations from texts attributed to Leo I described the communicant as becoming the flesh of the one "who was made our flesh" (*qui caro nostra factus est*). Another text identified the sacramental flesh with that born of Mary.[14] This was the closest Anselm came to providing an explanation of the Real Presence.

A change is evident with the collections ascribed to Ivo of Chartres (d. 1115), which reflect his interest in the Eucharist. Although it is

[8] *Das Sendhandbuch des Regino von Prüm*, 34–35.

[9] *Das Sendhandbuch des Regino von Prüm*, 86–87.

[10] *Das Sendhandbuch des Regino von Prüm*, 176–179.

[11] Greta Austin, *Shaping Canon Law Around the Year 1000: The Decretum of Burchard of Worms* (Farnham, 2009), 224–227.

[12] Burchardus Wormatiensis, *Decretum*, PL 140.753C, cited from the *Patrologia Latina Database*, accessed on August 5, 2012. The text derives from the False Decretals; see Hinschius, 99. The *Lay Folks Mass Book* attributes to Alexander part of the wording of the canon of the mass; see *Pastors and the Care of Souls*, 166.

[13] Burchardus Wormatiensis, *Decretum*, PL 140.756A–B.

[14] Anselm of Lucca, *Collectio canonum una cum collectione minore*, ed. Friedrich Thaner (Innsbruck, 1906–1915; Aalen, 1965), 461 with c. 6 by Leo, but cc. 7–9 by Ambrose.

unlikely that all three collections (*Decretum, Panormia*, and *Tripartita*) are his, Ivo's interest in the sacraments opened the canon law to more theological themes.[15] In one of his letters Ivo emphasized the ability of a priest to "invisibly consecrate and transform into the truth of Christ's body and blood." He also identified this transformation with the words of consecration.[16] The minister was unable to effect this "unless he first was consecrated into the order of priests" (*nisi primum fuerit in ordine sacerdotali consecratus*).[17] Jesus conferred this power only on His disciples, and through them on priests, but not on the laity.[18]

The *Decretum* of Ivo contains an unusual number of extensive excerpts from patristic texts on the sacrament, including works of Ambrose and Augustine. One text mentioned the transformation of the elements, while another emphasized the unity of the Church with Christ and, through Him, with the Father in the Eucharist.[19] Ivo and his circle were well aware of recent controversies about the Real Presence. An extensive excerpt from one of the writings of Lanfranc of Bec and the first recantation by Berengar of Tours also appeared in the *Decretum*.[20]

The *Panormia*, which was more widely circulated than Ivo's *Decretum*, also included patristic texts about the sacraments. One chapter attributed to Augustine said a newly baptized catechumen took communion "in commemoration of the Lord's death" (*in commemoratione mortis Domini*), dying together with Christ.[21] The *Panormia* required following Christ's practice at the Last Supper, offering bread and watered wine, but it rejected communion by intinction as like the morsel He gave to Judas (John 13:26). The water had to be present representing humanity, or "the

[15] Christof Rolker, "The Earliest Work of Ivo of Chartres: The Case of Ivo's Eucharist *Florilegium* and the Canon Law Collections Attributed to Him," *Zeitschrift der Savigny-Stiftung für Rechtsgeschichte, Kanonistische Abteilung* 124 (2007), 109–127.

[16] Ivo Carnotensis, *Epistola 63*, PL 162.78D, cited from the *Patrologia Latina Database*, accessed on September 7, 2012, "sic divina virtus sacramenta hujus temporis a legitimis sacerdotibus ministrata invisibiliter consecrat et in veritatem Christi corporis et sanguinis transformat." On the words of consecration, see Ivo, *Epistola 63*, PL 161.80A–B.

[17] Ivo Carnotensis, *Epistola 63*, PL 162.79C. Only priests had "the keys of the kingdom of heaven" (*claves regni coelorum*) as successors of the disciples; see Ivo, *Epistola 63*, PL 161.80B–C.

[18] Ivo Carnotensis, *Epistola 63*, PL 162.80A.

[19] Ivo Carnotensis, *Decretum*, PL 161.135A–136A, 136D–140C, 142D–147C, cited from the *Patrologia Latina Database*, accessed on September 7, 2012. One text of Ambrose (146D) says, "Sermo igitur Christi qui potuit ex nihilo facere quod non erat, non potest ea quae sunt in id mutare quod non erant? Non enim minus est novas res dare, quam mutare naturas ... Ante benedictionem verborum coelestium alia species nominatur, post consecrationem corpus significatur ... Ante consecrationem aliud dicitur; post consecrationem sanguis nuncupatur ... Primo omnium dixit tibi de sermone Christi, qui operatur ut possit mutare, et convertere genera et instituta naturae."

[20] Ivo Carnotensis, *Decretum*, PL 161.152C–162A.

[21] *Panormia* c. 107, cited from the *Panormia Project*, accessed on September 15, 2012.

blood of Christ would begin to be without us" (*sanguinis Christi incipit esse sine nobis*).[22] The text of Clement on consuming the offerings was adapted for use in this collection.[23] The recantation of Berengar of Tours, but not the text of Lanfranc found in the *Decretum* of Ivo, appeared in the *Panormia*, along with texts of Ambrose and Augustine, giving attention to the Real Presence in a way not found in earlier collections.[24] A text attributed to "Eusebius of Emesa" (actually Caesarius of Arles) was added. It spoke of Christ converting the elements: "The invisible priest converts visible creatures into the substance of His body and blood with His word by a secret power, saying thus, *Take and eat. This is My body.* And, by a repeated sanctification, *Take and drink. This is my blood.*"[25]

When the *Decretum* of Gratian took its final shape in the twelfth century, the teaching of laws at the University of Bologna was new, and the *Decretum* or *Concord of Discordant Canons* became the textbook for canonists. In its final version, the collection had three major parts: the *Distinctiones*; the *Causae*; and a tract on sacramental law, the *Tractatus de consecratione ecclesiae*, which probably was added later. The tract contains not just conciliar canons and papal letters but excerpts from patristic texts. This brought to the attention of students of canon law reflections on the Real Presence not usually found in earlier canonistic collections.[26] The *De consecratione*, as taught in university circles, had five distinctions. These focused on churches and altars; together with the central rites performed by the clergy; especially the Eucharist; the central medieval sacrament; and baptism, the gateway to all of the Church's salvific rites. The Eucharist was discussed first, both because the mass followed consecration of a church and because it was regarded as having greater dignity than any other sacrament, even baptism. The *De consecratione* exposed students, many probably lacking theological background, to the concept of the Real Presence of Christ in the consecrated Eucharistic elements, bread and wine. It also reflected the concern of the Gregorian Reform with simony, the buying and selling of spiritual gifts, and the sexual purity expected of priests as celebrants of the mass.

[22] *Panormia* c. 146.

[23] *Panormia* cc. 148–149. The prohibition of women carrying viaticum from the Council of Reims also appears, as c. 153.

[24] *Panormia* c. 126. The Ambrose texts appear as cc. 123–125, 127–128.

[25] *Panormia* c. 129, "Invisibilis sacerdos visibiles creaturas in substantiam corporis et sanguinis sui verbo suo secreta potestate convertit, ita dicens, Accipite et comedite, hoc est corpus meum. Et, sanctificatione repetita, Accipite et bibite, hic est sanguis meus."

[26] Anders Winroth, *The Making of Gratian's Decretum* (Cambridge, 2000), 7, 12, 14, 128, 144. For an argument that the *De consecratione* was part of Gratian's original project, see John Van Engen, "Observations on *De consecratione*," in *Proceedings of the Sixth International Congress of Medieval Canon Law, Berkeley, California, 28 July–2 August 1980*, ed. Stephan Kuttner and Kenneth Pennington (Città del Vaticano, 1985), 309–320.

Despite criticism of simony as a type of heresy, the Church eventually reached consensus that priestly actions were valid despite the sins of individual ministers. This particularly meant that a mass celebrated by a simoniac priest still effected consecration of the elements, bread and watered wine.[27]

Distinction 2 of the *De consecratione* included an excerpt from the canon of "Pope Alexander" saying no offering was more worthy than that of the body and blood of Christ (De cons. D. 2 c. 8). The Real Presence was addressed in a series of excerpts from older texts, many included in previous collections. Certain of these texts can be understood as endorsing some version of the corporeal presence of Christ on the altar. For example, one canon, attributed to Gregory the Great, said of the species that a similitude of the elements, but not their substance, remained after the consecration during the canon of the mass (De cons. D. 2 c. 34): "These are the species and similitude of those things that were bread and wine before ... The priest certainly asks that the body of Christ, which now is exhibited under the species of bread and wine, be revered thus whenever it is grasped by a manifest vision."[28]

A text of Augustine said the faithful honored the invisible Christ under the species of bread and wine, which had become his flesh and blood (De cons. D. 2 c. 41):

> We honor, however, under the species of bread and wine that we see, invisible things, flesh and blood. Nor do we value similarly these two species, as we valued them before the consecration, since we faithfully confess that they were bread and wine, which nature formed, but after the consecration they are the body and blood of Christ that the blessing consecrated.[29]

One of the most Paschasian texts in this Distinction was a longer version of the discussion of conversion of the elements attributed to "Eusebius of Emesa" (De cons. D. 2 c. 35). It included the passage about the

[27] Stanley Chodorow, *Christian Political Theory and Church Politics in the Mid-Twelfth Century. The Ecclesiology of Gratian's Decretum* (Berkeley, 1972), 9–13, 90–95, 113–114; Kathleen G. Cushing, *Reform and the Papacy in the Eleventh Century: Spirituality and Social Change* (Manchester, 2005), 95–99.

[28] Friedberg 1.1324–1325, "Species et similitudo illarum rerum uocabula sunt, que ante fuerunt, scilicet panis et uini, ... Postulat quippe sacerdos, ut corpus Christi, quod sub specie panis et uini nunc geritur, manifesta uisione, sicuti reuera est, quandoque capiatur." Gratian probably had this text, which had been used by Lanfranc in his argument for a more corporeal interpretation of the presence of Christ, from one of the collections attributed to Ivo of Chartres; see Friedberg 1.1324, n. 404.

[29] Friedberg 1.1328, "Nos autem in specie panis et uini, quam uidemus, res inuisibiles, id est carnem et sanguinem, honoramus, nec similiter pendimus has duas species, quemadmodum ante consecrationem pendebamus, cum fideliter fateamur, ante consecrationem panem esse et uinum, quod natura formauit; post consecrationem uero Christi carnem esse et sanguinem, quod benedictio consecrauit."

conversion of the elements previously included in the *Panormia*. A text of Ambrose (De cons. D. 2 c. 55) said that what was bread before the consecration (literally, *ante uerba sacramentorum*) became Christ's body afterward. The *De consecratione* also included the first, literal-minded recantation by Berengar of Tours, the one imposed on him by Cardinal Humbert of Silva Candida (De cons. D. 2 c. 42).

The early Decretists had little to say about the *De consecratione*, as Paucapalea did,[30] or said nothing at all. Serious discussion of the tract and its sacramental doctrines may have begun with Rufinus, who taught in Bologna in the mid-twelfth century. Rufinus drew on the *Decretum* of Burchard of Worms in his writings to supplement Gratian's collection. Thus he quoted Burchard as endorsing communion for the sick by intinction, but he rejected it for general reception by the faithful.[31] Rufinus explained that the Eucharist followed baptism in sequence but preceded it in the *De consecratione* because of its greater excellence.[32] The sacrament of the Eucharist was instituted by Christ at the Last Supper, not by the Church itself.[33]

The mass, according to Rufinus, involved three mysteries: the sacrament itself with its signs of bread and wine; the sign and its reality (*res*) together, the body and blood of Christ; the reality achieved in the sacrament, the unity of the Church. Rufinus apparently was the first canonist to use this categorization, which would become common among the canonists.[34] The whole Christ, God and man, had to be present in the

[30] *Die Summa des Paucapalea über das Decretum Gratiani*, ed. Johann Friedrich von Schulte (Giessen, 1890; Aalen, 1965), 144–146. Nothing is written about the tract in *Summa Magistri Rolandi*, ed. Friedrich Tanner (Innsbruck, 1874; Aalen, 1962) or the *Summa Parisiensis on the Decretum of Gratian*, ed. Terence P. McLaughlin (Toronto, 1952).

[31] Rufinus, *Summa decretorum*, ed. Heinrich Singer (Paderborn, 1902; Aalen, 1963), 553: De cons. D. 2 c. 7. Burchard also was the source of the formula Rufinus gave for communion, " 'Corpus et sanguinis Domini nostri Iesu Christi proficiat tibi' etc."

[32] Rufinus, *Summa decretorum*, 551: De cons. D. 2 c. 1, "Cum sacramentum baptismatis prius sit tempore sacrificio altaris, ordine temporis commonente agendum prius fuerat de baptismo quam de eucharistia. De hoc tamen prius agit in hac secunda distinctione et propter dignitatis excellentiam – hoc enim sacramentum dignius est baptismate."

[33] Rufinus, *Summa decretorum*, 555: De cons. D. 2 c. 39, "*Non est sacramentum religionis*, i. e. ab ecclesiastica religione inventum, sed tantum a Christo in cena institutum."

[34] Rufinus, *Summa decretorum*, 552: De cons. D. 2 c. 1, "Denique triplex misterii continentia in hoc cognoscitur, quia sunt in hoc sacramento tria: unum, quod est sacramentum tantum, scil. species panis et uini; aliud, quod est sacramentum et res sacramenti, videlicet ipsum essentialiter corpus et sanguinis Domini; tertium, quod est res sacramenti tantum, utique unitas ecclesie." The possibility that Rufinus borrowed this vocabulary requires further exploration. Among theologians, this idea was popularized by Peter Lombard; see Marilyn McCord Adams, *Some Later Medieval Theologies of the Eucharist: Thomas Aquinas, Giles of Rome, Duns Scotus and William of Ockham* (Oxford, 2012), 266. Even earlier, Alger of Liège distinguished between *sacramentum, res sacramenti*, and *effectus*; see Hans Geybels, *Adelman of Liège and the Eucharistic Controversy* (Louvain, 2013), 11, 30, 34.

Eucharist for it to be effective. Thus the bread that was consecrated represented the body, and the wine the blood, but body and blood were not truly separated underneath these signs. Both species represented things spiritual and intelligible, although hidden from humanity (*inuisibilis nobis*).[35] Water was poured into the chalice along with the wine because both blood and water flowed from Christ's pierced side (John 19:34) and because this mixture represents the nature all humanity shared with Him and His divinity, symbolized by water and wine respectively.[36]

Rufinus employed language rooted in the Fathers and probably from early Scholasticism in his own sacramental theology. Christ was present essentially or substantially (*essentialiter*) in the Eucharist, something Rufinus did not explain clearly; but he used the same adverb to describe humanity's natural unity with Christ.[37] Glossing *Ego Berengarius* (De cons. D. 2 c. 55), the canonist faced the excessive literalism of the text as Cardinal Humbert had written it. Rufinus accepted the canon's rejection of a purely spiritual presence of the Savior in the Eucharist, but his idea of the Real Presence was nuanced to the edge of being vague. He said that the priest, when breaking the bread, did not divide Christ *secundum se*. Christ was truly present, but His body was not injured in the fraction of the host. The priest, according to Rufinus, divided the host with Christ present under the sign (*in sacramento*) before he gave communion to the faithful: "The [true] body of Christ [born of the Virgin], which is there [on the altar], is not in itself (*secundum se*) crushed and divided, but rather [such division] occurs only on the level of the sacrament [i.e., the outward appearances]."[38]

[35] Rufinus, *Summa decretorum*, 556: De cons. D. 1 c. 48, "*carne et sanguine, utroque inuisibili spirituali intelligibili*, i. e. duplici specie representante corpus et sanguinem spiritualia et intelligibilis et inuisibilis nobis." See also 555. The doctrine of concomitance was intended to counter literal-minded interpretations of the Eucharist, according to Caroline Walker Bynum, *Christian Materiality: An Essay on Religion in Late Medieval Europe* (Boston, 2011), 209.

[36] Rufinus, *Summa decretorum*, 552: De cons. D. 2 c. 2, "*Sic* etc. *sine Christo*. i. e. sine totali Christi sacramento, quia ex eius latere etiam aqua profluxit."

[37] Rufinus, *Summa decretorum*, 560: De cons. D. 2 c. 82, "Alia enim essentialiter naturalis unitas est, qua nos sumus unum cum Christo; et alia, qua Christus est unum cum patre." The Scholastics were settling a theology of the Incarnation in this period, dismissing any idea that Christ had two persons, not one, as heretical; see Walter Principe, *Philip the Chancellor's Theology of the Hypostatic Union* (Toronto, 1975), 194–195.

[38] Translation by Ian Levy. Rufinus, *Summa decretorum*, 555: De cons. D. 2 c. 42, "Sed aliud est putare sacramentum ibi esse sine veritate corporis et sanguinis Domini, et ideo dici in solo sacramento tractare: quod hic improbatur; aliud est credere corpus Domini quod ibi est, non secundum se, sed in sacramento conteri et dividi." Rufinus's gloss was excerpted in the *Distinctiones Si mulier eadem hora seu Monacenses*, ed. Rosalba Sorice (Città del Vaticano, 2002), 146–147.

In communion the faithful were indeed united to Christ by means of that same humanity they shared with Him. Through Jesus they were united to the Father, to whom Jesus was united "by unity of nature and substance" (*unitate nature et substantie*). Thus the Eucharist was the sacrament of unity, although human unity with Christ could not be perfect.[39] Communion was offered in the broken bread without bloodshed (*sine cruore*), unlike the bloody Old Testament sacrifices.[40] Believers were able to enjoy the benefits of spiritual eating (*manducatio spiritualis*), something denied to unbelievers.[41]

Rufinus had an influence in Cologne and vicinity; but the same region was open to influences from Paris with its university, rich in professors of theology and canon law. Attached to the *Summa* of Stephen of Tournai in the edition by Schulte is a commentary on the *De consecratione, Fecit Moyses tabernaculum*. That commentary adopted, from the Scholastic language used in Paris, the term "transubstantiation," and it was one of the earliest Decretist texts to do so. Following Rufinus, the author said that the mass involved three mysteries. One was a sign but not the thing signified, the bread and wine employed in the mass; the second was both signifying and signified, the body and blood of Christ that He assumed from the Virgin Mary; and the third was signified without signifying something else, the unity of the Church.[42] The body of Christ was made up of many members, the faithful, as the Eucharistic bread was made of many grains.[43]

39 Rufinus, *Summa decretorum*, 557–560: De cons. D. 2 c. 82.

40 Rufinus, *Summa decretorum*, 557: De cons. D. 2 c. 78, "*Ubi pars est corporis*, id est illius specie, in qua latet corpus, *est totum* essentialiter ipsum corpus Christi . . . *Incruentem*, id est sine cruore." This sentiment was not new; see Aelfric's letter to the bishop of Sherbourne in *Councils & Synods*, 1/1.200.

41 Rufinus, *Summa decretorum*, 560: De cons. D. 2 c. 92. The same idea appears in writings of theologians like Bonaventure; see Adams, *Some Later Medieval Theologies of the Eucharist: Thomas Aquinas, Giles of Rome, Duns Scotus and William of Ockham*, 260.

42 The text appears in Stephen of Tournai, *Die Summa über das Decretum Gratiani*, ed. Johann Friedrich von Schulte (Giessen, 1891; Aalen, 1965), 272: De cons. D. 2 c. 32, "Ad quid dixerat visibile sacrificium, cum appellatione corporis domini ad tria porrigitur, quorum primum est signum et non significatum, scil. forma panis et vini, aliud significatum et significans, corpus scil. quod traxit de virgine, tertium significatum non signum, scil. unitas fidelium? De signo visibili in his duobus cap. fit mentio." On the origins of this work, see Peter Landau, "Die Dekretsumme *Fecit Moyses tabernaculum* – ein weiteres Werk der Kölner Kanonistik," *Zeitschrift der Savigny-Stiftung für Rechtsgeschichte, Kanonistische Abteilung* 127 (2010), 602–608. For Rufinus's appearance in another work from Cologne, see, for example, *Summa "Elegantius in iure divino" seu Coloniensis*, ed. Gérard Fransen and Stephan Kuttner, 2 (Città del Vaticano, 1978), 72–73.

43 *Die Summa über das Decretum Gratiani*, 272–273: De cons. D. 2 c. 36, "Sicut enim de pluribus granis unus panis fit, et sicut ex pluribus purissimis membris immaculatum Christi corpus conficitur, ita ex pluribus fidelium personis sacrosancta constat ecclesia, cuius membra sunt singuli quique fideles." This same theme appears in the *De expositione missae* by Hildebert of Lavardin; see PL 171.1166A, cited from the *Patrologia Latina Online*, accessed on April 4, 2011.

The anonymous canonist said of the mass that it was not impossible for God to change the species into the body and blood of Christ.[44] The transformation took place with the words of consecration, which had to be said in their entirety to be effective. These effected "entire transubstantiation" (*tota transsubstantiatio*) of the elements into the sacrament of the Eucharist.[45] A priest who omitted proper words or gestures was to be deposed if he acted without true faith in Christ's presence, rather than from ignorance. He only could be restored to his office when properly instructed in sacramental theology.[46] If the words were said correctly, the author affirmed, Christ's body was to be found under the appearances of the consecrated bread and wine, which retained the accidents of color, taste, odor, and roundness. The consecrated bread even could satisfy human hunger if consumed in a sufficient quantity.[47]

The author of *Fecit Moyses* did not give an exact definition of the term "transubstantiation," but he did make reference to Parisian disagreements about the Real Presence. After mentioning the *Sentences* of Peter Lombard, he cited Robert of Melun and Richard of Saint Victor as saying, "What once was bread is now the body of the Lord" (*id quod fuit panis nunc esse corpus domini*). Then the canonist noted the objections of others, especially Adam Parvipontanus, that something that was not the Lord's body could not become it.[48] The canonist summarized the affirmative case, using the developing language of transubstantiation: "That which was bread etc. is converted, transformed, transubstantiated into the body of Christ."[49] The canonist went on to discuss the differences among the

[44] *Die Summa über das Decretum Gratiani*, 272: De cons. D. 2 c. 35, "Plurium inductio ostendit, deo non esse impossibile, visibiles has species in corpus suum et in sanguinem commutare."

[45] *Die Summa über das Decretum Gratiani*, 273: De cons. D. 2 c. 39, "De consecratione panis et vini certum est, quia ad verba Christi: Hoc est corpus meum, hic e. s. etc. fit transsubstantiatio."

[46] *Die Summa über das Decretum Gratiani*, 273: De cons. D. 2 c. 39, "Sic ergo celebrantem sine spe restitutionis credimus deponendum, quod consecravit neque asserendo quod non sit corpus Christi religione sumendum, nisi certa in hoc articulo auctoritas instruatur."

[47] *Die Summa über das Decretum Gratiani*, 272: De cons. D. 2 c. 32, "Et nota quod, cum principaliter dici soleat in specie panis et vini tria accidentia post consecrationem remanere, scil. colorem, saporem, odorem, remanet tamen et alia, ut in pane rotunditas, in utroque vis satiandi, si quantitative sumatur, et multa alia." Roundness was tied to the idea of the host as Christ's coin; see Roger E. Reynolds, "Christ's Money: Eucharistic Azyme Hosts in the Ninth Century According to Bishop Eldefonsus of Spain: Observations on the Origin, Meaning, and Context of a Mysterious Revelation," *Peregrinations: Journal of Medieval Art & Architecture* 4/2 (2013), 1–69.

[48] *Die Summa über das Decretum Gratiani*, 273–274: De cons. D. 2 c. 40.

[49] *Fecit Moyses* attributes the words to Richard of Saint Victor; see *Die Summa über das Decretum Gratiani*, 273: De cons. D. 2 c. 40. See also *Die Summa über das Decretum Gratiani*, 274: De cons. D. 2 c. 40, "Determinabat autem eam sic: Id quod fuit panis etc.

theologians before refusing to take sides in a dispute between such learned men because of his own infirmity.[50] Instead, he affirmed that the body of Christ was on any altar in the form of bread. This fact overcame all the arguments of the philosophers and was to be considered something beyond the grasp of human reason: "Therefore, in this singular and excellent body all arguments of the philosophers become quiet. Nothing is effected here according to the ordinary course of nature. Nothing is judged comprehensible by human reason."[51] The author also said that many authorities proved that what was consumed at the altar was indeed the body and blood, which was demonstrated, according to Gratian, by the communicant becoming of one nature with Christ through participation in the sacrament.[52]

This strong affirmation of Eucharistic presence had practical consequences for the canonist. The author of *Fecit Moyses* discussed the proper punishment for a priest who erred in how he filled the chalice, especially by using only wine or water. He argued that a mixture was used at the Last Supper and thus was necessary for the sacrament.[53] Discussing the reception of communion, the canonist affirmed the doctrine of concomitance, the belief that the whole Christ was received under either species.[54] The canonist, like Rufinus before him, limited communion by intinction to the sick. Otherwise, only the priest received the consecrated wine, because he personified Christ Himself.[55] In all cases, both good and bad persons might receive communion with very different results according to their states of soul.[56]

It is not possible to treat all commentaries on the *De consecratione* at this time. However, we can see how "transubstantiation" became an accepted

convertitur, transformatur, transubstantiatur in corpus Christi." The author used transubstantiation loosely, as a synonym for other terms implying transformation; see Ian Christopher Levy, "The Eucharist and Canon Law in the High Middle Ages," in *A Companion to the Eucharist in the Middle Ages*, ed. Levy, Gary Macy, and Kristen Van Ausdall (Leiden, 2012), 399–445 at 420–422.

50 *Die Summa über das Decretum Gratiani*, 274: De cons. D. 2 c. 40, "Tantorum virorum aliquem praeferre alteri nostrae non est infirmitatis."

51 *Die Summa über das Decretum Gratiani*, 274: De cons. D. 2 c. 44, "In hoc ergo singulari et superexcellenti corpore omnia philosophorum argumenta conquiescant, nihil hic solito cursu naturae efficitur, nihil humana ratione comprehensibile aestimatur."

52 *Die Summa über das Decretum Gratiani*, 276: De cons. D. 2 c. 82, "Verum Christi corpus et sanguis in altari nos summere quod iam multis auctoritatibus probatum est et hic probat gratianus per hoc, quod sacramento hoc participantes unius cum Christo naturae officimur."

53 *Die Summa über das Decretum Gratiani*, 270: De cons. D. 2 c. 2.

54 *Die Summa über das Decretum Gratiani*, 271: De cons. D. 2 c. 12, "sub utraque enim totus Christus sumitur."

55 *Die Summa über das Decretum Gratiani*, 269–270: De cons. D. 1 c. 1.

56 *Die Summa über das Decretum Gratiani*, 276: De cons. D. 2 c. 92.

term among Italian canonists. This can be seen in the works of Simon of Bisignano and Sicard of Cremona, and later in the *Summa* composed by Huguccio of Pisa.[57] Simon may have been the first Italian canonist to use the language of transmutation or transubstantiation. He wrote about the words of consecration: "Here are those words through which transmutation of the bread into flesh and the wine into blood occurs."[58] Simon also used the language of transformation (*transire*) elsewhere in his *Summa*.[59] His *Summa* also says at c. *Species et similitudo* (De cons. D. 1 c. 34) that those opening words of the canon were used because, "after the consecration the substance of bread and wine is not there, but only the species and resemblance."[60]

Although Sicard had studied in Paris, he used much the same language in his *Summa*, borrowing heavily from Simon's text. Writing about the effect of the words said by the priest, he said almost exactly the same thing.[61] Sicard also used the language of transition (*transire*).[62] He said that the body of Christ "was made from bread" (*ex pane fit corpus Christi*).[63] Perhaps most indicative of the canonist's opinion is a reference to the accidents remaining after substitution.[64] Both canonists thought that the Eucharist was celebrated at the Last Supper to bring the old rites to an end, while inaugurating the new, more effective sacraments.[65]

[57] Huguccio's commentary on the *De consecratione* was added in the third stage of his *Summa*; see Wolfgang P. Müller, *Huguccio: The Life, Works and Thought of a Twelfth-Century Jurist* (Washington, D.C., 1994), 74.

[58] *Summa in decretum Simonis Bisianensis*, ed. Petrus V. Aimone Braida (Città del Vaticano, 2014), 55: De cons. D. 2 c. 55, "Hec sunt uerba illa per que fit transmutatio panis in carnem et uinum in sanguinem." In Augsburg Staats- und Stadtbibliothek MS 1, fol. 1ra–72vb at fol. 68va, the word "transubstantiatio" is used instead of "transmutatio."

[59] *Summa in decretum Simonis Bisianensis*, 510: De cons. D. 2 c. 1. The same passage uses the word "mutat," which also is borrowed from the text of De cons. D. 2 c. 55.

[60] *Summa in decretum Simonis Bisianensis*, 520: De cons. D. 1 c. 34, "Species et similitudo ideo dicit quia post consecrationem non est ibi substantia panis et uini, sed species tantum et similitudo." Elsewhere Simon says that the accidents of taste and weight remain; see *Summa in decretum Simonis Bisianensis*, 514: De cons. D. 1 c. 1.

[61] Sicardus Cremonensis, *Summa decretorum*, Bamberg Staatsbibliothek Can. MS 38: De cons. D. 1 c. 55, 102B, "*Accipite*. scilicet. uerba illa per que fit transubstantiatio panis in carnem et uinum in sanguinem." See also 102A: De cons. D. 2 c. 23, "unde corpus transubstantiatur." On Sicard's use of Simon, see Rudolf Weigand, "The Transmontane Decretists," in *The History of Medieval Canon Law in the Classical Period, 1140–1234: from Gratian to the Decretals of Pope Gregory IX*, ed. Wilfried Hartmann and Kenneth Pennington (Washington, D.C.), 174–210 at 190–191.

[62] Sicardus Cremonensis, *Summa decretorum*, 102A: De cons. D. 2 c. 23.

[63] Sicardus Cremonensis, *Summa decretorum*, 102B–103A: De cons. D. 2 c. 55.

[64] Sicardus Cremonensis, *Summa decretorum*, 101A: De cons. D. 2 c. 1, "remanent ergo illa accidentia per se substituta."

[65] *Summa in decretum Simonis Bisianensis*, 512: De cons. D. 2 c. 1, 526: De cons. D. 2 c. 80; Sicardus Cremonensis, *Summa decretorum*, 100B–101A: De cons. D. 2 c. 1.

In his *Mitralis de officiis* Sicard[66] used the term without any reference to theological controversies over its meaning. Sicard said Christ established the mass at the Last Supper "when he transmuted bread and wine into body and blood." The canonist went on to say that this occurred with the words *Hoc est corpus meum*. These words gave priests the power "by which bread is changed, that is transubstantiated, into the body and wine into blood."[67]

Sicard's discussion of the canon of the mass said that the bread was divinely transubstantiated. He said, however, that creation from nothing was more wondrous than the transubstantiation of something already created.[68] Sicard also said logic, mathematics, and physics could not grasp this reality.[69]

Although Huguccio did not write directly on the liturgy, his *Summa* included a detailed discussion of the Eucharist. His exposition of *De consecratione* D. 2 displayed a literal-minded approach to the correspondence between Christ's body and His presence in the sacrament. Thus, commenting on the first canon of that Distinction, he identified three things converted during the mass: bread, wine, and water. These become Christ's body, blood, and other humors. The third he called the "watery humor" (*aquaticum humorem*).[70] Advancing an opinion that would be rejected by Innocent III, Huguccio said that, in the chalice, the wine, signifying Christ, became blood, while the water became "other watery humors" (*alios humores aquaticos*), signifying the faithful united to Him. This opinion was based on a belief that a sacrament, as sign, had to

[66] *Sicardi Cremonensis episcopi Mitralis de officiis*, ed. Gábor Sarbak and Lorenz Weinrich (Turnhout, 2008). Timothy Thibodeau, "The Influence of Canon Law on Liturgical Exposition c.1100–1300," *Sacris erudiri* 37 (1997), 185–202. The theologian and liturgist Johannes Beleth also used the term "transubstantiation," distinguishing it from sanctification, like the blessing of holy water; see *Iohannis Beleth summa de ecclesiasticis officiis*, ed. Heribert Douteil (Turnhout, 1976), 183–184.

[67] *Sicardi Cremonensis episcopi Mitralis*, 127, "Missam instituit dominus Iesus, *sacerdos secundum ordinem Melchisedech*, quando panem et uinum in corpus et sanguinem transmutauit, dicens: *Hoc est corpus meum. Hic est sanguis meus.* Ecce quod Dominus missam instituit, id est hęc uerba constituit eisque uim substantiuam dedit, quibus panis in corpus et uinum mittitur, id est transubstantiatur, in sanguinem." Sicard, like other writers on the mass, identified the priest's acts with those of Christ, Whom he represented; see *Sicardi mitralis*, 195.

[68] *Sicardi Cremonensis episcopi Mitralis*, 190, "Sed mirabilius est, de nichilo cuncta creare quam creaturam in creaturam transsubstantiare." He continued that this happened in natural processes.

[69] *Sicardi Cremonensis episcopi Mitralis*, 190, "Huc enim logica non ascendit; hoc mathematica non inquirit; in hoc physica deficit."

[70] Huguccio, *Summa decretorum*, Admont Stiftsbibliothek MS 7, fol. 422ra: De cons. D. 1 c. 1, "Numquid sunt sacramenta unitatis et eiusdem in rei. nota ergo distingue in corpore Christi est caro et sanguis et iii. alii humores causa facilioris doctrine de cetero appellabimus aquaticum humorem."

resemble what it signified.[71] Huguccio said that transubstantiation of the species occurred when Christ pronounced the words of consecration at the Last Supper. This same form of words effected transubstantiation during the mass.[72] Huguccio considered and then rejected an argument that some other blessing said before these words effected change. He concluded that the body of Christ "began to be" when the priest used the Savior's words at the Last Supper.[73]

The Italian Decretists saw the Eucharist as building unity. Simon of Bisignano regarded the Eucharistic elements as signifying something else, it was the sign or "sacrament of the unity of the faithful" (*sacramentum alteri rei. scilicet. unitatis fidelium*), because the body of Christ was made up of purified persons, become like the pure body of the Savior.[74] Like other writers, he emphasized the way bread was made from many grains and wine from many grapes as making the Eucharist the sacrament of the Church's unity.[75] Likewise, the mixing of water into the wine in the chalice signified the people united to Christ.[76] Simon saw this sign as based on similitude between these species and the Church's unity, which they effected.[77] His vision of unity included the faithful adhering to Christ

[71] Huguccio, *Summa decretorum*, Admont Stiftsbibliothek MS 7, fol. 422ra: De cons. D. 1 c. 1, "Species uini est sacramentum sanguinis Christi. Species aque est sacramentum aquatici humoris in corpore Christi. species enim panis significat carnem Christi. species uini significat sanguinem Christi. species aque significat alios humores in corpore Christi. sed quia omne sacramentum debet habere aliquam similitudinem cum re illa cuius est sacramentum. uideamus que similitudo inter has species et illa significata possit assignari." See also *Summa decretorum*, fol. 422rb: De cons. D. 1 c. 1, "uinum enim conuertitur in sanguinem et illum significat. aqua conuertitur in alios humores aquaticos et illos significat." Huguccio (loc. cit.) added an argument that it was watery humor, not water, that flowed from Christ's pierced side on the cross (John 19:34).

[72] Huguccio, *Summa decretorum*, Admont Stiftsbibliothek MS 7, fol. 426rb: De cons. D. 2 c. 25, "Nota cum in canone profertur hec uerba. hoc est corpus meum. hic est sanguinis ex uirtute horum uerborum fit transubstantio."

[73] Huguccio, *Summa decretorum*, Admont Stiftsbibliothek MS 7, fol. 426va: De cons. D. 2 c. 25, "Quibus Christus usus est in cena quibus uerbis Christus tantam uim et efficaciam tribuit quod ad prolationem eorum factam a sacerdote ut debet fieri corpus Christi incipiat esse."

[74] *Summa in decretum Simonis Bisianensis*, 511: De cons. D. 2 c. 1, "Item etiam est sacramentum alterius rei, scilicet unitatis fidelium, quia ut corpus Christi constat ex multis membris purissimis et immaculatis, ita societas ecclesie ex multis personis a crimine puris consistit."

[75] *Summa in decretum Simonis Bisianensis*, 511: De cons. D. 2 c. 1, also saying the unity of the Church was "res et non sacramentum," an end and not a sign toward an end. Simon also tied the invisible but unifying body of Christ to the body born of the Virgin; see *Summa in decretum Simonis Bisianensis*, 519: De cons. D. 2 c. 32.

[76] *Summa in decretum Simonis Bisianensis*, 514: De cons. D. 2 c. 1, 515: De cons. D. 2 c. 2.

[77] *Summa in decretum Simonis Bisianensis*, 520: De cons. D. 2 c. 34, "Species et similitudo ideo dicit quia post consecrationem non est ibi substantia panis et uini, sed species tantum et similitudo."

in love, as Christ inhered in them through grace.[78] This created a unity not just of nature (with Christ's humanity) but of will, which the *sacramentum unitatis*, the Eucharist, promoted.[79] Those lacking that unity with the Church signified by Christ's flesh would not have eternal life.[80] Sicard thought the Church was visible, even palpable (*palpabile*), because Christ had been visible when He suffered scars (*cicatrices*) for the salvation of the people.[81] He also repeated Simon's words about the elements representing something else, "the unity of the faithful."[82]

Huguccio addressed this at greater length, using a version of the terminology of signifier and thing signified, which had become common among both theologians and canonists. He said the species were "very much a sign" (*tantum sacramentum*). The Real Presence was both the signified and signifier, Christ's body being both the thing in itself and the sign of ecclesiastical unity. The Church's unity was the thing effected (*res*), as the faithful became parts of the body of Christ.[83] In the Church were virtues and other natural gifts signified by water.[84] The Church's unity was made up of many persons united by charity. This unity was signified by the wine, made from many grapes.[85] Huguccio said, "Thus the Church is united to Christ by a unity of faith and charity." This required both Christ, signified by the sacrament of the Lord's body, and the faithful, signified by the water used in making bread.[86]

By the end of the twelfth century, transubstantiation was a term known to canonists on both sides of the Alps. The question arises: When did the language of transubstantiation gain approval from the papacy and episcopate? There is a common supposition that the Fourth Lateran Council

[78] *Summa in decretum Simonis Bisianensis*, 522: De cons. D. 2 c. 46.
[79] *Summa in decretum Simonis Bisianensis*, 526–527: De cons. D. 2 c. 82.
[80] *Summa in decretum Simonis Bisianensis*, 522–523, "Ita 'nisi manducaueritis carnem meam', idest nisi uniti eritis unitati ecclesie per carnem meam significate non habetis uitam eternam."
[81] Sicardus Cremonensis, *Summa decretorum*, 102B: De cons. D. 2 c. 48.
[82] Sicardus Cremonensis, *Summa decretorum*: De cons. D. 2 c. 1, 99B.
[83] Huguccio, *Summa decretorum*, fol. 422ra: De cons. D. 1 c. 1, "Notandum quod in sacramento eucharistie tria sunt. unum quod est tantum sacramentum. scilicet. species panis. species uini. species aque que uidetur facta conuersione. Aliud quod est tantum res sacramenti. scilicet. unitas ecclesie. et est res species panis et uini. id est. fidelium. tertium quod est sacramentum et res sacramenti ut corpus Christi quod est sacramentum unitatis ecclesie et est res species panis et uini et aque. Item species panis et uini et aque est sacramentum illarum duarum rerum. scilicet. corporis Christi et unitatis ecclesie."
[84] Huguccio, *Summa decretorum*, fol. 422ra: De cons. D. 2 c. 1.
[85] Huguccio, *Summa decretorum*, fol. 422ra: De cons. D. 2 c. 1, "Ita unitas ecclesie constat ex diuersis personis glutino caritatis coniunctis. species uini significat unitatem ecclesie. id est. gratiam caritatis qua fideles uniuntur."
[86] Huguccio, *Summa decretorum*, fol. 422va: De cons. D. 2 c. 2, "Ita ecclesia per unitatem fidei et caritatis unitur Christo. uel *sine Christo*. id est. sine sacramento corporis Christi. id est. sine aqua que est sacramentum ecclesie."

(1215) defined transubstantiation as a dogma explaining the Real Presence of Christ in the Eucharist. The decree *Firmiter credimus*, the first of the conciliar canons formulated at the Lateran, did mention transubstantiation, as a past participle (*transubstantiatis*) near the end of the text:

> There is indeed one universal church of the faithful, outside of which nobody at all is saved, in which Jesus Christ is both priest and sacrifice. His body and blood are truly contained in the sacrament of the altar under the forms of bread and wine, the bread and the wine having been changed in substance, by God's power, into his body and blood, so that in order to achieve this mystery of unity we receive from God what he received from us. Nobody can effect this sacrament except a priest who has been properly ordained according to the church's keys, which Christ gave to the apostles and their successors.[87]

Firmiter, however, was primarily concerned with the doctrine of the Trinity taught by Peter Lombard, only affirming the priesthood and the sacraments near its end. No detailed exposition of the term was offered; and other opinions were not condemned, as the contrary doctrine of the Trinity taught by Joachim of Flora was censured by the council.[88] The Lateran canons were circulated as a group, inserted into *Compilatio quarta* and distributed under topical titles in the *Decretals of Gregory IX*. *Firmiter credimus* appeared in the *Extra* as the first canon under the title "On the Supreme Trinity and the Catholic Faith" (*De summa Trinitate et fide catholica*, X 1.1.1).[89] However, transubstantiation did not enter medieval canon law through the Lateran canons. The term originated at the University of Paris, where it was created by theologians wrestling with the theology of the Real Presence in a Scholastic context;[90] and, as we have seen, it had entered medieval canon law in discussions of Gratian's *Decretum*.

[87] *Decrees of the Ecumenical Councils*, 1.230–231 at 230, "Una vero est fidelium universalis ecclesia, extra quam nullus omnino salvatur, in qua idem ipse sacerdos et sacrificium Iesus Christus, cuius corpus et sanguinis in sacramento altaris sub speciebus panis et vini veraciter continetur, transubstantiatis pane in corpus et vino in sanguinem potestate divina, ut ad perficiendum mysterium unitatis accipiamus ipsi de suo, quod accepit ipse de nostro. Et hoc utique sacramentum nemo potest conficere, nisi sacerdos, qui fuerit rite ordinatus secundum claves ecclesiae, quas concessit apostolis et eorum successoribus Iesus Christus."

[88] For the decree *Damnamus*, see *Decrees of the Ecumenical Councils*, 1.231–233. Compare R. N. Swanson, *Religion and Devotion in Europe, c. 1215–c. 1515* (Cambridge, 1995), 21–25 with Gary Macy, "The Dogma of Transubstantiation in the Middle Ages," *Journal of Ecclesiastical History* 45 (1984), 11–51.

[89] *Constitutiones Concilii quarti Lateranensis*; *Quinque Compilationes Antiquae nec non Collectio canonum Lipsiensis*, ed. Emil Friedberg (Leipzig, 1882; Graz, 1956), 135–150.

[90] Joseph Goering, "The Invention of Transubstantiation," *Traditio* 46 (1991), 147–170.

How then are we to interpret the reference to transubstantiation in the decree *Firmiter credimus*? Some scholars believe Innocent III played a direct role in drafting the decree. If so, that may account for the reference to transubstantiation. Innocent, as Lothar of Segni, had studied theology in Paris. It is less certain if he also studied law in Bologna.[91] A Parisian education may explain the presence of the language of transubstantiation in his description of the nuptial banquet in "Book on the Fourfold Nature of Marriages" (*Liber de quadrapartita specie nuptiarum*).[92] Lothar's "Six Books on the Sacrament of the Altar" (*De sacro altaris mysterio libri sex*) discussed the Real Presence in more detail, including a chapter on "When Transubstantiation Occurs" (*Quando fiat transsubstantiatio*). There he emphasized the transformation that occurred with the words of consecration. Lothar also added a chapter in which he said the transubstantiated bread was "more to be venerated than discussed" (*magis veneranda quam discutienda*).[93] He also discussed the miraculous return to materiality once a host, its accidents existing without a subject, was "corroded, as when eaten" (*quamvis hujus accidentia sine subjecto possunt sic corrodi, sicut edi*).[94] Lothar thought simple faith should suffice.[95] With his knowledge of Parisian terminology, Innocent may have presumed the council was speaking in language familiar to learned clerics. In that case, *Firmiter credimus* was neither defining the concept, nor, as Philip Hughes once claimed, was this the first official use of the term. Innocent, as we shall see, already had used it in a decretal.[96]

The Decretalists did pick up on this concept, but they did not identify it strongly at first with *Firmiter credimus*. The *casus* literature on the decree emphasized only the necessity of having an ordained priest celebrate the mass.[97] The apparatus of Vincentius Hispanus on the Lateran decrees pointed elsewhere in our examination of the language of transubstantiation. Vincentius, glossing *Firmiter*, said the accidents miraculously remained when Christ was present *sub speciebus*.[98] He referred the reader,

[91] Kenneth Pennington, "The Legal Education of Pope Innocent III," *Bulletin of Medieval Canon Law* 4 (1974), 70–77.

[92] *Liber de quadrapartita specie nuptiarum*, PL 217.945, cited from the *Patrologia Latina Database*, accessed on January 2, 2012.

[93] *De sacro altaris mysterio libri sex*, PL 217.859–861, 868–870, cited from the *Patrologia Latina Database*, accessed on January 2, 2012. Innocent also discussed the recantation of Berengar of Tours, saying he understood the flesh of Christ too literally, seeing it as potentially divided into morsels; PL 217.862A–863A.

[94] PL 217.863B. [95] PL 217.863C.

[96] Philip Hughes, *The Church in Crisis: A History of the General Councils 325–1870* (Welwyn Garden City, 1961), 215.

[97] *Constitutiones Concilii quarti Lateranensis*, 466, 477.

[98] *Constitutiones Concilii quarti Lateranensis*, 288, "*sub speciebus*: Et ita albedo, rotunditas et alia accidentia sunt ibi sine subiecto et hoc miraculose, uel sunt in aere."

however, to Innocent III's decretal *Cum Marthae*, which made reference not just to bread and wine but to the water added to the chalice as being changed.[99]

Cum Marthae originated as a letter of Pope Innocent addressed to the archbishop of Lyon, dated November 29, 1202. The extensive text of the decretal addressed the biblical or extra biblical origins of the words of consecration. Innocent, as was typical, noted three aspects of the sacrament: "We must, however, distinguish accurately between three things which are different in this sacrament, namely, the visible form, the truth of the body, and the spiritual power. The form is of the bread and wine; the truth, of the flesh and blood; the power, of unity and of charity." Then the pope invoked the distinction already used by Rufinus between the species as "sacrament and not reality," Christ's flesh and blood as "sacrament and reality," and the unity of the Church as "the reality and not the sacrament." Thus Innocent embraced teachings already known to the canonists.[100] *Cum Marthae* advocated transubstantiation as an explanation of the Real Presence, and he explained of the changing of the wine: "Therefore, it can happen that the accidents change subject, just as it can happen that the subject changes accidents." The pope added the telling phrase: "Obviously, nature gives way to miracle, and power overcomes custom."[101]

Innocent also carefully addressed the status of the water added to the chalice, asking whether it was "transubstantiated" (*transsubstantiatur*) with the wine, becoming Christ's blood, not His phlegm. The pope summarized conflicting opinions before saying it was "more probable" (*probabilior*) that the water too was "transmuted" (*transmutari*): "However, among the aforesaid opinions the most probable one is judged to be the one that asserts that the water is transmuted with the wine to better show forth the special character of the sacrament."[102]

[99] *Constitutiones Concilii quarti Lateranensis*, 288, "*panis et vini*: cum aqua, extra iii. de celebrat. missar. Cum Marthe."

[100] Heinrich Denzinger, *The Sources of Catholic Dogma*, trans. Roy J. Deferrari (Fitzwilliam, N.H., 2002), 163. Friedberg 1.638, "Distinguendum est tamen subtiliter inter tria, quae sunt in hoc sacramento discreta, videlicet formam visibilem, veritatem corporis, et virtutem spiritualem. Forma est panis et vini, veritas carnis et sanguinis, virtus unitatis est caritatis. Primum est sacramentum, et non res. Secundum est sacramentum et res. Tertium est res et non sacramentum."

[101] Friedberg 2.639, "cedit quippe natura miraculo, et virtus supra consuetudinem operatur."

[102] Friedberg 2.638–639 "Quaesivisti etiam, utrum aqua cum vino in sanguinem convertatur. Super hoc autem opiniones apud scholasticos variantur. Aliquibus enim videtur, quod, quum de latere Christi duo praecipua fluxerint sacramenta, redemptionis in sanguine, ac regenerationis in aqua, in illa duo, vinum et aqua, quae commiscentur in calice, divina virtute mutantur, ut in hoc sacramento plene sit veritas et

Innocent's reason for this conclusion was ecclesiological: "for we are joined with an insoluble nexus so that the one who is one with the Father by an ineffable unity may be made one with us by an admirable union, and through this, with Him generally mediating, we may be made one with the Father."[103]

This decretal passed into *Compilatio tertia* under the title "Concerning the Celebration of Masses, the Sacrament of the Eucharist and the Water Which Issued from the Side of Christ" (*De celebratione missarum et sacramento eucharistiae et aqua que exivit ex latere Christi*).[104] In 1234, *Cum Marthae* (X 3.41.6) entered the *Liber extra* under the title "Concerning the Celebration of Masses, the Sacrament of the Eucharist and Divine Offices" (*De celebratione missarum et sacramento eucharistiae et divinis officiis*). (An additional denial that the water became Christ's phlegm was sent to Huguccio of Pisa in 1209. That decretal, *In quadam*, also entered canon law (X 3.41.8).[105]) Thus transubstantiation entered the *Extra* earlier by a different route. In fact, *Cum Marthae* proved more important in the writings of the earlier Decretalists than was *Firmiter* in affirming transubstantiation.[106]

The Decretalists, beginning at least with Johannes Teutonicus's gloss on *Compilatio tertia*, offered three accepted formulations of the Real Presence when discussing *Cum Marthae*. One of these opinions was that bread and wine were transformed into Christ's body and blood

figura. Alii vero tenent, quod aqua cum vino transsubstantiatur in sanguinem, quum in vinum transeat mixta vino, licet physici contrarium asseverent, qui aquam a vino per artificium posse asserunt seperari. Preterea potest dici, quod aqua non transit in sanguinem, sed remanet prioris vini accidentibus circumfusa ita, quod vini saporem assumit . . . Verum inter opiniones praedictas illa probabilior iudicatur, quae asserit, aquam cum vino in sanguinem transmutari, ut expressius eluceat proprietas sacramenti." See Innocent III, *Register*, Bk. V letter 121 for the original version. Macy, "Transubstantiation in the Middle Ages," 26. The decretal may have been at least partly a rebuke of Huguccio, who thought the water became phlegm; see Levy, "The Eucharist and Canon Law," 422–426; Charles de Miramon, "Innocent III, Huguccio de Ferrare et Hubert de Pirovano: Droit canonique, théologie et philosophie à Bologne dans les années 1180," in *Medieval Church Law and the Origins of the Western Legal Tradition*, 320–346.

103 Friedberg 2.639, "tam insolubili nexu coniugimus, ut, qui est unum cum Patre per ineffabilem unitatem, fiat unum nobiscum per admirabilem unitatem, ac per hoc ipso communiter mediante cum Patre unum efficimur."

104 *Quinque compilationes antiquae nec non Collectio canonum Lipsiensis*, ed. Emil Friedberg (Leipzig, 1882; Graz, 1956), 125: 3 Comp. 3.33.5.

105 Müller, *Huguccio*, 24–27.

106 Much of Innocent's sacramental theology also was quoted almost verbatim by the older Guillelmus Durantis; see, for example, *Guillelmi Duranti rationale divinorum officiorum I–IV*, ed. Anselm Davril and Timothy M. Thibodeau (Turnhout, 1995), 446–447, 450–451; William Durand, *Rationale IV: On the Mass and Each Action Pertaining to It*, trans. Timothy M. Thibodeau (Turnhout, 2013), 338–339, 343–344. Thibodeau, "The Doctrine of Transubstantiation in Durand's *Rationale*," *Traditio* 51 (1996), 308–317.

(transubstantiation proper or transformation). The second said the substance of bread and wine was annulled, being replaced by the body and blood, while the accidents of taste, color, and weight remained (annihilation or substitution). The third was that body and blood coexisted with bread and wine together in the same place (consubstantiation or coexistence). The third option rapidly fell out of favor, while the other two remained acceptable for many years.[107] These opinions about Innocent's decretal received their widest distribution in the Ordinary Gloss on the *Extra* by Bernard of Parma. Teutonicus had said the elements ceased to be bread and wine. When glossing the word *transubstantiatur*, Bernard said wine and water ceased to be present after the consecration. Where the pope said the transformation of the water was more probable, the Gloss treated the text as establishing beyond question that the water was transubstantiated with the wine. This could not be true in nature, but it could through a miracle. Here the Gloss echoed the words of Innocent's decretal.[108]

Similarly, Pope Innocent IV said in his commentary on the *Gregorian Decretals* that the bread was transubstantiated into the body and the wine and water into the blood. He included the water in this statement about the sacrament for ecclesiological reasons. The combination of wine with a little water represented the joining of Christ with the Church.[109] Innocent was forthright too about concomitance, the belief that the whole and entire Christ (*Christus integer*) was present under the species of bread and wine with water, changed into the body and blood, since there could not be body without blood or blood without body.[110]

In the same period, Geoffrey of Trani wrote a *summa* on the titles of the *Decretals*. Like the Gloss, Godfrey stated three opinions on the Real Presence. One was that the substance of the bread and wine was transformed into Christ's body and blood. The second said the substance of

[107] *Apparatus glossatorum in compilationem* tertiam ad 3 Comp. 3.33.5, ed. Kenneth Pennington, work in progress found at http://faculty.cua.edu/pennington, accessed on December 21, 2011. On the terminology for the Real Presence, see Macy, "Transubstantiation in the Middle Ages," 13. Teutonicus's ideas on transubstantiation with the same discussion of signs and signified authored by Rufinus were imported by Teutonicus into his Ordinary Gloss on the *Decretum* with a specific reference to *Cum Marthae*; see Ordinary Gloss at De cons. D. 2 a. c.1.

[108] Ordinary Gloss at X 3.41.6.

[109] *Commentaria Innocentii quarti Pont. Maximi super libros quinque Decretalium* ... (Frankfurt, 1570; Frankfurt, 1968), fol. 269va: X 3.41.6, "*Aqua cum vino*) veritas videtur, quod panis transsubstantiatur in corpus, & vinum & aqua simul in sanguinem ... Coniunctio enim aquae & vini significat coniunctionem Christi & ecclesiae."

[110] *Commentaria Innocentii quarti Pont. Maximi super libros quinque Decretalium*, fol. 269va: X 3.41.6, "Et no. quod licet tantum panis transsubstantietur in corpus, & vinum, & aqua in sanguinem, tamen sub utraque specie Christus integer est, non enim est corpus sine sanguine & anima, nec sanguinis sine corpore & anima."

bread and wine ceased to be, being replaced by the body and blood with the accidents of taste, color, and weight remaining. Godfrey said this was the position of the Lateran Council. The third was that body and blood and the bread and wine remained under the same species. Godfrey cited c. *Cum Marthae* as reproving this third doctrine. In the sacrament were the forms of bread and wine and the unity of the body and blood under the species, as well as the sacrament of unity between signified and signifier, Christ and the Church. Godfrey rejected a fourth opinion, that Christ was present only in an image, not in reality, as worse than any of the other three.[111] Like some other canonists, Godfrey tied the water in the chalice to the other crucial sacrament, baptism. Also, he affirmed that the water was transformed together with the wine, adopting Innocent III's more probable opinion on this topic.[112]

Henricus de Segusio (Hostiensis) wrote an extensive *summa* on the titles of the *Decretals* and an even longer Commentary on the *Liber Extra*. The *summa* said little about the Real Presence when discussing the title on the Trinity. Hostiensis did say the sacrament could only be confected by a priest who was rightly ordained into the apostolic succession. In that case, nature gave way to the miracle God provided to the faithful.[113] The cardinal addressed the sacraments in the title "On the Non-Repeatable Sacraments" (*De sacramentis non iterandis*). There he said the Eucharist was greater than the others in substance, although baptism was greater in effect, being the root of the others.[114] Hostiensis emphasized the priest's role in penance and the Eucharist even when the latter was not administered at an altar.[115]

The canonist discussed the mass and the Eucharistic elements in greater detail when discussing the title "On the Consecration of a Church or an Altar" (*De consecratione ecclesiae vel altaris* = X 3.40). This discussion also covered issues usually addressed under the title "On the Celebration of Masses." The role of the duly consecrating priest, whose actions were effective *ex opere operato*, was reaffirmed.[116] Hostiensis also said that where bread had been, the flesh of Christ was present, although

[111] *Summa perutilis et valde necessaria do. Goffredi de Trano super titulis decretalium* ... (Lyon, 1519; Aalen, 1968), fol. 161vb–162ra: X 3.41. Reproof of the fourth opinion also appears in the Ordinary Gloss to the *Decretum* at De cons. D. 2 a. c. 1; see Levy, "The Eucharist and Canon Law," 433–434.

[112] *Summa Goffredi de Trano super titulis decretalium*, fol. 162ra: X 3.41.

[113] *Summa domini Henrici cardinalis Hostiensis* ... (Lyon, 1537; Aalen, 1962), fol. 4rb: X 1.1.

[114] *Summa domini Henrici cardinalis Hostiensis*, fol. 36ra: X 1.16, "eucharistie vero sacramentum maius est in substantia: baptismus quo ad effectum: quia radix est aliorum."

[115] *Summa domini Henrici cardinalis Hostiensis*, fol. 36rb: X 1.16.

[116] *Summa domini Henrici cardinalis Hostiensis*, fol. 184va: X 3.40.

the appearance of bread remained.[117] The *Summa* restated the three ideas of the Real Presence found in the *Decretals* commentaries of Johannes Teutonicus and others. Like Godfrey, Hostiensis believed that Lateran IV supported annihilation of the bread or substitution of Christ's flesh for it, rather than the transformation of the substance of the host. He rejected even more firmly the fourth and worse opinion that only an image, not the truth of Christ's flesh and blood, was present on the altar.[118]

Hostiensis's *Commentary on the Decretals* had more to say about the Eucharist when discussing *Firmiter credimus* than did most works of medieval canon law. The cardinal said that the priest had to follow the *forma ecclesiae*, using bread, wine, and water, and the *forma verborum*, the words of consecration.[119] The cardinal cited the three opinions on the Real Presence used by Johannes Teutonicus and other writers. Then he went on to cite *Cum Marthae* as reproving a fourth and worse opinion that there was "no truth of the body and blood" (*corporis & sanguinis veritatem*) on the altar.[120] Hostiensis went on to say that both *Firmiter* and *Cum Marthae* endorsed the opinion that the species were replaced by the body and blood of Christ.[121]

Hostiensis wrote extensively on transubstantiation at c. *Cum Marthae*. Much of what he said was traditional, discussing the need for the sign or sacrament (bread and wine), the sacrament together with the reality (body and blood), and the reality that was not a sign (the union of Christ and the Church).[122] Hostiensis wrote most extensively in this context, because of the issue addressed in Innocent's decretal, about the conversion of the water in the chalice. The cardinal was careful to explain that the water was not transformed on its own. It was transubstantiated after being absorbed by the wine, being converted in union with the wine. They were converted together (*simul*).[123] Like Innocent IV, Hostiensis

117 *Summa domini Henrici cardinalis Hostiensis*, fol. 185rb: X 3.40.

118 *Summa domini Henrici cardinalis Hostiensis*, fol. 185ra: X 3.40. Macy, "Transubstantiation in the Middle Ages," 29.

119 *Henrici de Segusio Cardinalis Hostiensis Decretalium commentaria*, 6 vols. (Venezia, 1581; Turin, 1965), 1, fol. 6va: X 1.1, "nam ad vocem sacerdotis fit transubstantiatio." He added "non ergo ad vocem laici."

120 *Hostiensis Decretalium commentaria*, 1, fol. 6va: X 1.1, "Quarto asserunt in sacramento altaris non ese corporis & sanguinis veritatem hoc reprobatur de cele. mis. cum Marthę. ¶. quęsivisti."

121 *Hostiensis Decretalium commentaria*, 1, fol. 6va: X 1.1, "opinio vero secundorum ibi approbatur, & hic, vt sequitur."

122 *Hostiensis Decretalium commentaria*, 3, fol. 163ra–b: X 3.41.6.

123 *Hostiensis Decretalium commentaria*, 3, fol. 163rb: X 3.41.6, "Intelligas tamen, quod aqua non transubstantiatur per se, sed tantum inquantum est, mixta vino, & ideo verius dicitur, vinum cum aqua mixtum transubstantiari . . . hoc igitur modo transubstantiatur vinum & aqua simul in sanguinem." See also *Commentaria*, 3, fol. 163va: X 3.41.6.

was interested in the ecclesiological dimensions of the Eucharist. He said more wine than water had to be in the chalice "because Christ is not changed into the Church, but the Church into Christ."[124]

Hostiensis consistently maintained that it was miraculous that the accidents remained without a subject,[125] and he affirmed that the risen body of Christ remained *integrum et glorificatum* in the sacrament as long as the species were not corrupted.[126] The idea that the consecrated host might decay or turn back into bread was controversial. Guitmund of Aversa had denied that the sacrament was subject to digestion;[127] and the Decretist Bazianus denied the host could nourish the body, instead leaving anyone who only received the Eucharist physically weak.[128] However, Hostiensis limited the duration of the miracle to the period while the host remained unspoiled.

Johannes Andreae, the early fourteenth-century Bolognese canonist, added the last significant contribution of the Decretalists to the discussion of transubstantiation. Johannes, a layman, writing a century after Lateran IV, addressed in his commentary not just the texts contained in the *Extra* but the interpretations of those texts in the Ordinary Gloss. His gloss on *Firmiter* emphasized the necessity of ordination according to the *forma ecclesiae*.[129] When Johannes discussed both the text and the Gloss at c. *Cum Marthae*, he emphasized, as was usual, the use of wheat to make the host; and he said pure wine, not vinegar or spiced wine, was preferable for celebrating mass.[130] His gloss followed the opinion of Hostiensis in saying the water in the chalice was not transubstantiated on its own (*per se*) but "only as far as it is mixed into the wine" (*sed tantum inquantum est mixta uino*).[131] Johannes too emphasized the

[124] *Hostiensis Decretalium commentaria*, 3: X 3.41.6, fol. 163rb, "quia Christus non mutetur in ecclesia, sed ecclesia in Christum."

[125] *Hostiensis Decretalium commentaria*, 3, fol. 163vb: X 3.41.6, "ut hic dicit, quod est valde miraculosum. i. quod accidentia sunt sine subiecto."

[126] *Hostiensis Decretalium commentaria*, 3, fol. 163vb: X 3.41.6.

[127] See Lanfranc, Archbishop of Canterbury, *On the Body and Blood of the Lord*; Guitmund of Aversa, *On the Truth of the Body and Blood of Christ in the Eucharist*, 17–18.

[128] Müller, *Huguccio*, 102–103.

[129] Johannes Andreae, *In quinque decretalium libros novella commentaria*, 5 vols. (Venezia, 1581; Turin, 1963), 1, fol. 8va: X 1.1.1, "necesse est enim in ordinatione seruare formam ecclesię, sicut in baptismo, vt hic, & i[a]. de bap. c. i."

[130] Johannes Andreae, *In quinque decretalium libros novella commentaria*, 3, fol. 220ra: X 3.41.6.

[131] Johannes Andreae, *In quinque decretalium libros novella commentaria*, 3, fol. 220rb: X 3.41.6. Johannes went on to emphasize that there was water in Christ's wine at the Last Supper (*in calice domini*). He also followed tradition by identifying the wine with Christ and the water with the Church united to Him, "Coniunctio enim uini & aquae significant unionem Christi, & ecclesiae."

words of consecration, *Hoc est corpus meum*;[132] and he also taught the doctrine of concomitance, using exactly the same words found in the commentary of Innocent IV.[133]

Andreae gave considerable attention to the Gloss on *Cum Marthae*. Looking at the opinions Bernard had listed on the Real Presence, he referred the reader to the *Sentences* of Peter Lombard.[134] His commentary here was more than a repetition of earlier texts. Discussing the opinion that the species were annihilated and replaced with the body and blood of Christ, Johannes raised the objection of Thomas Aquinas, whom he quoted briefly, that the words of consecration did not mean this, but that the body could not be present in the sacrament "unless by conversion of the substance of the bread into it" (*nisi per conuersionem substantiae panis in ipsum*).[135] Johannes gave a detailed reply, presenting the case for annihilation of the elements. Then he quoted Hostiensis to the effect that both opinions on the Real Presence had Catholic supporters. He went on, however, to say, with the cardinal, that the material, bread, "was not, is not nor will be the body of Christ. If, however, it denotes conversion, it is true. Wherefore he always says this: it is changed or transformed entirely, or it changes or is transubstantiated."[136] Johannes was not completely firm in his discussion of these two Catholic options, mostly letting the Angelic Doctor and his opponents speak for themselves.

Johannes Andreae was much firmer in offering Thomas's objections to consubstantiation. Johannes said Thomas abhorred this option (*sed tho. illam abhorret*). He then copied at length from the *Summa theologiae* an argument that coexistence of the elements with the body and blood is not fitting, as well as one that the body does not move about, since it is everywhere, and thus does not arrive where the bread is located. Nor does it cease to be present in heaven. Thomas said the body only could be

[132] Johannes Andreae, *In quinque decretalium libros novella commentaria*, 3, fol. 220rb: X 3.41.6.

[133] Johannes Andreae, *In quinque decretalium libros novella commentaria*, 3, fol. 220rb: X 3.41.6, "tamen sub utraque ipse Christus integer est, non enim est corpus hominis uiui sine sanguine, nec sanguis sine corpore & anima."

[134] Johannes Andreae, *In quinque decretalium libros novella commentaria*, 3, fol. 221vb: X 3.41.6 refers to Book IV D. 11 cc. 1–3 of the *Sentences*; see Peter Lombard, *The Sentences*, trans. Giulio Silano, 4 vols. (Toronto, 2010), 4.54–58.

[135] Johannes Andreae, *In quinque decretalium libros novella commentaria*, 3, fol. 221va: X 3.41.6. See *Summa theologiae*, III, art. 75 in *S. Thomae de Aquino Summa theologiae*, 4 (Ottawa, 1944), 2937a–2948b, esp. 2941b. Levy, "The Eucharist and Canon Law in the High Middle Ages," 443–444.

[136] Johannes Andreae, *In quinque decretalium libros novella commentaria*, 3, fol. 221va: X 3.41.6, "Panis fit corpus Christi, duplex est, si denotat materiam, est falsa. Panis enim nec fuit, nec est, nec erit corpus Christi. Si uero conuersionem denotet, uera est. vnde hoc semper dicit, mutatur uel commutatur, uel transit, uel transubstantiatur."

present by conversion of the species.[137] Johannes also argued that the body of Christ could not have arrived at the altar by motion, since He would have to leave heaven. Moreover, Christ would have to travel to many altars at one time. Although Duns Scotus is not mentioned by name, the canonist may have had his teaching on transubstantiation in mind, even if not subtly understood. Johannes affirmed, citing Thomas Aquinas, that only conversion of the elements could avoid problems in explaining transubstantiation.[138]

Thomas Aquinas himself had written a brief commentary on *Firmiter credimus*. In it he criticized the theory of consubstantiation, but he also denounced the idea that Christ was present on the altar only as a *figura*. Christ was present miraculously (*miraculose*) by divine power. Moreover, the Angelic Doctor, when discussing ordination according to the form of the Church, denounced the Waldensians for not following it.[139] (Similarly, John XXII later condemned the Fraticelli for teaching that a priest ordained "according to the form of the Church" cannot consecrate validly if "weighed down by any sins."[140])

Later canonists showed little or no interest in the sacraments, even after the heresies of John Wyclif and Jan Hus were condemned.[141] Ironically, Wyclif had used the canon law against the doctrine of transubstantiation. He quoted the case of Berengar of Tours via c. *Ego Berengarius* to support his own ideas on the Eucharist, a doctrine sometimes called

[137] Johannes Andreae, *In quinque decretalium libros novella commentaria*, 3, fol.222ra–b: X 3.41.6. Johannes also quoted Hostiensis summary of this opinion. See *S. Thomae de Aquino Summa theologiae*. 4.2940a–b.

[138] Johannes Andreae, *In quinque decretalium libros novella commentaria*, 3, fol. 221vb: X 3.41.6, "Constat autem corpus Christi non incipere esse etiam in hoc sacramento per motum localem: quia quod localiter mouetur, non peruenit ad locum, nisi priorem deserat, secundum quod desineret esse esse in cęlo. Item corpus localiter motum transit media, quod hic dici non potest. Item esse impossibile corpus localiter motum terminari simul ad diuersa loca, cum tamen in sacramento corpus Christi simul in diuersis locis esse incipiat. Ex hic concluditur, corpus Christi non posse incipere esse in hoc sacramento nisi per conuersionem substantiae in ipsum. Id autem, quod in aliquid conuertitur, conuersione facta non manet, per quod relinquitur facta conuersione. i. post consecrationem sacramenti ueritatem, salua substantia panis ibi manere non posse, imò nec remanet forma substantialis panis, ut ibi probat arti. 7" (Aquinas III q. 75 art. 2). On Scotus, see Adams, *Some Later Medieval Theologies of the Eucharist*, 138–151.

[139] *S. Thomae Aquinatis Opera Omnia ut sunt in Indice Thomistico*, ed. Roberto Busa, 3 (Stuttgart, 1980), 525a–528a at 527a.

[140] Peters, *Heresy and Authority*, 246.

[141] The commentary by the Dominican cardinal Juan de Torquemada on the *Decretum*, which interprets the *De consecratione* in depth, is treated here as a theological more than a legal contribution to the study of the sacraments; see *Commentaria super decreto*, 5 vols. (Venezia, 1579). Thomas Kaeppeli, *Scriptores Ordinis Praedicatorum medii aevi*, 4 vols. (Roma, 1970–1993), 3.37–38 no. 2731. For his other writings on the Eucharist, see *Scriptores Ordinis Praedicatorum* 3.29–30 no. 2711, 33 no. 2720, 4.175 no. 2720.

"remanence," the bread and wine not being changed on the altar. This, he said, was the theology of the Church before Innocent III "deviated into madness." Wyclif also blamed the "sect" of the friars for teaching the false doctrine of transubstantiation.[142] Denunciations of Wyclif's sacramental theology began in his lifetime. English councils soon listed errors found in books like the *Trialogus*, and the reading of these texts was prohibited.[143] English articles condemning Wyclif were confirmed by a Prague council in 1408, during the time when Jan Hus was being accused of heresy, partly for not rejecting Wyclif's writings outright.[144] Wyclif's thought was denounced at the Council of Constance, which took up the articles already extracted from his works as proof of heresy. In Session 8 (May 4, 1415), the assembly condemned Wyclif, using these accusatory articles nearly verbatim. He was convicted posthumously for denying transubstantiation and believing that the elements remained on the altar after the consecration. He was condemned too for believing the accidents could not remain without the substance and that the sacrament was not identical with Christ's body. The decree also condemned Wyclif for believing that a sinful priest could not ordain, consecrate, or baptize effectively.[145]

Martin V, at the end of the Council of Constance, issued a bull that required inquisitors to question suspected followers of Wyclif or Hus if they believed neither bread nor wine remained on the altar after consecration, "whether they believed the true body of Christ is on the altar." He also was supposed to ask if the whole Christ is present "under only one species, bread, apart from wine" (*sub sola specie panis tantum, et praeter speciem vini*).[146] Some local synods in Germany also affirmed the

[142] Wyclif, *Trialogus*, trans. Stephen E. Lahey (Cambridge, 2013), 195–224 esp. 199, 209–210. R. N. Swanson, *Church and Society in Late Medieval England* (Oxford, 1989), 318–319.

[143] For some of the papal letters and other official documents concerned with Wyclif, see Mansi 26.562–568, 718–722, 1037–1038, Articles extracted from the *Trialogus* appear at Mansi 26.808–810. The third article is drawn from the passage about *Ego Berengarius*. John XXIII forbade reading Wyclif's *dialogum, trialogum, & alios plures libros*; see Mansi 27.505–508.

[144] *Concilia Germaniae*, ed. Johann Friedrich Schannat and Joseph Hartzheim, 5 (Köln, 1763), 29A, accessed via Google Books on February 13, 2014. Controversy in Bohemia over Wyclif began in 1403 in the cathedral chapter and the university; see Thomas A. Fudge, *The Trial of Jan Hus: Medieval Heresy and Criminal Procedure* (Oxford, 2013), 116–119, 150–151.

[145] *Decrees of the Ecumenical Councils*, 1.411; Denzinger, *Sources of Catholic Dogma*, 208–209. A more detailed set of articles was condemned in Session 15; see *Decrees of the Ecumenical Councils*, 1.422–423. Session 21 condemned Jerome of Prague despite his claiming to accept transubstantiation while rejecting the errors of Wyclif and Hus; see *Decrees of the Ecumenical Councils*, 1.433–434.

[146] Mansi 27.1204–1215 at 1207. The inquisitor also was supposed to ask if the accused believed a bad priest could validly celebrate the sacraments.

condemnation of Wyclif, Hus, and Jerome of Prague for heresy.[147] One, from Eichstät in 1446, combined a condemnation of Wyclif, Hus, and the Waldensians.[148] Other local decrees focused, without naming Wyclif or Hus, on the erroneous denial by heretics that a sinful priest could consecrate the elements.[149]

Denial of transubstantiation could indeed be perilous. Among the earliest men condemned to death for following Wyclif's doctrines was William Sawtrey, a priest of Norwich. He affirmed remanence, was denounced, recanted temporarily, and then relapsed, eventually being condemned to burning. John Badby, an artisan, too was burned for denying transubstantiation.[150] A cleric of Norwich denied that ordained priests could consecrate, saying unchanged bread remained on the altar.[151] Other Lollards are recorded as if recycling topoi found in Continental inquisitors' registers, possibly because a common fund of texts denouncing heresy was available to the clergy. Thus they are reported to dismiss the host as something they could bake at home and make between two irons. Others were said to wonder whether a mouse received the real Presence if it ate a consecrated host. One curate who was accused of heresy managed to repeat an opinion close to Wyclif's when he contended that the Corpus Christi was simply a *res figurata*. Popular heresy and learned dissent came together in this testimony.[152]

These sacramental issues had an echo in papal ceremonial. By the late fifteenth century, Agostino Patrizzi could explain the utterance of the solemn excommunications of the Church's enemies on Holy Thursday by saying it was fitting to exclude the unworthy from the sacrament on that day on which the institution of the Eucharist at the Last Supper was commemorated.[153]

A few examples of the later canonists' failure to address these major theological challenges to the sacrament will suffice. Antonius de Butrio

[147] *Concilia Germaniae*, 5.153B–154A (Bratislava, 1416), 208A–209(Mainz, 1423), 220B–221A (Cologne, 1423), 223A–224A (Trier, 1423), 451A (Constance, 1463), 546A–B (Constance, 1483).

[148] *Concilia Germaniae*, 5.363B–364A.

[149] *Concilia Germaniae*, 5.172B (Salzburg, 1420), 274A–B (Freising,1440), 521A–B (Besançon, 1481, citing the Salzburg decree).

[150] Both cases are discussed in Peter McNiven, *Heresy and Politics in the Reign of Henry IV: The Burning of John Badby* (Woodbridge, 1987). For synodal documents in the Sawtrey case, including Latin and English texts of his recantations, see Mansi 26.939–951.

[151] *Pastors and the Care of Souls*, 279. Similarly, see Swanson, *Church and Society*, 331.

[152] Anne Hudson, "The Mouse in the Pyx: Popular Heresy and the Eucharist," *Trivium* 26 (1991), 40–53.

[153] Patrizzi, *Caeremoniale*, fol. CXLI^{r}, "Nunc id fit tantum in caena Domini. Causas, cur in istis diebus potissimum fiant, istas dicunt. in cęna Domini habuit principium Christi Sacramentum: congruit ut in illa die excludantur ab ecclesia, quam ei sacramento indignos se reddiderunt."

quoted Johannes Andreae's long discussion of the major opinions on the Real Presence verbatim, complete with its quotations from the *Summa theologiae*, adding nothing to it.[154] He did write briefly, citing *Cum Marthae*, about the *materiale elementum*.[155] Antonius, glossing *Cum Marthae*, listed ten miracles occurring in transubstantiation. These included that transubstantiation in masses worldwide made no increase in Christ's body or diminution with many communions. The canonist backed this list with similes like a comparison of concomitance with a reflection in a mirror that was the whole image of the person looking into it. The subtlety of Scholastic theology is lacking in these comparisons.[156] Panormitanus affirmed the Real Presence of the body born of the Virgin without discussing transubstantiation.[157] Other late medieval commentaries, like John of Imola, simply ignored texts like *Firmiter credimus* and *Cum Marthae*. This illustrates how the canonists were losing creative impulse in their discussions of texts related to the sacraments, even while challenges to orthodoxy mounted.

The question remains: when did *Firmiter credimus* become an authority to cite in the discussion of Eucharistic presence? A cautious reply, short of being able to examine many more texts, is that it can be found earliest in the *Ordinary* Gloss to the *Decretum*. Johannes Teutonicus cited c. *Cum Marthae* to prove the transformation of the elements occurs miraculously (*miraculose*).[158] Explaining the miraculous change, the Gloss cited the decree *Firmiter credimus* briefly to argue that the substance of bread and wine were replaced by the body and blood (annihilation), rather than being transformed.[159] The reference is very brief, and it does not present the decree as the final word on the Real Presence. *Firmiter* appears instead as an authority to be cited, part of the language of transubstantiation that had entered canon law even before the theologians had settled on their own understanding of the term. In fact, the canon was used by Johannes

154 *Excellentissimi Antonii de Butrio … In librum tertium decretalium commentaria* (Venezia: Apud Iuntas, 1578; Torino, 1967), fol. 191vb: X 3.41.6.

155 *Excellentissimi Antonii de Butrio … Super prima parte primi decretalium commentarii*, fol. 186rb: X 1.16.3.

156 *Excellentissimi Antonii de Butrio … In librum tertium decretalium commentaria*, fol. 192vb: X 3.41.6.

157 Nicholas de Tudeschis, *Prima pars Abbatis Panormitani super primo Decretalium …* (Lyon?, 1521), fol. 13va: X 1.1.1.

158 Ordinary Gloss at De cons. D.2 c. 38 v. Non nascitur.

159 Ordinary Gloss at De cons. D.2 c.11 v. Quia diuisio provides an extensive discussion of transubstantiation without citing Innocent III's texts. See, however, Ordinary Gloss at De cons. D.2 ante c. 1 v. In sacramentum, supporting annihilation or substitution, "Secunda opinio verior est, vt extra de sum. tri. firmiter. ¶. vna." The Gloss at De cons. D. 2 c. 33 v. Sunt only summarizes the acceptable theories.

Teutonicus to support an opinion that would not predominate later among Scholastic theologians.[160]

An inquiry is in order whether the term "transubstantiation" penetrated down to the parish level. What did bishops expect their priests to know, and what they were to teach the faithful about the Real Presence? Local councils and synods often adapted texts from the canons of Lateran IV when drafting local statutes.[161] These statutes frequently offered basic teachings on the sacraments, in general or about each individually, to the local clergy to guide their pastoral care of the laity. Occasionally, the message was simple: tell the parishioners that there are seven sacraments.[162] A typical teaching on the Eucharist can be found in the 1287 statutes from Exeter. The statute on the article of faith said to teach the laity "that the true body and true blood of Christ are in the sacrament of the altar."[163] Occasionally the texts made direct use of *Firmiter credimus*, as the statutes of Wells (ca. 1258) did in emphasizing the sacramental role of a rightly ordained priest (*rite secundum claves ecclesie ordinati*).[164] The 1236 provincial statutes of Canterbury added an affirmation of concomitance, saying "The whole Christ is under either form."[165]

Only on rare occasions did a statute use the language of transubstantiation, while numerous other texts emphasized the Real Presence without resorting to such technical language. Thus the first statutes of Salisbury (ca. 1217–1219) reused the language of *Firmiter*, saying Christ refreshed the faithful with species transubstantiated into His body and blood "refreshing them truly with His body and blood under species of bread and wine transubstantiated by divine power, bread into body and wine into blood."[166]

[160] Macy, "Transubstantiation in the Middle Ages," 26–27.

[161] Local councils also used the statutes of the diocese of Paris; see C. R. Cheney, *English Synodalia* (London, 1968); Pixton, *The German Episcopacy*, 83–85. For an example of adaptations of a Lateran canon, see Thomas M. Izbicki, "Forbidden Colors in the Regulation of Clerical Dress from the Fourth Lateran Council (1215) to the Time of Nicholas of Cusa (d. 1464)," *Medieval Clothing and Textiles* 1 (2005), 105–114.

[162] For example, see the instructions of Robert Grosseteste to his clergy; see *The Electronic Grosseteste* [http://www.grosseteste.com/], 155–156, accessed on June 21, 2007.

[163] *Councils & Synods*, 2/2, 1076, "quod in sacramento altaris est verum corpus et verus sanguis Christi, verus deus et verus homo."

[164] *Councils & Synods*, 2/1, 592.

[165] Mansi 23,397, "Tamen sub utraque forma est totus Christus."

[166] *Councils & Synods*, 2/1, 77, "corpore et sanguine suo eos *veraciter* reficiens *sub speciebus panis et vini transubstantiatis, pane in corpus et vino in sanguinem, potestate divina*." The italics, marking use of *Firmiter credimus*, are mine. This passage from *Firmiter* was repeated, together with the passage about priests rightly ordained, in the second statutes of Salisbury (ca. 1238–1242); see *Councils & Synods*, 2/1, 371.

Another set of English statutes emphasized veneration of the elevated host: "when the bread has been transubstantiated into the true body of Christ."[167]

At greater length, the Exeter statutes of 1287 recited the words of consecration, warning that elevation before transubstantiation could lead the people into idolatry, adoring a mere creature: "Because the bread is transubstantiated into the body by these words, *This is My body*, and not by other words, the priest should not elevate the host earlier than the time of displaying it fully lest a creature be venerated by the people as the creator."[168] There is no evidence that, even if the parish priest understood transubstantiation, such complex terminology was conveyed to the faithful in sermons or other teachings.

Similarly, transubstantiation appears only sporadically in manuals for parish priests. It does not appear in the popular *Manipulus curatorum*, either in the chapters on the Eucharist or among the matters to be taught to parishioners. The Real Presence is affirmed, but not in technical language beyond mention of the species of bread and wine in the section instructing priests about the sacraments.[169] This attitude differed little from that of Innocent IV, who thought inferior clergy needed to know just a little more than the uneducated laity did. These lesser clergy had to know just a bit more because they confected the true body of Christ daily.[170]

Transubstantiation did enter into the *Occulus sacerdotis* of William of Pagula. Discussing the material of the Eucharist in his instructions to parish priests, William denied that any other grain but wheat could be transubstantiated. He added a reference to Huguccio as saying leavened bread could not be changed either. This was the most negative opinion in the West, where the use of leavened bread by the Greeks was accepted grudgingly by others, although it was considered by almost everyone as contrary to Christ's use of unleavened bread at the Last Supper. William

[167] *Councils & Synods*, 2/1, 143, "quando panis in verum corpus Christi transsubstantiatur."

[168] *Councils & Synods*, 2/2, 990, "Quia vero per hec verba: hoc est enim corpus meum, et non per alia, panis transsubstantiatur in corpus, prius hostiam non levet sacerdos, donec ipsa plene protulerit, ne pro creatore creatura a populo veneratur." The 1277 Council of Trier expressed this slightly differently, saying not to elevate the host *ante transubstantiationis verba*; see Mansi 24.194.

[169] Guido de Monte Rocherii, *Manipulus curatorum* (London, 1508), fol. xx^{v}–xxvi^{r}, xl^{r}–xlii^{v}, clxi^{r-v}, cited from *Early English Books Online*, accessed on November 29, 2014; Guido, *Handbook for Curates*, 49–63, 87–102, 276.

[170] *Commentaria Innocentii quarti Pont. Maximi super libros quinque Decretalium*, fol. 2ra, "quod eis sufficiat scire sicut simplicibus laicis, & aliquantulum plus sicut de sacramento altaris, quia oportet eos credere quod in sacramento altaris conficitur verum corpus Christi, & hoc ideo, quia circa illud quotidie & continue versantur plus, quam laici."

also said that use of honey or any other liquid but water in making hosts prevented transubstantiation.[171] William emphasized the words of consecration as Christ's, not merely the priest's. The creator, who made all things from nothing, could make such changes.[172] The *Occulus* required a priest to instruct the people that the host he elevated was the body of Christ and that His blood was in the chalice after consecration. Anyone who did not believe this was a heretic. William cited the canon *Sane* of Honorius III (X 3.41.10), together with a text from the *Decretum*; however, he avoided bringing the language of transubstantiation as found in the *Liber Extra* into the teaching of the faithful.[173]

John de Burough, a Cambridge-educated theologian, quoted Thomas Aquinas at length in his *Pupilla occuli*. Particularly he used the Angelic Doctor's texts to explain how the accidents of the bread and wine, including the ability to satisfy hunger, remained after the consecration of the host.[174] Like those writing before him, John affirmed that the body and blood remained hidden under the appearences of bread and wine.[175] Discussing the mass, John de Borough said a priest's intention to

[171] William of Pagula, *Oculus sacerdotis*, University of Pennsylvania MS Codex 721, fol. 7rb, "Et si alia farina admisceatur non transubstantiatur. Et dicit Hugo quod de pane fermentato non potest confici corpus Christi. Quidam tamen dicunt quod potest licet fieri non debeat. Item non potest confici ex farina sola sed ex farina et aqua ex quibus fit panis. Et si ex melle uel ex alio liquore fuerit aspersa non transubstantiatur ille panis in corpus Christi. de con. di. ii c. ii in glo." On William, see Leonard E. Boyle, "The *Oculus Sacerdotis* and Some Other Works of William of Pagula, *Transactions of the Royal Historical Society* 5 (1955), 81–110. On the controversy over fermented bread and azymes, see Christopher Schabel, "The Quarrel over Unleavened Bread in Western Theology, 1234–1439)," in *Greeks, Latins, and Intellectual History 1204–1500*, ed. Martin Hinterberger and Schabel (Leuven, 2011), 85–127.

[172] William of Pagula, *Oculus sacerdotis*, fol. 7va, "Per hec uerba Hoc est corpus meum de pane fit uerum corpus Christi et hoc fit propter efficaciam illorum uerborum Christi. Nam quando istud sacramentum conficitur iam non suis sermonibus sacerdos utitur sed sermonibus Christi ergo sermo Christi conficit hoc sacramentum. Ille qui ex nichilo creauit omnia satis potest hoc commutare."

[173] William of Pagula, *Oculus sacerdotis*, fol. 72rb, "Quantum sacramentum est eukaristia. Et credere debet quilibet christianus illud uerum deum et hominem esse quod sacredos rite ordinatus in celebracione missarum eleuat sub specie panis et ostendit populo adorandum. Et illud quod continetur in calice est uerus sanguis Christi. Debet eciam firmiter credere et aliter est hereticus quod illud idem corpus est quod Christus filius dei habuit de maria uirgine gloriosa et quod pependit in cruce die ueneris benedicti. Illud idem corpus est in sacramento altaris quod non solum sumit sacerdos sed eciam omnes fideles qui sunt extra mortale peccatum percipiunt secundum illud augustini Crede et manducasti extra de cele. miss. c. sane et in glo. et de conse. di. ii c. ut quid paras."

[174] John de Burough, *Pupilla oculi omnibus presbyteris precipue Anglicanis summe necessaria . . .* (London, 1510), fol. xi$^{va–b}$, cited from *Early English Books Online*, accessed on August 19, 2012. John de Burough also used the works of Scotus and other theologians along with those of Aquinas and the canon law. Henry Ansgar Kelly, "Penitential Theology and Law at the Turn of the Fifteenth Century," in *A New History of Penance*, ed. Abigail Firey (Leiden, 2008), 239–317 at 243–253, 267–303.

[175] John de Burough, *Pupilla oculi*, fol. xiiii^{rb}.

consecrate could cover only so much bread. He could transubstantiate what was near him, and he could change only what he needed to use in the spiritual feeding of the faithful.[176] All of these issues, with others about the minister, materials, and words, were fitting to educated clerics, but not to the uneducated clergy, let alone to the laity. John wanted the laity taught that the church, with its sacraments and laws, was regulated by the Holy Spirit (*regulata per spiritum sanctum*) for the salvation of souls.[177] His exposition of the articles of faith presumed simple instruction of parishioners in those sacraments and laws.

Guides for confessors often contained basic information on the sacraments for the guidance of parish priests.[178] Thomas of Chobham, writing in the time of the Fourth Lateran Council, argued briefly for annihilation, not consubstantiation, as causing the presence of the body and blood. He did not, however, use such technical terminology as transubstantiation.[179] Raymond of Peñafort, in his widely circulated *summa*, said much less. He simply treated the Eucharist as one of the sacraments that can be repeated.[180]

Theology entered the literature of pastoral care very directly in the *Summa confessorum* by John of Freiburg, a Dominican friar, in the later thirteenth century. His *summa*, which updated Raymond's book, also brought the ideas of Albertus Magnus and Thomas Aquinas to pastors and confessors. John taught not just Christ's presence on the altar but His ability to be on many altars at the same time. The idea of concomitance, Christ present even in a fractured host, was affirmed. The Real Presence, however, departed once the consecrated host lost the appearance of bread.[181] The presence of Christ made the Eucharist greater even than baptism "by reason of its dignity and sanctity."[182]

Writing at the end of the century, John of Erfurt provided the priest with a chapter on the Eucharist, as well as giving practical advice

[176] John de Burough, *Pupilla oculi*, fol. xv^{va}.

[177] John de Burough, *Pupilla oculi*, fol. cxxvi^{rb}.

[178] Pierre Michaud-Quantin, *Sommes de casuistque et manuels de confession au Moyen Age (XII–XVI siècles)* (Louvain, 1962).

[179] *Thomae de Chobham summa confessorum*, 103, "Sed quia non possit intelligi quod ille novus panis et illud novum vinum creentur ibi de nihilo, quia prior panis et prius vinum desierunt esse, tutius est primam sequi opinionem." Thomas did say the accidents remained by a miracle (*per miraculum*); see *Thomae summa*, 123.

[180] *Summa S^{ti} Raymvndi de Peniafort Barcinonensis ord. praedator. de poenitentia et matrimonio cum glossis Ioannis de Fribvrgo* (Roma, 1502; Farnborough, 1967), 317–321.

[181] Johannes de Friburgo, *Summa confessorum* (Paris, 1519), fol. cxxiii^{va} (q. lxxxv), cxxv^{vb}–cxxvi^{ra} (q. cxii). Leonard E. Boyle, "The *Summa Confessorum* of John of Freiburg and the Popularization of the Moral Teaching of Saint Thomas and Some of His Contemporaries," in *St. Thomas Aquinas, 1274–1974: Commemorative Studies*, ed. Armand A. Maurer, 2 (Toronto, 1974), 245–268.

[182] Johannes de Friburgo, *Summa confessorum*, fol. cxxvii^{vb} (q. cxxxviii).

elsewhere on the mass and the discipline of the sacraments. John repeated the need for the sacrament and the *res sacramenti* found in so many canonistic texts. This went along with an argument about the need for a duly ordained priest.[183] The Real Presence was described as effected by transubstantiation, but this was mentioned only in a disciplinary context. Liquid was not converted if it was added to the consecrated wine in the chalice after the fact. He said that "The power of transubstantiating consists of the words. Therefore, when the words of consecration have not been said, nothing is converted into blood."[184]

More than a century later, Antoninus of Florence said the confessor could ask the penitent about doubting in matters of faith. A particular issue was doubt about "the sacrament of the altar." Involuntary doubts were one thing, but voluntary and willful doubt was a mortal sin.[185]

A York priest's notebook affirmed transubstantiation in a series of notes saying flesh, which is God, appears on the altar, brought from "bread created." Denial of this was dismissed as "godless." The change could not be seen by the senses. The presence was hidden "because, were it apparent, you would be awestruck and afraid to eat."[186]

Nothing even that sophisticated appeared in vernacular instructions about the mass and sacraments. Thus the English priest John Mirk, in his *Instructions for Parish Priests*, told them to teach the faithful to respond to the elevation of the host without urging instruction in sacramental doctrine.[187] Various versions of *The Lay Folks Mass Book* offered the literate believer instructions on how to act at the elevation; however, no explanation of Christ's presence was given.[188] Even the local pastor, unless well educated, probably could not follow the subtleties pastoral writers like William of Pagula, John de Burough, and John of Erfurt included among the things every priest should know. What the simple priest needed to celebrate mass under canon law were the character imprinted by his ordination, the proper materials (bread, wine, and

[183] Johannes de Erfordia, *Die Summa confessorum des Johannes von Erfurt*, ed. Norbert Brieskorn. 3 vols. (Frankfurt, 1980–1981), 3.868–869.

[184] Johannes de Erfordia, *Die Summa confessorum*, 3.875, "virtus autem transsubstantiandi consistit in verbo; ideo cum non dicantur verba consecratoria, nihil convertitur in sanguinem." John went on to discuss how much additional liquid might dissolve the sacrament (*solvitur sacramentum*).

[185] Antoninus of Florence, *Confessionale "Defecerunt scrutantes scrutinio"* (Köln, 1470), *De infidelibus*. "Potes tamen interrogare prout videtur. si habuit aliquid dubium in hiis que sunt fidei. Vt de sacramento altaris et huiusmodi: et si de hoc habet displicentiam: non curandum. Si autem voluntarie et sponte dubitat esset mortale."

[186] *Pastors and the Care of Souls*, 159.

[187] John Mirk, *Instructions for Parish Priests*, ed. Edward Peacock (London, 1868), 9–10.

[188] *The Lay Folks Mass Book*, 144.

water), and the right form of the sacrament,[189] that is, the words of consecration, together with the right intention, not subtle doctrine.[190]

Guillelmus Durantis, however, in his *Rationale divinorum officiorum* affirmed transubstantiation as the right interpretation of the Real Presence. He regarded this as miraculous and listed eleven miracles that occurred at the consecration. The first was the transubstantiation of the bread and wine into Christ's body and blood. The accidents remained even after transubstantiation (*remanent accidentia panis*). This change added nothing to God, and consuming it removed nothing from divinity. "The immense body" (*corpus immensum*) of Christ was contained in something small as a host. Like the light of sun and moon, the entire body of Christ was present in many places at once. Guillelmus also confirmed concomitance, saying, that, even when divided, the sacrament remained "whole and intact" (*totus et integer*).

Communion under one species meant reception of the whole Christ. There was no need for receiving both (*duplex sumptio corporis*). Bodily food became spiritual nourishment. It could be eaten by the criminous without physical injury, and it was mortal to them, not life giving, while the priest and communicants who received worthily were carried up to heaven.[191]

The minister of the Sacrament

The celebration of the mass and consecration of the Eucharist was the province of priests and bishops. The Eucharistic role was the most important spiritual power of the priesthood, including the episcopate, placed highest in the hierarchy of holy orders. Extensive discussions of this role and the norms expected of priests abounded in the Middle Ages.[192] Hugh of St. Victor was among the many theologians who saw bishops as successors to the apostles and priests as successors to the seventy disciples. No other cleric in holy orders could do these things, and bishops had to ordain priests according to the accepted Roman rite to provide these powers by imposing a permanent sacramental character. As part of the rite, the bishop gave a newly ordained priest a paten full of hosts and a full chalice as a sign of the Eucharistic power he was

[189] Note that Rufinus used *forma* to mean the materials; see *Summa decretorum*, 551: De cons. D. 2 c. 1.

[190] Right intention also excluded an extra host that happened to be on the altar, according to Johannes de Friburgo, *Summa confessorum*, fol. cxxv[vb] (q. cix).

[191] *Guillelmi Duranti rationale divinorum officiorum I–IV*, 447–449 William Durand, *Rationale IV*, 337–341. The order above is not that in the *Rationale*.

[192] Aelfric said the presbyter's roles were consecrating the Eucharist and teaching the people; see *Councils & Synods* 1/1.204–205, 283.

receiving.[193] Hildebert of Lavardin saw the priest as acting with divine power (*cum virtute divinitatis*). By the end of the twelfth century, theologians recognized holy orders as one of the seven sacraments. This list became canonical in the fourth book of the *Sentences* of Peter Lombard, which became the university student's textbook of sacramental theology. The sacrament of holy orders was not as crucial for salvation as baptism or as worthy as the Eucharist, but it was essential for creating a succession of ministers for these and other sacred rites.[194] Peter reached back to Isidore of Seville for a statement about the priestly power to consecrate, make offerings, and bless. He too mentioned the gift of a full paten and chalice as part of the rite of ordination.[195] Thomas Aquinas distinguished between the dignity of the priest, his office, and the power to consecrate the Eucharist that was bestowed by ordination.[196] One sermon compared the power to consecrate to Elijah calling fire down from heaven.[197]

In line with this theology, the need for the appropriate minister to consecrate the Eucharist was emphasized in canon law, especially in the decree *Firmiter credimus*. The canon says, "Nobody can effect this sacrament except a priest who has been properly ordained according to the church's keys, which Christ gave to the apostles and their successors."[198]

The early canonists, when they commented on the text at all, emphasized the necessity of using the form approved by the Roman church in ordination. The earliest commentaries on *Firmiter* usually were silent on the matter. However, the *Casus Fuldenses* said the daily offering of the mass belonged only to a priest rightly ordained according to the keys.[199] The *Casus Parisienses* said a priest confected three sacraments, the Eucharist (*sacrificium corporis & sanguinis Christi*), baptism, and penance.[200] The *casus* on *Firmiter* in the Ordinary Gloss repeated the

193 *Hugonis de Sancto Victore De sacramentis Christianae fidei*, ed. Rainer Berndt (Münster, 2008), Bk. II pt. III c. XI. Giovanni Tabacco, *Le metamorfosi della potenza sacerdotale nell'alto Medioevo*, ed. Grado Giovanni Merlo (Brescia, 2012). The degradation of an erring priest began with depriving him of chalice and paten; see Bernard Gui, *Manuel de l'inquisietur*, ed. Guillaume Mollat, 2 vols. (Paris, 1964), 2.144; Gui, *The Inquisitor's Guide: A Medieval Manual on Heretics*, trans. Janet Shirley (Welwyn Garden City, 2006), 187.

194 Peter Lombard, *The Sentences*, 4.138–150: Bk. IV D. 24. Peter Lombard did not distinguish between priesthood and episcopate in his discussion of this sacrament.

195 Peter Lombard, *The Sentences*, 4.146–147: Bk. IV D. 24 c. 11.

196 *Scriptum super sententiis*, Bk. IV D. 24 q. 2 a. 1. The *Lay Folks Mass Book* emphasized the diligence of the priest and his abstinence from worldly occupations; see *Catholic England: Faith, Religion and Observance before the Reformation*, trans. R. N. Swanson (Manchester, 1993), 80–81.

197 *Pastors and the Care of Souls*, 15.

198 *Decrees of the Ecumenical Councils*, 1.230–231 at 230.

199 *Constitutiones Concilii quarti Lateranensis*, 483.

200 *Constitutiones Concilii quarti Lateranensis*, 466.

same material, quoting the text of the canon in the process.[201] The Gloss declared that the priest could not confect the Eucharist without ordination, a summary of accepted doctrine widely circulated in the glossed text.[202] (Neither Godfrey of Trani nor Innocent IV, however, discussed the power of the priest at that place in the *Liber Extra*.[203])

Hostiensis gave more attention to the priesthood in his *Summa*, when commenting on the title *De Trinitate*. He said, employing the words of *Firmiter*: "It appears that that the secret mystery that is hidden under the species of bread only a priest rightly ordained according to the keys granted to the apostles and their successors can confect."[204]

Discussing the mass, Hostiensis referred to *Firmiter* in an argument that the rite had to be celebrated by a priest ordained according to ecclesiastical tradition. No one else could do this.[205] His *Commentary* made much the same point, emphasizing the priest's role in pronouncing the words of consecration, a power not given to the laity: "for at the priest's voice transubstantiation into the body occurs." The cardinal added, following Innocent's text, that, at the consecration, "Nature gives way to miracle."[206]

Among the later Decretalists, Johannes Andreae held the same opinion as Hostiensis. Glossing *Firmiter*, he too cited *Cum Marthae* to show that nature gave way to miracle at the consecration.[207] At the word *rite*, rightly ordained, Johannes argued that the form of the Church had to be followed in an ordination ceremony.[208] Antonius de Butrio added to this teaching the idea that the ordained priest had to use the form authorized by the

201 Ordinary Gloss at X 1.1.1 *casus*.

202 Ordinary Gloss at X 1.1.1 v. Claves ecclesiae, "Nota hic, quod non potest conficere corpus Christi nisi fuerit ordinatus in forma ecclesiae."

203 Geoffrey did say, glossing the title *De presbytero non bapitzato* (X 3.43), that anything done in good conscience by a priest who thought he was validly baptized was firm (*rata*); see *Summa Goffredi de Trano super titulis decretalium*, fol. 165va: X 3.41.

204 *Summa domini Henrici cardinalis Hostiensis*, fol. 4rb: X 1.1, "apparet ne illud secretum mysterium quod sub specie panis latet quod non potest conficere nisi sacerdos rite secundum claues ecclesie concessas apostolis et suis successoribus ordinatus. infra. e. firmiter. ¶. una." He goes on to say "Vbi cedit natura miraculo."

205 *Summa domini Henrici cardinalis Hostiensis*, fol. 184va: X 3.40, "Debet autem missa celebrari a presbytero rite ordinato secundum traditionem ecclesiasticam quia per alium perfici non potest. Supra de sum. tri. c. I ¶. Vna." He also cited texts from the *De consecratione*.

206 *Hostiensis Decretalium commentaria*, 1, fol. 6va: X 1.1.1, "nam ad vocem sacerdotis fit transubstantiatio. non ergo ad vocem laici."

207 Johannes Andreae, *In quinque decretalium libros novella commentaria*, 1, fol. 8va: X 1.1.1, "[*Potestatem*] quia cedit natura miraculo. i^{a}. de cele. mis. Cum Marthę."

208 Johannes Andreae, *In quinque decretalium libros novella commentaria*, 1, fol. 8va: X 1.1.1, "[*rite*] ... necesse est enim in ordinatione servare formam ecclesię, sicut & in baptismo, vt hic, &. i^{a}. de bap. c. i."

Church when celebrating mass.[209] He also discussed at length the place of the gift of chalice and paten in the rite of ordination. This gift, together with the imposition of hands by the bishop, conferred the priest's principal power, that of consecrating the Eucharist. Antonius added that "If the forms are observed, a certain character is imprinted on the soul, a certain intellectual, indelible character."[210]

Panormitanus repeated the words of *Firmiter* before saying that Christ conferred the power to consecrate at the Last Supper. He then quoted the Ordinary Gloss on the *Extra* as saying not even the pope could confer this sacramental power on a non-priest. He went on to say that the priest had to be ordained *secundum solemnitates ecclesiae*.[211]

In principle, there was nothing new in a concern with priestly ordination, although most of the early collections of canons did not focus on orders as a sacrament; nor did they mention a character imprinted on the soul. The closest they ordinarily got was discussing whether a priest was rightly ordained. Thus Regino of Prüm listed among the questions to ask a parish priest his parentage, home village, the bishop who ordained him, and the "title" or benefice he was ordained for. He did not, however, offer a theology of the priesthood.[212] Burchard said a lesser cleric could not confer anything an ordained priest could except by delegation from that priest, as an assistant to the minister.[213] Burchard's idea of the priesthood included the traditional view, drawn from the False Decretals, that priests succeeded the disciples and that the priest exercised a legation on behalf of Christ. Burchard, however, did not pursue the question of a priest's sole power to consecrate the Eucharist, perhaps because he lacked relevant texts among his sources.[214]

The Gregorian Reform added a polemical edge to Regino's emphasis on who was rightly ordained. Anselm of Lucca said the sacraments of heretics are valid only where they had something in common with the accepted sacraments, "because they are not human but divine" (*quia non humana*

209 *Excellentissimi Antonii de Butrio . . . Super prima parte primi decretalium*, 1, fol. 7va: X 1.1.1. See also *Excellentissimi Antonii de Butrio . . . In librum tertium decretalium*, fol. 192vb–193ra: X 3.41.6, using words from c. *Firmiter*.

210 *Excellentissimi Antonii de Butrio . . . In librum prmium decretalium commentarii*, fol. 186ra–b at 186rb: X 1.16.3, "Si vero formae seruantur, quidam character imprimatur animae. id est. figura quaedam intellectualis indelibilis. Per quem ostenditur fuisset collatum & ordinatus a non ordinato in die iudicii discernetur."

211 Nicholas de Tudeschis, *Prima pars Abbatis Panormitani super primo Decretalium*. fol. 13va: X 1.1.1.

212 *Das Sendhandbuch des Regino von Prüm*, 34.

213 Burchardus Wormatiensis, *Decretum*, PL 140.759A.

214 Burchardus Wormatiensis, *Decretum*, PL 140.550D, 568C, "Sacerdotes vero vice Christi legatione funguntur in Ecclesia."

sunt sed divina).[215] The *Collection in Seventy Four Titles* was more condemnatory, saying that sacrilegious laying on of hands wounded the ordinand in the head and brought only damnation.[216] Deusdedit offered, in a slightly more liturgical vein, a single passage from the False Decretals saying that the Lord chose priests to make sacrifices and offerings.[217] The *Decretum* of Ivo of Chartres included a passage from Pope Nicholas I saying a polluted priest could not pollute the sacraments he administered.[218] Canons drawn from the works of Augustine said the sacraments were to be venerated even if the minister was evil, since they were the sacraments of Christ and the Church.[219] Only in one of his letters did Ivo address the sacramental role of the priest directly, quoting Jerome on Christians having the keys and Augustine as agreeing that "no one can bless unless he was ordained" (*benedicere non possit quis, nisi fuerit ordinatus*).[220]

Gratian's *Decretum* had a good deal of material on the choice of clergy and their respective roles, especially those of deacons, priests, and bishops; but it offered no specific theology of holy orders. A *palea*, added in the vulgate version of the text, took up a canon from Burchard saying a lesser cleric cannot do the things an ordained priest ordinarily did except by delegation from that priest, as an assistant to an ordained minister (D. 24 c. 1). Distinction 93 included texts about the various orders, minor and major, with requirements that clergy be in union with Rome and that inferiors obey superiors (D. 93 c. 5). The Distinction gave a great deal of space to texts from Jerome explaining the relationship of deacons to priests and priests to bishops. Bishops were distinguished from priests only by their power to ordain (D. 93 c. 24 ¶. 1).[221]

Among the Decretists, Rufinus once again was a key interpreter of the relevant texts. His theology of the priesthood emphasized its mediatory role. The priest acted on behalf of Christ, the mediator between God and humanity, with the people transmitting prayers, vows, and offerings through him.[222] Rufinus also identified the priesthood with the ministry

[215] Anselm of Lucca, *Collectio canonum*, 479.

[216] *The Collection in Seventy-Four Titles: A Canon Law Manual of the Gregorian Reform*, trans. John Gilchrist (Toronto, 1980), 197. Several regulations about who could or could not be ordained can be found in *Collection in Seventy-Four Titles*, 149–162.

[217] *Die Kanonessammlung des Kardinals Deusdedit*, ed. Victor Wolf von Glanvell (Paderborn, 1905; Aalen, 1967), 205.

[218] Ivo Carnotensis, *Decretum*, PL 161.179AC.

[219] Ivo Carnotensis, *Decretum*, PL 161.182D–183D.

[220] Ivo Carnotensis, *Epistola 63*, PL 161.80B–C.

[221] Friedberg 1.328, "Quid enim facit excepta ordinatione episcopus, quod non facit presbyter?"

[222] Rufinus, *Summa decretorum*, 548: De cons. D. 1 c. 51, "et vocatur missa quasi transmissa vel quasi transmissio, eo quod populus fidelis per ministerium sacerdotis, qui mediatoris vice fungitur inter Deum et homines, preces et vota et oblations Deo transmittat."

"of blessing and consecration of the Eucharist" (*benedictionis et consecrationis eucharistie*).[223] He explained the obedience deacons owed bishops and priests, which included giving out the Eucharist only by the priest's command, in the light of this sacred function.[224] The priest was superior in the sacraments, although a deacon might be superior in some matter of business in which he represented a patriarch or metropolitan.[225] Stephen of Tournai also emphasized the Eucharistic ministry of the priesthood, although the priest might have the deacon distribute communion to the people.[226] The commentary *Fecit Moyses tabernaculum* more clearly than most expositions of the *De consecratione* identified the priest with Christ as His agent, saying, "But the priest, who bears the figure of Christ, alone should consume it [the contents of the chalice]."[227]

Even in the Ordinary Gloss, which was completed after the Fourth Lateran Council, there was little discussion of priestly orders except in terms of rules for ordination and generalities about ministry. The exposition of Distinction 93 asserted the hierarchy of orders with the acceptable qualification that a deacon might be superior in administration, especially if acting on behalf of a metropolitan or patriarch.[228] The Gloss permitted deacons to baptize or communicate the sick, but only in a case of necessity.[229] Otherwise he only gave communion if authorized by a priest.[230] Restating the belief that the ministry of the priest is that of consecrating the Eucharist, Johannes Teutonicus, when glossing the *De consecratione*, emphasized the fact that Christ, not the minister, effected transubstantiation.[231] Thus he said, in line with Augustine's theology, that this did not happen by the priest's merits.[232] Nor could anyone but Christ have consecrated the elements, bread and wine, during His time on Earth. The power to consecrate was conferred at the Last Supper with an eye toward the time after the Resurrection. This explained, the Gloss said,

223 Rufinus, *Summa decretorum*, 187: D. 93 c. 33.
224 Rufinus, *Summa decretorum*, 185: D. 93 a. c. 13, "nec presente presbitero, nisi ab eo iussi, eucharistiam alicui tradere."
225 Rufinus, *Summa decretorum*, 188: D. 93 a. c. 24.
226 Stephen of Tournai, *Die Summa über das Decretum Gratiani*, 114: D. 93 c. 22, "*ministratio*, i. e. eucharistiae consecratio *dispensatio*, i. e. mensae dominicae compositio, vel quia iubente presbytero possunt sacramentum dominici corporis populo dispensare."
227 *Die Summa über das Decretum Gratiani*, 271: De cons. D. 2 c. 22, "sed solus sacerdos eam sumere debet, qui figuram Christi gerit."
228 Ordinary Gloss ad D. 93 a. c. 1 v. Obedientiam.
229 Ordinary Gloss ad D. 93 c. 12 v. Necessitas.
230 Ordinary Gloss ad D. 93 c. 14 v. Non oportet.
231 Ordinary Gloss ad D. 93 c. 22 v. Ministratio, "Minestratio. id est, consecratio eucharistiae."
232 Ordinary Gloss at De cons. D. 2 c. 71 v. Sacerdos, "Sacerdos. i. ad ostendendum quod non in merito sacerdotis &c."

Jesus's reference to performing the Eucharistic rite in memory of Him.[233] Johannes explained the institution's being done after – or at the end of – dinner as "confirming" – and thus ending – the sacraments of the Old Testament, including the sacrifice of the Paschal lamb.[234] What occurred when the priest spoke the words of consecration was effected not by his voice but Christ's own words.[235] A non-Catholic priest could not confect the sacrament.[236]

Firmiter credimus brought into the canon law a somewhat more sophisticated idea of holy orders as a sacrament than was found in the *Decretum* and its commentaries. Hostiensis gave considerable attention to the sacraments, including the difference between the external imprint of the ecclesiastical rite and the internal imprint made by the Holy Spirit[237] This teaching then was communicated to local sees and their parishes. The Lateran canon's reference to a priest rightly ordained found its way, quoted or paraphrased, into local statutes. Thus the first statutes of Salisbury said of the Eucharist: "And assuredly any priest rightly ordained according to the keys of the Church receives this power of confecting the sacrament, which the Lord himself granted to the apostles and their successors."[238]

The second statutes of Salisbury said "the Only Begotten Son was offered for us at the altar in the form of bread and wine transubstantiated by divine power through the hands of a priest rightly ordained." Here too the words of *Firmiter credimus* reached the local level, affirming the sacramental power of the priesthood.[239]

Pastoral manuals varied in whether they offered a theology of the sacrament of orders alongside their practical precepts. Thus Raymond

[233] Ordinary Gloss at De cons. D. 2 c. 24 v. Corpus. See also Ordinary Gloss at De cons. D. 2 c. 49 v. Huius & c. 50 v. Repraesentat.

[234] Ordinary Gloss at De cons. D. 2 c. 53 v. Namque saluatur, "Respondeo. Ideo coenatus dominus coenatus discipulis corpus suum tradidit, vt in hoc sacramento confirmationem omnium sacramentorum veteris testamenti, & agni paschalis quem ante manducauerant, & caeterorum monstraret."

[235] Ordinary Gloss at De cons. D. 2 c. 72 v. Ad sacerdotis, "Ad sacerdotis vocem. i. ad sermonem Christi voce sacerdotis enuntiatum, panis & vini substantia in carnem Christi sedentis at dexteram patris in caelis transubstantiari ministerio angelorum." See also Ordinary Gloss at De cons. D. 2 c. 82 v. Virga.

[236] Ordinary Gloss at De cons. D. 2 c. 72 v. Catholicus.

[237] *Summa domini Henrici cardinalis Hostiensis*, fol. 36vb.

[238] *Councils & Synods*, 2/1, 77, "Et hoc utique sacramentum conficiendi potestatem recipit quilibet sacerdos qui rite fuerit ordinatus secundum claves ecclesie, quas ipse dominus concessit apostolis et eorum successoribus."

[239] *Councils & Synods*, 2/1, 371, "et ipse scilicet unigenitus dei filius offertur pro nobis manibus sacerdotis in altari sub speciebus panis et vini transubstantiatis, pane in corpus et vino in sanguinem, potestate divina ministerio sacerdotis qui rite secundum claves ecclesie fuerit ordinatus."

of Peñafort had much to say about the laws governing ordination, but he presented nothing substantive about the power conferred with the character imposed on the soul by the sacrament.[240] John of Freiburg, however, wrote on the powers of a validly ordained priest. He could consecrate the sacrament unless deposed from office. Even then he had the power, but he sinned by using it. John said it was better to attend the mass of a good priest than that of a bad one, but the bad priest still had to celebrate on feast days and occasions when the people were to receive communion.[241] Thomas of Chobham too discussed the character imposed "in ordination according to the institution of the church with the honor of dignity and honesty for the exercise of certain ecclesiastical offices."[242] Thomas also described ordination as conferring on humanity a power denied to the angels, the power to confect the body of Christ.[243]

John of Erfurt, discussing the imposition of the priestly character, identified it with the laying on of hands. He noted, however, that some thought the handing over of the chalice was the essential moment:

> because the principal act of the priest is consecrating the body and blood of Christ.[244]

John noted that the bishop's laying on of hands imposed the character, but the priests present imposed their hands to signify the grace they shared in common.[245] If a heretic bishop, one who was validly consecrated before falling into error, tried to ordain someone, he could confer the character but not its use. If not validly consecrated, he could not ordain anyone.[246]

The *Manipulus curatorum* offered a more detailed discussion of the minister of the Eucharist, which turned its focus on who could or could not celebrate mass. This included an ordained priest being unable to celebrate or having been prohibited from celebrating for a valid reason. An example of the former is a cleric who was not validly ordained if there was a defect in the ceremony. Such a man was not rightfully ordained

240 *Summa Raymvndi de poenitentia*, 275–317. Raymond did quote Augustine from the *De consecratione* about the species of bread and wine as the visible sacrifice of the Church, as well as the invisible source of grace; see *De poentientia*, 317.

241 Johannes de Friburgo, *Summa confessorum*, fol. cxxvi^{vb}–cxxvii^{ra} (qq. cxxiii–cxxv).

242 *Thomae de Chobham summa confessorum*, 111, "Ordo est character impressus in ordinatione secundum institutionem ecclesie cum honore dignitatis et honore honestatis ad aliquod officium ecclestiasticum exercendum." This passage derives from the *Sentences* of Peter Lombard Bk. IV D. 24 c. 13; see Peter Lombard, *The Sentences*, 4.148. The priest's need for ordination to celebrate the Eucharist is stated briefly at *Thomae de Chobham summa confessorum*, 101.

243 *Thomae de Chobham summa confessorum*, 99, "quia ex virtute ordinis potest homo facere quod non potest angelus, scilicet conficere corpus Christi."

244 Johannes de Erfordia, *Die Summa confessorum*, 3.907, "quia principalis actus sacerdotis est consecrare corpus et sanguinem Christi."

245 Johannes de Erfordia, *Die Summa confessorum*, 3.925.

246 Johannes de Erfordia, *Die Summa confessorum*, 3.928.

according to the norms imposed in *Firmiter credimus* and other canons. Some of the reasons why a priest ought not to celebrate included mortal sin, irregularity, excommunication, schism, or heresy. The author also said a priest should not undertake celebration of a mass, a requiem especially, for monetary reasons, especially if he equated the mass with the sum offered. (Such thinking by a priest smacked of simony, although Guido did not use the term in this context.) The priest would have to repent and confess before celebrating again.[247] When discussing the sacrament of holy orders, Guido discussed at length the character imposed on the soul. It was because of this character that the priest could celebrate mass, something no one not rightly ordained could do. This, in turn, required that the ordinand had received the character imposed in baptism.[248] The *Manipulus curatorum* also, following Thomas Aquinas, emphasized the handing over of chalice with wine and paten with bread as a crucial factor in imposing the priestly character.[249]

In England, William of Pagula quoted the text of *Firmiter* as an explanation of the priest's Eucharistic role.[250] The author of the *Oculus sacerdotis* expected the faithful to accept the priestly role in effecting the Real Presence. Here too William emphasized right ordination.[251] The *Pupilla oculi* described all orders as oriented toward "one act, the consecration of the Eucharist."[252] The subdeacon, deacon, and priest received a sacramental character because they were "ordered" to the sacrament of the Eucharist.[253] The supreme order, the priesthood, was focused on the consecration of the sacrament.[254] John de Burough, like other authors,

[247] Guido de Monte Rocherii, *Manipulus curatorum*, fol. xviii^{r}–xx^{r}; Guido, *Handbook for Curates*, 44–49.

[248] Guido de Monte Rocherii, *Manipulus curatorum*, fol. xlvi^{v}–xlvii^{v}; Guido, *Handbook for Curates*, 111–114. See also John de Burough, *Pupilla oculi*, fol. lxxii^{va}.

[249] Guido de Monte Rocherii, *Manipulus curatorum*, fol. xviii^{r}–xx^{r}; Guido, *Handbook for Curates*, 44–49.

[250] William of Pagula, *Oculus sacerdotis*, fol. 7ra, "Nemo potest conficere corpus Christi nisi sacerdos qui rite fuerit ordinatus secundum claues ecclesie. Extra De sum. trinita. et fide catho. c. i ver. Una."

[251] William of Pagula, *Oculus sacerdotis*, fol. 72rb, "Quartum sacramentum est eukaristia. Et credere debet quilibet christianus illud uerum deum et hominem esse quod sacredos rite ordinatus in celebracione missarum eleuat sub specie panis et ostendit populo adorandum."

[252] John de Burough, *Pupilla oculi*, fol. lxxi^{va}, "quia omnes ordinantur ad unum. s. ad unum actum consecrationis eukaristie."

[253] John de Burough, *Pupilla oculi*, fol. lxxi^{vb}. These were involved with the materials, distribution of communion and consecration respectively; see *Pupilla oculi*, fol. lxxii^{ra}. John referenced Thomas Aquinas about the priestly character; see John de Burough, *Pupilla oculi*, fol. lxxii^{va}.

[254] John de Burough, *Pupilla oculi*, fol. lxxii^{ra}, "Primus gradus et supremus disponit ad consecrationem eukaristie et est sacerdotium."

emphasized the importance of giving a chalice and paten to the newly ordained. That act was the sign of the new priest's sacramental role.[255]

Works discussing ecclesiastical offices, some of them by canonists, occasionally touched on the ordination of the minister, although they tended not to discuss the character imprinted on the priest's soul.[256] Johannes Beleth said the priests of the New Law acted instead of those of the Old Law and "offer the sacrifice of the altar to God for us and are bound to teach the words of faith to the people entrusted to them."[257] Beleth wrote that an ordained priest was not to say the canon unless he was dressed in proper vestments and was at a consecrated altar.[258]

Innocent III, while still a cardinal, wrote on the mass and its mysteries. He described the priestly office as disposed to do the things that were done by Christ (*quae per Christum gesta sunt*).[259] Bishops and priests shared the priesthood, the one group succeeding the apostles and the other the disciples.[260] All were able to confect the sacrament (*conficere*); but only a bishop could ordain others, conferring that power. Innocent too cited the handing over of chalice and paten as conferring the power to offer sacrifice. The priest's office received the power to consecrate from Christ at the Last Supper, just before He, as the supreme priest, offered Himself as sacrifice on the altar of the cross.[261]

Sicard of Cremona offered a similar interpretation of the origin of the priesthood. He emphasized, in his discussion of the rite of ordination, the anointing of the hands: "The hands are anointed so that they may be clean for offering victims for sins and so that priests, who are chosen for the power of consecrating from the consecrated Lord, may imitate the example of the crucified Christ in the works of mercy."[262]

Sicard likewise discussed the sacramental significance of conferring a paten and chalice on the ordinand. These gestures conferred the power to celebrate mass and dispense of the body of the Lord (*corpus Domini*

255 John de Burough, *Pupilla oculi*, fol. lxxii^{va}.

256 An exception is Antonius de Butrio, who wrote that the indelible character imprinted on the soul would be discerned on the Day of Judgment (*in die iudicii discernetur*); see *Excellentissimi Antonii de Butrio ... Super prima parte primi decretalium commentarii*, fol. 186rb: X 1.16.3.

257 *Iohannis Beleth summa de ecclesiasticis officiis*, 33, "Horum uicem nostri tenent sacerdotes, qui sacrificium altaris pro nobis Deo offerunt et populum sibi commissum uerba fidei edocere teneantur."

258 *Iohannis Beleth summa de ecclesiasticis officiis*, 82.

259 *De sacro altaris mysterio libri sex*, PL 217.774A, cited from the *Patrologia Latina Database*.

260 *De sacro altaris mysterio libri sex*, PL 217.777A–D.

261 *De sacro altaris mysterio libri sex*, PL 217.7779C, 780B–C.

262 *Sicardi Cremonensis episcopi Mitralis*, 85, "manus inunguntur, ut mundę sint ad offerendum hostias pro peccatis et ut Christi crucifixi uestigia sacerdotes in misericordię operibus imitentur, qui potestatem consecrandi a consecrato Domino sortiuntur."

dispensare) to the faithful.[263] In addition, when discussing the canon of the mass, Sicard said that Christ's blessing of the bread at the Last Supper conferred on the apostles the power to transubstantiate it.[264]

The most extensive exposition of the mass and other ecclesiastical offices, that of Guillelmus Durantis Senior, like most such works, said the bishops succeeded the apostles and the priests the disciples.[265] Priests and deacons were instituted in the Primitive Church for the ministry of the altar, with other, lesser, orders added later as the Church grew in numbers.[266] In Durantis's theology of the priesthood, priests acted in Christ's place as mediator.[267] At his ordination, each priest received from the bishop "the chalice with wine and the paten with the host," showing he received "the power of offering acceptable sacrifices, and the Body and blood of Christ." The bishop told him he was receiving the power to offer sacrifices and celebrate mass.[268] As a celebrant of the mass, the priest enacted Christ's sacrifice of Himself to the Father.[269] This brought Durantis, the canonist, fully into the common theology of the priesthood in his age, which treated the priest as Christ's agent on earth. This role of representing Christ helps explain why priests were expected to have no physical defects, natural or based on injury, especially those which would cause scandal. Even minor ones required a papal dispensation for the ordinand, as petitions to the Apostolic Penitentiary show.[270] One test for

263 *Sicardi Cremonensis episcopi Mitralis*, 85–86.

264 *Sicardi Cremonensis episcopi Mitralis de officiis*, 190, "id est gratiam multiplicationis infudit, sic etiam hic credimus intelligendum 'Benedixit', id est gratiam transsubstantiandi infudit, ut panis transubstantiaretur in carnem. "

265 *Guillelmi Duranti rationale divinorum officiorum I–IV*, 166–167 (*minores sacerdotes*); William Durand, *On the Clergy and Their Vestments: A New Translation of Books 2 – 3 of the Rationale divinorum officiorum*, trans. Timothy M. Thibodeau (Scranton, 2010), 66–67, 116. Durantis also saw the priesthood as succeeding Aaron, Moses, and Melchisedek; see *Guillelmi Duranti rationale*, 165–166.

266 *Guillelmi Duranti rationale divinorum officiorum I–IV*, 136; William Durand, *On the Clergy and Their Vestments*, 76.

267 *Guillelmi Duranti rationale divinorum officiorum I–IV*, 169; William Durand, *On the Clergy and Their Vestments*, 119.

268 *Guillelmi Duranti rationale divinorum officiorum I–IV*, 169; William Durand, *On the Clergy and Their Vestments*, 120. Hostiensis thought the gift of these vessels might not be essential to ordination, but he though doing this was "safer" (*tutius*); see *Hostiensis Decretalium commentaria*, 1, fol. 114rb: X 1.16.3. Antonius de Butrio noted the opinion of some that this gift was essential, but he focused on the idea that the laying on of hands by other priests was supplemental, not essential; see *Super prima parte primi decretalium commentarii*, fol. 186ra: X 1.16.3.

269 *Guillelmi Duranti rationale divinorum officiorum I–IV*, 170–171; William Durand, *On the Clergy and Their Vestments*, 121–122.

270 *Repertorium Poenitentiariae Germanicum*, 2 no. 889, 5 no. 959, 6 no. 3058, 2183. Kirsi Salonen and Jussi Hanska, *Entering a Clerical Career at the Roman Curia, 1458–1471* (Washington, D.C., 2012), 122–129. This concern with bodily defects was found

a priest or ordinand was the ability to break a consecrated host during mass.[271]

Although we have much normative material about the priesthood – as has been outlined above, it is harder to discern how most priests saw their calling. Priests were numerous in every Latin Christian land, and those assigned to parishes or chantries usually were not university trained in theology or canon law.[272] However, a minimum knowledge of theology, liturgy, and law was expected of any priest. Stephen Langton, for example, expected a priest to know the *opus Dei*. William Lyndwood interpreted this as meaning knowing how to perform the office and the sacraments, as well as what to teach their parishioners.[273] Later John Peccham issued the statutes *Ignorantia sacerdotis* and *Altissimus*, found in Lyndwood's *Provinciale*. Among the things a priest was supposed to know were the articles of faith and the seven sacraments. He was to teach the faithful about the faith and the sacraments, including the Eucharist, both basic doctrine and discipline.[274] More than a century earlier, Cardinal Otto, on his legation to England in the early thirteenth century, issued a statute requiring candidates for the priesthood to be examined on their knowledge of these basics of the priestly calling; and he required archdeacons to instruct priests in the performance of the sacraments.[275]

Motivations for seeking orders could be as different as the educational and social backgrounds of the ordained. Whether trained at a university or in a local song school, each ordinand was supposed to pass an examination, in the diocese or even at the papal curia; and they were expected to have some financial support, a living. However, their real knowledge might vary wildly, including limits to their competence in Latin, let alone

early on in the penitentials; see *Medieval Handbooks of Penance: A Translation of the Principal "libri poenitentiales" and Selections from Related Documents*, ed. John T. McNeill and Helena M. Gamer (New York, 1938), 239. For examples of priests who needed graces on account of wounds affecting their hands, see *Repertorium Poenitentiariae Germanicum*, 9 no. 1793, 3138.

271 *Repertorium Poenitentiariae Germanicum*, 7 no. 2051, 2055.

272 On university studies by parish priests, see most recently F. Donald Logan, *University Education of the Parochial Clergy in Medieval England: the Lincoln Diocese, c.1300–c. 1350* (Toronto, 2014).

273 Lyndwood, *Provinciale seu Constitutiones*, 226 "a *Opus Dei*. Quod consisit in his quae pertinent ad Divinum Officium exequendum, & administrationem Sacramentorum, & ad doctrinam & eruditionem Subditorum."

274 *Lyndwood's Provinciale: The Text of the Canons Therein Contained, Reprinted from the Translation Made in 1534*, ed. J. V. Bullard and H. Chalmer Bell (London: Faith Press, 1929), 1–3, 14–15; Lyndwood, *Provinciale seu Constitutiones*, 1–10, 42–45. On the teaching role of the clergy, describing Ignorantia sacerdotis as a syllabus, see Andrew Reeves, "Teaching the Creed and Articles of Faith in England, 1215–1281," in *A Companion to Pastoral Care in the Middle Ages (1200–1500)*, ed. Ronald J. Stansbury (Leiden, 2010), 41–72.

275 *Constitutiones Domini Ottonis*, in Lyndwood, *Provinciale seu Constitutiones*, 8–10.

in theology and canon law. All of these priests were expected to celebrate mass and administer the other sacraments. Some of them failed to perform even their most basic functions or perform them competently, as visitations to local churches too often show. At the most lowly levels, concubinage was common, even though all priests were expected to be celibate, especially under the norms of the Gregorian Reform. Many members of the clerical proletariat differed little from their parishioners, living close to the earth in rural villages and small towns.[276]

In the matter of priestly powers and prerogatives, as in other issues concerning the sacraments, there was occasional dissent with respect to their status. Criticism might cross the line into open dissent and outright heresy. Thus the Waldensians were suspected by inquisitors like Jacques Fournier of denying that a sinful priest could consecrate the Eucharist *ex opere operato*.[277] Fournier also accused the Waldensians of equivocating when asked about that during questioning.[278] Bernard Gui too thought the Waldensians held this opinion about a sinful priest's inability to consecrate the sacrament: "They err about the sacrament of the Eucharist, saying, not publicly in their secrecy, that bread and wine are not made into the body and blood of Christ if the priest celebrating or consecrating is a sinner."[279]

John Wyclif later challenged traditional thinking about priestly powers in a somewhat different way. He raised a doubt whether the prayers of unworthy priests, especially those who were not among the elect, were as efficacious as those of a priest predestined to be saved.[280] Martin V, following the condemnation of Wyclif's errors at Constance, ordered inquisitors to ask suspected Lollards or Hussites questions about belief in the Real Presence. He also wanted suspects asked about belief in the priest's power to consecrate even when he was in a state of mortal sin. This question presupposed the priest's use of the right materials and form with the right intention (*et cum intentione faciendi*), but it focused on the supposed ability of sinful humans to impede sacramental actions *ex opere operato*.[281] A Lollard like Walter Brut rejected the entire medieval

[276] Margaret Bowker, *The Secular Clergy in the Diocese of Lincoln 1495–1520* (Cambridge, 1968), 38–84; Dorothy M. Owen, *Church and Society in Medieval Lincolnshire* (Lincoln, 1971), 132–142; Denys Hay, *The Church in Italy in the Fifteenth Century* (Cambridge, 1977), 49–57.

[277] *Regestre d'inquisition de Jacques Fournier*, 1.42–43, 72–73.

[278] *Regestre d'inquisition de Jacques Fournier*, 1.72–73.

[279] Bernard Gui, *Manuel de l'inquisietur*, 1.42; Gui, *The Inquisitor's Guide*, 54. Gui added that the Waldensians thought everyone but themselves sinners.

[280] Stephen E. Lahey, *John Wyclif* (Oxford, 2009), 188–189.

[281] *Catholic England: Faith, Religion and Observance before the Reformation*, trans. R. N. Swanson (Manchester, 1993), 268.

theology of the priesthood, especially the idea of the priest offering Christ in the sacrament. Small wonder his judges thought him a heretic.[282]

The materials of the Sacrament

All medieval canonists believed that the Eucharist was instituted at the Last Supper. The synoptic gospels recorded Christ as having said of the bread, "This is my body," and over the cup, "This is my blood" (Matthew 26:26–28: Mark 14:22–24; Luke 22:19–20; also 1 Cor. 11:24–26). By the twelfth century, the Eucharistic supper had become the mass, often interpreted as a reenactment of Christ's Passion. Duly ordained priests were expected to celebrate the mass with due decorum, using vestments, vessels, and altar linens. The essential materials of the rite were wheat bread made with a little water and wine into which a little water was mixed.[283] The bread, by the late eighth century, was being replaced with hosts, small rounds of unleavened wheat dough baked between two irons. By the eleventh century, these small round objects were in universal use among Latin Christians.[284] These, with the priest and the right words, were the essentials of the mass. Nonetheless, the canonists worried about the right materials, including whether the bread could be leavened or unleavened and what became of the water combined with the wine. Of these concerns, only that about using yeast in the Eucharistic bread was grounded in an ongoing conflict, the long-standing disagreement with the Greeks over whether one followed a literal meaning of the Bible, using unleavened bread, or accepted a symbolic interpretation, with the yeast representing the action of the Holy Spirit. Latin opinion, like that of Thomas Aquinas, could grudgingly tolerate the use of yeast. The Angelic Doctor, as summarized in the *Summa theologiae*, said Latin practice was Christ's but that yeast had been added to combat the Ebionite heresy, which retained too many Jewish practices.[285] However, the canon law also conveyed the more negative opinion of Huguccio. That canonist said that priests had to do as Christ did, using unleavened bread when

[282] David Aers, "Walter Brut's Theology of the Sacrament of the Altar," in *Lollards and Their Influence in Late Medieval England*, ed. Fiona Somerset, Jill C. Havens, and Derrick G. Pitard (Woodbridge, 2003), 115–126.

[283] This was stated in a canon of a Council of Carthage, which entered canonistic collections like the *Decretum* of Burchard of Worms as an offering the Lord used; see Burchardus Wormatiensis, *Decretum*, PL 140.753A–B. A brief summary of these necessities for mass, together with a priest intending to consecrate, appears in a York priest's notebook; see *Pastors and the Care of Souls*, 161.

[284] Aden Kumler, "The Multiplicity of the Species: Eucharistic Morphology in the Middle Ages," *Res* 59/60 (2011), 179–191 with pictures of surviving irons in figures 6–8; Reynolds, "Christ's Money," 104–11, 137.

[285] Thomas Aquinas, *Summa theologiae*, III q. 74 art. 4.

confecting the Eucharist.[286] Huguccio went farther, saying that adding yeast made the bread no longer what Christ had used. Then consecration could not occur. Any addition to bread or wine that made the elements "impure" impeded transubstantiation.[287]

Official reactions too could be purely condemnatory. The Fourth Lateran Council condemned in the canon *Licet Graecos* (X 3.42.10) the Greek practice of washing altars once used by Latin priests to celebrate mass, probably because of these differences over the Eucharistic bread.[288] Johannes Teutonicus interpreted the Lateran text as meaning the Greeks were subject to Rome, apparently including obedience in sacramental practice.[289] Another text, c. *Literas tuas* (X 3.41.10), from a decretal of Honorius III, threatened a Latin priest who used leavened bread with deposition. More positive efforts were made later to resolve this and other divisive issues by compromise at the Second Council of Lyon (1272) and the Council of Florence (1439): but these failed, being rejected in the East.[290] This difference about the Eucharistic bread was not just a theological dispute. Collisions in lands like Cyprus could lead to inquisitorial inquiries, suffering, and death.[291]

The canon law was slow to adopt a theology of the priestly ability to consecrate the Eucharist, but discussion of the materials appeared early. A key text was the letter attributed to "Pope Alexander" in the Pseudo-Isidorean Decretals, already mentioned, in which it was stated that "And, to repel all superstitious opinions, only bread and wine mixed with water are offered in sacrifice."[292] The text states that water must be mixed with the wine in the chalice because blood and water issued from Christ's side

[286] Huguccio, *Summa decretorum*, Admont Stiftsbibliothek MS 7, fol. 422vb: De cons. D. 2 c. 3, "Et ideo propter iudeorum credendus est Christus tunc usus fuisse tantum azimis et ideo nos in sacramento altaris azimis uti debemus."

[287] Huguccio, *Summa decretorum*, Admont Stiftsbibliothek MS 7, fol. 423ra: De cons. D. 2 c. 5," Distinguo id solum quod est de pura substantia uel materia frumenti conuertitur in corpus Christi et nichil aliud siue sit de pipere uel sale uel alia specie. uel ordeo. uel lolio. uel uicia. et huiusmodi queritur non fit ita si fermentum addatur. quia ibi nichil remanet azimi cuius possit fieri consecratio. Et ideo nichil conuertetur de uuis dicit. id est. de uino uuarum quia est uinum de moris et de prunis et huiusmodi sed de ullo uino nisi de uuis conficitur sanguis Christi." This passage was checked against Klosterneuburg MS 89, fol. 346vb.

[288] See also the *Casus Fuldenses* in *Constitutiones Concilii quarti Lateranensis*, 484.

[289] *Constitutiones Concilii quarti Lateranensis*, 191.

[290] Joseph Gill, *Byzantium and the Papacy, 1198–1400* (New Brunswick, N.J., 1979), 120–141; Gill, *The Council of Florence* (Cambridge, 1959), 265–267, 270–275, 278, 280–281, 284, 286, 349–388.

[291] Christopher Schabel, "Martyrs and Heretics, Intolerance of Intolerance: The Execution of Thirteen Monks in Cyprus in 1231," in Schabel, *Greeks, Latins, and the Church in Early Frankish Cyprus* (Farnham, 2010), study no. III, 1–33.

[292] Hinschius, 99, "ita ut repulsis opinionibus superstitionum panis tantum et vinum aqua permixtum in sacrificio offerantur."

on the cross. "Alexander" then recited the narrative of the blessing of bread and wine at the Last Supper.[293] Another text, attributed to "Pope Julius," reaffirmed the use of bread and the chalice against wrong practices like using milk or "a flax cloth dipped in partially fermented grape juice" (*panem lineum musto intinctum*). It also required using watered wine, saying the wine represented Christ and the water the people united to him. Both were necessary, or the Lord's chalice (*calix Domini*) of the Last Supper would not be on the altar.[294]

Regino of Prüm wanted each parish priest asked whether he mixed water into the wine at mass.[295] He backed this question with a decree from a Council of Worms saying "the master of truth" (*magister veritatis*), Christ, commended to His disciples the use only of bread and wine mixed with a little water. Nothing else was to be offered.[296] The decree said, as many would say later, that the water represented the people and the wine represented Christ. The mixture in the chalice of the Lord showed the joining of the believing people (*credentium plebs*), inseparably united to their Savior.[297] Regino followed this text with others from a Council of Reims about the proper quality of the materials employed in making the chalice, paten, and corporal for use at the altar.[298] Similarly, the Canons of Edgar required the use of pure bread, wine, and water. The priest who began mass without all of these was threatened with divine wrath.[299]

Burchard of Worms included in his *Decretum* the texts attributed to Alexander and Julius about the materials of the Eucharist.[300] A text of "Pope Anicius" said that the offerings of bread, wine, and water, which were necessary for the Eucharist, were to be kept clean so that nothing vile

[293] Hinschius, loc. cit., treats this narrative as derived from Matthew 26:26–28.

[294] For this text from the Third Council of Braga, see Hinschius, 434.

[295] *Das Sendhandbuch des Regino von Prüm*, 32, "Si aquam cum vino misceat in sacrificio Domini."

[296] *Das Sendhandbuch des Regino von Prüm*, 66, "Cum igitur magister veritatis verum salutis nostrae sacrificium suis commendaret discipulis, panem tantum et calicem sub hoc sacramento praebuisse cognoscimus, ideoque praeter panem et vinum cum aqua mixtum aliud offeri non debet."

[297] *Das Sendhandbuch des Regino von Prüm*, 66, "Ergo quando vino aqua miscetur, Christo populus adunatur et credentium plebs ei, in quem credidit, copulatur et iungitur, quae copulatio et coniunctio aquae et vini sic miscetur in calice Domini, ut commixtio illa non possit separari."

[298] *Das Sendhandbuch des Regino von Prüm*, 68. For reasons of space, this issue will not be pursued here.

[299] *Councils & Synods*, 1/1.327. These canons required the chalice be of metal and not of wood; see *Councils & Synods*, 1/1.327–328. Northumbrian priests were to be fined for using a wooden chalice; see *Councils & Synods*, 1/1.456.

[300] Burchardus Wormatiensis, *Decretum*, PL 140.751A–752B, 753C–754A. See also texts echoing the Alexander letter, c. 3 and 4, in Burchardus, *Decretum*, PL 140.753A–B.

was found in them.[301] The collection also includes a text of "Pope Melchiades" saying any offering that could not be used at the altar according the apostolic custom, were to be carried to the priest's house to be blessed and shared.[302] Burchard added the text from a Council of Worms that Regino had used about mixing water into wine. He rejected any idea that water alone could be used "on account of sobriety" (*sobrietatis causa*). This text too said that the mixture represented the blood and water that flowed from Christ's pierced side. This canon also reflected in its phrasing the "Pope Alexander" text. The mixture also could represent the union of Christ (represented by wine) with the people (represented by water). The combination of elements was such that "it could not be separated," since Christ might then be thought separable from the people in the mass.[303]

Anselm of Lucca began his book on the sacraments with an abridged version of the text of "Pope Alexander" about the Eucharistic elements, affirming the use only of bread and watered wine.[304] Anselm also quoted Cyprian of Carthage on the necessity of putting water into the chalice. Otherwise, Christ (represented by wine) would begin to be there without the people (water).[305] The *Decretum* of Ivo of Chartres contained the "Julius" text about materials to avoid in the Eucharist, affirming the use of only wheat bread and watered wine. It also contained the decree of the Council of Worms about not offering only water or wine. Likewise a

[301] Burchardus Wormatiensis, *Decretum*, PL 140.758A–B, "Panes quos Deo in sacrificium offertis, aut a vobismetipsis, aut a vestris pueris coram vobis nitide ac studiose fiant, et diligenter observetur, ut panis, et vinum, et aqua, sine quibus Missae nequeunt celebrari, mundissime atque studiose tractentur, et nihil in eis vile, nihil non probatum inveniatur, juxta illud quod ait Scriptura: Sit timor Domini vobiscum, et cum diligentia cuncta facite."

[302] Burchardus Wormatiensis, *Decretum*, PL 140.754A–B, "Haec species quas non licet offerre super altare juxta constitutionem apostolorum eorumque successorum, ad domum sacerdotum deferantur, et a sacerdotibus benedicantur, et simplici benedictione benedicta demum a populis sumantur."

[303] Burchardus Wormatiensis, *Decretum*, PL 140.753A, "Quae copulatio et coniunctio aquae et vini sic miscetur in calice Domini, ut commixtio illa non possit separari. Nam si vinum tantum quis offerat, sanguis Christi incipit esse sine nobis. Si vero aqua sit sola, plebs incipit esse sine Christo."

[304] Anselm of Lucca, *Collectio canonum*, 459, "In sacramentorum oblationibus, quae inter missarum sollempnia Domino offeruntur panis tantum et vinum aqua permixtum in sacrificium offerantur. Non enim debet in calice Domini aut vinum solum aut aqua sola offerri, sed utrumque permixtum ex latere eius sua in passione perfluxisse legitur."

[305] Anselm of Lucca, *Collectio canonum*, 460, "Nam si vinum tantum quis offerret, sanguis Christi incipit esse sine Christo." The author follows the reading *sine nobis* from the *Patrologia Latina Database*, accessed on September 11, 2012, rather than *sine Christo* in Thaner's edition. The text also says the host was made only with flour and a little water. That water added to the wine represents the people also appears in a text of Cyprian included in *The Collection in Seventy-Four Titles*, 189–190.

canon of a Council of Carthage and a text from another African council were used, the latter saying milk and honey could be offered for their own blessing, but not for consecration.[306] The decree of "Alexander," with its gospel narrative of the institution of the sacrament, was quoted at length.[307] The *Panormia* too contained the "Julius" decree split into three parts, one saying that only bread and watered wine were to be offered, another warning against giving communion by intinction, and a third stating the ecclesiological meaning of wine and water – Christ represented together with the Christian people.[308]

Distinction 2 of the *De consecratione* in Gratian's *Decretum* began with an excerpt from "Pope Alexander," saying only bread and wine with a little water were to be offered (De cons. D. 2 c. 1). There followed texts attributed to Saint Cyprian (De cons. D. 2 c. 2 and 3), Pope Martin (c. 4), and a Council of Carthage (c. 5) saying similar things. The entire canon of "Pope Julius" was included (c. 7). All of these texts emphasized the use of bread and watered wine. A text of Gregory the Great identified the chalice offered by the priest with the cup Christ gave to the apostles (De cons. D. 2 c. 73). Another text, by Ambrose, emphasized the use of watered wine in Biblical terms, mentioning Melchisedek and Moses (c. 83).[309] None of these texts reflected collisions with the Greeks in eastern Mediterranean lands.

The Decretists were slow to deal with these issues. Paucapalea, for example, only mentioned other texts about Abraham in the *Decretum*, emphasizing his giving tithes to Melchisedek and the punishment of Dathan, Abiram, and Korah for trying to usurp the honor of the priesthood.[310] Rufinus treated the sacrament in depth. He said, "The form of sacrificing always is this: wine and water with bread are offered in this sacrament, and nothing else."[311] Water was used because it had flowed from Christ's side, and bread became Christ's body.[312] The canonist said, quoting Burchard of Worms, that nothing vile was to be permitted to enter into the bread, wine, or the water that were offered at

[306] Ivo Carnotensis, *Decretum*, PL 161.162B–174A. Texts about other offerings presented for blessing appear in Ivo, *Decretum*, 161.164D–165A.

[307] Ivo Carnotensis, *Decretum*, PL 161.164B–D. [308] *Panormia Project*, 87–89.

[309] Melchisedek appears in other texts as anticipating Christ's priesthood and the Eucharist; see, e. g., Hildebert of Lavardin, *De expositione missae*, PL 171.1165C–D.

[310] *Die Summa des Paucapalea über das Decretum Gratiani*, 144–145: De cons. D. 2 cc. 83 and 26.

[311] Rufinus, *Summa decretorum*, 551: De cons. D. 1 c. 1, "Forma vero sacrificandi hec est: semper vinum et aqua cum pane in hoc sacramento, et nichil aliud offeratur." The text rejects use of grapes but accepts partially fermented wine in a case of necessity (*si necessitas fecerit*).

[312] Rufinus, *Summa decretorum*, 552: De cons. D. 2 c. 2.

the altar.[313] He also said that only grapes and wheat, from which wine and bread could be made, were to be used in the Eucharist.[314] Rufinus repeated the condemnation by "Julius" of errors like using milk in place of wine.[315]

By the thirteenth century, there was a continuing tradition of commentary on the *De consecratione* in Italy. Simon of Bisignano said only wheat bread could be used in the Eucharist; and he listed vinegar, spoiled wine, together with other liquids that could not be added to the wine.[316] He also said that yeast represented corruption, and so the Greeks were repressible for using it in the Eucharist.[317] Sicard of Cremona said the same thing, using Simon's words.[318] Huguccio required pure elements in the sacrifice, especially unadulterated wheat in the making of the bread. The wine was not to be sour or mixed without other liquids. Nor were spices to be added to it.[319] Huguccio concluded that "Nothing is changed into the body of Christ except bread made of wheat, and wine from grapes with water."[320]

The Ordinary Gloss on Distinction 2 of the *De consecratione* made it clear from its beginning that bread, wine, and water were the basic materials of the sacrament.[321] They were made from "fruits of the earth" (*ex fructibus terrae*) consecrated by a mystical prayer.[322] The bread, made from many grains, represented the body of Christ, made up of many members, that is, holy Church made up of many persons.[323] The necessity of using water in making the bread was affirmed, and the utility of any other liquid was denied.[324] The Gloss affirmed that Latin

[313] Rufinus, *Summa decretorum*, 552: De cons. D. 2 c. 1, "et postquam facte fuerint, diligenter observentur, ut nichil in eis – vel in vino vel in aqua – vile, nihil non probatum inveniatur, ut in Burch. l. V. ex decreto Annitii pape cap. Panes."

[314] Rufinus, *Summa decretorum*, 552–553, "Si est *in sacrificiis*, talis est sensus, ut non omnino conformetur de aliis frugibus terre aliquid, nisi de uva et tritico, ut de uvis vinum et de frumento fiat panis."

[315] Rufinus, *Summa decretorum*, 553.

[316] *Summa in decretum Simonis Bisianensis*, 515–516: De cons. D. 2 c. 1.

[317] *Summa in decretum Simonis Bisianensis*, 513–514: De cons. D. 2 c. 1, "Non enim ibi apponi debet fermentum, per quod corruptio designatur et ob hoc reprehensibilis uidetur esse Grecorum ecclesia que conficit in fermento."

[318] Sicardus Cremonensis, *Summa decretorum*, 101A: De cons. D. 2 c. 1.

[319] Huguccio, *Summa decretorum*, fol. 423ra: De cons. D. 2 c. 5.

[320] Huguccio, *Summa decretorum*, fol. 423ra: De cons. D. 2 c. 5, "nichil transit in corpus Christi preter panem frumenti et uinum uuarum cum aqua."

[321] Ordinary Gloss at De cons. D. 2 a. c. 1 v. In sacramentorum. The Gloss cited (loc. cit.) the decretal *Cum Marthae* to say the water signified regeneration.

[322] Ordinary Gloss at De cons. D. 2 c. 59 v. Corpus & sanguinem.

[323] Ordinary Gloss at De cons. D. 2 c. 35 v. Vnum, "siue vnum panem ex pluribus granis, siue vnum corpus Christi ex pluribus membris purissimis: cuius figuratum est ecclesia sacrosancta, quę ex pluribus personis adunatur."

[324] Ordinary Gloss at De cons. D. 2 c. 1 v. Calix. The use of honey was mentioned specifically at v. Nisi utrunque.

priests had to employ unleavened bread as Scripture required, denying the Greeks' use of yeast.[325] Scripture also required that the wine be watered in imitation of the Lord, as learned men advised.[326] Johannes Teutonicus said that bread and wine were used as others did, that these materials were used "So that there would not be the horror of flesh and blood and to avoid seeming ridiculous to pagans."[327]

The thirteenth-century papacy on occasion issued its own decrees about the Eucharistic elements; but it focused its most influential decretals on the wine and water in the chalice, not on the bread. Innocent III's *Cum Marthae* was the most influential of these, but it was more theological than practical. Honorius III, however, added to the canon law a letter to the archbishop of Uppsala, *Perniciosus* (X 3.41.13), warning against a local usage employing more water than wine at mass. The archbishop was warned to follow "the reasonable general custom of the Church" (*secundum rationabilem consuetudinem ecclesie generalis*) by using more wine than water when celebrating mass.[328]

The early Decretalists wrote a little about the material of the sacrament. Vincentius Hispanus cited *Cum Marthae* about the use of bread and wine "with water" (*cum aqua*).[329] Innocent IV cited the *Decretum* to argue that the Lord's chalice (*calix Domini*) contained not wine or water alone but both. Both had to be present for symbolic reasons. Wine without water meant Christ without the Church. Water without wine meant the Church without Christ. The joining of both represented the "conjunction of Christ and the Church."[330] Priestly negligence in this matter could result in a true but imperfect sacrament. The small amount of water was absorbed, as Church was not changed into the Church but the Church into Christ.[331]

325 Ordinary Gloss at De cons. D. 2 c. 2 v. Scriptura, "verissimile enim est, quod dominus azymis vsus est propter ritum Iudaeorum. & nos azymis vti debemus." The *Gloss* continues saying the Greeks did not use yeast in their homes and attributes the adoption of leavened bread to "some of their doctors."

326 Ordinary Gloss at De cons. D. 2 c. 4 v. Tradidit. Jewish priests also were forbidden unwatered wine; see Ordinary Gloss at De cons. D. 2 c. 81 v. Et vinum.

327 Ordinary Gloss at De cons. D. 2 c. 42 v. Hoc dicerent, "Et ne esset horror carnis & sanguinis. Et ne ridiculum fieret paganis. infra. ead. panis etc." See also Ordinary Gloss at De cons. D. 2 c. 44 v. Inuisibiliter & c. 63 v. Panis est.

328 Revised from *The Sources of Catholic Dogma*, 174–175.

329 *Constitutiones Concilii quarti Lateranensis*, 288, "*panis et vini*: cum aqua, extra iii. de celebr. missar. Cum Marthe."

330 *Commentaria Innocentii quarti Pont. Maximi super libros quinque Decretalium*, fol. 453va–b, "Calix domini non est tantum vinum, nec est tantum aqua, sed vinum & aqua. de conse. dist. 2. C. 1 & c. 2. Quia si est ibi tantum vinum: est ibi tantum Christus sine nobis, si est ibi tantum aqua incipit esse ibi ecclesia sine Christo. Coniunctio enim aquae & vini significat coniunctionem Christi & ecclesia."

331 loc. cit., "et debet tam parvum ibi poni de aqua, quod vinum eam absorbeat, quia Christus non mutatur in ecclesia sed ecclesia in Christum."

Godfrey of Trani wrote briefly about the materials of the Eucharist in his *Summa*. Discussing the materials for the mass, he focused on the bread to be used. Godfrey cited Huguccio of Pisa as saying that unleavened bread was to be used and that even a little yeast or leavened bread impeded transubstantiation. Anything else mixed in, such as pepper, would not be transubstantiated.[332] The canonist, as was usual, said more wine than water was to be put into the chalice. He said, citing *Cum Marthae*, that both wine and water were transformed in the mass, leaving out Pope Innocent's words about this being the more probable opinion.[333]

Hostiensis wrote more extensively on the Eucharistic elements, using the existing body of texts. He said, "In the sacrament of the altar nothing else is offered except bread and wine mixed with water." Then he went on to specify that the wine be made from grapes and the bread from wheat flour. New wine not entirely fermented could be used in place of wine, but he insisted on unleavened bread. Hostiensis sided with Huguccio, denying that bread with yeast could be consecrated, and he quoted Scripture to support this opinion. Hostiensis said the Greeks held the contrary opinion, but they should follow Roman custom.[334] The cardinal said neither darnel nor vinegar could be used. Any pepper mixed in would not be transubstantiated with the bread.[335] He also followed Godfrey of Trani in saying transformation would not occur if leavened and unleavened bread were mixed when making the dough.[336] Hostiensis followed c. *Perniciosus* in saying there should be more wine than water in the chalice.[337]

Writing about defects in the mass, as many canonists did, Hostiensis wrote about what to do if only water were found in the chalice after a

332 *Summa Goffredi de Trano super titulis decretalium*, fol. 161va–b: X 3.41. This passage is one of the many in canonistic writings reflecting controversies over the bread to be used in the Eucharist; see Schabel, "The Quarrel over Unleavened Bread in Western Theology, 1234–1439," 85–127.

333 *Summa Goffredi de Trano super titulis decretalium*, fol. 162ra: X 3.41, "Hec duo vinum et aqua in sanguinem transmutantur. vt. infra. eo. cum marthe. ¶. que fuisiti."

334 Hostiensis, *Summa*, fol. 185ra, "In sacramento altaris nihil aliud offeratur nisi panis et vinum aqua mixtum. Vinum. scilicet. de uvis et panis de frumento. de cons. di. ii. in sacramento. Sed si necesse fit botrus exprimi potest in calice et illud vinum consecrabitur. De conse. di. ii cum omne. Nec est celebrandum in pane fermentato et cypho ligneo nec sine igne et aqua. infra. eo. ti. c. i. Quid si conficiat quis de fermentato nihil aget secundum hug. de conse. dist. ii. in sacramento. iuxta illud non in fermentato veteri: sed in azymis synceritatis et veritatis. Greci tamen tenent contrarium: sed debent sequi consuetudinem roma. eccl."

335 Hostiensis, *Summa*, fol. 185ra: X 3.40.

336 Hostiensis, *Summa*, fol. 185ra: X 3.40, "Quid si panis fit ex fermentato et azimo simul mixto. Nihil agitur secundum gof."

337 Hostiensis, *Summa*, fol. 185ra: X 3.40.

particle of the broken host (*particula corporis Christi*) already had been added. He recommended taking it back to the sacristy instead of drinking from the chalice at the altar. Even then, the water was not to be treated vilely (*viliter*), such as by pouring it onto the ground.[338] Innocent IV had already said that, if the priest found only water there just after receiving the bread, he could add wine and repeat the entire consecration of the blood (*& repetet totam consecrationem sanguinis*). If he had added a particle of the host, however, the particle had to be kept (*custodienda*).[339]

The opinions of the later Decretalists differed little from those of their predecessors on this topic. Johannes Andreae repeated what had been said about darnel being incapable of being transubstantiated. He quoted John 12:24 on the necessity of a grain of wheat falling to the ground and dying so that it would not remain alone. Christ was represented, he said, by that grain. Thus darnel did not represent the Savior, but wheat did.[340] Johannes repeated what Hostiensis had said about the ecclesiological significance of the wine and water in the chalice. He too said a perfect sacrament would not result from an imbalance of the two liquids or the lack of wine.[341] Johannes Andreae too thought the addition of a particle of the host to a chalice containing only water after the fraction required placing the contents in the sacristy "on account of the particle of Christ's body" (*propter particulam corporis Christi*), not pouring it on the ground or drinking the water.[342]

Panormitanus was among those who reaffirmed the need to add more wine than water to the chalice. This was according to the general custom of the Church (*generalis ecclesie consuetudo*). This custom was attributable, he said, to Christ, the apostles, or the holy fathers. Nonetheless, custom required that water be used. Panormitanus added a summary of *Cum Marthae*, with its Gloss, saying the water denoted the people united to Christ through charity.[343]

[338] *Henrici de Segusio Cardinalis Hostiensis Decretalium commentaria*, 3, fol. 163rb–va: X 3.41.6.

[339] *Commentaria Innocentii quarti Pont. Maximi super libros quinque Decretalium*, fol. 453va–b: X 3.41.6.

[340] Johannes Andreae, *In quinque decretalium libros novella commentaria*, 3, fol. 220ra: X 3.41.6, "quia & Christus fuit granum frumenti, sicut ipse dicit Ioann. 12. Nisi granum frumenti cadens in terram mortuum fuerit ipsum solum manet. unde nec de lolio conficeretur." He denied the "expert" opinion that darnel was born from wheat, or perhaps the contrary.

[341] Johannes Andreae, *In quinque decretalium libros novella commentaria*, 3, fol. 220rb: X 3.41.6.

[342] Johannes Andreae, *In quinque decretalium libros novella commentaria*, 1, fol. 221rb: X 3.41.6.

[343] Nicholas de Tudeschis, *Abbatis Panormitani super tertio Decretalium*, fol. 217va: X 3.41.6.

Synodal decrees were in this matter, as in others, the conduits of the canons of general councils and papal decrees to local churches. The materials of the sacrament rarely were controversial except in areas with populations following different liturgical traditions. Thus in divided Cyprus, with its mixed population,[344] Latins, Greeks, and others, the materials of the Eucharist were controversial, with potential sources of conflict down to the parish level. Thus the thirteenth-century constitution instructing Greek priests on acceptable practices specifically said, loosely paraphrasing a letter of Pope Innocent IV,

> Concerning the sacrament of the Eucharist, they should also warn them that as long as it is done by the priest according to the procedure of the Church, it does not matter whether they perform it with leavened or unleavened bread, since the Lord Pope states, "As long as they believe" that in both ways it is the true body of Christ, which He assumed from the Blessed Virgin.[345]

A fourteenth-century Council of Nicosia prepared a detailed *Confessio fidei*. It included a statement on the Eucharist partly composed of excerpts from *Firmiter credimus* and partly of the *Professio fidei* of the Emperor Michael VIII Palaiologos (1267), which reflects his unsuccessful efforts to forge a union with the Western church. The text affirms both transubstantiation and priestly power, but it is less accommodating than were the instructions for the Greeks about leavened bread:

> "Another is the sacrament of the Eucharist, which the same Roman Church prepares with unleavened bread, holding and teaching that in" unleavened bread there is brought about and can be brought about the true body of Christ, "whose body and blood are truly contained in the sacrament of the altar under the forms of bread and wine, the bread being transubstantiated into the body and the wine into the blood by divine power." "And no one can effect this sacrament except a priest who has been duly ordained in accordance with the keys of the Church, which Jesus Christ himself granted to the apostles and their successors."[346]

[344] *The Synodicum Nicosiense and Other Documents of the Latin Church of Cyprus, 1196–1373*, ed. Christopher David Schabel (Nicosia, 2001), 250–251. This phrase is derived from canon 9 of the Fourth Lateran Council.

[345] *Synodicum Nicosiense*, 124–125, 127, "Admoneat etiam ipsos circa Eucharistiae sacramentum quod sive in fermento sive azymo pane conficiant, dummodo per sacerdotem fiat secundum ecclesiae formam non refert, cum Dominus papa dicat, 'dummodo credant' quod utroque modo esse verum corpus Christi quod de beata Virgine traxit." For Innocent IV's letter on the liturgical norms to be imposed on the Greek clergy, see *Synodicum Nicosiense*, 307–311.

[346] *Synodicum Nicosiense*, 256, "Aliud est Eucharistiae sacramentum, quod 'ex azymo conficit eadem Romana ecclesia, tenens et docens quod in' azymis" verum conficitur et potest confici corpus Christi, 'cuius corpus et sanguis in sacramento altaris sub speciebus panis et vini veraciter continetur, transsubstantiatis pane in corpus et vino in sanguinem potestate Divina.' Quod 'utique sacramentum nemo potest conficere nisi

This issue could emerge in visitations, as it did when Matthew, Greek bishop of Lefkara, and his clergy were questioned by the Latin bishop of Limassol about their avoidance of the use of unleavened bread in the Eucharist.[347] Denial of Latin practices by the Greeks could even be considered heresy.[348]

Western synods occasionally said something about the materials of the sacrament, but the texts are more concerned with practical or pedagogical details than with theological issues. The statutes of Paris mandated keeping the ampoules for wine and water "clean and whole."[349] Bishop Odo of Sully said that a priest who consecrated unmixed wine was to be regarded as having consecrated validly, but unmixed water was not transformed. Negligence involving use only of water, since no consecration occurred, required a greater penance than using only wine.[350] The 1287 statutes of Liège, using language similar to that of the Paris statutes, required not just labeling the ampoules for wine and water but frequent renewal of the wine.[351] The statutes of Tournai specified not just the proper keeping of the ampoules but that it was better to use red wine, not white, when celebrating mass.[352] The 1239 statutes of Tarragona required that the host be made of pure wheat flour without yeast or salt.[353] Similarly, a French statute forbade use of hosts not made of "pure, clean and chosen wheat grain" (*de puro et mundo et electo grano frumenti*).[354]

A more detailed discussion of the materials appears in a "precept" of the statutes of Soissons. The statute specified bread made with flour, wine from the vine, and natural water (*aqua naturalis*), not made "by art" (*non per artem facta*). This statute required a priest to add wine to water, if he found only that in the chalice, and repeat the complete words for the consecration of the wine before finishing his own communion. Also, if he failed to add water to the wine, he was to do penance.[355] The second statutes of Salisbury specified bread made from the purest flour and

sacerdos rite fuerit ordinatus secundum claves ecclesiae, quas ipse concessit apostolis et eorum successoribus Iesus Christus.'"

347 *Synodicum Nicosiense*, 331–332.

348 *Synodicum Nicosiense*, 142–145 at 142. The heading of this canon describes it as to be used "ad extirpandum haereticam pravitatem."

349 Odette Pontal, *Les statuts synodaux français du XIIIe siècle*, 1 (Paris, 1971), 58.

350 *Pontal, Les statuts synodaux francais du XIIIe siècle*, 1.78.

351 Mansi 24.896. See also the statutes of Cambrai in Joseph Avril, *Les statuts synodaux francais du XIIIe siècle*, 4 (Paris, 1975), 39.

352 Avril, Les statuts synodaux francais du XIIIe siècle, 4.329.

353 Mansi 23.515.

354 Pontal, *Les statuts synodaux*, 2.326.

355 Avril, *Les statuts synodaux francais du XIIIe siècle, 4.294. Similarly see the statutes of Cambrai in Avril, Les statuts synodaux francais du XIIIe siècle*, 4.40.

water, specifying its roundness (*rotunditatem*). This statute said the wine was to be pure but was accepting of either white wine or red. It was to be rejected, however, if it had turned to vinegar. A "modicum" of water was to be added to the chalice during the mass.[356] The same thing was said of soured wine in the 1287 statutes of Exeter.[357] A statute of Tournai said a priest should select hosts that were whole, solid, and not too old to consecrate.[358] A synod of Constance (1300) said the priest was to choose *manu electo* a white host in circular form.[359] One visitation in the archdeaconry of Josas told the parishioners of Evry-Petit-Bourg to provide "less black bread" (*panem minus nigrum*) for the mass.[360]

Manuals for priests also discussed the right materials in some detail but with differing emphases. Thus Thomas of Chobham listed the purity of the materials (*puritas materie*) among the things necessary for celebrating mass.[361] Thomas, like Johannes Andreae, quoted John 12:24, *Unless a grain of wheat falls to the ground and dies, it remains alone*, to prove wheat flour was essential for making the host. He added, "If, however, a grain of a different sort is mixed in, there is danger, because, unless there is so little of it that it is absorbed by the wheat flour, consequently the body of Christ is not confected."[362] The wine had to be real wine in which one was not required to mix so much water "that the essence of wine perishes" (*quod pereat essentia vini*). Instead the wine should absorb the water. The wine should also not have turned to vinegar.[363] Thomas gave the usual symbolic meanings for the wine and water, the blood and the water from the side of Christ representing the Savior and the people united to Him.[364]

The *Manipulus curatorum* compared the spiritual food in the Eucharist with terrestrial food and drink. Wheat and pure water had to be baked into hosts, since dough could not be consecrated. Liquids like wine, milk, or rose water could not be used; any other grain could also not be used. Following the custom of Rome, the bread had to be unleavened. Leavened bread could be consecrated, but the Latin priest who used it

[356] *Councils & Synods*, 2/1.372. [357] *Councils & Synods*, 2/2.990.

[358] Pontal, *Les statuts synodaux francais du XIIIe siècle*, 1.329. See also the 1287 statutes of Liège in Mansi 24.896. The same statute said to inspect wine and water for any odor.

[359] Mansi 25.35. The diocese of Bayeux added the requirement that hosts be breakable (*frangibilis*); see Mansi 25.62.

[360] *Visites archdidiaconales de Josas*, ed. J.-M. Alliot (Paris, 1902), 337.

[361] *Thomae de Chobham summa confessorum*, 100.

[362] *Thomae de Chobham summa confessorum*, 100, "Si autem grana alterius generis commixta sint periculum est, quia nisi granum admixtum tam paucum sit quod penitus absorbeatur a frumento non conficitur inde corpus Christi."

[363] *Thomae de Chobham summa confessorum*, 101.

[364] *Thomae de Chobham summa confessorum*, 101–102. Thomas added the usual warning that a priest sinned if he absentmindedly omitted the water when filling the chalice; see *Thomae de Chobham summa*, 102.

sinned gravely.[365] The wine had to be made from grapes, not pomegranates, mulberries, or apples. New wine not yet fermented (*botrus*) could be used, but not vinegar. Vinegar had become a different "species" from wine, even slightly sour wine.[366] This was the way in which Christ wanted the sacrament to be celebrated. Wheat bread would strengthen the believer, and wine would make hearts glad. Moreover, multiple grains and many grapes in the materials represented the many believers spiritually united with Christ. The mixing of the water into the wine represented the union the people could attain with Christ through the sacrament.[367]

John of Erfurt too repeated the need for wheat bread and wine squeezed out of grapes. He discussed a very practical problem: what the priest should do if the wine froze. He said the priest should try to thaw it before consecration, but it was validly consecrated if he did not notice until later. Frozen wine only differed in an accidental quality (*accidentali qualitate*) from its liquid form.[368] The priest sinned if he used unbaked dough or bread made with rose water. Dough could not be consecrated; and, although he thought that bread made with rose water could be consecrated, John also thought the priest sinned gravely in doing so.[369] If the priest realized the host was not made of good wheat, but inferior flour or spelt, he was to replace it with a good host before consecrating. If he only realized this after consuming the host, he was not to drink from the chalice, since he no longer was fasting. The chalice would have to be set aside to the next day's mass or given to another priest to receive with the wine he had consecrated.[370]

John of Freiburg addressed many of these same issues. He also considered the possibility that the host might have decayed before being used at mass. He said that this, like adding grain other than wheat to the flour, changed the nature of the bread and impeded transubstantiation. If a priest discovered at the altar that his host was not made of pure wheat, he could send for another made properly. If he had already consecrated it, he could consume if after he had received the replacement host.[371] A Latin

[365] Guido de Monte Rocherii, *Manipulus curatorum*, fol. xx^{v}–xxi^{r}; Guido, *Handbook for Curates*, 49–50.

[366] Guido de Monte Rocherii, *Manipulus curatorum*, fol. xxi^{r}; Guido, *Handbook for Curates*, 50.

[367] Guido de Monte Rocherii, *Manipulus curatorum*, fol. xxi^{r-v}; Guido, *Handbook for Curates*, 50–51.

[368] Johannes de Erfordia, *Die Summa confessorum*, 2.135. Johannes Beleth allowed the priest even to use fire to thaw the wine; see *Iohannis Beleth summa de ecclesiasticis officiis*, 228.

[369] Johannes de Erfordia, *Die Summa confessorum*, 2.136–137.

[370] Johannes de Erfordia, *Die Summa confessorum*, 2.135–136.

[371] Johannes de Friburgo, *Summa confessorum*, fol. cxxiiii^{vb}–cxxv^{ra} (qq. xci–xcii).

priest, following the "more probable" (*probabilior*) usage, had to use unleavened bread or he sinned; but a Greek priest sinned if he did not used leavened bread, thus "perverting the rite of his church" (*peruertens sue ecclesie ritum*).[372] John offered all the usual cautions about using good wine and pure water, but he added the observation that concomitance permitted priests in countries having no wine still to celebrate mass using bread alone.[373]

William of Pagula, as noted above, said only wheat bread could be transubstantiated. Following Huguccio, he said leavened bread could not be changed, since its use was contrary to Christ's use of unleavened bread at the Last Supper. William also said that use of honey or any other liquid but water in making hosts prevented transubstantiation.[374] Likewise, the *Pupilla occuli* says that the bread had to be made with natural water, not wine, honey, or "artificial water" (*aqua artificiali*). Dough did not suffice, nor did a mixture of grains suffice unless the additional grain was but a small part of the whole. The author was inclined to blame any such problem on the one who made the host, allowing a priest who trusted that person, believing the bread was correctly made, to go without blame.[375] The bread had to be unleavened, because Christ was free of *the leaven of malice* (1 Cor. 5:8). A Latin priest who knowingly used leavened bread sinned gravely. The Greeks, who did not follow the custom of the Roman church, also sinned seriously.[376] Watered wine was to be employed, but not with so much water that the wine was lost in the mixture. That mixture could not be transubstantiated. The water had to be absorbed into the wine in order to be consecrated. The wine also had to be made from grapes and no other fruit. John de Burough cited c. *Perniciosus* to support these conclusions. A priest who acted against these traditions with contempt or from negligence also sinned.[377] John also said vinegar had changed too much from wine to be used, becoming a cold rather than a hot substance. Nor was mere grape juice sufficient, although partially fermented juice could suffice.[378] The *Pupilla* also allowed remedies for failures to put the right balance of wine and water into the chalice

[372] Johannes de Friburgo, *Summa confessorum*, fol. cxxv^{ra} (q. xciiii).
[373] Johannes de Friburgo, *Summa confessorum*, fol. cxxv$_{va}$ (q. cv).
[374] William of Pagula, *Oculus sacerdotis*, fol. 8ra, "Non licet sacerdoti celebrare cum pane fermentato." loc. cit., "Et si alia farina admisceatur non transubstantiatur. Et dicit Hugo quod de pane fermentato non potest confici corpus Christi . . . Et si ex melle uel ex alio liquore fuerit aspersa non transubstantiatur ille panis in corpus Christi. de cons. di. ii. c. ii in glo." William's discussion of wine without water or vinegar in the chalice follows.
[375] John de Burough, *Pupilla oculi*, fol. xiii^{rb-va}.
[376] John de Burough, *Pupilla oculi*, fol. xiii^{va}.
[377] John de Burough, *Pupilla oculi*, fol. xiii^{va-vb}.
[378] John de Burough, *Pupilla oculi*, fol. xiv^{ra}.

at mass, and even measures to be taken if poison (*venenum*) or a spider were found in the chalice.[379]

Writing in the fifteenth century, Nicholas of Ausimo updated the *Summa Pisanella* or *Magistrutia*, an alphabetical manual refashioned from John of Freiburg's work by Bartholomew of San Concordio, an early fourteenth-century Dominican. Nicholas, a Franciscan Observant, repeated much of what others had said about use of wrong materials, corrupted species, or the wrong proportion of water in the chalice. Nicholas too thought Latin use of unleavened bread was more reasonable (*rationabiliter*), but he admitted a Greek priest would sin in using it.[380] More interesting is his comment that even a country that cannot make its own wine can import enough of it for the celebration of mass.[381]

Liturgical treatises addressed the symbolism of the elements as well as the instructions for celebrating mass. Innocent III discussed the theology and symbolism of the mass in more than one work. In his book *Book on the Fourfold Nature of Marriages*, Innocent said the bread was eaten and not consumed. The one who is eaten, Christ, incorporated the one who eats.[382] The bread referred to Christ's body and the wine to His blood. The one was offered for the body and the other for the soul.[383] In his widely distributed *Six Books on the Sacrament of the Altar*, he argued for the Real Presence, via the transformation of bread and wine, against unspecified heretics, possibly the Cathars.[384] Innocent III distinguished in this work between the Paschal lamb as prefiguring Christ's body and the unleavened bread of Passover as representing a sincere work (*opus sincerum*).[385] His interpretation of the unleavened bread said the Church followed Christ's practice, which meant he consecrated unleavened bread at the Last Supper.[386] The text included a detailed discussion of the error of the Greeks, who thought the Last Supper did not fall on Passover and thus could have included leavened bread.[387] Innocent added an affirmation that Rome was founded upon apostolic faith (*super*

379 John de Burough, *Pupilla oculi*, fol. xli^{v}–xlii^{r}. Johannes Beleth allowed a priest to discard the wine if a fly or spider fell into it; see *Iohannis Beleth summa de ecclesiasticis officiis*, 228.

380 Nicholas of Ausimo, *Supplementum Summae Pisanellae* (Venezia, 1489), fol. I-2vb–3ra.

381 Nicholas of Ausimo, *Supplementum Summae Pisanellae* (Venezia, 1489), fol. I-3rb, "Non est aliqua terra ad quam non possit tantum portari de vino quantum sufficeret ad celebrandum."

382 *Liber de quadrapartita specie nuptiarum*, PL 217.945C–D.

383 *Liber de quadrapartita specie nuptiarum*, PL 217.946C–D.

384 *De sacro altaris mysterio libri sex*, PL 217.860A.

385 *De sacro altaris mysterio libri sex*, PL 217.860A, "Nam paschalis agnus absque dubio figurabat corpus Dominicum, sed azymus panis, opus sincerum."

386 *De sacro altaris mysterio libri sex*, PL 217.854D–855A, "Et ita panem azymum in corpus suum sine dubio consecravit."

387 *De sacro altaris mysterio libri sex*, PL 217.855A–857D.

apostolicae fidei fundamentum), whereas Constantinople was leavened with heresy.[388] Innocent also said both bread and wine had to be consecrated, not just one species, in order to enact the "mystery of unity" (*mysterium unitatis*).[389] As he would do in *Cum Marthae*, Innocent denied the water in the chalice became phlegm. His test of the sufficient amount of water in the wine was flavor, whether the taste of wine predominated. Then the contents of the chalice could be transubstantiated.[390]

Sicard of Cremona referred to the materials of the sacrament, the offerings, as "the terrestrial and material substance" of the sacrifice in the Eucharist.[391] Addressing the significance of the materials, Sicard interpreted the bread made of many grains and the wine made from many grapes as representing the Church and the body of Christ, made up of many believers.[392] The water mixed with the wine also represented the people redeemed by the Savior's blood. It also represented the water from the side of Christ crucified and baptismal water.[393] Sicard said that he left the question whether the water too was transubstantiated to the theologians and to his own discussion of the *Decretum*. He affirmed, however, that "We know, nevertheless, that neither is the people saved without blood, nor is this mystery enacted except on account of the people."[394] Sicard, as a canonist, did look occasionally at more practical matters, interspersed into his symbolic readings of the actions in the mass. He addressed the dispute over leavened and unleavened bread. Reciting arguments already long established, Sicard said the use of unleavened bread was not Judaizing but imitated Christ's actions at the Last Supper.[395] Only flour and water were used in making the host and only wine and water were in the chalice.[396]

Guillelmus Durantis, like other writers, said the priest's offerings were bread, wine, and water. He argued from the Old Testament that the bread

388 *De sacro altaris mysterio libri sex*, PL 217.857D–858A.
389 *De sacro altaris mysterio libri sex*, PL 217.872B–D.
390 *De sacro altaris mysterio libri sex*, PL 217.875D–876D.
391 *Sicardi Cremonensis episcopi Mitralis*, 170, "Offerunt autem ministri panem, uinum et aquam. Hęc est enim huius sacrificii terrena et materialis substantia."
392 *Sicardi Cremonensis episcopi Mitralis*, 171.
393 *Sicardi Cremonensis episcopi Mitralis*, 172. Sicard referenced the decree of "Pope Alexander" in this context.
394 *Sicardi Cremonensis episcopi Mitralis*, 172, "Vtrum alterum sine altero transsubstantietur, et quid acqua transsubstantietur? Si transsubstantiantur, quomodo est? Sed exploratoribus theologicis, quos labor exagitat inquirendi, ad pręsens reliquimus, cum et de his etiam alibi super decretis et in theologię disputationibus studiose tractauerimus. Scimus tamen, quod nec populous sine sanguine saluatur, nec, nisi populi causa, hoc misterium agitur."
395 *Sicardi Cremonensis episcopi Mitralis*, 173–174.
396 *Sicardi Cremonensis episcopi Mitralis*, 186, "'Hęc dona' quoad panem, in quo sunt farina et aqua. 'Hęc munera' quoad uinum, in quo sunt uinum et aqua."

should be unleavened, as with the showbread (Leviticus 24:5–9), and that hosts should be made, like the showbread, by the priests themselves.[397] The roundness of the host was to represent God, without beginning or end.[398] After invoking the offering of Melchisedek, Durantis said the bread represented both the offering of Christ's body and the "pious desires of the faithful" (*pia desideria fidelium*).[399] The wine represented the blood of Christ, which became separated from His body. The deacon held the chalice, but only the priest could consecrate it.[400] Durantis cited "Pope Alexander" as declaring that water must be added to the wine to represent the people. There were, he said, many waters and many people. Just as blood and water flowed from Christ's side, the water added to the chalice showed inseparable union: "When, therefore, water is mixed with wine, then the people is gathered to Christ."[401] Like other writers, Durantis said there had to be more wine than water, since the people are incorporated into Christ.[402]

The issue of leavened and unleavened bread was temporarily resolved at the Council of Florence. *Laetentur coeli*, the decree of union with the Greeks (1439), said, "Also, the body of Christ is truly confected in both unleavened and leavened wheat bread, and priests should confect the body of Christ in either, that is, each priest according to the custom of his western or eastern church."[403] In the same year, the decree of union with the Armenians affirmed seven sacraments, each made up of matter, "words as form," and the minister.[404] The Eucharist was to be celebrated with wheat bread and wine from grapes as the matter. The Lord, according to the Fathers and doctors, used watered wine, not unmixed wine. Bread became body and wine became blood, but "the whole" Christ was

[397] *Guillelmi Duranti rationale divinorum officiorum I–IV*, 382; William Durand, *Rationale IV*, 247.

[398] *Guillelmi Duranti rationale divinorum officiorum I–IV*, 382–383, "ipsa sui forma significet illum qui principio caret et fine"; William Durand, *Rationale IV*, 246–247, "through its form is signified He who has no beginning or end."

[399] *Guillelmi Duranti rationale divinorum officiorum I–IV*, 384–386; William Durand, *Rationale IV*, 250–253.

[400] *Guillelmi Duranti rationale divinorum officiorum I–IV*, 386; William Durand, *Rationale IV*, 253–254.

[401] *Guillelmi Duranti rationale divinorum officiorum I–IV*, 386–387 at 387, "Cum ergo aqua cum uino miscetur, tunc Christo populus adunatur"; William Durand, *Rationale IV*, 253.

[402] *Guillelmi Duranti rationale divinorum officiorum I–IV*, 388; William Durand, *Rationale IV*, 254–255.

[403] *Decrees of the Ecumenical Councils*, 1.527, "Item, in azymo sive fermentato pane tritico, corpus Christi veraciter confici, sacerdotesque in altero ipsum Domini corpus conficere debere, unumquemque scilicet iuxta sue ecclesię sive occidentalis sive orientalis consuetudinem."

[404] *Decrees of the Ecumenical Councils*, 1.542.

present in either species. Those who received the sacrament were given increased grace and made members of Christ.[405] The minister, a priest, received "a chalice with wine and a paten with bread" at his ordination. The sacrament was conferred with the laying on of hands and these actions.[406] The decree for union with the Copts (1441) added an affirmation of the words of consecration to be said over wheat bread by a priest intending its consecration.[407] The Maronites' metropolitan was to affirm not just that there were seven sacraments, as the Roman church taught, but that he never would employ oil (*oleum*) in the Eucharist.[408]

Of these four decrees, only *Laetentur coeli* received learned commentary. Fantinus Vallaresso, who had participated in the council and signed the decree, discussed the clause about the Eucharistic at length. He presented an argument that Christ instituted the sacrament at the Last Supper without specifying leavened or unleavened bread. The Bible simply said "He took bread" (*accepit panem*). Fantinus said it did not matter whether the bread was "white or black, square or round in form" (*albus vel niger aut in forma quadratra vel rotunda*): "Therefore, Christ did not wish to restrain this sacrament to unleavened or leavened bread alone, but He granted and conceded power that it could be confected from any wheat bread."[409] Fantinus still concluded, after reviewing all arguments, that Christ actually had used unleavened bread; but he still accepted the council's conclusion about the use of either type of bread as valid.[410] Juan de Torquemada, in his commentary on the decree, also argued that Christ used unleavened bread. His exposition affirmed the need for wheat bread without other grains.[411] Torquemada used canon law and the works of Thomas Aquinas in an exposition that treated Latin practice as "more reasonable" (*rationabilior*), but accepted the custom of the Greeks too. Quoting Thomas Aquinas, he described Greek practice as having "reason and significance" (*rationem & significationem*).[412] Torquemada stated a

405 *Decrees of the Ecumenical Councils*, 1.546–547.

406 *Decrees of the Ecumenical Councils*, 1.548–549.

407 *Decrees of the Ecumenical Councils*, 1.581.

408 *Decrees of the Ecumenical Councils*, 1.590.

409 Fantinus Vallaresso, *Libellus de ordine generalium conciliorum et unione florentina*, ed. Bernardus Schultze (Roma, 1944), 61, "Non ergo ad azimum tantum vel fermentatum tantum voluit Christus hoc sacramentum restringere, sed de quocumque pane triticeo hoc posse confici virtutem dedit atque concessit."

410 Fantinus Vallaresso, *Libellus de ordine generalium conciliorum et unione florentina*, 69, "et in utroque vere conficitur, sicut dicitur in ipsa tercia diffinitione sancte unionis."

411 Juan de Torquemada, *Apparatus super decretum florentinum unionis Graecorum*, ed. Emmanuel Candal (Roma, 1942), 66–70.

412 Juan de Torquemada, *Apparatus super decretum florentinum unionis Graecorum*, 70–71. Most of this section is a patchwork of quotations from Torquemada's sources.

similar opinion in his commentary on Gratian's *Decretum*.[413] Thus the West grudgingly accepted Greek practice, although Greek opinion still tended to treat Latin practice as Judaizing and thus erroneous.[414]

At the parish level, the issue of the right materials usually was one of quality, supply, and costs, not doctrine. Thus Robert Grosseteste wanted visitors to ask if a priest used sour wine at the mass.[415] The London statutes of ca. 1245–1259 wanted the archdeacon to determine whether the wine used at the altar was adequate (*competens*).[416] During a visitation at Worley in the diocese of Hereford in 1397, a dispute arose over whether the vicar was obligated to supply bread, wine, and candles to each chaplain who celebrated in his church. He denied being obliged to provide these things.[417] At Compton Hawry and Haydon in the diocese of Salisbury pensions were left to the abbot of "Shirbourne" who was supposed to provide bread and wine for mass.[418] At Ramsbury, a married cleric served as deacon and parish clerk, the former office obliging him to provide bread and wine.[419] Wills could include bequests for support of the mass, like one by a priest in the register of a dean of Salisbury that provided wax for candles, as well as bread and wine, to an altar of the cathedral.[420] In the diocese of Lincoln on the eve of the Reformation, one priest lacked good wine for mass.[421] In the same period the abbess of Elnestone refused to provide bread and wine to the parish of Clamefeld because of a squabble with the parishioners.[422] These issues of obligation and costs mattered more at the parish level than did theology or arguments of Latins and Greeks over the materials of the Eucharist.

[413] Juan de Torquemada, *Commentaria super decreto*, 5.61A–B.
[414] Deno J. Geanakoplos, "The Council of Florence (1438–9) and the Problem of Union between the Byzantine and Latin Churches," *Church History* 24 (1955), 324–346.
[415] *Pastors and the Care of Souls*, 290.
[416] *Councils & Synods*, 2/1.649.
[417] *Pastors and the Care of Souls*, 293. There are other examples from Hereford involving providing the grain for the bread; see A. T. Bannister, "Visitation Returns of the Diocese of Hereford in 1397," *The English Historical Review* 44 (1929), 279–289, 444–453, 45 (1930), 92–101, 444–463 at 29.449, 30.99.
[418] *The Register of John Chandler Dean of Salisbury 1404–1417*, ed. T. C. B. Timmins (Devizes, 1984), 22 no. 38, 25 no. 47.
[419] *The Register of John Chandler Dean of Salisbury*, 35 no. 71.
[420] *The Register of John Chandler Dean of Salisbury*, 160 no. 556.
[421] *Visitations in the Diocese of Lincoln 1517–1531*, ed. A. Hamilton Thompson, 3 vols. (Hereford, 1940), 3.141.
[422] *Visitations in the Diocese of Lincoln 1517–1531*, 2.51.

2 The form of the sacrament and the elevation of the host

The form of the sacramental words

Hoc est enim corpus meum, the words used for the consecration of the host in the canon of the Latin mass, and *Hic est enim calix sanguinis mei*, the words for the consecration of the chalice, were rooted in the Bible's narratives of the Last Supper (e.g., Matthew 26:26–28). These words came to be regarded in the twelfth and thirteenth centuries as bringing about the transubstantiation of the bread and wine into Christ's body and blood.[1] These words, said by a rightly ordained bishop or priest, provided the form of the sacrament to consecrate the elements or materials, wheat bread and watered wine. The importance of the words of the canon of the mass is illustrated by the statement of the canonist Henricus Bohic that the priest needs "The words by which transubstantiation occurs."[2] Among the possible defects in the celebration of mass, he said, was having a priest who is a mute.[3] The consecrated elements were elevated to arouse the devotion of the congregation, but only once the words had been said over them.

The issue of the right words eventually became familiar down to the parish level by the later Middle Ages. A schema for the celebration of mass from a York notebook for parish priests said the celebrant needed, in ascending order of importance, the right gestures, the right form of words said without mispronunciation, and the right intention.[4] Canon

[1] Theologians did debate the timing of the change, whether all the words had to be said first; see Marilyn McCord Adams, *Some Later Medieval Theologies of the Eucharist: Thomas Aquinas, Giles of Rome, Duns Scotus and William of Ockham* (Oxford, 2010), 62–65.

[2] Henricus Bohic, *Opus preclarissimum distinctionum henrici bohic … super quinque libris decretalium* (Lyon, 1498), Tertius, fol. xciii^{rb}: X 3.41.6, "necessaria sunt verba per que fit transubstantiatio." Bohic repeated (loc. cit.) the need for "intentio et materia et forma debita," that last meaning the words.

[3] Henricus Bohic, *Opus preclarissimum distinctionum henrici bohic … super quinque libris decretalium*, Tertius, fol. xciii^{ra}: X 3.41.6.

[4] *Pastors and the Care of Souls*, 154–155. Thomas of Chobham called this *intentio conferentis*; see *Thomae de Chobham summa confessorum*, ed. F. Broomfield (Louvain, 1968), 100.

law could not regulate the internal intentions of the priest except by enjoining him not to let his mind wander and not to try consecrating too much bread.[5] The right form of the words, however, could be taught. Moreover, a diocese could try having missals and other liturgical books with correct texts available in all parishes, as they were obligated in the province of Canterbury following the statutes of Archbishop Walter Reynolds.[6]

The words of Christ at the Last Supper were quoted often by early writers; however, the first collections of canon law did not treat them as transformative. A canon attributed to "Pope Euticianus" only said the offerings were blessed by the priest "with a simple blessing" (*simplici benedictione*) before being consumed by the people.[7] Otherwise, the Pseudo-Isidorean decretals emphasized, in a text of "Pope Alexander," the priest's role of offering of Christ for the forgiveness of sins.[8] A text from the Penitential of Theodore, archbishop of Canterbury, later attributed to "Pope Fabian," said not to accept the sacrifice from the hand of a priest unable to read the prayers, lections, and other observances of the mass.[9] So did the texts attributed to "Alexander" and "Fabian."[10] The need for liturgical books for the mass had become important by the time of Regino of Prüm. Among his questions for a visitation was whether a church had a missal, lectionary, and antiphonary:

> For without these mass is not celebrated perfectly.[11]

The text of "Euticianus," credited to "Pope Melchiades," on the blessing of offerings appeared in the *Decretum*.[12] Burchard also said, quoting "Pope Fabian," that an illiterate priest should not celebrate mass.[13]

At first the Gregorian Reform, although dedicated to improving the worthiness of priests, offered nothing new about the words of institution. This changed with Ivo of Chartres. Quoting Jerome in a letter, Ivo emphasized the ability of a priest to "invisibly consecrate and transform

[5] On the latter point, see the discussion of quantity and intention in Nicholas of Ausimo, *Supplementum Summae Pisanellae* (Venezia, 1489), I-2^{ra-va}, which said excess material or any not included in the intention to consecrate is not consecrated.

[6] *The Register of John Chandler Dean of Salisbury 1404–1417*, ed. T. C. B. Timmins (Devizes, 1984), xxxii. Lyndwood, *Provinciale seu Constitvtiones*, 52; *Lyndwood's Provinciale*, 19.

[7] Hinschius 209. [8] Hinschius, 99.

[9] Burchardus Wormatiensis, *Decretum*, V c. 36, PL 759B, "Ex decr. Fabiani papae, capite 10."

[10] Burchardus Wormatiensis, *Decretum*, V c. 5, PL 140.753C–754A, V c. 36, PL 759B.

[11] *Das Sendhandbuch des Regino von Prüm*, 26, "Nam sine his missa perfecte non celebratur."

[12] Burchardus Wormatiensis, *Decretum*, V c. 7, PL 140.754A–B.

[13] Burchardus Wormatiensis, *Decretum*, V c. 36, PL 140.759B. See also Ivo Carnotensis, *Decretum*, PL 161.170A.

the elements into the truth of Christ's body and blood." He also identified this transformation with the words of consecration.[14] Ivo's *Decretum* gathered numerous texts about the Eucharist and the mass. One patristic text, drawn from the works of Augustine, said that the invisible priest, Christ, converted the elements "by His word with a hidden power," using the words of institution.[15] Another text repeated the idea that the sacrament was "confected by Christ's word" (*Christi sermone conficitur*). A question was raised whether Christ, who created things from nothing, could effect this change. Ivo replied, "It is no less a matter to create new things than to change natures."[16] The text went on to say that divine power could do this, veiling the flesh and blood under the elements to avoid "the horror of gore" (*cruoris horror*), while providing grace for redemption (*gratia redemptionis*).[17]

The *Panormia* provided a quotation from Ambrose that places the change of the Eucharistic species to Christ's body and blood at the blessing with the divine words of the institution. This could be understood as the words changing the species. Then Christ was in the sacrament.[18] The same collection contained another excerpt from Ambrose about the "horror of gore" being omitted in order to offer redeeming grace rather than cause offense.[19] Likewise, it offered a text by Eusebius of Emesa about Christ as the "invisible priest" whose words of institution effected change "by secret power."[20] None of these texts offered a theology of the instrumental role of the priesthood, focusing on the words of Christ said by the duly ordained over the species.

Gratian's *Decretum* differs little in this regard. The text about Christ as the "invisible priest" appears as part of a longer canon of "Eusebius of Emesa" in the second Distinction of the *De consecratione* (De cons. D. 2 c. 35) The Ambrose text about the "benediction" of the species appeared

[14] Ivo Carnotensis, *Epistola 63*, PL 161.78D, "sic divina virtus sacramenta hujus temporis a legitimis sacerdotibus ministrata invisibiliter consecrat et in veritatem Christi corporis et sanguinis transformat." On the words of consecration, see Ivo Carnotensis, *Epistola 63*, 80A–B.

[15] Ivo Carnotensis, *Decretum*, PL 161.139D–140A, "Nam et invisibilis sacerdos visibiles creaturas in substantiam corporis et sanguinis sui, verbo suo secreta potestate convertit, ita dicens, Accipite et comedite; HOC EST CORPUS MEUM: et sanctificatione repetita: accipite et bibite; hic est sanguinis meus."

[16] Ivo Carnotensis, *Decretum*, PL 161.146D, "Sermo igitur Christi qui potuit ex nihilo facere quod non erat, non potest ea quae sunt in id mutare quod non erant? Non enim minus est novas res dare, quam mutare naturas."

[17] Ivo Carnotensis, *Decretum*, PL 161.147B–C.

[18] *Panormia* c. 124, cited from the *Panormia Project*, "Ante benedictionem verborum coelestium alia species nominatur, post consecrationem corpus significatur. Item: In illo sacramento Christus est."

[19] *Panormia* c. 127. [20] *Panormia* c. 129.

(De cons. D. 2 c. 11) not far distant from that by "Eusebius."[21] Another text of Ambrose asked, "The consecration occurs by means of what words, and whose? Those of the Lord Jesus." This is the same text which referred to the ability of Christ to create the heavens, the land, and sea. That text also referred to the use of bread and wine to avoid the "horror of gore" (De cons. D. 2 c. 55).[22]

Early commentaries on the *Decretum* also say little about the words of consecration. Rufinus, commenting on a text by Ambrose (De cons. D. 2 c. 39), mentioned consecration of the gifts without discussing the words to be employed. He simply said the consecration was "apostolic." This was instituted by the apostles "in secret."[23] Rufinus contrasted the bloodless sacrifice of the New Testament to those of the Old Testament that were not offered, he said, without gore.[24]

The development of a theology of transubstantiation required serious thought about the transformative power of words, especially those of Christ. The Decretists eventually tackled this issue. *Fecit Moyses tabernaculum* brought together the past emphasis on Christ's words with an interest in the exact timing of the conversion of the elements, saying, "Concerning the consecration of the bread and wine it is certain, because at Christ's words *Hoc est corpus meum* ... transubstantiation occurs. Sound faith believes and preaches, that once all those words have been said entire transubstantiation is brought about."[25]

Sicard of Cremona discussed the timing of consecration against the pronunciation of the words of institution, which were more important than the other words of the canon.[26] As we saw in the context of transubstantiation, Huguccio considered whether Christ's exact words were to be said by the priest at the consecration, and he concluded that they had to be pronounced to the last one. He considered problems with word order in the different biblical accounts and the necessity of saying all the words,

[21] A text attributed to Augustine said only the bread that receives the blessing of Christ becomes His body (De cons. D. 2 c. 61).

[22] Friedberg 1.1334–1335 at 1334, "Consecratio autem quibus uerbis, et cuius sermonibus est? Domini Iesu Christi."

[23] Rufinus, *Summa decretorum*, ed. Heinrich Singer (Paderborn, 1902; Aalen, 1963), 555: De cons. D. 2 c. 39, "que ab apostolis est instituta in secreta."

[24] Rufinus, *Summa decretorum*, 557: De cons. D. 2 c. 80, "*Incruentem*, id est sine cruore. Hoc dicit ad differentiam sacrificii veteris testamentis, ubi sine cruore hostia non offerebatur."

[25] Stephen of Tournai, *Die Summa über das Decretum Gratiani*, ed. Johann Friedrich von Schulte (Giessen, 1891; Aalen, 1965), 273: De cons. D. 2 c. 39, "De consecratione panis et vini certum est, quia ad verba Christi: Hoc est corpus meum, hic e. s. etc. fit transubstantio ... hoc sana fides credit et praedicat, ut omnibus verbis illis dictis tota transubstantiatio facta sit."

[26] Sicardus Cremonensis, *Summa decretorum*, 102B–103A: De cons. D. 2 c. 55.

concluding that the entire form of the words was of the very substance of the sacrament.[27]

The Ordinary Gloss on the *Decretum*, which reached its final form after *Cum Marthae* was issued, tackled the issue of the timing of transubstantiation during the canon. The Gloss quoted different opinions on this question, focusing especially on the transubstantiation of the bread. Some, it said, thought the change came with the pronunciation of the last syllable of the formula. Others said the change was conditional until the chalice too had been consecrated. Yet others were doubtful when, "according to the nature of things" (*in rerum natura*), the host truly became Christ's body. Johannes Teutonicus allied himself in somewhat conditional language with those who said the pronunciation of the very last letter of the one formula "transubstantiated the body," while the other "transubstantiated the blood."[28] The Gloss revisited this matter elsewhere. Glossing "Eusebius Emisanus," it noted a difference of opinions whether there was only one form of consecration rather than two, one for each element. Teutonicus gingerly said both body and blood were present, but not before transubstantiation. This left the issue of concomitance, with body and blood together in heaven even if divided by their earthly signs, unresolved except by a reference to the blood being with the body by mixture (*per mistionem*).[29] Elsewhere, however, the Gloss embraced the idea that both body and blood were received by the faithful in communion under the species of bread.[30]

Decretum commentaries, however, were not as important for this change of emphasis as papal decretals and their commentaries were. Innocent III made the most important contribution when he devoted a large portion of the decretal *Cum Marthae* to defending the exact form of words used in the canon. This was the focus of the original inquiry by the archbishop of Lyon to the pope. Most of the words of consecration in the canon of the mass were biblical, but not the expression *mysterium fidei*. As Innocent summarized the question:

[27] Huguccio, *Summa decretorum*, Admont Stiftsbibliothek MS 7, fol. 426va: De cons. D. 2 c. 25, "Quibus Christus usus est in cena quibus uerbis Christus tantam uim et efficaciam tribuit quod ad prolationem eorum factam a sacerdote ut debet fieri corpus Christi incipiat esse. ibi prolatio tantum hoc. uel hoc est corpus et dicendum. quod tota illa forma uerborum est de substantia sacramenti."

[28] Ordinary Gloss at De cons. D. 2 c. 6 v. Et seorsum, "Sed ego dico, quod si per copulatiuam duo dicuntur, tunc in prolatione huius vocis. Hoc est corpus meum transubstantiatur corpus, & in prolatione consequentis vocis siue locutionis, transubstantiatur sanguis si per copulatiuam tantum vnum dicatur, tunc fiet tantum in vltima litera transubstantiatio."

[29] Ordinary Gloss at De cons. D. 2 c. 35 v. Et sanctificatione.

[30] Ordinary Gloss at De cons. D. 2 c. 12 v. Aut integra. A longer affirmation is found at v. Quia diuisio.

You have asked (indeed) who has added the form of the words which Christ Himself expressed when He changed the bread and wine into the body and blood, that in the Canon of the Mass which the general Church uses, which none of the Evangelists is read to have expressed . . . In the Canon of the Mass that expression "mysterium fidei," is found interposed among His words.[31]

Pope Innocent warned against those who thought the expression meant believing only "the truth of the body and blood" was present. He said such persons thought that "only the image, species and figure" (*imaginem tantum, et speciem et figuram*) were present. This was the fourth opinion on the Real Presence which, as we have seen above, the canonists uniformly rejected. Innocent warned against this error, wishing it were far from the hearts of the faithful. He said it denied the death and Resurrection of Christ.[32] The pope pointed out that the canon contained other language not in the gospels – *novi et aeterni testamenti* and *qui pro vobis et pro multis effundetur in remissionem pecatorum* – resorting to the argument that the gospels do not contain all the Lord's words. Others came down from the Apostles outside the Scripture. This is evidence of the idea of Tradition that later became a point of conflict between Catholic and Protestant theologies.[33]

Cum Marthae almost inevitably became a place at which to stress the use of the form of words (*forma verborum*) authorized by the Church. Johannes Teutonicus, in his commentary on *Compilatio Tertia*, went farther than had Innocent III and said that the Church observed many things established not by the apostles but by long custom.[34] The *casus* to this decretal in the Ordinary Gloss summarized the archbishop's question about the term *mysterium fidei*. It then summarized the pope's reply, both his pointing out other words not in the gospels and his contention that other sayings of Jesus were handed down by the Apostles outside the New Testament or

[31] Heinrich Denzinger, *The Sources of Catholic Dogma*, trans. Roy J. Deferrari (Fitzwilliam, N. H., 2002), 163. Friedberg 2.637, "Quaesivisti *siquidem*, quis forma verborum, quam ipse Christus expressit, quum in corpus et sanguinem suum panem transsubstantiavit et vinum, illud in canone missae, quo ecclesia utitur generalis, adiecerit, quod nullus Evangelistarum legitur expressisse. Quum enim in Evangelio sic legatur: 'Accipiens calicem, gratias agens benedixit, et dedit discipulis suis, dicens: bibite ex hoc omnes; hic est enim sanguis meus novi testamenti, qui pro nobis, et pro multis *aliis* effundetur in remissionem peccatorum:' in canone missae sermo iste, videlicet 'mysterium fidei,' verbis ipsis interpositus invenitur."

[32] Friedberg 2.638, "Sed absit a fidelium cordibus error iste."

[33] Friedberg 2.637, "Sane multa tam de verbis quam de factis dominicis, invenimus ab Evangelistis omissa, Quae apostoli vel supplevisse verbo, vel facto expressisse leguntur." Yves Congar, *Tradition and Traditions: The Biblical, Historical, and Theological Evidence for Catholic Teaching on Tradition* (New York, 1967).

[34] *Apparatus glossatorum in compilationem tertiam* ad 3 Comp. 3.33.5, ed. Kenneth Pennington, work in progress found at http.//faculty.cua.edu/pennington, "*sane multa*: multa enim seruat ecclesia que nec ab apostolis sunt tradita, que tamen, cum sint longa consuetudine roborata, non sunt minor auctoritatis, ut xi. di. Ecclesiasticarum."

could be verified by consulting other gospel texts. Then the *casus* confirmed the added words *novi et aeterni testamenti* as biblical by looking elsewhere in the Scripture.[35] The Gloss said that the Church also observed many things not handed down by the Apostles but by long custom, which "are of no less authority" (*non sunt minoris auctoritatis*).[36] The *Summa* of Geoffrey of Trani had little to say about this issue when touching on *Cum Marthae* except that there were words in the canon not found in the gospels. Geoffrey said, "We believe these were added by the Apostles and holy fathers" (*sed ea credimus ab apostolis et sanctis patribus esse adiecta*).[37] Innocent IV merely referred to the words *mysterium fidei* (misprinted as *ministerium* in the available reprint edition) as the cause of the archbishop's inquiry to the pope about who had added them to the canon.[38]

Hostiensis said nothing about the words of the canon in his *Summa*. However, his commentary on the *Decretals* did address the issue raised by the archbishop of Lyon. He said that, if there were no error involved, the pope could add to the canon to declare the truth.[39] Hostiensis also endorsed the idea that there were long-standing customs of the Church which were not introduced by the Apostles, which were of no less authority.[40] Some customs could, as Innocent had declared, be presumed to have been introduced by an Apostle or some other "just author" (*vel alium iustum authorem*).[41] The cardinal concluded that words like *aeterni testamenti* could reasonably be added to the canon.[42]

Two commentaries written after that of Hostiensis gave more attention to the words of consecration. Johannes Andreae began his exposition of *Cum Marthae* with a *casus* summarizing the decretal. It said any words in the canon not found in the gospels should be believed to come from Christ, the apostles, or their successors.[43] Johannes discussed the

[35] *Ordinary Gloss at* X 3.41.6 *casus*. [36] *Ordinary Gloss at* X 3.41.6 v. Multa.

[37] *Summa Godfredi Tranensis*, fol. 162va.

[38] *Commentaria Innocentii quarti Pont. Maximi super libros quinque Decretalium* ... (Frankfurt, 1570; Frankfurt, 1968), 453va.

[39] *Henrici de Segusio Cardinalis Hostiensis Decretalium commentaria*, 6 vols. (Venice, 1581; Turin, 1965), 3, fol. 162vb: X 3.41.6, "Sol. verum est, quod nihil est apponendum contrarium, vel pro errore fouendo. Caeterum Papa potest addere aliqua declarando, vel ex ratione. infra. qui fil. sint. le. per venerabilem, ¶. rationibus. xxiiii. q. ii. quos Deus."

[40] *Hostiensis Decretalium commentaria*, 3, fol. 162vb, "Sane multa: ver. multa nempe seruat ecclesia, quae nec ab apostolis sunt introducta, nec minoris auctoritatis intelliguntur esse, cum sint longissima, & generalissima ecclesiae universalis consuetudine roborata."

[41] *Hostiensis Decretalium commentaria*, 3, fol. 162vb.

[42] *Hostiensis Decretalium commentaria*, 3, fol. 163ra, "Patet ergo, quod elevates oculis in cęlum, & aeterni testament potuit in canone rationabiliter interponi. ¶. Ex eo autem."

[43] Johannes Andreae, *In decretalium libros novella commentaria* ... (Venezia, 1581; Torino, 1966), 3, fol. 219vb, "Casus. Si qua uerba sunt in canone missae, quae ab euangelistis dicta non fuerint, credere debemus, quod a Christo apostoli, & ab ipsis eorum successores acceperint, hoc primo."

transforming power of the words, referring to a discussion of it by Hostiensis.[44] The canonist went on to say the canon should be said silently to avoid distracting the people from their prayers and because "it pertains to the priest alone" (*ad solum pertinent sacerdotem*).[45] Antonius de Butrio repeated the *casus* used by Johannes Andreae, noting that the pope was able to supply what was needed (*pape sit supplere*).[46] He noted that many other words were added to the canon before repeating what Johannes Andreae had said about why it was said silently.[47] Antonius argued that change occurred after the last syllable of the words of institution had been pronounced.[48]

The commentaries on the Florentine decree of union *Laetentur coeli* focused on the sacramental materials, but they did not ignore the words of consecration. Juan de Torquemada touched on this briefly. He quoted "Eusebius of Emesa" (De cons. D. 2 c. 35) as saying that the elements were converted "by the words of the Savior" (*verbis salvatoris*). Likewise, the words of Christ, not the priest, according to "Ambrose" (De cons. D. 2 c. 55), brought about the Real Presence.[49] Fantinus de Vallaresso devoted a brief chapter to the meaning of the Greek word *arthon* in the gospel narrative of the institution of the sacrament. He said the term was used by the Greeks to argue for "fermented" bread, requiring a third ingredient, yeast, to represent both the soul and the growth of Christ's body in the virgin's womb. Fantinus replied that one only needed unleavened bread, representing Christ's divinity (bread) and humanity (a little water). Thus the words of institution brought about the body of Christ, not the body of the virgin (*corpus virginis*).[50]

Writers on liturgy, like the canonists, at first said little about the words. Johannes Beleth simply said words were not to be added or omitted

[44] Johannes Andreae, *In decretalium libros novella commentaria*, 3, fol. 219vb *Canone*.

[45] Johannes Andreae, *In decretalium libros novella commentaria*, 3, fol. 219vb *Canone*[2]. Andreae also warned that the laity might say these words "*locis incongruis*" if they knew them well.

[46] *Excellentissimi Antonii de Butrio ... Super tertium librum decretalium ...* (Venezia, 1578; Torino, 1967), fol. 191rb.

[47] *Excellentissimi Antonii de Butrio ... Super tertium librum decretalium*, fol.191va "Quero quare in secreto dicitur canon," "Tertio ne impediatur populous orare ... Quinto, quia haec ad solum pertinent sacerdotem."

[48] *Excellentissimi Antonii de Butrio ... Super tertium librum decretalium*, fol. 192vb–193ra, "ita quod non transsubstantiatur pars corporis Christi post partem syllabarum, vel dictionum, *sed in ultima verborum ipsorum probatione, ad quam ordinariam omnium verborum precedentium prolatione fit transsubstantiatio corporis*. Idem de vino" (emphasis mine).

[49] Johannes de Torquemada, *Apparatus super decretum florentinum unionis Graecorum*, ed. Emmanuel Candal (Roma, 1942), 69.

[50] Fantinus Vallaresso, *Libellus de ordine generalium conciliorum et unione florentina*, ed. Bernardus Schultze (Roma, 1944), 68–69.

except that the names of the persons for whom mass was offered might be included in the canon of the mass.[51] By the end of the twelfth century, however, more was said. Sicard of Cremona interpreted the words of the canon in terms of transubstantiation: "And see that at the saying of those words *This is my body* the bread is divinely transubstantiated into flesh. Indeed the divine material substance of this sacrifice is the word that, approaching the element, perfects the sacrament."[52] Sicard said the priest prays for the host to be transubstantiated and, after transubstantiation, offers the transubstantiated to the Father (*et transubstantiate Patri obtulerit*).[53] Innocent III was more systematic about the words. He said that once the priest pronounced the words of Christ, "the bread and wine are converted into flesh and blood."[54] Innocent went on to discuss how the elements consecrated at the saying of the words of Christ did not separate the unity of body and blood under these signs.[55] Elsewhere, Innocent said that consecration happened when the priest said the very words Christ had said.[56] He said that, at the Last Supper, Jesus probably acted with divine power before teaching the apostles the form of the sacraments.[57]

Guillelmus Durantis gave a detailed explanation of the canon, including the words of consecration. He said the conversion of the bread "into the substance of Christ's body" (*in substantiam corporis Christi*) happened "by the blessing of heaven and the power of the word" (*benedictione celesti et uirtute uerbi*).[58] Looking at the Last Supper, Durantis said there were differing opinions on the right order of saying the words and breaking the bread. The gospels said Jesus broke it first, but the established Western

[51] Johannes Beleth, *Summa de ecclesiasticis officiis*, ed. Heribert Douteil (Turnhout, 1976), 82.

[52] *Sicardi Cremonensis episcopi Mitralis de officiis*, ed. Gábor Sarbak and Lorenz Weinrich (Turnhout, 2008), 190, "Et uide quod ad prolationem istorum uerborum: 'Hoc est corpus meum', panis diuinitus transsubstantiatur in carnem, diuina etenim materialis substantia huius sacrificii est uerbum, quod accedens ad elementrum perfecit sacramentum." Sicard compared this change not just with the Word becoming united with Christ's flesh, and with the making of vinegar from wine by heating it.

[53] *Sicardi Cremonensis episcopi Mitralis de officiis*, 193.

[54] *Liber de quadrapartita specie nuptiarum*, PL 217.859, "Cum enim illa Christi verba pronuntiat: *Hoc est enim corpus meum*, et *hic est sanguis meus* (Matth. XXVI), panis et vinum in carnem et sanguinem convertuntur."

[55] *Liber de quadrapartita specie nuptiarum*, PL 217.867–869.

[56] *De sacramento altaris mysterio libri sex*, PL 217.859, "Benedixit. Cum ad prolationem verborum istorum: Hoc est corpus meum, hoc est sanguis meus (Matth. XXVI) sacerdos conficiat, credibile judicatur, quod et Christus eadem verba dicendo, confecit."

[57] *De sacramento altaris mysterio libri sex*, PL 217.859.

[58] Guillelmus Durantis senior, *Rationale divinorum officiorum*, ed. Anselm Davril and Timothy M. Thibodeau (Turnhout, 1995), 445–446; William Durand, *Rationale IV: On the Mass and Each Action Pertaining to It*, trans. Timothy M. Thibodeau (Turnhout, 2013), 336–337.

rite had the words said before the fraction of the host. The canonist compromised by saying that Christ consecrated first by using "divine power hidden from us" (*uirtute diuina nobis occulta*). Only then did He show the apostles the right form, especially the words, by which the sacrament was confected. Like Sicard of Cremona before him, Durantis said, "Therefore, at the pronunciation of those words the bread, through Divine power, is transubstantiated into flesh" (*Ad prolationem ergo uerborum diuinitus transsubstantiatur in carnem*). It was the saying of the words that confected the sacrament.[59] Durantis said the same thing about the conversion of the watered wine. He too affirmed concomitance, saying, "The Blood exists in the Body through the change of the bread, and the opposite as well; but not that bread changes into Blood, or wine changes into the Body, but because neither of them can exist without the other."[60]

Guillelmus discussed in depth the exact meanings of the gospel texts from which the words of consecration were drawn. Particularly he asked about the consequences of any change in the words by addition, subtraction, or changed order. The priest who did anything like that, he said, sinned gravely (*grauiter peccat*), especially if he intended to change the form or tried to introduce heresy (*heresim introducere*). Durantis said that "the form of the words that Christ used must be inalterably observed by everyone."[61] If the priest could not complete the canon for reasons of illness between saying the words over the bread and saying them over the wine, the *Rationale* said, in case of doubt about consecration of the host, a new priest could repeat the words. It was safer, however, to repeat the whole canon with new bread and have the bread previously on the altar consumed after the mass.[62] The elevation of the bread was to happen only after the words of consecration had been said.[63]

The impact of this line of thought, with increasing attention to the words of consecration, was felt in local regulations about the celebration of mass. The early eleventh-century Canons of Edgar permitted the priest to look at his book to avoid making a mistake with the words.[64] Robert Grosseteste, bishop of Lincoln, writing much later, simply told his clergy

[59] *Rationale divinorum officiorum*, 446–447; William Durand, *Rationale IV*, 339.

[60] *Rationale divinorum officiorum*, 456, "sed sub forma panis sanguis existit in corpore per mutationem panis in corpus et, e converso; non quod panis in sanguinem, uel uinum mutetur in corpus, sed quia neutrum potest existere sine reliquo."; William Durand, *Rationale IV*, 350–351.

[61] *Rationale divinorum officiorum*, 456–458 at 458, "quia forma uerborum quam Christus expressit per omnia debet illibata seruari."; William Durand, *Rationale IV*, 351–353 at 352.

[62] *Rationale divinorum officiorum*, 458–459; William Durand, *Rationale IV*, 353–354.

[63] *Rationale divinorum officiorum*, 461; William Durand, *Rationale IV*, 356–357.

[64] *Councils & Synods*, 1/1.324–325. The text continues by saying the priest needs "good and indeed correct books."

that the text of the canon had to be "rightly corrected" (*rite correctus*).[65] Similarly Guiard of Laon, bishop of Cambria before the middle of the thirteenth century, said the canon had to be read attentively and distinctly, saying only what was supposed to be said.[66] The second statutes of London required the archdeacon to determine whether the priest knew the words of the canon and the form of baptism.[67]

William Lyndwood warned against altering the form of the words of consecration. Any change in these words might deprive the form of its rightful meaning.[68] He particularly discussed, when glossing a canon of Stephen Langton, what was essential in the words for the consecration of the bread. In the formula *Hoc est enim corpus meum*, the word *enim* was not a substantial part of the form but fitting to include in the canon. Omission of any other word, however, would vitiate transubstantiation. His exposition drew upon Innocent III's decretal *Cum Marthae*, while the distinction between fitting and essential was grounded in the theology of Thomas Aquinas.[69]

Occasionally more attention was paid to providing the correct text of the canon. In the early eleventh century, Aelfric said he had seen examples of the text terribly changed *contra fidem*, and he said these errors should be corrected "by means of right examplars" (*per recta exemplaria*).[70] In 1195 Hubert Walter, archbishop of Canterbury, tasked archdeacons with seeing that each church had a "true and approved exemplar of the canon of the mass" corrected diligently.[71] A statute attributed to Stephen Langton in Lyndwood's *Provinciale* similarly said the words of the canon were to be "plainly spoken and whole": "The words also of the Canon shall be plainly spoken and whole, especially in the Sacraments of the Body and Blood."[72]

[65] *Letter 52bis*, cited from *The Electronic Grosseteste* [http://www.grosseteste.com/], 155, 162, 166, accessed on June 21, 2007.

[66] Joseph Avril, *Les statuts synodaux français du XIIIe siècle*, 4 (Paris, 1995), 40. This is repeated in the statutes of Tournai; see Pontal, *Les statuts synodaux francais du XIIIe siècle*, 1.329.

[67] *Councils & Synods*, 1/2.649.

[68] Lyndwood, *Provinciale seu Constitvtiones Angliæ*, 227 m *Integré*.

[69] Lyndwood, *Provinciale seu Constitvtiones*, 227, "k *Consecratione*. i. e. *In verbis Consecratoriis*, In quibus propriè consistit Canon Missae, secundum *Hosti. extra. eo. c. cum Marthae. in prin.* Forma enim verborum quoad corpus est talis: Hoc est enim corpus meum, haec tamen Conjunctio enim non est de substantia Formae, sed de bene esse, unde non debet omitti. Aliud namque est Forma necessaria, sine qua non potest fieri Transubstantiatio; aliud est Forma debita, sine qua non potest fieri, secundùm *Tho. li. de veritate. parte 6 c. ii.*"

[70] *Councils & Synods*, 1/1.254.

[71] *Councils & Synods*, 1/2.1048, "archidiaconorum sollicitudine provideat ut in singulis ecclesiis ad verum et probatum exemplar canon misse cum omni diligencia corrigatur."

[72] *Council & Synods*, 2/1.109; Lyndwood, *Provinciale seu Constitvtiones*, 227, "Verba quoque Canonis, praesertim in Consecratione Corporis & Sanguinis Christi, plenè et integrè proferantur."; *Lyndewood's Provinciale*, ed. J. V. Bullard and H. Chalmer Bell (London, 1929), 94.

Langton did decree that the canon was to be according to the custom of Canterbury. It was to be written roundly (*rotunde*), allowing the priest to say the words distinctly.[73] The 1222 Council of Oxford said archdeacons were to see that the canon was "amended" (*canon misse emendetur*). Likewise, the priest was to know the words of both the canon and the form of baptism.[74] The first statutes of Salisbury (1217–1219) of Bishop Richard Poore addressed this issue in detail. Every priest was expected to have the correct text of the canon of the mass "according to the custom of the church of Salisbury" (*secundum consuetudinem Saresbiriensis ecclesie*). The words of the canon were to be said smoothly and distinctly (*rotunde et distincte*) so that words were not cut off or indistinct on account of hurry.[75] When Poore moved to Durham in 1228, he issued a similar statute saying the canon was to be read according to the use of York.[76] The second statute of Salisbury specified a missal according to the Sarum use.[77] A synod of Exeter in 1287 simply said a good missal was one of the books needed for mass.[78] Archbishop Winchelsey issued three lists of the "ornaments" a church should have. Each listed a missal, along with books like the manual for special services, among the books necessary for the liturgy.[79]

On the Continent, a priest also was expected to know his books.[80] Dealing with the missal, the statutes of Cambrai said the priest was to read "attentively and distinctly" (*attente et distincte*); and he was to say what was supposed to be said in reciting the canon.[81] Even the care of the missal might be regulated. Guiard of Laon required that the missal be placed on the altar housed in clean linen. This decree was reenacted in the diocese of Tournai.[82] Similarly the 1287 statutes of Liège required that the book be placed on the altar housed in clean linen.[83] In 1310 Antonio Biliotti, bishop of Florence, wanted each mass book checked against the cathedral's copy.[84] Bishops continued issuing

[73] *Councils & Synods*, 2/1.29. [74] *Councils & Synods*, 2/1.115.

[75] *Councils & Synods*, 2/2.79. [76] *Councils & Synods*, 2/2.442.

[77] *Councils & Synods*, 2/1.379. The "constitutions of a certain bishop" said the canon should be correct "secundum consuetudinem ecclesie nostre"; see *Councils & Synods*, 2/1.186.

[78] Mansi 24.800. The same synod said the parish was to provide books for the main altar; see *Councils & Synods*, 24.801. Similarly see *Councils & Synods*, 2/1.296 (Worcester III).

[79] *Councils & Synods*, 2/2.1385–1388.

[80] The province of Narbonne (1310) required this, see Mansi 25.360.

[81] Avril, *Les statuts synodaux français du XIIIe siècle*, 4.40.

[82] Avril, *Les statuts synodaux français du XIIIe siècle*, 4.38; Odette Pontal, *Les statuts synodaux français du XIIIe siècle*, 1 (Paris, 1971), 328. The Paris statutes said there should be a towel by the missal to prevent a priest dribbling from mouth or nose onto his vestments; see Pontal, *Les statuts synodaux* 1.82.

[83] Mansi 24.895.

[84] Richard Trexler, *Synodal Law in Florence and Fiesole, 1306–1518* (Città del Vaticano, 1971), 57.

regulations about missals well into the sixteenth century, even before the Roman curia, following up on the decrees of the Council of Trent, issued the "Tridentine Missal" in 1570. Thus Spanish sees, like that of Tuy, required clergy to have missals and other appropriate books;[85] and the 1553 synod of Astorga issued regulations for mass books to be used in the diocese.[86]

Pastoral manuals usually gave only limited attention to the form of the words. Thomas of Chobham addressed the matter briefly. He said, "The sacred words pronounced by the Lord in the gospel are necessary, because without them the Eucharist is not consecrated."[87] Thomas went on to address briefly the question of the exact form of the words, since the wording varied between gospels. He opted for the form approved by the Church, "because the authority of the Church is great" (*quia magna est auctoritas ecclesie*).[88] John of Erfurt warned that if the priest changed the words of consecration or omitted them, nothing happened. This was especially true if the changes affected the means of signifying (*modus significandi*). John did admit that Latin was not necessary for consecration, just as was the case with the use of another tongue when baptizing.[89] John made provision for making good failure to consecrate the chalice after the elevation of the host or dealing with doubt whether the words of consecration had been said at all.[90] William of Pagula summarized the institution of the Eucharist, emphasizing the words of consecration said over the bread, transforming it as Christ had done at the Last Supper. These words of Christ remained the *forma conficiendi* employed by the priest.[91] Once the words had been said, Christ was truly, perfectly present in the form of

[85] *Synodicon Hispanum*, 1.375, 484. By 1543 the bishop of Orense was blaming the tardiness of printers for lack of books like the Manual for his see; see *Synodicon Hispanum*, 1.160.

[86] *Synodicon Hispanum* 3.131–132.

[87] *Thomae de Chobham summa confessorum*, 101, "Verba etiam sacra constituta a domino in evangelio ad hoc necessaria sunt, quia sine illis non consecratur eucharistia."

[88] *Thomae de Chobham summa confessorum*, loc. cit.

[89] *Die Summa confessorum des Johannes von Erfurt*, ed. Norbert Brieskorn, 3 vols. (Frankfurt, 1980), 2.137, "forma debita: puta si mutat verba consecratoria vel omittit; tunc enim nihil fit, maxime, si non remanet eadem significatio et idem modus significandi; secus si utrumque horum maneret, sicut in qualibet tingua potest baptizari, ita in qualibet lingua potest confici." See also *Summa confessorum des Johannes von Erfurt*, 3.875.

[90] *Die Summa confessorum des Johannes von Erfurt*, 2.137.

[91] William of Pagula, *Oculus sacerdotis*, University of Pennsylvania MS Codex 721, fol. 8ra, "Istud sacramentum eukaristie fuit institutum a domino yhesu Christo et in cena domini quando comedit agnum paschalem cum discipulis suis. Et hec est forma conficiendi corpus Christi per hec uerba. Hoc est corpus meum. et in ultimo instant istorum uerborum fit translacio panis in corpus Christi. et est ibi Christus perfectus sub specie panis."

bread.[92] The words of Christ Himself effected this change, not the priest's own utterance of them.[93]

The *Manipulus curatorum* discussed the form of the words in greater depth. Each sacrament, it said, consists of "certain limited words." Only some of those used in the mass were essential. The most important words, those necessary for the sacrament, were the words of institution pronounced by Christ at the Last Supper. The priest might omit other words, but even the intention to consecrate could not overcome the lack of Christ's words.[94] The *Manipulus* discusses the exact words needed and the time of the transformation. Guido concludes that "This is my body" must be said, and the change occurred when the last syllable was pronounced.[95] For the timing of the consecration of the chalice, Guido said that it is not elevated until every word of the formula has been said, even those not in the gospels. He also quoted *Cum Marthae* to verify the form of words used in the canon.[96] The exposition of the mass in the *Manipulus* threatened the person who dared pronounce the words of the canon without being an ordained priest with anathema.[97]

John of Freiburg expected the form used to be "according to the use of the Roman church" (*secundum usum romane ecclesie*), an opinion he attributed to both Albertus Magnus and Thomas Aquinas. He said no other words were to be used than Christ's, even if the changed wording would express the same thing. Other words were added in the canon, and these were not to be omitted. If the consecration was made using only the words of institution, it was valid; but the priest was liable to punishment for not following the right order of service.[98] John also considered the possibility that the priest might forget he had said these words, permitting him to act according to his degree of uncertainty, going on with the mass or possibly

92 William of Pagula, *Oculus sacerdotis*, University of Pennsylvania MS Codex 721, fol. 8ra–b, "Et hec est forma conficiendi corpus Christi per hec uerba. Hoc est corpus meum. et in ultimo instant istorum uerborum fit translacio panis in corpus Christi. et est ibi Christus perfectus sub specie panis."

93 William of Pagula, *Oculus sacerdotis*, University of Pennsylvania MS Codex 721, fol. 7va, "Per hec uerba Hoc est corpus meum de pane fit uerum corpus Christi et hoc fit propter efficaciam illorum uerborum Christi. Nam quando istud sacramentum conficitur iam non suis sermonibus sacerdos utitur sed sermonibus Christi *ergo sermo Christi conficit hoc sacramentum*. Ille qui ex nichilo creauit omnia satis potest hoc commutare" (emphasis mine).

94 Guido de Monte Rocherii, *Manipulus curatorum* (London, 1508), fol. xxii^{r}–xxvi^{r}; Guido, *Handbook for Curates*, 53–63.

95 Guido de Monte Rocherii, *Manipulus curatorum*, fol. xxiii^{v}; Guido, *Handbook for Curates*, 56–57.

96 Guido de Monte Rocherii, *Manipulus curatorum*, fol. xxiv^{v}; Guido of Monte Rochen, *Handbook for Curates*, 58–59.

97 Guido de Monte Rocherii, *Manipulus curatorum*, fol. xl^{r}; Guido, *Handbook for Curates*, 96.

98 Johannes de Friburgo, *Summa confessorum* (Paris, 1519), fol. cxxii$^{ra–b}$ (qq. liiii–lvi, lviii).

repeating himself.[99] An additional concern of this Dominican was whether the right words could consecrate the wrong materials, which he denied, following the teachings of Thomas Aquinas.[100]

The presence of adequate liturgical books, especially a good missal, often was a topic for archdeacons making visitations of parishes. The French manual for archdeacons focused attention on the missal, especially on the correct text of the canon, but also noted the need to inspect other books used in the liturgy.[101] Visitation records from the diocese of Exeter in 1301 and 1330 noted not just the quality of the missals but whether musical notes had been added.[102] The 1297 visitation of the parishes dependent on St. Paul's, London, abounds in such references. The record for the parish of Aldbury carefully noted that the canon of the mass was "well corrected" in the missal (*cum canone bene correcto*).[103] The visitation records of John Chandler, dean of Salisbury, make numerous references to missals, with or without music, including the condition of some. Among the problems uncovered in these visits were parishes lacking missals and others with service books in need of repair. Sometimes these faults were blamed on the church wardens or the people.[104] However, the parish priest might be found at fault instead.[105] Missals might also be involved in fights over inheritance between parishes and the executors of wills, or they might even be stolen.[106]

In the fifteenth century, Nicholas of Cusanus's instructions for visitors in the diocese of Brixen included what missals (*quot missalia*) and other books a parish church had.[107] Among the defects his visitors found in the

99 Johannes de Friburgo, *Summa confessorum*, fol. cxxii^{va} (q. lxi).

100 Johannes de Friburgo, *Summa confessorum*, fol. cxxv^{vb} (q. cviii).

101 Elizabeth Kay Todd, "*Libellus pastoralis de cura et officio archidiaconi*: A Thirteenth-Century Handbook for Archdeacons; a Critical Edition and Introduction," PhD Dissertation, Ohio State University, 1993, 104–106.

102 *Pastors and the Care of Souls*, 301, 305.

103 *Visitations of Churches belonging to St. Paul's Cathedral, in 1297 and in 1458*, ed. W. Sparrow Simpson (London, 1895; New York, 1966), li. One parish, Twyford, even had a missal of the Ambrosian rite; see *Visitations of Churches*, l, 63. The 1458 visitation is less detailed but gives the *dictiones probatoriae* on the second folios of the missals, e.g., *Visitations of Churches*, 105.

104 *The Register of John Chandler Dean of Salsbury*, 2 no. 2, 36 no. 72, 119 no. 353. In one case (*Register of John Chandler*, 118 no. 349), the wardens were threatened with a fine if they did not have the binding of a missal repaired. Similarly, see *Visitations in the Diocese of Lincoln 1517–1531*, ed. A. Hamilton Thompson, 3 vols. (Hereford, 1940), 1.98, 2.62. Both text of canon and binding were insufficient in a missal from the parish in the archdeaconry of Totnes; see G. G. Coulton, "A Visitation of the Archdeaconry of Totnes in 1342," *The English Historical Review* 26 (1911), 108–124 at 113.

105 *The Register of John Chandler Dean of Salsbury*, 30 no. 58.

106 *The Register of John Chandler Dean of Salsbury*, 4 no. 4, 28 no. 54, 90–91 no. 247. For a simple bequest of a missal, see *Register of John Chandler*, 144 no. 449.

107 *Akten zur Reform des Bistums Brixen*, ed. Heinz Hürten, Cusanus-Texte 5, fasc. 1 (Heidelberg, 1960), 26.

parish of Albeins was the lack of the right books. They specified that a good missal should be provided for the principal church and noted that the existing missals were particularly incorrect (*presertim incorrecti sunt*). The curate and keepers of the fabric of the church were to see that they were to be corrected quickly, the costs being charged to the fabric fund.[108]

Cusanus was not the only fifteenth-century clerical authority concerned with the presence of a good missal on the altar. The 1427 visitation of the archdeaconry of Madrid added a local variant to these concerns. The visitation records the presence not just of missals but of books called *mixto*, combining material for celebrating mass in both the Roman and Toledan rites.[109] The visitations conducted on behalf of Jean de Courcelles, archdeacon of Josas in the diocese of Paris, in the 1460s and early 1470s contain several instructions to parishes to repair missals, including threats to penalize those who failed to do so. Two parishes were told especially to repair or renew the text of the canon.[110] Even good books did not guarantee the proper celebration of mass. Robert Grosseteste instructed his visitors to be sure priests said the canon correctly. His worries extended to the possibility that rectors, vicars, or other priests might be "woefully illiterate."[111] The canons of Hubert Walter emphasized devotion and the right materials, but they also said about the mass: "It is not to be celebrated without a literate minister."[112]

The English bishops were among those who examined ordinands to determine if they were sufficiently literate to fulfill their duties.[113] Similar requirements can be found on the Continent, for example in the 1329 statutes of Tarragona.[114]

The elevation of the host

The emphasis on the words of institution became coupled eventually with the elevation of the consecrated host and the chalice. This became the

[108] *Akten zur Reform des Bistums Brixen*, 35.
[109] Gregorio de Andrés, "Actas de la visita al arcedianazgo de Madrid en 1427," *Hispania Sacra* 38 (1986), 153–245 at 164, 180, 186, 189, 206, 208, 211, 239, 243.
[110] *Visites archidiaconales de Josas*, ed. J.-M. Alliot (Paris: Picard, 1902), 33, 66–67, 85, 232, 271, 274, 342, 345. Two parishes were told to obtain supplemental texts for newer feasts; see *Visites Josas*, 74, 235.
[111] *Pastors and the Care of Souls*, 290, 289.
[112] E.g. *Councils & Synods*, 1/2.1048, "nec sine ministro literato celebretur."
[113] *Pastors and the Care of Souls*, 42–43. For an example of a priest who could not construe the Latin of the canon of the mass, see *Pastors and the Care of Souls*, 61.
[114] Mansi 25.875–876.

most distinctive feature of a late medieval mass, beginning in the twelfth century. The elevation of the host after its consecration was a dramatic act, showing the consecrated species to the faithful. The elevation emphasized the Real Presence of Christ in the Eucharist, especially when it came to be explained as the transubstantiation of the elements, bread and wine, into the body and blood of Christ, while the accidents remained visible.[115] The elevation emphasized the very corporeal presence of Christ to be adored at the altar. It is an aspect of what Caroline Walker Bynum has called "Christian materiality," the most important form of material presence of Christ on Earth after the Incarnation itself.[116] Thus the act of elevation became an affirmation of God present in the local church, not just in heaven. Devotional art came to emphasize this act, for example in some surviving representations of the Mass of Saint Gregory with Christ as Man of Sorrows appearing on the altar with the instruments of the Passion during the liturgy.[117]

Elevation after the consecration began as a small thing, possibly based on Jewish practices, and gradually grew. Eventually it eclipsed the elevation of bread and wine together during the concluding doxology of the canon of the mass. One of the common symbolic interpretations of that act was that it represented the raising up of Christ on the cross, part of an increasingly dramatic reading of the mass as reenacting the Savior's sacrifice.[118] This dramatic act, which became common during the twelfth century, may have reflected in part efforts to refute the more spiritual, less literal emphasis of Berengar of Tours. Another possible explanation is the rejection of Cathar ideas that the material world was evil, countered by reverencing God truly present in the Eucharistic elements of bread and wine.[119] The practice of elevation was promoted in the twelfth century by the Cistercians, and preachers trained in Paris. It was promoted in the thirteenth century especially by the Franciscans, who drew much of their

[115] The origin of this practice can be traced as early as the Cistercian statutes of 1152; see Pontal, *Les statuts synodaux français du XIIIe siècle*, 1, 83 n. 1.

[116] Caroline Walker Bynum, *Christian Materiality: An Essay on Religion in Late Medieval Europe* (New York, 2011).

[117] Susan Leibacher Ward, "Who Sees Christ?: An Alabaster Panel of the Mass of St. Gregory," in *Push Me, Pull You: Imaginative and Emotional Interaction in Late Medieval and Renaissance Art*, ed. Sarah Blick and Laura D. Gelfand, 1 (Leiden, 2011), 347–381, figures 10.1, 10.3, 10.6.

[118] Jozef Lamberts, "Liturgie et spiritualité de l'eucharistie au XIIIe siècle," in *Fête-dieu (1246–1966)*, 1: *Actes du colloque de Liège, 12–14 septembre 1996*, ed. André Haquin (Louvain-la-Neuve, 1999), 81–95 at 94.

[119] Jessalyn Bird, "The Construction of Orthodoxy and the (De)construction of Heretical Attacks on the Eucharist in *Pastoralia* from Peter the Chanter's Circle in Paris," in *Texts and the Repression of Medieval Heresy*, ed. Caterina Bruschi and Peter Biller (York, 2003), 45–61.

liturgy from that of the Roman curia, where the friars were in high favor at the time.[120] The elevation became an established feature of the Roman Rite throughout the West, and texts of the mass included rubrics for the raising up of host and chalice.[121] Likewise, the chasubles worn by priests while celebrating mass were cut in such a way to make lifting the consecrated bread and wine easier.[122] The discipline of the elevation deserves study as it entered canon law and, through the law, became a regulated practice. It is necessary to identify the theological concerns that lay behind the norms adopted to regulate the elevation, and to comprehend the message taught the laity about their proper response to this liturgical action.[123]

Coming during the canon of the mass, said in Latin facing away from the people, the elevation of the host was a dramatic moment in which the faithful could see the white round of consecrated bread raised up. This moment was made all the more dramatic by the ringing of bells and the lighting of lights,[124] and occasionally by the use of incense. A dark curtain behind the altar might even be used to create a contrast of the light host and the dark cloth.[125] Music was added, including the sound of trumpets or the singing of motets based on texts like *O sacrum convivium*.[126]

Depiction of the elevation became a prominent feature of illuminated missals and books of hours in manuscript.[127] The elevation was also depicted in the Mass of Gregory the Great, in which the pope sees the

[120] Stephen J. P. Van Dijk, *The Ordinal of the Roman Court from Innocent III to Boniface VIII*, ed. John Hazelden Walker (Fribourg, 1975), 512, noting an instruction of Gregory IX that a bell be rung during the canon (n. 1), as well as the copying of rubrics about the elevation into some mass books used in the curia.

[121] *Tracts on the Mass*, ed. J. Wickham Legg (London, 1904), 10–12, 80–82, 155–160, 222–225.

[122] Cordelia Warr, *Dressing for Heaven: Religious Clothing in Italy, 1215–1545* (Manchester, 2010), 23–24.

[123] The elevation is discussed in many books, especially Miri Rubin, *Corpus Christ: The Eucharist in Late Medieval Culture* (Cambridge, 1991; but the provisions of canon law are not studied in depth. On its possible connection with the refutation of Berengar and the Cathars, see G. J. C. Snoek, *Medieval Piety from Relics to the Eucharist: A Process of Mutual Interaction* (Leiden, 1995), 47–48, 55.

[124] Wax or formed candles were provided as gifts and bequests for the elevation in both England and Italy; see *Pastors and the Care of Souls*, 247; also Robert Brentano, *A New World in a Small Place: Church and Religion in the Diocese of Rieti, 1188–1378* (Berkeley, 1994), 28. Wax also was bought, e.g., for Corpus Christi; see Brentano, *A New World in a Small Place*, 316.

[125] Joseph A. Jungmann, *The Mass of the Roman Rite: Its Origins and Development*, rev. ed., trans. Francis A. Brunner (New York, 1959), 426.

[126] Andrew Kirkman, *The Cultural Life of the Early Polyphonic Mass: Medieval Context to Modern Revival* (Cambridge, 2010), 130–131, 198–201. Kirkman argues that music deliberately concealed the canon; see Kirkman, *Polyphonic Mass*, 193–198.

[127] Rubin, *Corpus Christi*, 49–63, 131–134; Rogers S. Wieck, *Illuminating Faith: The Eucharist in Medieval Life and Art* (New York, 2014), 22, 27, 32, 59; Elizabeth Saxon,

Man of Sorrows with the instruments of His Passion.[128] At least one altarpiece, Roger van der Weyden's Seven Sacraments Altarpiece, showed a priest elevating the host in the background of a Crucifixion scene.[129] Some canon law manuscripts also are found with the elevation illustrating the sacramental function of the clergy in their relationship to lay worshipers.[130] The attendants of the priest can be shown with lighted candles or ringing bells at the elevation.[131] The elevation also could be depicted in sculpture, whether directly or indirectly, in the image of the Christ Child held aloft before the congregation by the Virgin Mary.[132]

With reception of communion infrequent, usually at Eastertide, and when confession and communion were made obligatory, this spiritual communion became extremely important in the life of medieval Christians in the West. Devotional viewing seems to have spread rapidly in the late twelfth century.[133] The elevation also can be seen as a moment of community solidarity, with all or at least most of the congregation, educated or not, gazing intently at the elevated host.[134] With this drama of elevation and devotion went the belief of the learned that the individual

The Eucharist in Romanesque France: Iconography and Theology (Woodbridge, 2006), 149, discussing a possible early example from Tours.

[128] Wieck, *Illuminating Faith*, 71.

[129] Caterina Limentani Virdis and Mari Pietrogiovanni, *Great Altarpieces, Gothic and Renaissance* (New York: Vendome Press, 2002) 73–75.

[130] Rubin, *Corpus Christi*, 132; Alixe Bovey, "Communion and Community: Eucharistic Narratives and Their Audience in the Smithfield Decretals," in *The Social Life of Illumination: Manuscripts, Images and Communities in the Late Middle Ages*, ed. Joyce Coleman, Mark Cruse, and Kathryn A. Smith (Turnhout, 2013), 53–82 at 60–63; Aden Kumler, "The Multiplicity of the Species: Eucharistic Morphology in the Middle Ages," *Res* 59/60 (2011), 179–191 in figure 4. A baby elevated as the host appears in an illustrated life of Edward the Confessor in figure 1.

[131] Bovey, "Communion and Community," 54–55, figures 5–6. A custodian of the parish of Calonge in the archdiocese of Tarragona was accused in a 1314 visitation of failing in his duty to ring bells at the appropriate hours; see Christian Guillere, "Les visites pastorales en Tarraconaise à la fin du Moyen-Age (XIVe–XVe siècle)," *Mélanges de la Casa Velázques* 19 (1983), 125–162 at 158.

[132] Saxon, *The Eucharist in Romanesque France*, 91–92.

[133] Rubin, *Corpus Christi*, 63–80; Saxon, *The Eucharist in Romanesque France*, 219. On Easter Duty, see the decree *Omnis utriusque sexus* of the Fourth Lateran Council (1215), found in the *Decretals of Gregory* IX as X 5.38.12; see *Corpus Iuris Canonici*, ed. Emil Friedberg, 2 vols. (Leipzig, 1879; Graz, 1959), 2.887–888. Spiritual communion occasionally was urged as a substitute for frequent reception where a zealous lay person desired it; see the example from fifteenth-century Basel cited in *Medieval Christianity in Practice*, ed. Miri Rubin (Princeton, 2009), 126–131. However, there may have been a reaction toward reception of the host during the fifteenth century; see A. Goossens, "Résonances eucharistiques à la fin du Moyen Âge," in *Fête-dieu*, 1.173–191 at 180–182, 185–187, emphasizing the theology of Gabriel Biel.

[134] For a brief summary of the contrast drawn by some scholars of the elevation with the use of books of hours, see Eamon Duffy, *Marking the Hours: English People and Their Prayers 1240–1570* (New Haven, Conn., 2006), 98–99.

was touching Christ, truly present, with a visual ray of sight.[135] The practice of elevation was sufficiently common by the thirteenth century that it was discussed by theologians and mystics, like the nuns of Helfta.[136] The texts of the Devotio Moderna included instructions by Geert Grote on devout participation in the mass, not just when a person could see the host but when it could not be seen.[137]

Many Christians believed that seeing the host also had a practical impact, of saving the Christian from harm or conferring benefits like good digestion. This made beholding the elevation all the more desirable. Complaints consequently were recorded about pressures on the priest to hold the host higher and longer, and others about people trying to obtain places where a better view might be obtained. Another complaint was that people rushed from one mass to another to see the elevation. It is unclear, as R. N. Swanson has observed, whether we should regard this practice as "real adoration of Christ in the Host" or as simply "toting up repetitions of the *Pater Noster* during the elevation as a means of curtailing time in Purgatory."[138] Purgatory may have been the destination of the woman in a sermon *exemplum* who ended up in the flames for leaving mass after the elevation but before communion to protect her possessions. A thief cut the woman's throat, but she appeared to her sister and revealed her plight.[139] Nonetheless, whatever warning may have been issued, the devout could find consolation in this form of communion as they did in the contemplation of Christ's Passion, whereas they might receive host with fear that they were unworthy.[140]

[135] Margaret R. Miles, *Image as Insight: Visual Understanding in Western Christianity and Secular Culture* (Boston, 1985), 96–97. This idea of sight, in this case, was supposed to touch a deeper reality than the appearances of bread and wine; see Gwenfair Walters Adams, *Vision in Late Medieval England: Lay Spirituality and Sacred Glimpses of the Hidden Worlds of Faith* (Leiden, 2007), 122–124.

[136] Édouard Dumoutet, *Le désir de voir l'hostie et les origines de la dévotion au Saint-Sacrement* (Paris, 1926), accessed online from the Center for Research Libraries on May 6, 2011.

[137] *Devotio Moderna: Basic Writings*, ed. John Van Engen (Mahwah, N.J.: Paulist Press, 1988), 72–73. Grote also treated passing to Pax as a substitute for communion; see *Devotio Moderna*, 72.

[138] Charles Zika, "Hosts, Processions and Pilgrimages: Controlling the Sacred in Fifteenth-Century Germany," *Past and Present* 118 (1988), 25–64 at 32; Jungmann, *The Mass of the Roman Rite*, 90–91; R. N. Swanson, *Religion and Devotion in Europe c. 1215–c. 1515* (Cambridge, 1995), 100; Swanson, *Church and Society in Late Medieval England* (Oxford, 1989), 276. For a warning of what we cannot learn of parish life from official records, see Eamon Duffy, *The Voices of Morebath: Reformation and Rebellion in an English Village* (New Haven, Conn., 2001), 65–66.

[139] *Friars' Tales: Thirteenth-Century Exempla from the British Isles*, ed. David Jones (Manchester, 2011), 65–66.

[140] John Van Engen, "Multiple Options: The World of the Fifteenth-Century Church," *Church History* 77 (2008), 257–284 at 278.

There is no recorded enactment by ecclesiastical authorities initially authorizing the elevation of the host or the chalice. Nor was the elevation important enough at first to be mentioned by some important twelfth-century theologians writing about the mass. Hugh of Saint Victor did not discuss it in his treatise on the sacraments, although he made a reference to Christ being present: "Finally, in sight, in touch, in taste (*in uisu in tactu in sapore*), He is with you corporeally."[141] Nor did the theologian and liturgist Johannes Beleth, who was educated in Chartres, make any mention of the practice.[142] Hildebert of Lavardin's exposition of the mass offers us little evidence of the practice.[143] Most importantly, the *Sentences* of Peter Lombard did not mention the elevation. It discussed the fraction of the host, but not its raising up for devout public viewing.[144] Significantly, Lothar of Segni, the future Pope Innocent III, although he affirmed transubstantiation in his tract on the mass, made no mention of elevations as significant actions during the canon.[145]

Discussions of the elevation can be found, at last, in some late twelfth-century texts. Radulphus Ardens described "the elevations of the bread and chalice" as the form of the mass together with the words of the canon.[146] The canonist Sicard of Cremona focused on the elevation of host and chalice at the end of the canon. He identified this act with the deposition of Christ from the cross. Sicard identified the priest holding up the host with Nicodemus and the deacon holding the chalice with Joseph of Arimathea.[147] Sicard also specified the setting down of the chalice as signifying the entombment of Jesus. The mixing of the two elements signified the Resurrection, but the fraction of the host represented Christ's breaking of the bread at Emmaus (Luke 24:30–31).[148]

In 1219, however, the practice was approved by Pope Honorius III. His decretal *Sane*, addressed to the archbishop and bishops of Sweden, a land which may have adopted the practice at a comparatively late date,

[141] Hugh of Saint Victor, *On the Sacraments of the Christian Faith (De sacramentis)*, trans. Roy J. Deferrari (Cambridge, Mass., 1951), 304–315 at 314; *Hugonis de Sancto Victore De sacramentis Christiane fidei*, ed. Rainer Berndt (Münster, 2008), 400–412 at 410.

[142] Johannes Beleth, *Summa de ecclesiasticis officiis*, 82.

[143] The discussions of elevation in *Liber de expositione missae* only appear in the notes at PL 171.1165 n. 88, 1177 n. 97. Saxon, *The Eucharist in Romanesque France*, 145–147.

[144] Peter Lombard, *The Sentences*, book 4: *The Sacraments*, trans. Giulio Silano (Toronto, 2007), 41–69: Distinctions VIII–XIII, especially 61–64: Distinction XII c. 2–4.

[145] Innocentius III, *De sacro altaris mysterio libri sex*, PL 217.833, 859, 868–870.

[146] Radulphus Ardens, *The Questions on the Sacraments, Speculum universal 8.31–92*, trans. Christopher P. Evans (Toronto, 2010), 102–103, "The form of action is the elevations of the bread and chalice and the signs of the cross that are made there."

[147] *Sicardi Cremonensis episcopi Mitralis de officiis*, 198–199. Sicard also identified this elevation with the Resurrection; see *Mitralis*, 204.

[148] *Sicardi Cremonensis episcopi Mitralis de officiis*, 219.

appeared in *Compilatio quinta* (5 Comp. 3.24.1).[149] Then it entered the *Gregorian Decretals* as Chapter 10 in the title "On the Celebration of Masses, the Sacrament of the Eucharist and Divine Offices" (*De celebratione missarum, et sacramento eucharistiae et divinis officiis*, X. 3.41). The original decretal began with a long reference to the keeping of manna in the Ark of the Covenant as a prefiguration of the Eucharist. This portion was edited out by Raymond of Peñafort, together with its lamentation that the Eucharist was not always kept carefully in churches. Raymond may have regarded this portion of the decretal as superfluous, especially since he added the canon *Statuimus* of the Fourth Lateran Council, treating the custody of the sacrament, elsewhere in the collection (X 3.44.1). As it entered the official collection, the text of *Sane* still required that a priest keep the reserved Eucharist devoutly and faithfully in a single clean and sealed place (*in loco singulari, mundo etiam et signato*). More to our point, *Sane* ordered priests to teach the people frequently to reverence the elevated host at least by bowing their heads. The same deference was enjoined on those who saw communion being carried to the sick (viaticum), "Any priest should frequently teach his people that, when the saving host is elevated in the celebration of masses, anyone should bow reverently, doing the same thing when the priest carries it to the sick."

Honorius told prelates they were to enforce *Sane*, including its provision for the safe keeping of the reserved Eucharist, in order to avoid his wrath and that of God (*divinam et nostram ... ultionem*).[150]

The Ordinary Gloss to *Sane* repeated in the *casus* or summary of the text[151] much of the text of Pope Honorius's decree. Bernard of Parma,

149 *Quinque compilationes antiquae nec non Collectio canonum Lipsiensis*, ed. Emil Friedberg (Leipzig, 1882: Graz, 1956), 178. On Honorius's pontificate, see Jane Sayers, *Papal Government and England during the Pontificate of Honorius III (1216–1227)* (Cambridge, 1984), 1–12.

150 See X 3.41.10 in *Corpus Iuris Canonici*, 2.642, "Sacerdos vero quilibet frequenter doceat plebem suam, ut, quum in celebratione missarum elevator hostia salutaris, quilibet se reverenter inclinet, idem faciens, quum eam defert presbyter ad infirmum." The omitted portions of the text were printed in italics. This passage is quoted in the Synodal Constitutions found in Cambridge, Corpus Christi College Manuscript 255, fol. 209vb, cited from the *Parker Library on the Web* [http://parkerweb.stanford.edu/parker/], accessed on November 7, 2012. For the canon law concerning safekeeping of the reserved sacrament, see Thomas M. Izbicki, "*Manus temeraria*: The Custody of the Eucharist in Medieval Canon Law," in *Proceedings of the Thirteenth International Congress of* Medieval Canon Law, Esztergom-*Budapest (Hungary), August 3–9, 2008*, ed. Peter Erdö and Szaboles Anselm Szuromi (Città del Vaticano, 2010), 539–552. Some canonists discussed custody of the Eucharist at c. *Sane*, but others addressed while commenting *Statuimus*; see *Corpus Iuris Canonici*, 2, col. 649.

151 *Ordinary Gloss at* X 3.41.10 *Casus*, "ut quando in celebratione Missarum Hostia elevatur. Se reverenter inclinet: & idem faciat cum portatur ad infirmum lumine pręcedente, & prelati huiusmodi mandati transgresores puniant, si et ipsi divinam volunt effugere ultionem." *Casus* also was used in law to mean the summary of a case to which a

the compiler of the Gloss, said, at the word *inclinet*, where the decree said to bow: "on bended knees" (*Flexibus genibus*). Bernard went on to recommend that the Christian say one of these prayers: *Salve lux mundi* or *Transsubstantientur res iste*. One said: "Hail, light of the world, word of the Father, true victim, living flesh, entire God etc." The other reads: "These things are transubstantiated into your body and blood, Lord, for the honor and glory of your name, for the confession of our sins, and the health of our souls." Bernard also encouraged saying the *Pater noster* at the moment of elevation. The prayers recommended in the Gloss are but two of the many in Latin or in the vernacular associated with the elevation of the host found in medieval books of hours and other manuscripts containing devotional works.[152] Among these is a French translation of the hymn *O salutaris hostia*.[153] Bernard added that the pious prayer about transubstantiation was to be said before the consecration of the wine in the chalice took place.[154] The Gloss also said the penalty for not enforcing *Sane* is left to the discretion of the judge.[155]

Canonists' commentaries on *Sane* and related texts varied in their interests. Some focused on the elevation, and some on viaticum processions. A question also arose in the *Commentary* of Hostiensis on the *Gregorian Decretals* whether a criminal, especially a perpetrator of homicide, might gain sanctuary where the host was being carried, not only at a church. He noted an objection that the Eucharist is food for the soul, and so it can liberate the soul. A church is corporeal, and so it can liberate a body. Hostiensis replied that the Eucharist is not just the food of the soul; but it can save the body "because, nevertheless, it is the Body of Christ, which is preferable to a corporeal church." The canonist said the creator of all was able to act for the saving of bodies (*in salvatione*

jurist replied in a *consilium*; see Peter Riesenberg, "The *consilia* Literature: a Prospectus," *Manuscripta* 6 (1962), 3–22.

152 For example, there are two versions of "O Jhesu Lorde, welcome thou be," plus *Anima Christi*, in the Roberts Hours; see Duffy, *Marking the Hours*, 85, 90, plate 59. Portions of the offices for Corpus Christi attributed to Thomas Aquinas also can be found marked for use at the elevation; see Thomas M. Izbicki, "The Bleeding Host of Dijon: Its Place In the History of Eucharistic Devotion," in *Saluting Aron Gurevich: Essays in History, Literature and Other Related Subjects*, ed. Yelena Mazour-Matusevich and Alexandra S. Korros (Leiden, 2010), 227–246.

153 Pierre Rézeau, *Répertoire d'incipit des prières françaises à la fin du Moyen Âge: Addenda et corrigenda aux répertoires de Donet et Sinclair, Nouveaux incipit* (Geneva, 1986), 324, 356.

154 *Ordinary Gloss at* X 3.41.10 v. Inclinet. "& potest dicere ista verba. *Salve lux mundi, verbum patris: Hostia vera, viva caro, deitas integra, verus homo.* Vel ista: Transsubstantientur res istae in corpus & sanguinem tuum Domine & laudem nominis tui, ad confessionem peccatorum, & ad salutem animarum nostrarum. Vel orationem dominicam." The instructions on when to say the second prayer follow.

155 *Ordinary Gloss at* X 3.41.10 v. Punire, in *Decretales Gregorii noni*, 1263.

corporum).[156] This question also was pursued by Johannes Andreae and Antonius de Butrio in their commentaries. Both agreed with Hostiensis, whom they quoted at length, on the ability of the body to save a life. Johannes specified that the host was being taken to a sick person (*ad infirmum*), linking this discussion of sanctuary to the rules for viaticum processions.[157] Henricus Bohic specified that this relief did not apply to prisoners to whom the Eucharist was taken. The seeker of sanctuary was free, but a man guilty of homicide or theft was not freed from prison by receiving communion. The host could not liberate him.[158]

Hostiensis gave serious consideration to the elevation of the host in his *Commentary*. He instructed parish priests to require their parishioners to send children for instruction in the rudiments of the faith.[159] The faithful were to learn to kneel, bow their heads, and worship after they, "believing and adoring," had seen the Lord's body. Hostiensis encouraged reciting *Salve lux mundi*.[160] He favored, however, deleting *Transsubstantientur res iste*, because that prayer did not specify by whom the change is effected; therefore "it seems to propagate the error of the heretics who say that anyone can confect. But it seems to do injury to the sacrament."[161] Hostiensis warned that the prayer might promote belief that the priest's own power effected transubstantiation, which could lead people into idolatry. He recommended saying the *Pater noster* instead of the prayers mentioned in the Gloss.[162]

156 *Hostiensis Decretalium commentaria*, 3, fol. 166rb, "Nec obstat, quod Eucharistia est cibus animae: quia nihilominus est corpus Christi. Quo est, & corporali ecclesiae praeferentium. Est etiam & creator omnium, & Dominus dominorum vnde & in saluatione corporum ipsum catholici milites recognoscunt. xi. q. iii. Iulianus." Hostiensis did warn against sacrilegious scuffles over custody of the guilty party that might land the host in the mud.

157 Johannes Andreae, *In decretalium libros novella commentaria*, 3, fol. 223vb; *Excellentissimi Antonii de Butrio . . . Super tertium librum decretalium*, fol. 194rb–va.

158 *Opus preclarissimum distinctionum henrici bouhic . . . super quinque libris decretalium . . .* (Lyon, 1498), fol. xciii[va–b].

159 *Hostiensis Decretalium comentaria*, 3, fol. 166ra, "[*Doceat plebem.*] . . . clericus suos pueros qui & eosdem parochianos moneat, ut pro fide discenda ad ecclesiam filios suos mittant." See also fol. 166ra v. Idem faciens.

160 *Hostiensis Decretalium comentaria*, 2, fol. 166ra, "[*Inclinent.*] flexis genibus, demissis oculis in terram adorando, & commotis visceribus ac capite inclinato dicit, si novit, salve Lux mundi . . . Quod autem dicit. Supra inclinato capite & demissis oculis intelligas postquam ipsis elevatis viderit corpus Christi firmiter credendo & adorando."

161 *Hostiensis Decretalium comentaria*, 2, fol. 166ra, "Haec oratio penitus est delenda: quia cum dicat transubstantientur, & non dicat per quem, videtur fovere errorem haereticorum dicentium, quod quilibet potest conficere: sed & videtur facere iniuriam sacramento." At fol. 166ra–b Hostiensis, after saying the prayer was "against gospel truth" (*contra evangelicam veritatem*), offers a corrected wording of it, "Fiat hoc sacrificium tuum domine ad honorem tuum & salutem animae meae & omnium fidelium animarum." Hostiensis may have meant to condemn the Waldensians here, but the identity of the heretics is not clear from this text.

162 *Hostiensis Decretalium comentaria*, 2, fol. 166rb.

Later canonists built on what Hostiensis had taught when commenting on c. *Sane*. Johannes Andreae briefly told priests to teach the faithful to bow their heads before the host.[163] Commenting on the recommendation to pray at the elevation, he gave a long list of prayers, almost all derived from the works of earlier canonists. Johannes added the hymn *Ihesu nostra redemptio* to the list.[164] He commented on the recommendation that the *Pater noster* could be used, saying that it was fitting because *A disciple is not above his master* (Luke 6:40).[165] Johannes concluded with Hostiensis's recommendation that *Transsubstantientur res iste* be dropped from the list of acceptable prayers to be said at the elevation.[166] Antonius de Butrio built, in turn, on the commentary of Johannes Andreae, listing many prayers and the hymn *Iesu nostra redemptio*. Antonius, however, dropped Hostiensis's objection to *Transsubstantientur res iste*.[167]

The canon *Sane* had an echo in an episcopal letter. Robert Grosseteste, writing in 1238 to the priests of his diocese with cure of souls, said that the faithful should be taught frequently to bow their heads at the elevation, an exact quotation from Honorius III.[168] Two years later, in 1240, a Council of Worcester held by Bishop Walter de Cantilupe praised the superlative character of the Eucharist and emphasized the duty of venerating it: "This is, therefore, the sacrament, excelling all veneration that, nevertheless, should be venerated by us with all our strength despite the tiny measure of our littleness."[169] The council ordered that the host be raised up so that the faithful standing by could see it. Moreover, he commanded those religious who did not yet follow the practice of elevation to adopt it. Bishop Walter and his council stated that the practice, signaled by the ringing of a bell,

163 Johannes Andreae, *In decretalium libros novella commentaria,* 3, fol. 223vb, "[*Idem faciens*] plebs se reverenter inclinando, et ad hoc per sacerdotem instruantur."

164 Johannes Andreae, *In decretalium libros novella commentaria,* 3, fol. 223vb–224ra, "Item hymnum, Ihesu nostra redemptio &c."

165 Johannes Andreae, *In decretalium libros novella commentaria,* 3, fol. 224ra [*& ibi, orationem dominicam*], citing Hostiensis on use of the *Pater noster* at the elevation.

166 Johannes Andreae, *In decretalium libros novella commentaria,* 3, fol. 224ra [*& in fine*], "posset sic corrigi sit hoc sacramentum domine ad honorem, &c. secundum Hostien."

167 Antonius de Butrio, *Super tertium librum decretalium,* fol. 194rb. By Antonius's day, the *Pater noster* was being displaced by prayers focused on the Passion at the elevation and communion, according to Stephen Mossman, *Marquard von Lindau and the Challenges of Religious Life in Late Medieval Germany: The Passion, the Eucharist, the Virgin Mary* (Oxford, 2010), 151.

168 Letter 52bis, *The Electronic Grosseteste,* 155, "Sacerdos vero quilibet frequenter doceat plebem suam, ut cum in celebratione missarum elevatur hostia salutaris, se reverenter inclinet; idem faciens cum eam portet presbyter ad infirmum, . . . "

169 *Councils & Synods,* 2/1.299, "Hoc *est igitur sacramentum omnem superexcell*ens venerationem, quod tamen debemus pro nostre parvitatis modulo totis viribus venerari."

would arouse devotion in tepid souls and further inflame the souls of those who had charity.[170]

The idea of elevation, not just of the host but of the chalice, was elaborated with the passing of time. By the late thirteenth century, the canonist and liturgist Guillelmus Durantis the Elder was able to discuss multiple elevations. Interpreting the elevation of the host, just after his exposition of the words of consecration, Durantis listed five reasons for this act. Four were symbolic, although none was the long-established identification of the elevation with the Crucifixion, which was then found in sermon literature.[171] One reason, Durantis said, was that the host represented the bread offerings made under the Old Law, showing that "there is no other worthy sacrifice" (*non est aliud dignum sacrificium*) than that of Christ enacted in the mass. The act signifies Christ as "the true bread" (*uerum panem*) foretold by the prophets, signifying the Resurrection of Jesus from the dead. The fifth meaning was pastoral:

> Fifth, the host is elevated so that the people, not being present at the consecration, will know through the elevation that it has been done and that Christ has come on the altar, and they will reverently prostrate themselves on the ground, following the text of Philippians, *At the name of Jesus, every knee shall bow*, and that everyone will adore Him with heart and mouth.[172]

Durantis also noted that different churches managed the elevation of the chalice so that the people might see it in different ways, covered with a pall to indicate the mystery of the Eucharist or uncovered to designate the visible shedding of Christ's blood.[173]

There was, Durantis explained, a third elevation at the end of the canon of the mass. Here the priest lifted a little (*aliquantulum*) of the chalice into which a fragment of the host had been placed. The priest said the formula *Per omnia secula seculorum* loud enough to signify the end of the canon to the congregation. The subsequent lifting and setting down of the chalice

[170] *Councils & Synods*, 2/1.299–300, "Cum autem, in celebratione misse corpus domini per manus sacerdotum in altum erigitur, campanella pulsetur ut per hoc devotio torpentium excitetur, et aliorum caritatis fortius inflammetur; quod etiam a religiosis illis quo ad elevationem in altum, ut videri possit ab astantibus, observari precipimus, qui non servaverunt ut dicitur, hactenus hoc statutum."

[171] See, for example, Radulphus Ardens in *Homelia XLVII*, PL 155.836. Ronald J. Stanbury, "Preaching and Pastoral Care in the Middle Ages," in *A Companion to Pastoral Care in the Late Middle Ages*, ed. Stanbury (Leiden, 2010), 23–39 at 33.

[172] Guillelmus Durantis senior, *Rationale divinorum officiorum*, 461–462 at 462, "Quinto, hostia eleuatur ut populus non proueniens consecrationem, sed ex hoc cognoscens illam factam esse et Christum super altare uenisse, reuerenter ad terram prosternantur, iuxta illud ad Philippenses: *In nomine Iesu omne genu flectatur* etc., et illum corde et ore adorent"; William Durand, *Rationale* IV, 357. Durantis allowed for the interpretation of the elevations after the canon as representing the Crucifixion and the deposition from the cross, but not where he discussed the words of institution; see *Rationale divinorum officiorum*, 502; William Durand, *Rationale IV*, 411.

[173] Durantis, *Rationale divinorum officiorum*, 478; William Durand, *Rationale IV*, 378–379.

represented the removal of Christ from the cross for burial. The priest, according to Durantis, represented Nicodemus; the deacon, holding the chalice that had received a fragment of the host, represented Joseph of Arimathea. The two requested from Pilate the body of Jesus for burial, but it was Joseph who placed the body and blood of the Crucified in the tomb. An interesting detail of the discussion of the elevation at the conclusion of the canon is the instruction, "He should raise his voice, and even raise the chalice a little." With the priest facing the altar, this elevation at the end of the canon could not be seen by the laity, although they would hear his words. The discussion of these elevations ends with instructions for the priest to hold the host with four fingers to signify the merits of the Passion: power over the devil, humility, chastity and submission to the deity, and loving both God and neighbor.[174] Durantis's biblical symbolism for priest and deacon was not new, being found in the *Ritus antiquus celebrandae missae*.[175] It also was found in a better-known work, the *De sacro altaris mysterio libri sex* of Pope Innocent III, who identified these clergy as representing Nicodemus and Joseph requesting the body of Christ from Pilate; but he did not specify which minister signified which biblical figure.[176]

The *Pupilla oculi* of John de Burough, one of the most popular English manuals for parish priests, also contained instructions on how to elevate the consecrated host properly. The action of the priest was to be continuous, without, at least voluntarily, any pause or "unsuitable interval" (*impertinens interuallum*). The priest also was warned, "Nor should he elevate it too long, nor kiss it, nor hold it before his eyes."[177] The priest also was instructed to avoid obscuring the host from the sight of the faithful or touching the host with any part of the body but his consecrated fingers (*nisi cum digitis consecratis*).[178]

Discipline for the celebration of these rites was left, for the most part, to local authorities. Councils, diocesan synods, and bishops issued statutes

[174] Durantis, *Rationale divinorum officiorum*, 502–503, "exaltat vocem, et etiam aliquantulum chalicem eleuat."; William Durand, *Rationale IV*, 410–411. Durantis feared spilling of the consecrated wine but thought the little elevation symmetrical with the elevation of the host and chalice, as well as fitting with Scripture; see Rubin, *Corpus Christi*, 55–56. On Durantis's approach to liturgical symbolism, see Andrea Denny-Brown, "Old Habits Die Hard: Vestimentary Change in William Durand's *Rationale divinorum officiorum*," *Journal of Medieval and Early Modern Studies* 39 (2009), 545–570.

[175] The *Ritus* is found appended to the works of Gregory the Great in PL 78.254.

[176] *De sacro altaris mysterio libri sex*, PL 217.895.

[177] Johannes de Burough, *Pupilla oculi omnibus presbyteris precipue Anglicanis summe necessaria* . . . (London, 1510), fol. xxiii$^{ra–b}$, "sic quod non voluntarie fiat nimia pausatio. vel impertinens intervallum. consecrata hostia elevet eam mature sacerdos et ostendat populo adorandum nec nimis diu teneat eleuatum. nec osculetur eam seu oculis suis apponat." The 1287 Council of Liège warned the priest to touch only the host or the corporal on which it rested between the *lavabo* and the elevation; see Mansi 24.895.

[178] Johannes de Burough, *Pupilla oculi*, fol. xxiii^{rb}.

that regulated the conduct of the clergy, at least in intention, and told them what to teach the faithful.[179] Certain concerns emerge from reading these enactments. One is the fear that the priest might fail to consecrate the host and yet would elevate it. The canonist Hostiensis articulated this concern in his *Commentary on the Decretals*. The cardinal said the priest should take care that he had raised up the body, not bread. Otherwise, a creature might be adored instead of the Creator: "The priest should take care that he elevate not bread but the body, so that a creature not be adored but God. That is first he said the words of the Canon by which the body of Christ is confected."[180] Any mistake in this process might lead the laity into idolatry. Likewise, a note in a French manuscript warned a priest against raising an unconsecrated host too high just before he spoke the words of consecration to avoid another occasion for adoration of an unconsecrated creature.[181] John de Burough issued a similar warning in the *Pupilla oculi*.[182]

Guido de Monte Rocherii warned in his manual for priests against another of the many defects possible in a mass. He warned that a priest should not simply eat a host without saying the words of consecration if he suddenly recalled a mortal sin he had not confessed while he was celebrating mass. This irreverent behavior toward the sacrament would offend God and could lead to idolatry if the congregation, deluded by the priest, reverenced the host he had failed to consecrate.[183] Guido offered curates a warning already issued by Hostiensis in his *Summa on the Titles of the Decretals*, that "A priest should not deceive the people – or rather himself – on account of consciousness of a sin gnawing [him] by pretending to confect and consume the body of Christ, not saying the

179 On local councils and their texts, see C. R. Cheney, *English Synodalia of the Thirteenth Century* (London, 1941); Pontal, *Les statuts synodaux*, 1.lvii–lxxvii; Pontal, *Les statuts synodaux* (Turnhout, 1975).

180 *Hostiensis Decretalium commentaria*, 3, fol. 166ra, "Debet enim cauere sacerdos, quod panem non elevet, sed corpus, ne creatura adoretur, sed Deus. Hoc est primo dicat verba canonis per quae conficitur corpus Christi." Hostiensis also warned against making the faithful more confused by repeating the prayer of consecration after a false elevation, turning a prayer into an execration. Hostiensis also emphasized the words of consecration as effecting transubstantiation; see *Decretalium commentaria*, 3, fol. 162va. Similarly, see the 1255 constitutions of Valencia, a region that was then recently wrested from Muslim control, in Mansi 22.1890.

181 V. L. Kennedy, "The Moment of Consecration and the Elevation of the Host," *Mediaeval Studies* 6 (1944), 121–150.

182 Johannes de Burough, *Pupilla oculi*, fol. xxiii[ra].

183 Guido de Monte Rocherii, *Manipulus curatorum*, fol. xlii[v], "Dicunt quidam quod talis sacerdos non debet dicere verba consecrationis sed simplicem hostiam debet sumere sed illud non est verum: immo erroneum quia talis deum illuderet facieno irreverentiam sacramento et populum deciperet quia faceret cum ydolatrice."; Guido, *Handbook for Curates*, 105–106. John de Burough was kinder to a priest who celebrated with what he thought good unleavened wheat bread but discovered was not the proper material for the sacrament; see Johannes de Burough, *Pupilla oculi*, fol. xiii[va].

words of the canon and consuming the bread from which the Eucharist was to be confected and pure wine."[184]

Local councils and synods did not often address the possibility of defects in the mass and their remedies; however, there are surviving canons about this from across Europe. Thus the Council of Oxford (1222) ordered that the canon be read "fully and entirely" (*plene et integre*), especially at the consecration, a text which was repeated in Lyndwood's *Provinciale*.[185] The 1227 provincial Council of Trier took a more admonitory approach, warning that a priest sinned mortally if he failed to confect the Eucharist properly, leading the people into idolatry by having them adore mere bread:

> Likewise the priest who celebrates mass should confect the body of Christ and read the Canon. Otherwise he sins mortally because he makes the people adore mere bread, which is idolatry.[186]

The Parisian statutes were among the earliest in date warning a priest to hold the host before his breast until he had said the words *Hoc est corpus meum*. Then and only then was he to raise it up for all to see. These synodal texts were widely read in England, where they frequently were paraphrased or reused verbatim.[187] Similarly, the statutes of Angers said the unconsecrated host was to be held before the priest's breast until the words of consecration had been said. Then the host was to be held up decently (*decenter*) so it could be seen.[188] The statutes of Bordeaux said the words of consecration were to be said continuously in secret before the

[184] Henricus de Segusio Cardinalis Hostiensis, *Summa una cum summariis et adnotationibus Nicolai Superantii* (Lyon, 1537; Aalen, 1962), fol. 185ra, "Sed et propter peccati conscientiam remordentem non debet sacerdos decipere populum vel potius seipsum fingendo se conficere et sumere corpus Christi: tacens verba canonis et sumens panem de quo conficienda erat eucharistia: et vinum purum."

[185] See above n. 72. Archbishop Walter Reynolds repeated this injunction in a statute on the celebration of the mass; see Lyndwood, *Provinciale seu Constitvtiones*, 235; *Lyndwood's Provinciale*, 98.

[186] Mansi 23.28, "Item Sacerdos, qui celebrat Missam debet conficere corpus Christi & canonem legere; alias peccat mortaliter, quia facit populum adorare panem simplicem, quod est idolatria." This provision was repeated in 1277; see Mansi 24.194. See also the 1268 Council of Claremont; see Mansi 22.1191, "hoc autem dictum est, ne purus panis adoretur: quod esset, si ante probationem verborum istorum hostia elevaretur." For a rare example of a priest who celebrated a fictional mass (*missam fictam*), see *Visites archidiaconales de Josas*, 389.

[187] Pontal, *Les statuts synodaux*, 1, 82–83; Mansi 22.682, "28. Praecipitur presbiteris, ut cum in canone Missae incoeperint, *Qui pridie*, tenentes hostiam, ne elevant eam statim nimis alte, ita quod posit ab omnibus videri a populo, sed quasi ante pectus detineant, donec dixerint: *Hoc est corpus meum*: & tunc eleven team, ut posit ab omnibus videri." On Odo's influence in England, possiblty via Paris-educated clergy, see Cheney, *English Synodalia*, 24–25, 55–5782–84.

[188] Pontal, *Les statuts synodaux*, 1.144. See also Brentano, *A New World in a Small Place*, 111.

elevation.[189] Likewise, a 1287 statute from Liège instructed a priest not to elevate the host before he had said the words of consecration, which words were copied verbatim into the synodal text to inform even an ignorant priest. After the consecration, the great bell (*campana magna*) was to be rung three times to call the faithful to adore wherever they might be (*ubicumque fuerint*).[190] Similarly, the 1287 statutes of Exeter stated that the priest was to say the words *Hoc est enim corpus meum* to effect transubstantiation. Otherwise the people might venerate a creature as the Creator when the host was raised up. Such warnings were issued as late as the fifteenth century. Thus Nicholas of Cusa included in his instructions for visitations an inquiry whether the host was shown to the people before it was consecrated.[191]

The consecrated host was, however, to be raised high (*levetur in altum*) once consecrated to be perceived by the worshipers standing by.[192] According to the Exeter statutes, this act would arouse the devotion of the faithful, who would receive an increase in merit. The parishioners were to be exhorted to bend their knees in adoration when the little bells (*campanellae*) and the great bell were rung, the latter thrice.[193] The Parisian statutes of Guillaume de Seignelay allowed the ringing of the bell a bit before (*paulo ante*) the elevation.[194] A statute of Fiesole said priests especially should warn "nobles" (*nobiles homines*) to prostrate themselves devoutly at the elevation.[195] The 1298 Council of Limassol warned the priest against raising the host twice if he discovered, after the elevation, there was no wine in the chalice.[196] (A priest of the diocese of

[189] Pontal, *Les statuts synodaux*, 2, 58.

[190] Mansi 24.896 Statute XXIII, "Sacerdos non elevet hostiam ad ostendendum populo, nisi postquam dixerit haec verba: *Hoc est enim Corpus meum*; & tunc pulsetur campana magna tribus ictibus ex una parte, ut fideles qui audierint, ubicumque fuerint, adorent." Similarly, a 1280 synod of Cologne ruled against elevating the host before the words of consecration had been said, and it required ringing the bell three times to announce the sacring to the faithful wherever they were to come and adore; see Mansi 24.350.

[191] *Akten zur Reform des Bistums Brixen*, 27, "Item si ostendit hostiam populo, antequam sit consecrate, uoniam hoc numquam debet fieri." Similarly see the 1408 instructions for Reims in Mansi 26.1070.

[192] *Councils & Synods*, 2/2.990, "Quia vero per hec verba: Hoc est enim corpus meum, et non per alia, panis transsubstantiatur in corpus, prius hostiam non levet sacerdos donec ipsa plene protulerit, ne pro creatore creatura a populo veneretur. Hostia autem ita levetur in altum ut a fidelibus circumstantibus valeat intueri."

[193] *Councils & Synods*, 2/2.990, "Per hoc etenim fidelium devotio excitatur et fidei meritum suscipit incrementum. Parochiani solicite exhortentur ut in levatione corporis Christi nedum reverenter se inclinent sed genua flectant et creatorem suum adorent omni devotione et reverenti; ad quod per campanelle pulsationem primitus excitentur, et in levatione ter tangatur campana maior."

[194] Pontal, *Les statuts synodaux*, 1.101.

[195] Trexler, *Synodal Law in Florence and Fiesole*, 202.

[196] *The Synodicum Nicosiense and Other Documents of the Latin Church of Cyprus, 1196–1373*, ed. Christopher David Schabel (Nicosia, 2001), 196–197.

Paris was reported to have left the altar when he found he had no wine and repeated the canon when he returned with it.[197])

A related worry was whether an unconsecrated host might be mistaken by a priest for a consecrated one.[198] A 1284 Council of Nîmes addressed one aspect of this problem: a priest might discover a host under the altar cloth (*sub palla altaris*) or a fragment of one on the altar that he was unsure had been consecrated. The statute said he could consume that host or fragment after he had received the consecrated wine.[199] In the *Pupilla oculi*, John de Burough resolved the problem by saying that any part of a host on the altar not included in the priest's intention to consecrate, whether he omitted it knowingly or not, was unconsecrated. John's understanding of consecration was very specific, allowing a host on the altar to remain bread if not included in the priest's intention.[200] When absolutely in doubt, John allowed the priest to leave a host on the altar for the next priest to include in his intention.[201] As various councils and bishops had done, John also warned against elevating the host if the words of consecration had not been said. He said it was a grave sin to celebrate while in mortal sin but worse to pretend consecration. That dissimulation would offend God and his neighbor by leading his people into idolatry.[202]

Problems with the elevation of the chalice seem to have been reported rarely, although one priest of the diocese of Paris was penanced for spilling its contents on himself.[203] Nicholas of Ausimo did worry, as others had before him, about elevating the chalice at the wrong moment. He advised priests not to raise it up until he said *unde et memores*, which, in the canon, followed the words said over the cup. He said this practice was safer (*tutior*).[204]

An additional worry focusing on sending wrong signals to the laity involved the distribution of unconsecrated hosts. A warning was issued

197 *Visites archdidiaconales de Josas*, 337.

198 A council around the end of the twelfth century warned against consuming unconsecrated hosts as consecrated ones; see Mansi 22.670. See also the 1217 statutes of Salisbury in Mansi 22.1119, which also warned against accidentally consecrating a host twice.

199 Mansi 24.536, "dicimus quod sacerdos in fine Missae post receptionem sanguinis potest eam recipere, & idem dicimus de aliqua parte hostiae, si ita inventa fuerit in altari, & dubitatur utrum fuerit consecrata."

200 Johannes de Burough, *Pupilla oculi*, fol. xv[va–b], "credibile quod consecraret illam medietatem super quam fertur suam intentionem et non super aliam."

201 Johannes de Burough, *Pupilla oculi*, fol. xvi[a].

202 Johannes de Burough, *Pupilla oculi*, fol. xvii[vb], "sed similando se conficere et non conficiendo peccat in deum et in proximum quem ydolatrare facit." For an example of a *missa ficta*, see *Visites archdidiaconales de Josas*, 389.

203 *Visites archdidiaconales de Josas*, 384. Another priest said stains on a corporal resulted from spilling unconsecrated wine; see *Visites Josas*, 154.

204 Nicholas of Ausimo, *Supplementum Summae Pisanellae* (Venezia, 1489), fol. I–1[vb].

at the 1277 Council of Trier against giving them to children, or even to adults, in place of consecrated ones.[205] A similar prohibition against giving unconsecrated hosts to children had been issued by a Council at Claremont in 1268.[206] One possible explanation of this practice in the case of adults can be found in the *Novella* of Johannes Andreae on the *Gregorian Decretals*. Discussing the decretal *De homine* (X 3.41.7), he warned priests against giving unconsecrated hosts to sinners who asked privately for communion. Giving a *hostiam non sacratam* could lead that sinner in yet another way into the sin of idolatry.[207] This opinion was repeated by Antonius de Butrio.[208] (Johannes also thought there was a danger of idolatry if the consecrated elements were believed by some not to be entirely transformed during mass and yet were adored by the people.[209])

John of Erfurt, in his pastoral manual, worried about the possibility of idolatry in different forms. A man who pretended to be ordained might celebrate mass, offering what should not be adored, mere bread, for adoration. In that case, the people were not guilty of deliberate worship of an idol. The devil also might delude people by a false manifestation, causing worship. Such manifestations should be greeted with a conditional form of adoration. If a priest elevated an unconsecrated host, he was the guilty party; but the bishop could absolve his offense.[210]

A major concern of local bishops who followed the universal canon law was the adequate education of the laity in reverence for the consecrated host. Even where the statutes mentioned above do not say it, the faithful had to be taught from one generation to another to reverence the elevated host and to respond to the clues offered by the great bell and the little bells. By 1208, Bishop William of Paris wanted congregations taught that they should respond to the bells "so that the minds of the faithful are excited to prayer."[211] A statute prepared between Stephen Langton's Council of Oxford (1222) linked teaching adoration of the elevated host to reverence for viaticum being carried to the sick. The canon specified that Christians were to display special reverence, "as if to their Lord

[205] Mansi 24.194, "Item, nullus sacerdos det hostias non consecrates pueris, vel aliis hominibus pro corpore Christi, quia nullo modo fieri debet."

[206] Mansi 23.1192.

[207] Johannes Andreae, *In decretalium libros novella commentaria*, 3, fol. 222ra.

[208] *Excellentissimi Antonii de Butrio ... Super tertium librum decretalium*, fol. 193va.

[209] Johannes Andreae, *In decretalium libros novella commentaria*, 3, fol. 221vb–222ra "Ite, ut dicit, esset contra uenerationem huius sacramenti, si aliqua substantia ibi esset, quae adorari non posset adoratione latriè."

[210] *Die Summa confessorum des Johannes von Erfurt*, 2.122–123.

[211] Mansi 22.768, "Praecipitur, quod in celebratione Missarum, quando Corpus Christi elevator, in ipsa elevatione, vel paulo ante, campana pulsetur, sicut alias fuit statutum: ut sic mentes fidelium ad orationem excitentur."

creator and their redeemer," at the elevation "When bread is transformed into the true body of Christ and what is in the chalice is transformed into His blood by a mystical blessing."[212]

A synodal constitution from Valencia (1254) required that the clergy preach about reverencing the host. It also said the priest should raise the host "cautiously" (*caute*) so that all the people could see it.[213] A fifteenth-century statute for the diocese of Olumouc too urged diligent teaching of the faithful concerning adoration of the host.[214]

Instructions about teaching the laity in pastoral manuals differed little over time and place. Thus William of Pagula, in his *Oculus sacerdotis*, listed among the duties of a priest with cure of souls to instructing parishioners to genuflect when he raised up "the saving host" and to say prayers, whether special ones or the *Pater noster*.[215] The instructions for a parish priest in the *Pupilla occuli* said he was to teach the faithful about adoration of the host and urge that they learn to say the prayer *Salva lux mundi*.[216] John of Freiburg added an instruction about how sinners should react at the elevation. He said they should strike their breasts (*percutere pectus*), expressing their unworthiness and penitence.[217]

This duty entered into the vernacular literature for the clergy and laity alike. Thus John Mirk, in his *Instructions for Parish Priests*, told the clergy to teach their flocks to kneel and raise their hands at the sound of the bell for elevation:

> Teche hem eft to knele downe sone;
> And whenne they here the belle rynge
> To that sakerynge
> Teche hem knele downe bothe ȝonge & olde,
> And bothe here hondes up to holde.

[212] *Council &Synods*, 2/1.142–143, "Sint rectores ecclesiarum et presbiteri diligentes ut summa reverential et honor maximus sacris alteribus exibeatur et maxime ubi sacrosanctum corpus domini reservatur et missa celebretur ... Item, frequenter moneabtur laici ut ubicumque viderint corpus domini defferri statim genua flectant tanquam domino creatori et redemptore suo et iunctis manisbus quousque transierit orent humiliter, et hoc maxime tempore consecrationis in elevatione ostie, quando panis in verum corpus Christi transubstantiatur et id, quod est in calice, in sanguinem mystica benedictione transformatur." A canon of the 1261 provincial Council of Mainz also tied these two acts of veneration, reverencing viaticum and the elevated host, to one another; see Mansi 23.1082. See also the 1410 *Liber synodalis* of the diocese of Salamanca in *Synodicon Hispanum*, 4.130.

[213] Mansi 23.1890.

[214] Pavel Krafl, *Synody a statuta Olomoucké diecéze období středověku* (Praha, 2003), 220.

[215] *Pastors and the Care of Souls*, 146. The reverence to be shown a priest carrying viaticum also was to be taught to the faithful.

[216] Cambridge, Corpus Christi College MS 255, fol. 207ra.

[217] Johannes de Friburgo, *Summa confessorum*, fol. cxxiii[ra] (q. lxxi).

The prayer they were to teach the faithful to use at this moment was "O Jhesu Lorde, welcome thou be."[218] The various versions of *The Lay Folks Mass Book* offer directly to the literate believer instructions on how to act at the elevation. The "litel belle" was to focus the attention of lay persons, who were to kneel, bow their heads, and lift up their hands. Short prayers, including the *Pater noster* and the Creed, could be employed. Some versions of the *Mass Book* recommend instead the popular prayer "Loued be thou, kyng."[219] The Vernon manuscript offered a brief version of such instructions for when "Godes flesh [the priest] raiseth up."[220] Rossell Hope Robbins has argued that these and other prayers in English, most of them not based on Latin originals, offered more emotional release than did the available Latin texts. Robbins also suggested that these be taught to the faithful by parish priests.[221] Although not legal in tone, the vernacular verse exposition of the mass by Gonzalo de Berceo said that the priest who elevated the host without Christ's Passion in his heart profaned the very words he said.[222] French books of hours frequently included elevation prayers among devotions to be used during mass, including familiar Latin texts like *Ave verum corpus* and a prayer often attributed to Pope Boniface VI offering 2,000 years of "true pardon" in Purgatory.[223]

Devout persons did not always react according to script. Medieval holy women were known to hunger for the Eucharist,[224] but some reacted dramatically to the elevation. Thus, when Ida of Nivelles saw the Christ Child in the elevated host at Christmas mass, she reacted with *fear and trembling* (Psalm 54:6). This is exactly the sort of wonder the *Pupilla oculi* and the *Liber synodalis* of Salamanca hoped to regulate but not to prevent.[225] Agnes Blannbekin, apart from her tasting sweetness at communion, saw

[218] John Mirk, *Instructions for Parish Priests*, ed. Edward Peacock (London, 1868), 9–10. Mirk also warned the laity to kneel when they saw the priest carrying "Goddes body"; see *Instructions for Parish Priests*, 10. Mirk went on to detail the practical benefits of seeing the host. Among the other things he thought a chaplain should know was how to bear viaticum fittingly; see *Instructions for Parish Priests*, 57.

[219] *The Lay Folks Mass Book; or, The Manner of Hearing Mass* . . ., ed. Thomas Frederick Simmons. (London, 1879), 36–43; *Catholic England: Faith, Religion and Observance before the Reformation*, trans. R. N. Swanson (Manchester, 1993), 88–89.

[220] *The Lay Folks Mass Book*, 144.

[221] Rossell Hope Robbins, "Levation Prayers in Middle English Verse," *Modern Philology* 40 (1942), 131–146.

[222] *The Collected Works of Gonzalo de Berceo in English Translation*, trans. Jeannie K. Bartha, Annette Grant Cash, and Richard Terry Mount (Tempe, Ariz., 2008), 459.

[223] Virginia Reinberg, *French Books of Hours: Making an Archive of Prayer, c. 1400–1600* (Cambridge, 2012), 188–198 at 192–193.

[224] Caroline W. Bynum, *Holy Feast and Holy Fast: the Religious Significance of Food to Medieval Women* (Berkeley, 1987).

[225] *The Life of Ida the Compassionate of Nivelles, Nun of La Remée*, in *Send Me God*, ed. Martinus Cawley (Turnhout, 2003), 62–64. Ida realized that the priest consumed the host with "trembling reverence"; see *Life of Ida*, 63. Such visions, except one example

visions at the elevation. In one case she saw demons appear to boast how they tried to distract the celebrant of the mass with "fantasies of bad thoughts." She also saw angels present who stayed through that mass. In another instance, Agnes saw "a human face of miraculous beauty" in the elevated host. Agnes feared, when the face turned away from the people to the priest, that this might be "because of Resentment"; but she received her usual consolation at communion. Occasionally there were physical manifestations accompanying her visions. Once, Agnes moved around in a friars' church just after the elevation to see the host, and "her bodily senses fell asleep," possibly a swoon, at the light emitted by the consecrated bread.[226] More intriguing is the story of how she was having a vision of Jesus and, when a "devout woman" nearby nudged her to pay attention to the elevation, Agnes ceased to see the Lord.[227] Although priests may have found the visionary experiences of these women troubling at times, there is no history of synods issuing rules for dealing with them. This is not for lack of concern for women's conduct, such as efforts to discourage them from following viaticum processions in case they might disrupt the solemnity of the proceedings.[228] The local authorities, especially after Clement V issued the decree *Ad nostrum* discussed later, may have left this issue to inquisitors appointed by papal authority.

A vital part of the veneration of the elevated host was alerting the faithful to the event in time to look devoutly toward the altar. This required, as noted above, the ringing of a bell or bells at the Sanctus and the elevation. The use of a small bell in this context was recorded as early as 1216 in the acts of a synod of Segovia.[229] In England the small bell was called the "sacring bell," named from a term commonly used for the consecration of the Eucharistic elements. This bell became an important liturgical object, and a parish was supposed to have at least one. Thus the 1268 legatine constitutions of Cardinal Ottobono Fieschi for England require a parish to have bells for the altar and for use in processions.[230] The statutes of Robert Winchelsey, archbishop of Canterbury, also require parishes to have bells.[231] The bells to be rung included the large

from the ninth century, Became common together with the practice of elevation; see Mossman, *Marquard von Lindau*, 211, citing Peter Browe.

[226] Ulrike Wiethaus, *Agnes Blannbekin, Viennese Beguine: Life and Revelations* (Cambridge, 2002), 48–49, 52, 129.

[227] Wiethaus, *Agnes Blannbekin*, 101.

[228] A Council of Münster threatened women with censures for causing disruptions; see Mansi 24.315. Similarly the 1280 synod of Cologne warned women away from viaticum processions; see Mansi 24.351. Other rules might be applied to devout women, like the prayer to be said before the elevated host, at communion, or when visiting the reserved sacrament in the *Ancrene Wisse*; see Snoek, *Medieval Piety from Relics to the Eucharist*, 245–246.

[229] *Synodicon Hispanum*, 6.258. [230] *Councils & Synods*, 2/2.287.

[231] *Councils & Synods*, 2/2.1385–1386.

ones hung in steeples. Thus the 1282 Council of Lambeth ordered ringing of bells "on one side" of the church to alert the populace, often taken up with daily cares, whether they were in the fields or at home, to the sacring. They were to kneel wherever they were on hearing the sound of the bell. The council also noted that many bishops granted indulgences for honoring the Eucharist thus.[232] Similarly, the 1287 statutes of Exeter, as noted above, specified ringing of the great bell, not just the little one, at the elevation.[233] William Lyndwood glossed a constitution of John Peccham, archbishop of Canterbury, which mentioned ringing bells at the elevation. The text of the statute said: "After the lifting up of Christ's body let the bells be rung at the least of the one side." This was to be done, the archbishop said, to alert workers in the fields and persons still at home to the rite: "That the common people which may not daily hear Mass, wheresoever they be either in the fields or in their houses, may kneel down and receive the indulgences granted by many Bishops." They were to kneel wherever they were, and indulgences might be earned for doing this. (Note that the indulgences came from bishops, not from the pope.) Lyndwood noted that, despite the plural word "bells" in its text, the constitution meant that each parish was to ring one bell. There was no need to ring more than one per church. Lyndwood added that the bell most likely to be heard at a distance should be used for this purpose.[234] The ringing of the "great bell" would explain the case of the accused heretic who mocked a coworker in the fields who heard the elevation bell and began to pray.[235] Lyndwood thought that the faithful should adore at least in the heart.[236] One text of the Devotio Moderna, composed by John Kessel, said hearing the Sanctus bell was an occasion for devout prayer during the work day.[237]

232 *Council & Synods*, 2/2.894, "In elevatione vero ipsius corporis domini pulsentur campane in uno latere, ut populares, quibus celebrationi missarum non vacat cotidie interesse, ubicunque fuerint seu in agris seu in dominibus, flectant genua, indulgentias concessas a pluribus episcopis habituri."; Lyndwood, *Provinciale seu Constitvtiones*, 230–231; *Lyndwood's Provinciale*, 96. Bishops still gave indulgences in the fourteenth century; see C. R. Cheney, "Illuminated Collective Indulgences from Avignon," in *Palaeographica diplomatica et archivistica: Studi in onore di Giulio Battelli*, 2 vols. (Roma, 1979), 2.353–373.

233 See n. 192.

234 Lyndwood, *Prouinciale seu Constitutiones*, 231, "p. *Campanae*. Non intelligas de pluribus illo tempore simul pulsandis in una Ecclesia, quia sufficit unam sonari; sed pluraliter loquitur respectu plurium Ecclesiarum. Et haec pulsatio fieri debet de Campanis illis quae longius possent audiri, quod satis patet per rationem quae sequitur." Lyndwood added a long discussion of indulgences at *Prouinciale seu Constitutiones*, 231–232.

235 John H. Arnold and Caroline Goodson, "Resounding Community: The History and Meaning of Medieval Church Bells," *Viator* 43/1 (2012), 99–130 at 130.

236 Lyndwood, *Prouinciale seu Constitutiones*, 231 "r. *Flectant genua*. Saltem Cordis."

237 *Devotio Moderna*, 207.

In areas where Latin Christians did not predominate, such as on the island of Cyprus, another issue could arise: the failure of non-Latin Christians to respond "properly" to the elevation. Thus a provincial Council of Nicosia ca. 1252, held by Archbishop Hugh, required every priest to teach the faithful to reverence the host at the elevation and when it was carried to the sick. The statute also ordered prelates and priests of the Greek nation and any other to uncover their heads and bow to the elevated host when they were in Latin churches and to do the same when a viaticum procession passed by:

> [3] Again, we admonish and exhort, for the salvation of their souls, and we also order, for the honor of the Christian faith, that all Greek prelates or priests and those of other nations who cherish the name of the Christian religion should admonish and exhort the common people and the populace to show reverence when the host of the Eucharist is raised at the altar in the churches of the Latins, bowing and uncovering their heads, and to do the same when a priest brings [the host] to the sick and when they read the gospel.[238]

This instruction on response to the elevation was repeated in a "Constitution Instructing the Greeks and Others." This text also extended recognition to the leavened bread used by the Greeks, while stating that the use of unleavened bread by the Latins also was valid.[239] The issue of Greek responses to Latin rites surfaced again in the 1340 Council of Nicosia presided over by Archbishop Elias of Nabinaux, a Franciscan master of theology trained in Paris. The council ordered the Greek clergy to "settle on a certain sign" for the faithful to display due reverence "at that hour in which they complete [*or* perfect] the body of Christ, when they are celebrating at the altar." These canons aimed at having reverence paid to the Eucharist according to the liturgical norms of the West, with their emphasis on unleavened bread, transubstantiation, and the elevation of the host signaled with bells.[240]

Cyprus had another issue based on differing liturgical norms. John XXII complained of reverence being shown to unconsecrated bread

[238] Translated, facing the Latin text, in *Synodicum Nicosiense*, 98–101 at 100–101.

[239] *Synodicum Nicosiense*, 126–127. This text quotes a letter of Innocent IV, dated 1254, found in *Synodicum Nicosiense*, 307–311, which urges teaching the faithful to use the prayer *Ave salus mundi.*

[240] *Synodicum Nicosiense*, 262–263, "IV. *Ut aliquo signo admoneantur fideles perfectum esse corpus Christi.* Item, statuimus, et ordinamus, ac etiam mandamus omnibus episcopis Graecis et aliis praesulibus quarumlibet nationum et sacerdotibus earumdem quod debeant ordinare quoddam signum quod possit omnibus audientibus Divinum officium notum esse illa hora qua perfecerint corpus Christi, quando celebrant in altari, ita quod illo tempore corpori Christi exhibeatur reverentia tam debita quam devota." The council's confession of faith reaffirmed transubstantiation; see *Synodicum Nicosiense*, 254–257.

"after the benediction and before the consecration" in Eastern rites. The pope wanted the faithful to be clear that the bread had not been consecrated and thus was not to be given the honor to be paid in Western practice to a consecrated host. John said he was afraid the people would be led into "idolatry or heresy."[241]

Despite the synodal enactments of Archbishops Hugh and Elias, liturgical harmony was not achieved. Nor did the Council of Florence achieve harmony by saying in the 1439 decree of union with the Greeks that "Also, the body of Christ is truly confected in both unleavened and leavened wheat bread, and priests should confect the body of Christ in either, that is, each priest according to the custom of his western, or eastern, church."[242]

This irenic viewpoint on liturgical practice was reflected by the Dominican cardinal Juan de Torquemada in his commentary on the Florentine decree of union. He said that wheat bread was necessary for the sacrament, but the type of bread was not an essential element in the mass. He also said, following Thomas Aquinas, that Greek priests were obligated to celebrate with leavened bread but Latin priests only with unleavened bread.[243] Torquemada said the same thing in his commentary on Gratian's *Decretum*.[244] However, this approach had no apparent traction on the ground in places like Cyprus. Jerome of Prague complained during the fifteenth century that Greek Christians on the island turned away at the elevation. They were taught that the Latins were heretics because the Eucharist was celebrated with unleavened bread.[245]

In a visitation, usually by the local archdeacon, inventories were made of liturgical objects; and any that were lacking or defective were noted.[246] Bells for use in the mass, viaticum processions, and funerals might be specified when a diocese, like that of Exeter, gave detailed instructions for

241 *Synodcum Nicosiense*, 341–345, Document 37.

242 *Decrees of the Ecumenical Councils*, 1.527.

243 Juan de Torquemada, *Apparatus super decretum florentinum unionis Graecorum*, ed. Emmanuel Candal (Roma, 1942), 66–71 at 68, "sacerdotes in altero ipsum debere corpus Christ conficere, ecclesie tamen sue sive Orientalia sive Occidentalia servata consuetudine." See also Torquemada, *Apparatus*, 70–71 on the duty of each priest to use the bread customary in his rite. He still declared the Latin custom "more reasonable" (*rationabilior*). Torquemada cited the recantation of Berengar of Tours to reaffirm the Real Presence; see *Apparatus*, 69.

244 Juan de Torquemada, *Commentaria super decreto* (Venezia, 1579), 5.61A–B.

245 Christopher David Schabel, "The Quarrel Over Unleavened Bread in Western Theology, 1234–1439," in *Greeks, Latins, and Intellectual History 1204–1500*, ed. M. Hinterberger and Schabel (Leuven, 2011), 85–127 at 127.

246 Noël Coulet, *Les visites pastorals* (Turnhout, 1977). English statutes routinely required archdeacons to look at books, vestments, and liturgical objects; see *Councils & Synods*, 2/1.128, 148, 379.

the care of ecclesiastical ornaments.[247] Archbishop Winchelsey made an effort to see that parishioners were not ignorant of their obligations to provide furnishings necessary for the liturgy, specifying, among other things, possession of a small bell for carrying communion to the sick, two bells to use when carrying corpses to church, and bells with ropes to hang in the church tower.[248] However, the archbishop had not ended all possibilities of squabbling within parishes. During a visitation of the diocese of Hereford in 1397, care of the tower bells and the ropes to ring them was a matter disputed between curate and parishioners at Worley, each saying it was the other's duty. This is but one example of many complaints from the same diocese in that year. One parish priest even was accused of letting two women who lived in his manse ring bells and serve at the altar. (These women were suspected too of being his concubines.)[249] Similarly, in fifteenth-century France, the visitations done on behalf of the archdeacon of Josas revealed concerns about bell towers, bells, and ropes. The concerns included whether the laity were to pay for repairs. One squabble was recorded over who was to tug the bell ropes to announce services.[250]

Records of visitations show equipment differing from one parish to another. Poor parishes especially might lack objects the bishops thought essential or have items in need of repair. The presence of hand bells is not always noted in English visitations records, as are books, vestments, sacramental vessels, and the steeple bells of a parish. These, when listed, might be called *campanulle, campanae manuales,* or *tintinnabula*. Some were indicated as having specialized uses, like *pro mortuis*; but most were simply noted as present with the number of them if there was more than one.[251] Thus an inventory of Saints Peter and Paul, Salle in the diocese of Norwich (1368), identified two hand bells but did not specify their uses. Possibly they served more than one function.[252] There are a few

[247] Mansi 24.800–801.

[248] *Pastors and the Care of Souls*, 220. A bishop might also impose care of bells and bell towers on monasteries; see Adam J. Davis, *The Holy Bureaucrat: Eudes Rigaud and Religious Reform in Thirteenth-Century Normandy* (Ithaca, 2006), 90. A parish in the archdeaconry of Totnes was found in 1342 to lack usable bells for elevation, viaticum, or burials; see Coulton, "A Visitation of the Archdeaconry of Totnes in 1342," 120.

[249] *Pastors and the Care of Souls*, 293. See also the complaint from Eardisley in *Pastors and the Care of Souls*, 300. On the women who rang bells, see A. T. Bannister, "Visitation Returns of the Diocese of Hereford in 1397," *The English Historical Review* 44 (1929), 279–289, 444–453, 45 (1930), 92–101, 444–463 at 45.447.

[250] *Visites archidiaconales Josas*, 122, 125, 134, 186, 188, 320, 400, 403.

[251] *Visitations of Churches belonging to St. Paul's Cathedral*, xxxvii. A few references in the 1458 Saint Paul's visitations distinguish *tintinnabula* from *campanae manuales* without any explanation; see *Visitations of Churches*, 72 (Navestock), 99 (Cadyngton).

[252] *Pastors and the Care of Souls*, 227.

references in the visitation inventories to defects in bells or bell towers. Thus the 1458 visitation of Kirkby found that the church had three *tintinabula*, including one lacking its clapper. It also had three *campane manuales* and a Sanctus bell.[253] (In Spain the 1427 visitation of Madrid included occasional notes on the presence of a small bell for the elevation of the host.[254])

Problems with bell towers and their bells also were noted and often in greater detail. Thus the rector of Codrington in the diocese of Hereford was accused during the visitation of 1397 of not just failing to supply bell cords but of using the bell tower to store hay.[255] The 1458 visitation of the churches subject to Saint Paul's Cathedral shows wide variances in towers, bells, and care for ropes. Most had bells, even if they needed new ropes or repairs to the steeple. However, Westlee had no tower; and Twyford had two bells hanging from trees.[256]

Dissent

Transubstantiation was not without critics in the late medieval West, with criticism occasionally directed at the elevation of the host. Attacks on belief in the Real Presence entered into inquisitors' records from the late thirteenth and early fourteenth centuries. Thus the depositions before the tribunal of Toulouse, atop concerns that individuals had eaten the "blessed bread" of the Cathars, included worries that the Church's sacraments were being rejected. More than one deposition said the heretics dismissed the consecrated host as "mere bread," not the body of Christ.[257] The case of Bernard of Souillac connected this accusation directly to the veneration of the host. Pons of Parnac, a Dominican inquisitor, listed among Bernard's errors that he believed "That the consecrated host which the priest elevates is not the true body of Christ but cooked dough." Bernard was accused of saying the same thing about the viaticum carried through the streets and that the body of Christ would have to be bigger than a mountain, since it would

253 *Visitations of Churches belonging to St. Paul's Cathedral*, xxvi, 86.

254 Andrés, "Actas de la visita al arcedianazgo de Madrid en 1427," 179, 193, 201, 205, 216, 241.

255 *Pastors and the Care of Souls*, 297. The deacon temporarily employed at Much Cowarne also was accused of failing to supply bell ropes; see *Pastors and the Care of Souls*, 298.

256 *Visitations of Churches belonging to St. Paul's Cathedral*, xxvi.

257 *Inquisitors and Heretics in Thirteenth-Century Languedoc: Edition and Translation of Toulouse Inquisition Depositions, 1273–1282*, ed. Peter Biller, Caterina Bruschi, and Shelagh Sneddon (Leiden, 2011), 301, 347, 415.

otherwise have been consumed already.[258] A long list of witnesses quoted Bernard as saying such things, as well as claiming he had grain in his chest at home as good as that used to make hosts.[259] One witness, Jean Moret, said that he and two other men hired to work in Bernard's vineyard stopped to pray at the sound of the Sanctus bell. Bernard, he said, asked whether they believed the elevated host was the body of Christ. Jean also reported that his employer claimed the body of Christ had to be bigger than "the Mount of *Vinhar*" not to have been eaten up long ago.[260]

Many of the same opinions can be found in the fourteenth-century inquisitorial register of Jacques Fournier, bishop of Pamiers. Testimony can be found to disbelief in the Real Presence, as well as the topos of the body of Christ needing to be bigger than a mountain.[261] The elevation entered into some cases. Aude Faure reported losing her faith in the Real Presence during the elevation, because she had seen the messy effects of childbirth.[262] Raimond Vaissière was reputed to have said the priest elevated a pastry (*paté*) baked between two irons.[263] Raimond Delaire was said to have denied that the bread shown to the people by the priest was the body of Christ.[264] It was said of Guillaume Bélibaste that he did kneel and uncover his head at the elevation but scarcely looked at the host.[265] Perhaps the most interesting story comes from the testimony concerning Pierre Péllicier. One witness told how, while at Arnaud Faure's workshop in Rabat, Morocco, he heard the Sanctus bell ring. Péllicier, who was present, said that the Muslims could mock Christians for eating the Lord they believe in and adore.[266] Even joking about the Eucharist could lead to trouble. A teenage farmhand named Pierre Aces was reported to inquisitors for joking with friends that the elevated host resembled "a radish or turnip," and that the cup looked like "a jar made of glass."[267]

258 *Inquisitors and Heretics in Thirteenth-Century Languedoc*, 657.
259 *Inquisitors and Heretics in Thirteenth-Century Languedoc*, 659, 661, 663, 667, 669.
260 *Inquisitors and Heretics in Thirteenth-Century Languedoc*, 663.
261 *Regestre d'inquisition de Jacques Fournier (éveque de Pamiers) 1318–1325*, ed. Jean Duvernay, 3 vols. (Paris, 1978), 1.260–261, 272, 278, 295, 364, 2.471, 572, 741, 3.932, 1117.
262 *Heresy and Authority in Medieval Europe*, ed. Edward Peters (Philadelphia, 1980), 262. Aude claimed to have recovered her faith when her nurse prayed for her; see Emmanuel Le Roy Ladurie, *Montaillou: The Promised Land of Error*, trans. Barbara Bray (New York, 1978), 307–308, 323. A friend told Aude a miracle tale, with a child replacing the host and blood in the chalice in place of the wine, in order to defend the Real Presence; see *Montaillou*, 304.
263 *Regestre d'inquisition de Jacques Fournier*, 1.355. Raimond denied the charge; see *Regestre Fournier*, 1.358.
264 *Regestre d'inquisition de Jacques Fournier*, 2.628.
265 *Regestre d'inquisition de Jacques Fournier*, 3.1010–1011.
266 *Regestre d'inquisition de Jacques Fournier*, 3.1075.
267 *Regestre d'inquisition de Jacques Fournier*, 3.1277; *Heresy and Authority*, 263.

Worries about Eucharistic errors made their way into manuals for inquisitors, although in more general terms. The Dominican inquisitor Bernard Gui, writing in the early fourteenth century, reported that the Modern Manichees (Cathars) rejected the sacrament of the Eucharist. He also warned that they substituted blessed bread for the Eucharist, a form of counter-sacrament.[268] The Waldensians were reported to dismiss consecration of the elements by a sinful priest; but they permitted any good person, women included, to consecrate. Gui's description of a Waldensian mass made no reference to elevation or other acts of adoration. According to Gui, the Waldensians used verbal tricks to avoid affirming transubstantiation and also avoided receiving Easter communion except as a means of avoiding suspicion of heresy.[269] Another whole category of error listed by Gui was the effort to use the host and holy oils for magical purposes.[270]

Nicholas Eimeric, another Dominican inquisitor, writing later in the same century, had much the same thing to say about the Cathars and Waldensians.[271] More unusually, Nicholas listed Eucharistic errors supposedly preached by Franciscans in the kingdom of Aragon just before 1370. These he referred to Pope Gregory XI (1370–1378), who had two cardinals issue a letter addressed to the archbishops of Tarragona and Cartagena. Their letter condemned three errors, each of which presumed the body of Christ went away, leaving bread behind, when something untoward happened: dropping the host into mud, having a mouse or other beast nibble one, or when a communicant, especially an unworthy one, chewed the communion he or she received. The Franciscans rallied to their own brothers; and Eimeric was driven out of Aragon for a time, not the only time he was expelled.[272]

268 Bernard Gui, *Manuel de l'inquisietur*, ed. Guillaume Mollat, 2 vols. (Paris, 1964), 1.12–13, 24–25; Gui, *The Inquisitor's Guide: A Medieval Manual on Heretics*, trans. Janet Shirley (Welwyn Garden City, 2006), 36, 44–45.

269 Gui, *Manuel de l'inquisietur*, 1.42–45, 72–73, 80–81; Gui, *The Inquisitor's Guide*, 54–55, 65–66, 75. The Waldensians were anti-sacerdotal, not anti-material, according to Bynum, *Christian Materiality*, 163–164.

270 Gui, *Manuel de l'inquisietur*, 2.22–23, 52–53. See also Gui, *The Inquisitor's Guide*, 153, 167–168

271 Nicholas Eimeric, *Directorium inquisitorum* ... ed. Francisco Peña (Roma, 1587), 273–274, 278–279. This edition includes many authoritative texts on orthodoxy belief drawn from the canon law, including the recantation of Berengar of Tours; see *Directorium inquisitorum*, 247–248 with Peña's notes on Berengar's repentance at 247–248. Eimeric also listed refusal to use unleavened bread in the Eucharist among the errors of the Greeks; see *Directorium inquisitorum*, 303.

272 Eimeric, *Directorium inquisitorum*, 44. Eimeric repeated this list, among other errors condemned by the inquisitors of the kingdom of Aragon, at *Directorium inquisitorum*, 262–264. Peña noted that beasts do not eat sacramentally; see *Directorium inquisitorum*, 44. On Eimeric's controversial actions and their consequences, see Gary Macy, "Nicolas Eymeric and the Condemnation of Orthodoxy," in *The Devil, Heresy and Witchcraft in the*

Other Eucharistic heresies arose after the outbreak of the Great Western Schism in 1378. The story of John Wyclif's death in 1384, as reported by Thomas Gascoigne, is unusual but intriguing in how it illustrates the issue as it arose in England. Wyclif had rejected the doctrine of transubstantiation in favor of a more complex theology, along with his other departures from accepted theological opinions. He also criticized as idolatrous the adoration of the host and other "materialistic" forms of piety.[273] According to Gascoigne, John Horn, who had been Wyclif's curate in his retirement, reported nearly forty years later that the reformer had his fatal stroke during mass, not just during mass but at the moment of elevation. This reads suspiciously like an affirmation of transubstantiation by showing the critic struck down by God.[274] Part of Gascoigne's reason for taking up the story may have been Wyclif's argument that the believer might see Christ's body with the "eye of the mind" (*oculum mentis*) or "mental eye" (*oculum mentale*) rather than the "bodily eye" (*oculum corporale*). Such a distinction might undermine the message to the laity that they were seeing God.[275]

Likewise, one of the accusations made against Jan Hus involved adoration of the sacrament. In a 1411 letter to Pope John XXIII denying the charges his foes lodged against him, Hus took up one about the elevation of the host. The Czech reformer denied saying the material substance of the host remained after consecration, a charge frequently made; however, he also denied saying the host was the body of Christ when elevated but not when the priest replaced it on the corporal.[276]

The Church authorities responded to these dissident beliefs and practices, as they understood them, with condemnation. In May of 1415 the Council of Constance approved four articles condemning Wyclif's ideas about the Eucharist and priestly powers. One article was supposed to prove that the Eucharistic body was not "identically and really" (*identice et realiter*) the same as Christ's body in His "proper corporeal person" (*in propria persona corporali*). Wyclif's doctrine, if presented accurately, removed the tight connection theologians had drawn between Christ

Middle Ages: Essays in Honor of Jeffrey B. Russell, ed. Alberto Ferreiro (Leiden, 1998), 369–381.

[273] Ian Christopher Levy, *John Wyclif: Scriptural Logic, Real Presence, and the Parameters of Orthodoxy* (Milwaukee, 2003), esp. 239–245.

[274] Andrew E. Larsen, "John Wyclif, c. 1331–1384," in *A Companion to John Wyclif: Late Medieval Theologian*, ed. Ian Christopher Levy (Leiden, 2006), 1–65 at 62.

[275] Stephen Penn, "Wyclif and the Sacraments," in A *Companion to Wyclif*, 241–291 at 269–270.

[276] *The Letters of John Hus*, trans. Matthew Spinka (Manchester, 1972), 54 Letter 18.

and the sacrament, including at the elevation.[277] In June of the same year, the council condemned additional articles, including one contending that Wyclif thought the host was bread naturally (*naturaliter*) and Christ's body figuratively (*figuraliter*).[278] Jan Hus was condemned in June, partially for rejecting the condemnation of Wyclif's teachings in the list of articles approved in May of that year, although he himself affirmed an orthodox belief about the sacrament.[279] In May of 1416 Jerome of Prague was condemned at Constance even though he claimed to accept transubstantiation and to believe Augustine, not Wyclif and Hus, on the Eucharist.[280]

This set of condemnations was intended to be enforced by bishops and inquisitors. Pope Martin V, elected at Constance to end the Great Western Schism, issued the bulls *Inter cunctas* and *In eminentis* on February 22, 1418. The first of these bulls, addressed to all archbishops, bishops, and inquisitors everywhere, promulgated articles to be used in interrogations to detect the errors of Wyclifites and Hussites. This text required that suspects affirm the condemnations of Wyclif and Hus issued at Constance. An important article on the Eucharist formulated a question whether the accused believed Christ, not bread and wine, was on the altar once the words of consecration had been said.[281]

The Hussite movement, in open revolt after the execution of Hus at the Council of Constance and the promulgation of the bulls of interrogation, focused intensely on the Eucharist, demanding – as will be discussed in the next chapter – communion under both species for the laity; and the Hussites defeated crusading armies sent against them by the popes. Consequently there was no overt persecution of Hussites in the period of their nearly united opposition to the Catholic authorities, clerical and lay.[282] The movement divided, however, over many issues, including whether to retain or abandon medieval sacramental theology and its expression in practice. The Taborites adopted more spiritual and less literal beliefs and rites than did the more conservative Utraquists, who desired to have communion administered under both species. Consequently, the Taborites questioned both transubstantiation and its

277 *Decrees of the Ecumenical Councils*, 1.411; *Unity, Heresy and Reform, 1378–1460: The Conciliar Response to the Great Schism*, ed. C. M. D. Crowder (New York, 1977), 85.

278 *Decrees of the Ecumenical Councils*, 1.422.

279 *Decrees of the Ecumenical Councils*, 1.431.

280 *Decrees of the Ecumenical Councils*, 1.434.

281 Mansi 27.1204–1215 at col. 1212, "Item, utrum credat, quod post consecrationem sacerdotis in sacramento altaris sub velamento panis & vini non sit panis materialis & vinum materiale, sed idem per omnia Christus, qui fuit in cruce passus, & sedet ad dexteram Patris."

282 Frederick G. Heumann, *John Žižka and the Hussite Revolution* (Princeton, 1950).

expression in the adoration of the consecrated host. Martin Húska, a Taborite theologian, denounced kneeling before the sacrament and adoring the elevated host. Húska claimed such practices were not evident in the primitive Church. Utraquist theologians in Prague argued the opposite case on these points; and Catholics were not the only ones who claimed Taborites emptied monstrances, stamping on consecrated hosts.[283]

Lollards, who looked to Wyclif as their founder, suffered persecution. There was no mendicant inquisition in England, but the bishops did take measures against religious dissent with backing from the Crown once the House of Lancaster was reigning. These inquiries uncovered many Lollards who had unorthodox opinions on Eucharistic theology and practice. They suffered penalties ranging from being compelled to receive communion from local priests to outright burning by the secular arm. One case among many, from 1509, specifically referenced the elevation of the host. William Baker of Cranbrook spoke of a gathering at which it was said of those who attended: "Everyche of theym commyned, held, concluded, and believed that the sacrament of the aulter that the preest did holde above his hede at the sacring tyme was not Christ's body, fleshe and bloode, but oonly brede."[284]

Much earlier, in 1428, Margaret Baxter accused the priests of causing the laity to commit the sin of idolatry, in adoring material bread. Idolatry came not from the priest failing to consecrate but from the teachings of the priests themselves.[285] Such dissident beliefs survived down to the time of the English Reformation. Some of the accused Lollards even used language reflecting Wyclif's Latin writings, while others affirmed sacramental reminiscence in their own terms.[286]

Late medieval and early modern academic canonists showed remarkably little interest in the issues arising at Constance. In fact, avoidance of theological topics is apparent beginning in the early fifteenth century. Commentary on the texts about the Trinity at the beginning of book one of the *Gregorian Decretals* (X 1.1), especially on the canon *Firmiter credimus*, became less frequent. Thus John of Imola commented on

283 Howard Kaminsky, *A History of the Hussite Revolution* (Berkeley, 1967), 407, 427, 455–456, 473.

284 Shannon McSheffrey, *Gender and Heresy: Women and Men in Lollard Communities, 1420–1530* (Philadelphia, 1995), 49–50. On the diversity of Lollard Eucharistic beliefs and practices, see John A. F. Thomson, *The Later Lollards 1414–1520* (Oxford, 1965), 246–247.

285 Sarah Beckwith, *Christ's Body: Identity, Culture and Society in Late Medieval Writings* (London: Routledge, 1993), 24.

286 Anne Hudson, "The Mouse in the Pyx: Popular Heresy and the Eucharist," *Trivium* 26 (1991), 40–53.

the title *De summa Trinitate* in his exposition of the *Decretals*, including a brief discussion of the Eucharist. That material was published in the printed version, but not in the one known Vatican manuscript of part one of book one.[287] Nicholas de Tudeschis, known as Panormitanus, left behind two versions of his commentary on the Gregorian collection. The version that omits the title *De summa Trinitate* is found more often in the Vatican manuscript collections.[288] The printed version of his commentary, which includes a discussion of the Trinity, says little about the Eucharist when discussing *Firmiter credimus*. Its chief message at that relevant passage (v. Una vero) is that only priests may consecrate the Eucharistic elements.[289]

John of Imola never finished his commentary on the third book of the *Decretals*, giving up in the title *De testamentis* (X 3. 26) when he turned to teaching Roman law. His one reference to the elevation said a priest should remove his hood (*caputium*) before elevating the host, also in the presence of his bishop or another ecclesiastical superior.[290] Felinus Sandeus has not left us a commentary on book three of the *Decretals*.[291] Panormitanus did discuss the entire title *De celebratione missarum, et sacramento eucharistiae et divinis officiis*; however, his commentary said nothing about Lollards or Hussites, even though he was writing after the Council of Constance and Martin V had condemned their errors. Panormitanus recited the established teachings of the canonists about the priest instructing the people to reverence the elevated host. He also repeated the past discussion of taking refuge with the Eucharist as it was carried through the streets, saying that the sacrament provided safety for the body, not just for the soul.[292]

Some other canonists showed no interest in these issues when treating the *Gregorian Decretals*. Francesco Accolti did not touch book three of the *Decretals*; and his commentaries on books one, two, and five of the collection avoided dealing with theological and pastoral issues.[293] Filippo Decio, writing on the Decretals early in the sixteenth century, covered what his printer regarded as the "principal" titles. None addressed issues about the

[287] *Johannes de Imola super primo decretalium* . . . (Lyon, 1549), fol. 10ra–b.

[288] Stephan Kuttner and Reinhard Elze, *A Catalogue of Canon and Roman Law Manuscripts in the Vatican Library*, 2 vols. (Città del Vaticano, 1986–1987), 2.103 (John of Imola), 1.282–283, 2.124 (Panormitanus).

[289] Nicholas de Tudeschis, *Prima pars Abb. Panor. super primo Decreti* . . . (Lyon, 1521), fol. 13rb–va.

[290] Johannes de Imola, *Super tertio decretalium* (Lyon, 1547), at fol. 8ra, commenting on regulations for clerical clothing at c. *Clerici* (X 3.1.15).

[291] Felinus Sandeus, *Commentaria* . . . *in V. lib. Decretalium* . . ., 3 vols. (Basel, 1567).

[292] Nicholas de Tudeschis, *Super tertio Decreti* . . . (Lyon, 1521), fol. 216vb–217rb.

[293] *Francisci Accolti,* . . . *In primi, secundi et quinti Decretal. Titulos commentaria* . . . (Venezia, 1581).

sacraments.[294] Even writing when the Reformation was in full flower, Agostino Berò avoided treating sacramental law in a commentary on selected passages of the *Decretals* that he dedicated to Pope Julius III (1550–1555).[295]

Only the Dominican cardinal Juan de Torquemada took up the Hussite challenge briefly via the canon law. Torquemada was a Thomist trained in Paris, and he learned canon law in order to refute the conciliarism propounded by the Council of Basel (1431–1449) as a dogma of the Church.[296] Unlike the professional canonists of his day, he was seriously interested in the sacraments, having involved himself in the debates with the Hussites at Basel and with the Greeks in Florence.[297] When glossing the *De consecratione*, Torquemada took aim briefly at the Utraquists. He argued from the doctrine of concomitance that Eucharist could be received under the species of bread alone because both the body and the blood of Christ were present under the appearance of either species. Consequently, the faithful did not need to receive the consecrated wine as well.[298]

Torquemada discoursed at length on transubstantiation, and this led him to a discussion of the adoration of the host and the possibility of falling into idolatry by reverencing one that had not been consecrated. Augustine had said, in a text excerpted in the canon *Nos autem* (De cons. D. 2 c. 41), that we adore the invisible Godhead under the visible species of bread and wine.[299] Torquemada argued that the human flesh of Christ was not to be adored *cultu latriae*, the form of adoration that belongs to God. (This was the form of adoration displayed at the elevation of the host.) However, since the flesh of Christ is hypostatically united to His divinity: "Then it is said that [Christ's flesh] must be adored with the adoration of *latria* with which the Word to Whom it is united is adored. Christ is adored with one adoration, in as far as there are the two natures, just as in the same adoration both head and feet are adored in one person."[300]

294 *Philippus Decius Mediolanensis super decretalibus solemnia atque utilissima commentaria* ... (Lyon, 1536). The principal titles mentioned in the subtitle are concerned with issues like rescripts and appeals.

295 *Avgustini Beroii ... decretalium commentarii* ... (Lyon, 1550–1551).

296 Thomas M. Izbicki, *Protector of the Faith: Cardinal Johannes de Turrecremata and the Defense of the Institutional Church* (Washington, D.C., 1981), 18–19. On the difficulties Torquemada had interpreting canon law, see Karl Binder, "Kardinal Juan de Torquemada Verfasser der *Nova Ordinatio Decreti Gratiani*," *Archivum Fratrum Praedicatorum* 22 (1952), 268–293.

297 Izbicki, *Protector of the Faith*, 4–5, 8, 12.

298 Torquemada, *Commentaria super decreto*, 5.60A–63B at 63B.

299 *Corpus Iuris Canonici*, 1.1328.

300 Torquemada, *Commentaria super decreto*, 5.115B, "Tunc dicitur, quod est adoranda adoratione latriae, qua adoratur ipsum verbum cui unita est, una enim adoratione adoratur Christus quantum ad vtramque naturam, sicut eadem adoratione adorantur

Torquemada devoted an entire question to the possibility than an unconsecrated host might be adored. He identified reasons there might be a failure to consecrate, including a man not ordained pretending to be a priest or an ordained priest failing to follow the form of the sacrament.[301] The cardinal allowed for the possibility of error, not just deception. A particle of an unconsecrated host might be found on an altar and adored as if consecrated.[302] Torquemada allowed that a person might adore a host out of habit (*habitualiter*). He quoted William of Auxerre to make the point that, if a believer approached an unconsecrated host with habitual reverence, thinking it might be consecrated, this was not a sin. Even a priest could be deceived into lifting up what he thought was a consecrated host.[303] Only knowingly adoring unconsecrated bread truly was idolatry.[304]

Even inquisitorial manuals made little mention of Lollards and Hussites. Thus Peña's additions to Eimeric's manual referred to Wyclif only twice. Once he said that the English heretic shared three condemned errors of the Franciscans of Aragon who had posited the withdrawal of the Real Presence under certain circumstances.[305] Adding to the discussion of procedures, part three of Eimeric's *Directorium*, Peña used Wyclif's condemnation at Constance as an example of posthumous condemnation of a heretic.[306] Peña added to the edition of Eimeric a set of *litterae apostolicae* about the punishment of heretics. It included Martin V's *Inter cunctas* and even Pius II's recantation of the conciliarist errors of his youth, *In minoribus*.[307]

A different penal issue arose in the context of the witch hunt. Johannes Nider said that an inquisitor in the diocese of Lausanne learned how a demon appeared in a gathering of witches, telling them not to "worship the host." They were to stamp on it instead.[308] A woman from Villars in the diocese of Geneva confessed being told by a demon not to worship

in vno caput, & pedes." He went on to say this union required *latria*, not merely *dulia*, the honor paid to saints.

301 Torquemada, *Commentaria super decreto*, 5.116A.

302 Torquemada, *Commentaria super decreto*, 5.116A, "aut potest occurrere casus, quod reperitur in altari hostiae particular aliqua, & adoraretur."

303 Torquemada, *Commentaria super decreto*, 116A: De cons. D. 2 c. 41, "Potest. n. decipi sacerdos, qui porrigit simplicem hostiam credens ibi esse corpus Christi." Torquemada said that it sufficed to know that an unconsecrated host was not to be adored, and he presumed a real priest would not willingly deceive the people; see Torquemada, *Commentaria*, 116B.

304 Torquemada, *Commentaria super decreto*, 116A: De cons. D. 2 c. 41.

305 Eimeric, *Directorium inquisitorum*, 44.

306 Eimeric, *Directorium inquisitorum*, 574–575.

307 Eimeric, *Directorium inquisitorum*, appendix, 69–76, 78–82. Also included was Innocent VIII's *Summis desiderantes*; see *Directorium inquisitorum*, 83–84.

308 *Witch Beliefs and Witch Trials in the Middle Ages: Documents and Readings*, ed. P. G. Maxwell-Stuart (London, 2011), 62.

Christ at the elevation.[309] Jupert of Bavaria was "instructed" to close his eyes at the elevation.[310] A woman of Laach in the Eifel region was accused of hiding under a veil her sneering at the elevated host.[311] Stamping on the host was among the accusations made by witch hunters. At least one of the accused had his foot amputated.[312]

Criticism of the elevation entered the penal aspects of canon law in another way. The Council of Vienne (1311–1312), convoked by Pope Clement V, legislated against errors supposedly embraced by certain Beguines and Beghards. In Clement's canon *Ad nostrum*, one error attributed to the Beguines and Beghards of Germany was that they were dismissive of the elevation in comparison to their mystical experiences:

> Eighthly, that at the Elevation of the body of Jesus Christ, they ought not to rise or show reverence to it; it would be imperfection for them to come down from the purity and height of their contemplation so far as to think about the ministry or sacrament of the Eucharist, or about the Passion of Christ as man.[313]

This condemnation was included in the *Clementine Constitutions*, reissued in 1317 after Clement's death by Pope John XXII, under the title *De haereticis* (Clem. 5.3.3).[314]

Guillelmus de Monte Lauduno, in one of the earliest commentaries on the *Clementines*, briefly reminded his readers that heretics confused the vulnerability of the human body of Christ with the perfection of God present in the sacrament.[315] The Ordinary Gloss of Johannes Andreae on *Ad nostrum* addressed this error too and in greater depth. Johannes accused these heretics of failing to give due honor to Christ's humanity, especially to His flesh, citing Augustine to support that point.[316] The canonist also extended the biblical argument for eating Christ's flesh in the sacrament to eating it spiritually. Johannes added that even the Virgin

[309] *Witch Beliefs and Witch Trials in the Middle Ages*, 165.

[310] *Witch Beliefs and Witch Trials in the Middle Ages*, 191.

[311] *Witch Beliefs and Witch Trials in the Middle Ages*, 218.

[312] *Witch Beliefs and Witch Trials in the Middle Ages*, 154, 166.

[313] *Decrees of the Ecumenical Councils*, 1.383–384 at 384. This error is one of those attributed to the so-called heresy of the Free Spirit, and it resembles one extracted from the *Mirror of Simple Souls* by Marguerite Porete; see Robert E. Lerner, *The Heresy of the Free Spirit in the Later Middle Ages* (Berkeley, 1972), 81–84.

[314] *Corpus Iuris Canonici*, 2.1183–1184. Elizabeth Makowski, *"A Pernicious Sort of Woman": Quasi-Religious Women and Canon Law in the Later Middle Ages* (Washington, D.C., 2005), 4, 25–26, 31.

[315] Guilelmus de Monte Lauduno, *Apparatus ... super Clementinas ...* (Paris, 1517), fol. cli[ra], accessed via Google Books, January 1, 2014.

[316] Ordinary Gloss at Clem. 5.3.3, "quoniam sanctum est. quod de Christi humanitate et specialiter de Christi carne exponit aug."

and the great saints were not without imperfection.[317] Paulus de Liazariis, commenting on the same text, said these heretics fatuously thought themselves superior not just to the pope and other prelates but to Christ Himself.[318] Paulus said their arrogant refusal to adore the sacrament "proceeds from an insane head" (*ab insano capite procedit*).[319]

The opinions of Johannes Andreae and Paulus de Liazariis were repeated by later writers. Franciscus de Zabarellis summarized the argument attributed to heretical mystics that contemplating God was more important than reverencing the Eucharist.[320] Zabarella repeated the opinion of Paulus de Liazariis that these heretics fatuously thought themselves superior even to Christ Himself, not admitting the unity of Christ's humanity and divinity. They did not understand that, in the order of nature, inferiors (themselves) should reverence superiors (Christ present in the sacrament).[321] John of Imola described that error about elevation as "insanity and heresy" (*insania et heresis*). Those who thought themselves too perfect to adore were denounced for failing to follow biblical teaching and thinking themselves more perfect than the saints.[322]

This error and others attributed to Beguines and Beghards later appeared in Juan de Torquemada's *Summa de ecclesia* in his enumeration of the heresies that had afflicted the Church from its earliest days to his own time.[323] Nicholas Eimeric, however, treated Beguines and Beghards as interchangeable with Fraticelli and only addressed the errors of the latter in his inquisitorial manual.[324]

Veneration of the Real Presence of Christ in the Eucharist had been encouraged by prelates and lawyers from the thirteenth century onwards. Medieval canon law had been slow at first to recognize the elevation of the host as a liturgical practice, but efforts were made eventually to regulate it. Mostly, these regulations focused on the priest's proper actions or how he was to teach the laity to react. The concern that the faithful not be led into

317 Ordinary Gloss at Clem. 5.3.3, "Sed qua ratione tenetur quis corpus Christi summere et spiritualiter manducare."

318 Paulus de Liazariis, *Super clementinis*, University of Notre Dame MS Latin e.3, fol. xliii[vb], "uel ex sui fatuitate dicebant se equales uel maiores Christo nedum pape et aliorum prelatorum."

319 Paulus de Liazariis, *Super clementinis*, fol. xlii[vb].

320 Franciscus de Zabarellis, *Lectura super clementinis* ... (Venezia, 1481), fol. [180][ra].

321 loc. cit. 322 Johannes de Imola, *Super clementinis* (Lyon, 1525), fol. 132rb.

323 Juan de Torquemada, *Summa de ecclesia una cum eiusdem Apparatu super decreto Eugenii papae IV in Concilio Florentino de unione Graecorum emanato* (Venezia, 1561), fol. 407v: Lib. IV, pars 2, c. xxxvi. Torquemada condemned the Eucharistic errors of the Cathars at Torquemada, *Summa*, fol. 406v: Lib. IV, pars 2, c. xxxv, but he ignored Waldensian rejection of the sacrament consecrated by a sinful priest. He listed the Eucharistic errors of Wyclif at Torquemada, *Summa*, fol. 410r: Lib. IV, pars 2, c. xxxviii.

324 Eimeric, *Directorium inquisitorum*, 282–298.

idolatry by defects in the mass surfaced early, and it explains the reasoning behind many of these enactments. The emphasis on the Real Presence required that only the transubstantiated host should be venerated, not mere bread, the Creator and not His creation. Dismissing the elevation as the exaltation of mere bread was among the errors inquisitors were charged with pursuing. All of these concerns required practical measures, including giving of signals to the laity whether Christ was or was not present. Thus efforts were made, at the local level, to see that bells were available to call attention to the most dramatic moment in the mass and incite the faithful to true devotion when Jesus was sacramentally present. This form of devotion was treated as efficacious apart from the infrequent reception of communion by most lay persons.

3 Communion

Union with Christ and unity in the sacrament

Communion became infrequent during the Middle Ages. Frequent communion was not discouraged in late Antiquity, but an increased fear of unworthy reception militated against it. This fear was tied to a Pauline text in 1 Corinthians (11:29) warning that anyone eating and drinking unworthily ate condemnation and could be "guilty of the Lord's body and blood."[1] This fear had to be juxtaposed against the idea that receiving communion identified loyal members of the Church. The requirement that communion be received on three major feasts, Christmas, Easter, and Pentecost, became a part of canon law; but a person conscious of sin might hesitate to receive even on those feasts. The rule of reception three times a year was displaced eventually by a new requirement, embodied in the canon *Omnis utriusque sexus* of the Fourth Lateran Council (X 5. 38.12), that the faithful had to confess and receive "reverently" at Easter. Thus confession and absolution preceded communion, which identified the faithful believer.[2] This Easter Duty, including its emphasis on both sacraments being administered by one's own pastor, the "proper priest,"[3] became an established part of canon law and pastoral practice. Its development ran alongside a move toward communion under a single species, the consecrated bread, especially since the consecrated wine, the Lord's blood, might be spilled by accident.[4] The doctrine of

[1] See, for example, Amalar of Metz, *On the Liturgy*, ed. Eric Knibbs, 2 vols. (Cambridge, Mass.: Harvard University Press, 2014), 2.226–227, where the text is used to promote fasting before communion.

[2] See a translation of the Lateran canon in *Heresy and Authority in Medieval Europe: Documents in Translation*, ed. Edward Peters (Philadelphia, 1980), 177–178. *Omnis utriusque* was so important that John Wyclif denounced it as compelling obedience to the Devil; see *Trialogus*, trans. Stephen E. Lahey (Cambridge, 2013), 335–336.

[3] John Peccham treated the two functions of a *proprius sacerdos* as inseparable; see *Quodlibeta quatuor*, ed. Girard J. Etzkorn and Ferdinand M. Delormen (Grottaferrata, 1989), 275. See also the Winchester Statutes of 1224 in *Council & Synods*, 2/1.129.

[4] Nicholas of Cusa argued against the Hussites that this was one reason why giving communion under both species ceased; see Nicholas of Cusa, *Writings on Church and Reform*, trans. Thomas M. Izbicki (Cambridge, Mass., 2008), 56–57, 80–83. Spilling was a major defect in the mass, which could cause priest and server to do penance; see Guido de

concomitance, the teaching that the risen Christ was whole in the sacrament, even if visibly separate in the two species, prevailed, helping explain why drinking from the chalice was not required. This remained true in practice through most of Europe despite the Hussite demand for communion from the chalice, not just the paten, also known as Utraquism.

Behind these doctrinal and disciplinary issues lay a more spiritual vision of the effects of receiving the Eucharist. This was spiritual feeding to build up the body of Christ in love. Thus a 1368 Council of Levaux in France, in a canon affirming the seven sacraments, described the Eucharist as the sacrament of charity, binding the faithful together, and a remedy against malice.[5]

Reception of the Eucharist and its effects

Many of the most influential canons concerning the Eucharist were inherited from Antiquity, but others were added to the canon law in the early Middle Ages. The Pseudo-Isidorean or False Decretals included some references to communion and related practices. "Pope Alexander" said the Passion of Christ was remembered, and thus sins were blotted out. This was true because there was no greater sacrifice than the body and blood of Christ. These gifts were to be offered and received "with a pure conscience" (*pura conscientia*).[6] A canon attributed to "Clement" required consuming the offerings made at the altar that were not used in the liturgy, but it warned against mixing those offerings with daily food.[7] An African council required that mass be celebrated "only by men who have fasted" (*a ieiunis hominibus celebratur*).[8] "Clement" wanted a priest not to go to his wife before going to the altar.[9] A text attributed to Leo I described the communicant as becoming the flesh of the one "who was made our flesh" (*qui caro nostra factus est*).[10] A canon from a Council of Carthage said a deacon could distribute communion in the presence of the priest "in a case of necessity" (*si necessitas cogit*).[11] A decree of "Pope Julius," actually a canon of the Third Council of Braga, forbidding communion by intinction, appeared. Each element was to be received separately, following the testimony of Scripture, except in the case of the

Monte Rocherii, *Manipulus curatorum* (London, 1508), fol. xlii^r; Guido, *Handbook for Curates*, 104–105.

5 Mansi 26.488, "Eucharistia, caritatis . . . Eucharistia contra malitiam."

6 Hinschius, 99, "Nihil enim in sacrifitiis maius esse potest quam corpus et sanguis Christi."

7 Hinschius, 47. 8 Hinschius. 299 (Third Carthage c. 29). 9 Hinschius, 48.

10 Hinschius, 572. 11 Hinschius. 304 (Fourth Carthage c. 38).

dipped morsel given to Judas at the Last Supper.[12] Other passages in the text attributed to "Julius" reaffirmed the use of bread and wine against wrong practices like using milk. It also required using watered wine, saying the wine represented Christ and the water the people united to him. Both of these were necessary, or the Lord's chalice (*calix Domini*) of the Last Supper would not be on the altar.[13] The Council of Agde said the laity should receive three times a year, on Christmas, Easter, and Pentecost. Otherwise they might not be regarded as Catholics.[14] (Later collections, like the *Decretum* of Burchard of Worms, included texts attributed to "Fabian," "Soter," and other popes represented in the Isidorean Decretals.)

Regino of Prüm prepared questions to be asked priests about the celebration of mass. Among these was an inquiry whether the priest celebrated at a fitting hour and did so fasting. Regino said celebrating after eating or drinking was presumptuous.[15] Another question was whether the priest sang mass but did not receive the sacrament.[16] Whether another's parishioner attended the parochial mass, except if that person was traveling, also was topic for inquiry.[17] Regino's questions included whether the priest warned the parish to receive communion three times in a year, at Christmas, Easter, and Pentecost.[18] The priest also was to teach abstaining from work from sunrise to sundown on Sundays and feast days.[19] He also was to teach the parish orthodox interpretations of the Creed and *Pater noster*.[20] Regino cited numerous canons in support of these inquiries about discipline, including a text of Augustine on frequency of communion, saying he neither accepted nor rejected daily communion.[21] More than one text included denounced exacting payment for the sacraments, while one forbade giving the sacraments to another's parishioners.[22] Those who did not receive communion were to be regarded as causing "disturbances of the Church"

[12] Hinschius, 434, "nec hoc prolatum ex evangelio testimonium recipit, ubi apostolis corpus suum et sanguinem commendavit, seorsum enim panis e sorsum calicis commendatio memoratur."

[13] loc. cit.

[14] Hinschius, 333, saying those who did not receive "catholici non credantur nec inter catholicos habeantur."

[15] *Das Sendhandbuch des Regino von Prüm*, 28, "Si presyter quod absit, postquam cibum aut potum sumserit, missam celebrare praesumat."

[16] *Das Sendhandbuch des Regino von Prüm*, 30.

[17] loc. cit.

[18] *Das Sendhandbuch des Regino von Prüm*, 32.

[19] *Das Sendhandbuch des Regino von Prüm*, 34.

[20] *Das Sendhandbuch des Regino von Prüm*, 36.

[21] *Das Sendhandbuch des Regino von Prüm*, 176–177.

[22] *Das Sendhandbuch des Regino von Prüm*, 72–73, 86–89, 138–139.

(*inquietudines ecclesie*); and they were especially to receive on Christmas, Easter, or Pentecost unless impeded by major crimes.[23] Regino's canons on communion required both celebrant and communicants to be fasting, and married persons were expected to refrain from sexual activity.[24] Penances were imposed on those who vomited up the host.[25]

In Burchard's *Decretum*, communion was treated, in a canon attributed to "Pope Clement," as the reception of the body and blood. Great discretion was urged by "Clement" about receiving communion, because unworthy reception could be harmful to the soul.[26] However, Burchard included Augustine's text saying he neither accepted nor rejected daily communion, since the effects depended on the communicant's state of soul. He did exhort the faithful to communicate on Sundays.[27] A canon of a Council of Rouen said the priest and his deacon or subdeacon should receive. The laity was not to touch the Eucharist; but the priest was to place a host in each mouth, while saying "The body and blood of the Lord benefit you for the remission of sins and eternal life." Any priest who transgressed this decree was to be "removed from the altar" (*ab altari removeatur*).[28]

Burchard included in his *Decretum* the canon from a Council of Carthage saying a deacon should distribute communion in the presence of the priest "in a case of necessity" (*si necessitas cogit*).[29] Burchard also included a text of "Pope Fabian," saying the laity should receive three times a year, unless "impeded by major crimes" (*nisi forte quia majoribus quibuslibet criminibus impediatur*).[30] Another text, attributed to "Pope Soter," added Holy Thursday to the days for obligatory communion.[31] The *Decretum* also required a man to abstain from intercourse with his wife three, five, or even seven days before receiving.[32] Burchard included texts imposing penances on those who vomited up the Eucharist, especially on account of drunkenness.[33]

[23] *Das Sendhandbuch des Regino von Prüm*, 112–113, 178–179. The latter text is from a Carolingian capitulary found in the collection of Ansegisus.
[24] *Das Sendhandbuch des Regino von Prüm*, 32, 110–111, 182–183.
[25] *Das Sendhandbuch des Regino von Prüm*, 100–101.
[26] Burchardus Wormatiensis, *Decretum*, V c. 14, PL 140.755B.
[27] Burchardus Wormatiensis, *Decretum*, V c. 15, PL 140.755C–D.
[28] Burchardus Wormatiensis, *Decretum*, V c. 76, PL 140.689D–690A at 690A, "Corpus Domini et sanguis prosit tibi ad remissionem peccatorum et ad vitam aeternam."
[29] Burchardus Wormatiensis, *Decretum*, V c. 14, PL 140.755B.
[30] Burchardus Wormatiensis, *Decretum*, V c. 14, PL 140.756A. See also the Council of Agde at Burchardus, *Decretum* V c. 23, PL 140.757A. A text of "Pope Silverius" said to receive daily during Lent; see Burchardus, *Decretum* V c. 19, PL 140.756C.
[31] Burchardus Wormatiensis, *Decretum*, V c. 20, PL 140.756C–D. This text appears in Gratian's *Decretum* as c. *In cena Domini* (De cons. D. 2 c. 17).
[32] Burchardus Wormatiensis, *Decretum*, V c. 22, PL 140.757A.
[33] Burchardus Wormatiensis, *Decretum*, V c. 46, 48 & 49, PL 140.761C & 762A.

The canonistic collections of the Gregorian Reform included some instructions about communion. Anselm of Lucca placed in his collection the requirement of an African council that mass be celebrated "only by men who have fasted" (*a ieiunis hominibus celebratur*).[34] According to Augustine, those made members of Christ in the Church's unity through baptism could not be denied participation in "the fellowship of Christ's body" (*consortio*), the Eucharist, receiving body and blood, bread and wine.[35] Anselm included texts of Leo the Great underlining the spiritual nourishment provided by communion, "the food of refreshment" (*cibus refectionis*).[36] A text by Augustine said the bad received but did not benefit spiritually. The text referenced both the morsel given to Judas and Paul's text about eating a condemnation as proofs of this truth.[37] Other passages from Augustine's works warned against participating in the sacraments of heretics, "because ours are not human but divine" (*quia non humana sunt sed divina*).[38]

Ivo of Chartres gave more attention to priestly powers and the Eucharist than had most of his predecessors. In his letter on these topics, quoting from Augustine, he said the power to consecrate followed the conferral of orders, not personal worth, assuring that Christians had access to the means of grace.[39] In Ivo's *Decretum*, an excerpt from Augustine's works emphasized the feeding the Eucharist provided, so that the faithful who were fed belonged to Christ. Those who received the sacrament of unity at Christ's table (*in mensa sua*), however, without adhering to the "bond of peace" (*vinculum pacis*) were witnesses against themselves.[40] Another canon treated the manna the Jews ate in the desert as a "figure" of Christ in the sacrament. Whoever understood this, received "spiritual food" (*cibum spiritualem*).[41] This food was eaten inwardly, not outwardly, with the heart rather than the teeth. The act of eating and drinking frequently at the Lord's Table promoted the unity of Christ's body. This was the sacrament of unity (*sacramentum, id est unitatis*).[42] The *Decretum* included a passage from Hilary of Poitiers saying a Christian was united to the Father via the flesh of the Son,

[34] Anselm of Lucca, *Collectio canonum una cum collectione minore*, ed. Friedrich Thaner (Innsbruck, 1906–1915; Aalen, 1965), 460.
[35] Anselm of Lucca, *Collectio canonum*, 467.
[36] Anselm of Lucca, *Collectio canonum*, 461.
[37] Anselm of Lucca, *Collectio canonum*, 462.
[38] Anselm of Lucca, *Collectio canonum*, 479–480. See also Ivo Carnotensis, *Decretum*, PL 161.136C.
[39] Ivo Carnotensis, *Epistola 63*, PL 161.80C–81A, 182D.
[40] Ivo Carnotensis, *Decretum*, PL 161.135A–C.
[41] Ivo Carnotensis, *Decretum*, PL 161.136A–B.
[42] Ivo Carnotensis, *Decretum*, PL 161.137D, 138B.

born of Mary, creating "a unity of will" (*voluntatis unitas*).[43] A text of Ambrose said remission of sins was granted those who ate worthily.[44] The larger intellectual context of this portion of Ivo's *Decretum* was established by the Berengarian controversy. Thus, a long passage from Lanfranc of Bec distinguishing the visible species from the invisible body and blood. The presence of the latter, the *res sacramenti*, was "a mystery of faith that can be believed wholesomely" (*Mysterium fidei credi salubriter potest*).[45]

Ivo provided, atop these more theological excerpts, plenty of practical material. The decree of "Pope Julius" forbidding communion by intinction appears.[46] The decree from Carthage about communion being given by a deacon in a case of necessity also was included.[47] The priest was required to receive under both species, so that the wholeness of the sacrament was maintained.[48] The "Clement" text offering cautions about unworthy reception being harmful to the soul was included in the *Decretum* of Ivo.[49] Augustine's discussion of the possibility of daily communion follows.[50] The requirement of "Pope Fabian" that communion was to be received on the three major feasts and that of "Pope Silverius" on reception on Holy Thursday also appear.[51] So too does a decree requiring abstention from marital relations for three days before reception of the sacrament.[52] The faithful also, according to Augustine, were to receive while fasting.[53] Familiar texts about vomiting the sacrament, including penalties for receiving while drunk, were present.[54] A decree attributed to Pope Gelasius said not to give communion to those possessed by demons or irrational passions.[55] The faithful, in turn, were supposed to avoid the sacraments of "pseudo-priests."[56] God, according to Jerome, hated the festivals of heretics.[57] No one, according to a canon

[43] Ivo Carnotensis, *Decretum*, PL 161.139A.

[44] Ivo Carnotensis, *Decretum*, PL 161.143A.

[45] Ivo Carnotensis, *Decretum*, PL 161.153A–B. The text of Berengar's recantation follows at Ivo, *Decretum*, PL 161.160D–162A.

[46] Ivo Carnotensis, *Decretum*, PL 161.162B–163B. See also Ivo, *Decretum*, PL 161.181A–B.

[47] Ivo Carnotensis, *Decretum*, PL 161.166A.

[48] Ivo Carnotensis, *Decretum*, PL 161.182A.

[49] Ivo Carnotensis, *Decretum*, PL 161.166B.

[50] Ivo Carnotensis, *Decretum*, PL 161.166C–D.

[51] Ivo Carnotensis, *Decretum*, PL 161.167A–B, 167C. See also Ivo, *Decretum*, PL 161.168B on those who do not communicate on the major feasts not being regarded as Catholics.

[52] Ivo Carnotensis, *Decretum*, PL 161.168A–B.

[53] Ivo Carnotensis, *Decretum*, PL 161.190D–191B.

[54] Ivo Carnotensis, *Decretum*, PL 161.172C–D, 173A–B.

[55] Ivo Carnotensis, *Decretum*, PL 161.181D–182A. A decree of "Pope Pius" said priests vexed by demons were not supposed to handle holy things; see Ivo, *Decretum*, PL 161.195C–D.

[56] Ivo Carnotensis, *Decretum*, PL 161.184A–C, 184C–186A.

[57] Ivo Carnotensis, *Decretum*, PL 161.189C–D.

attributed to Leo IX, was to exact payments for baptism, the Eucharist, visitation of the sick, or burial of the dead.[58] This text aligned Ivo with the Gregorian attack on simony, as did an extensive decree of Pope Paschal in the *Decretum*.[59]

The *Panormia* employed many of the same texts appearing in Ivo's *Decretum*. Thus an excerpt from Ambrose on the Eucharist emphasizes spiritual refreshment.[60] A text of Augustine says, "the Eucharist is the visible form of invisible grace" (*invisibilis gratie visibilis forma*).[61] The one who believed in Christ "ate" Him.[62] Eating and drinking brought to mind the liberating death of Jesus, whereas the fraction of the host showed Christ on earth, present at mass and in the tomb.[63] The collection includes a text of Augustine about the different effects on the worthy and the unworthy of receiving the Eucharist. The unworthy person incurs "a great torment" (*magnum tormentum*).[64] The *Panormia* also contains the prohibition of intinction as a form of communion,[65] also Augustine's discussion of daily communion.[66] "Pope Fabian" on reception on Christmas, Easter, and Pentecost follows immediately.[67] Also included is the rule of refraining from marital intercourse for three days before taking communion.[68] One of the texts about penances for vomiting the Eucharist is repeated.[69] Some copies contain the Carthage text about the deacon giving communion in the presence of the priest.[70]

Gratian's *Decretum* included passages about the reception of the Eucharist drawn from some of these earlier sources. The patristic texts excerpted were the most concerned with the spirituality of communion. A text from Augustine's exposition of the Psalms, c. *Prima quidem* (De cons. D. 2 c. 44), said that the sacrament should be received spiritually and not carnally. The former meant participation in the life-giving Spirit. The latter meant not just flesh, but dead flesh (*cadaver*). Augustine used the biblical text, "Unless you eat the flesh of the Son of Man and drink His blood, you have no life in you" (John 6:53), in this context. One of his letters, excerpted as c. *Non hoc corpus* (De cons. D. 2 c. 45), emphasized celebrating visibly but understanding invisibly. This fits with c. *Ut quid* (De cons. D. 2 c. 47), which treated believing as eating. Another text of Augustine, c. *Quid est* (De cons. D. 2 c. 46), said that many ate, but some ate unworthily. These canons threatened those who ate unworthily with

[58] Ivo Carnotensis, *Decretum*, PL 161.83B. See also Ivo, *Decretum*, PL 161.182C–D. However, offerings were to be given to priests after mass on major feasts; see Ivo, *Decretum*, PL 161.169D.

[59] Ivo Carnotensis, *Decretum*, PL 161.179C–181A. [60] *Panormia Project*, 72.

[61] *Panormia Project*, 76. [62] *Panormia Project*, 81. [63] *Panormia Project*, 84, 83.

[64] *Panormia Project*, 80–81. [65] *Panormia Project*, 88. [66] *Panormia Project*, 90–91.

[67] *Panormia Project*, 91. [68] *Panormia Project*, 92. [69] *Panormia Project*, 94.

[70] *Panormia Project*, 26.

damnation (e.g. c. *Timorem*, De cons. D. 2 c. 25). Another canon, c. *Hoc est* (De cons. D. 2 c. 48), distinguished between the visible elements and the invisible body and blood of Christ. Christ's body was both a sign (*sacramentum*) and the thing signified (*res sacramenti*). The body was offered on the cross for redemption. This was, as c. *Quia morte* (De cons. D. 2 c. 50) said, the death that we commemorate by sacramental eating. This body was offered daily, as Ambrose said (c. *In Christo*, De cons. D. 2 c. 53), as a memorial of Christ's self-offering. This commemoration required fasting before reception of the saving sacrament (c. *Liquido*, De cons. D. 2 c. 54). Another canon, from a Council of Toledo (c. *Omnis homo*, De cons. D. 2 c. 21), said any married man who wished to receive should abstain from intercourse with his wife for as much as a week before. The sacrament of the Eucharist also was the sign of unity. Those who wanted to live eternally had to be incorporated into the body through sacramental eating (c. *Hoc sacramentum*, De cons. D. 2 c. 63; c. *Panem*, De cons. D. 2 c. 54).

One of the most influential early commentaries on the *Decretum*, that by Rufinus, addressed communion. He commented on the prohibition of intinction, comparing it with the dipped morsel Jesus gave to Judas at the Last Supper (John 13:26). Otherwise, Rufinus emphasized reverence in receiving communion. The priest was to receive under both species. The others who received, if married, were to abstain from marital relations for at least three days before reception out of reverence. Communion was to be received by the worthy, but they had to receive at least three times a year: "He should not receive communion more rarely than three times in the year, that is, Christmas, Easter and Pentecost."[71] Rufinus allowed an exception to this rule for "unworthy" persons, who would eat a judgment on themselves. Such persons should be warned to "do penance" (*agere penitentiam*) to become worthy of communion. The canonist noted a statement of Burchard that communion could not be received before a penance was completed.[72] The sacrament was to offer the soul of the penitent "spiritual nourishment" (*spiritualis refectio anime*).[73] Worthy communicants were united to Christ "by the dignity of charity, innocence and justice" (*per dignitatem caritatis, innocentie et iustitie*).[74] The Eucharist effected perfect union with Christ, since it was the sacrament of unity.

[71] Rufinus, *Summa decretorum*, ed. Heinrich Singer (Paderborn, 1902; Aalen, 1963), 551–552 at 552: De cons. D. 2 c. 1, "rarius vero quam in tribus temporibus anni – scil. in nativitate, pasca, pentecoste – communicare non debet." Rufinus attributed this rule to "Pope Anacletus" at *Summa decretorum*, 553: De cons. D. 2 c. 10.

[72] Rufinus, *Summa decretorum*, 554: De cons. D. 2 c. 17, citing Burchard's *Decretum*, Bk. 5 c. 19.

[73] Rufinus, *Summa decretorum*, 555: De cons. D. 2 c. 39.

[74] Rufinus, *Summa decretorum*, 557: De cons. D. 2 c. 80.

Human beings already shared a "nature" with Christ, but this was not realized as fully as possible without the sacrament: "And just as the Father and the Son are one by unity of substance, so anyone is made one with them properly by unity of nature with the Son, with the Father in the same way, because we are made one with the Father by the natural unity which is between us and the Son."[75]

Recipients were to avoid "gluttony or drunkenness" (*voracitas vel ebreitas*). Anyone who vomited for one of these reasons was to be punished "harshly" (*acriter*), but even a sick person had to do seven days of penance.[76] Communicants who had received without fasting, unless receiving viaticum, had to do penance. Children were to do three days of penance, adults seven but clerics twenty, a rule Rufinus also attributed to Burchard.[77]

In the North, the commentary *Fecit Moyses tabernaculum*, which was influenced by Rufinus's work, said that many texts in the *Decretum* proved Christians who received the body and blood were enabled to be one with Christ.[78] However, even the wicked and reprobate received "the true body of Christ" (*veram Christi carnem*).[79] The author, in the light of this, noted the difference between sacramental and spiritual eating, the latter feeding only the faithful.[80] There were two aspects of the Corpus Christi, the body born of the Virgin and unity of the faithful (*de unitate fidelium*). The body on the altar and the "unity of faith" (*unitas fidei*) were the visible aspects of the sacrament.[81] (The *Distinctiones monacenses* said

[75] Rufinus, *Summa decretorum*, 558–559 at 559: De cons. D. 2 c. 82, "Et sicut pater et filius unum sunt unitate substantie, ita faciunt nos unum esse secum unitate nature cum filio quidem proprie, cum patre eodem modo, quia mediante illa naturali unitate, que est inter nos et filium, unum cum patre efficimur." Rufinus noted, citing Hilary, that the union of the Christian with the Father was via our "natural unity" with the Son; see *Summa decretorum*, 560: De cons. D. 2 c. 82, "Asserit ergo nos unum fieri cum filio, non tantum unitate voluntatis, sed etiam unitate nature et substantie, et hoc per sacramentum corporis et sanguinis eius. Et sic mediante filio unum efficimus cum patre quodam modo unitate nature, i. e. media naturali unitate, quam constat esse inter nos et filium esse."

[76] Rufinus, *Summa decretorum*, 552: De cons. D. 2 c. 1.

[77] Rufinus, *Summa decretorum*, 556: De cons. D. 2 c. 54, employing Burchard's *Decretum*, Bk. 5 c. 35.

[78] Corrected at the underlined words from *Die Summa über das Decretum Gratiani*, 276: De cons. D. 2 c. 82, "Verum Christi corpus et sanguis in altari nos sumere quod iam multis auctoritatibus probatum est et hic probat Gratianus per hoc, quod sacramento hoc participantes unus cum Christi natura efficimur." See also *Summa über Summa über das Decretum Gratiani*, 274.

[79] *Die Summa über das Decretum Gratiani*, 276: De cons. D. 2 c. 92.

[80] *Die Summa über das Decretum Gratiani*, 275: De cons. D. 2 cc. 46–47. "secundum quae duo hic inuuntur modi manducandi, sacramentalis scil. et spiritualis ... Spiritualis manducandi modus evidenter exprimitur [sequitur similis expositio]."

[81] *Die Summa über das Decretum Gratiani*, 275: De cons. D. 2 c. 45.

that what was consumed visibly in the sacrament was eaten and drunk spiritually in truth.[82]) *Fecit Moyses* affirmed concomitance, as evident in the fraction of the host into three pieces, each containing the whole Christ.[83] This also allowed the author to say that only the priest had to receive both species, because he represented Christ (*qui figuram Christi gerit*).[84]

In Italy, Simon of Bisignano addressed the effects of communion. In reply to the theology of Berengar of Tours, he said that the body of Christ was "handled and broken by the hands of priests" (*manibus sacerdotum tractari, frangi*), "ground by the teeth of the faithful" (*fidelium dentibus teri*) but only sacramentally (*sacramentaliter*). Simon treated this in terms of concomitance, saying it was consumed "under divided parts" (*sub partibus diuisis*).[85] Noting the problem of reception by the unworthy, Simon said the body of Christ fed and nourished "the interior man" spiritually.[86] By the end of the twelfth century, a Decretist like Simon could presume that communion under one species, bread, was sufficient and that intinction was reserved for communicating the sick.[87] Sicard of Cremona treated the same issues, drawing heavily on Simon's commentary. Sicard said the body and blood came to be on the altar, but "the taste and weight of the species" (*de speciebus uero sapore et pondere*) remained.[88] He also strongly endorsed the idea of concomitance, saying both species were received under one.[89] Like Simon, Sicard said both good and bad received; but only the good received spiritually.[90]

[82] *Distinctiones Si mulier eadem hora seu Monacenses*, ed. Rosalba Sorice (Città del Vaticano, 2002), 147, "Quod in sacramento uisibiliter sumitur, in ipsa ueritate spiritualiter manducatur et bibitur."

[83] *Die Summa über das Decretum Gratiani*, 269–270.

[84] *Die Summa über das Decretum Gratiani*, 271. The author also denied the utility of communion by intinction.

[85] *Summa in decretum Simonis Bisianensis*, ed. Petrus V. Aimone Braida (Città del Vaticano, 2014), 512: De cons. D. 2 c. 1. Simon tied this teaching to the recantation of Berengar of Tours, see *Summa in decretum Simonis Bisianensis*, loc. cit. He added that the breaking of the host only affected the species and the accidents; see *Summa in decretum Simonis Bisianensis*, 521: De cons. D. 2 c. 42.

[86] *Summa in decretum Simonis Bisianensis*, 511: De cons. D. 2 c. 1, "sic caro Christi et sanguis interiorem hominem spiritualiter reficit et satiat."

[87] *Summa in decretum Simonis Bisianensis*, 513: De cons. D. 2 c. 1; 516: De cons. D. 2 c. 7, 518: De cons. D. 2 c. 22.

[88] Sicardus Cremonensis, *Summa decretorum*, Bamberg Staatsbibliothek Can. MS 38, 101A: De cons. D. 2 c. 13.

[89] Sicardus Cremonensis, *Summa decretorum*, 102A: De cons. D. 2 c. 22, "et quia sub una specie utroque accipitur." See also *Summa decretorum*, 101A. At *Summa decretorum*, 99B: De cons. D. 2 c. 1, Sicard too related the unity under the breaking of the host to the case of Berengar.

[90] Sicardus Cremonensis, *Summa decretorum*, 101A: De cons. D. 2 c. 1, "qui boni et mali manducant alter spiritualiter quo soli boni manducant." This difference of results is depicted in an Italian book of hours; see Rogers S. Wieck, *Illuminating Faith: The Eucharist in Medieval Life and Art* (New York, 2014), 35.

Huguccio of Pisa wrote at length about communion. The Eucharist was a sacrament of the Church that effected what it "figured." This included effecting the unity of the Church, the Mystical Body of Christ, united by faith and charity.[91] In the sacrament, the body of Christ was "broken, divided, ground" (*frangitur diuiditur teritur*), a statement that affirmed the Real Presence very corporeally.[92] The priest was supposed to receive the sacrament he confected, receiving both species, not one without the other. The others present could receive, and they were to do so reverently (*cum ea reuerentia*).[93] Those men who were married were supposed to refrain from sexual relations with their wives for at least three days.[94] Elsewhere he warned against overeating and drunkenness before receiving communion. Huguccio not only wanted those who erred in this way to do penance, he said the Real Presence did not include complete digestion and excretion. The presence vanished with the taste of bread once the host left the mouth for the stomach, where it might be mixed with common foodstuffs.[95] The worthy could receive, even frequently; but the unworthy needed to do penance first.[96] Those who received unworthily when in mortal sin risked a judgment, damnation.[97] Only those who received worthily received really or spiritually (*realiter siue spiritualiter*) for their benefit, receiving remission of sins.[98]

Huguccio too emphasized concomitance, permitting communion under only one species. The whole and entire Christ still was received. He specified that this reception by the laity was under the species of bread.[99]

91 Huguccio, *Summa decretorum*, Admont Stiftsbibliothek MS 7, fol. 427rb: De cons. D. 2 c. 32, "Sed queratur an corpus Christi cum sit sacramentum noui testamenti effitiat quod figurat. Respondetur si aperte intelligatur totum uere efficit quod figurat. Christus enim efficit unitatem ecclesie." See also *Summa decretorum*, fol. 432rb: De cons. D. 2 c. 57.

92 Huguccio, *Summa decretorum*, fol. 425va: De cons. D. 2 c. 22.

93 Huguccio, *Summa decretorum*, fol. 423vb: De cons. D. 2 c. 8. The consecrated wine was to be handled carefully to avoid spilling; see *Summa decretorum*, loc. cit.

94 Huguccio, *Summa decretorum*, fol. 423vb: De cons. D. 2 c. 8, "ut coniugati saltem et tribus diebus ab uxoribus abstineant."

95 Huguccio, *Summa decretorum*, fol. 426ra: De cons. D. 2 c. 23, 427ra: De cons. D. 2 c. 28.

96 Huguccio, *Summa decretorum*, fol. 423vb: De cons. D. 2 c. 8.

97 Huguccio, *Summa decretorum*, fol. 426rb: De cons. D. 2 c. 25, "*Timorem*. domini. uel cauendi ne indigne corpus Christi sumamus. Iuditium. cum eo quod est ei ad iuditium. id est. ad dampnationem. scilicet. cum peccato mortali."

98 Huguccio, *Summa decretorum*, fol. 427va: De cons. D. 2 c. 34, "Ita etiam realiter siue spiritualiter sumamus. Sumitur enim corpus et sanguis Christi et sacramentaliter. et hoc tam a malis quam a bonis." The bad received sacramentally but not spiritually; see *Summa decretorum*, fol. 430rb: De cons. D. 2 c. 46, "Mali enim manducant tantum sacramentaliter. id est. sub specie uisibili carnem Christi de uirgine sumpta et sanguine pro nobis fusum sumitur. sed non misticam."

99 Huguccio, *Summa decretorum*, fol. 424va: De cons. D. 2 c. 12, "Sed ecce sub specie panis sumitur corpus et sanguis Christi. Immo totus Christus sumitur sub specie uno." Huguccio went on to explain that reception under the species of wine after receiving the bread was superfluous for the laity; see *Summa decretorum*, fol. 424va–b: De cons. D. 2 c. 12.

In Huguccio's theology, under the species of bread one received not just flesh but soul and divinity (*deitas*).[100] The canonist also gave the fraction of the host, apart from concomitance, a threefold significance for the Church as Mystical Body of Christ: the living members of the Mystical Body, those Christians quiet in their tombs, and the resurrected, that is, the risen, glorified Lord (*unum iam resurrexit*).[101] Huguccio also tied this to Christ's sacrifice "on the altar of the cross" (*in ara crucis*). This sacrifice united all liturgical acts, so that "Although [Christ] is offered in many places, there is only one victim, not many. There is one sacrifice, not many."[102] He added that the sacrifice was "powerful, that is efficacious" (*potens. idest. efficax*), wherever it remembered and represented the offering made only once.[103]

Pastoral manuals dealt with issues of worthy reception. Thomas of Chobham said this was laudable in the perfect person (*perfectus*) receiving out of devotion but worthy of rebuke (*vituperabile*) in others.[104] John of Erfurt emphasized faith. He said that "intention regulated by faith" (*intentio regulatam per fidem*) was essential in reception. Anyone who ate consecrated bread only as bodily food did not receive it "as a sacrament" (*ut sacramentum*). One had to know that something spiritual was hidden under that species (*aliquod spirituale lateat sub illa specie*). If one knew this, even if he or she was a heretic who denied the Real Presence, reception was sacramental.[105] One who received without realizing he or she was in mortal sin was delivered from that sin by receiving devoutly.[106]

Liturgical tracts reflected a general belief in the salutary aspect of receiving communion. Thus Hildebert of Lavardin, in his discussion of the canon of the mass, glossing the word *communicantes*, said that it referred to the desire to have "communion and a share in perennial

[100] Huguccio, *Summa decretorum*, fol. 424vb: De cons. D. 2 c. 12, "Sed ecce sub specie panis est totus Christus. scilicet. caro sanguis et anima et deitas."

[101] Huguccio, *Summa decretorum*, fol. 425va: De cons. D. 2 c.22. Huguccio wrote about Christ's glorified body at *Summa decretorum*, fol. 432va: De cons. D. 2 c. 58.

[102] Huguccio, *Summa decretorum*, fol. 431rb: De cons. D. 2 c. 53, "Christus semel est oblatus hostia in ara crucis. Cotidie offertur in sacramento. et licet in multis locis offeratur. una est tantum hostia et non plures. Unum est sacrificium et non plura."

[103] Huguccio, *Summa decretorum*, loc. cit. Huguccio compared Christ to the Paschal lamb at *Summa decretorum*, fol. 431va: De cons. D. 2 c. 54, "Ideo quia celebrato cum discipulis tipico pascha. id est. agno paschali commesto quodam memoriale eis Christus commedare uolens sub specie panis et uini. Corpus et sanguinem suum eis tradidit. ut ostenderet ueteris legis. idest. sacramenta. Inter que precipuum erat agni paschalis sacrifitium. In morte sua terminari. et noue legis sacramenta substitui. in quibus excellit misterium eucharistie."

[104] *Thomae de Chobham summa confessorum*, 103–104. Thomas applied the same rule to reception by priests celebrating mass; see *Thomae de Chobham summa confessorum*, 106.

[105] *Die Summa confessorum des Johannes von Erfurt*, ed. Norbert Brieskorn, 3 vols. (Frankfurt, 1980), 3.870–871.

[106] *Die Summa confessorum des Johannes von Erfurt*, 3.871.

beatitude" (*ut communionem et partem habeamus in perenni beatitudine*). Hildebert emphasized the identification of the bread with Christ's body that "is broken and eaten here" (*hic frangitur et comedatur*).[107] Fasting should precede communion, because it pleased the Holy Spirit that, in honor of so great a sacrament, the host should enter the mouth before any other food.[108] Nor should anyone seek daily communion. Whoever honored the sacrament would not dare to receive it daily.[109]

Lothar of Segni, the future Innocent III, said that in communion the incorruptible was given and the incorruptible eaten.[110] He said, after discussing how Christ was both able to suffer and yet be impassible under the form of the sacrament: "Now, however, the immortal and impassible is consumed by us ... What, therefore, was passible was eaten and yet not harmed."[111] Lothar treated the dipped morsel Christ gave to Judas at the Last Supper (John 13:26) as explaining why intinction was not practiced in communion.[112] He said that communion was received in two ways, the True Body received sacramentally (*sacramentaliter*) under the species and the Mystical Body spiritually. Communicants too received doubly: "In this way both the good and the bad eat the body of Christ. But only the good eat for salvation. The bad, however, eat for judgment."[113] This latter statement reflects indirectly Paul's belief that one could become guilty by receiving the sacrament unworthily. Belief and eating salvifically went together, and eating incorporated believer more firmly into Christ's body. What was eaten served to incorporate whoever ate properly.[114]

Innocent also gave communion an ecclesiological significance. He wrote that there were two lives, celestial and terrestrial (*coelestis videlicet et terrena*). Thus there were also two powers, ecclesiastical and mundane (*ecclesiastica et mundana*). The one dealt with the soul, and the other with the body.[115] Innocent said that the clergy offered "bread for the body, wine for the soul

107 *Hildeberti liber de expositione missae*, PL 171.1163A–B, 1165A-B.
108 *Hildeberti liber de expositione missae*, PL 171.1174D.
109 *Hildeberti liber de expositione missae*, PL 171.1176B.
110 *De sacro altaris mysterio libri sex*, PL 217.863D.
111 *De sacro altaris mysterio libri sex*, PL 217.864D, "Nunc autem sumitur a nobis immortale et impassibile ... Quod ergo passibilis edabatur, et tamen non laedabatur."
112 *De sacro altaris mysterio libri sex*, PL 217.866A.
113 *De sacro altaris mysterio libri sex*, PL 217.866C, "Hoc modo tam boni quam mali corpus Christi manducant. Sed soli boni comedunt ad salutem, mali vero comedunt ad judicium."
114 *De sacro altaris mysterio libri sex*, PL 217.866D, "Qui credit in Deum, comedit ipsum; qui incorporatur Christo per fidem, id est membrum ejus efficitur, vel in unitate corporis ejus firmius solidatur. Alibi quod manducatur, incorporatur; et qui manducat, incorporat. Hic utem quod manducatur incorporat, et qui manducat incorporatur." Peter the Chanter said that adoration had to precede communion; see *Petri cantoris Parisiensis Verbum abbreviatum, textus confletus*, ed. Paul Tombeur and Monique Boutry (Turnhout, 2004), 206.
115 *De sacro altaris mysterio libri sex*, PL 217.844B–C.

and water for the people."[116] Communion refreshed the soul, but the Real Presence did not pass from the stomach to the latrine. Instead, Christ passed "from the mouth to the heart" (*de ore transit ad cor*).[117] Innocent used the familiar distinction between *sacramentum non res, sacramentum et res*, and *res non sacramentum*. Writing about the Mystical Body of Christ, in this context, he said, "Just as one bread is made up of many grains, and one wine flows from many grapes, so the body of Christ is made up of many members and ecclesiastical unity from diverse persons, the predestined, called, justified and glorified."[118] Ecclesiastical unity, beginning with right reception of communion, built up the body of Christ.

Sicard of Cremona emphasized unity in the reception of communion. The priest communicated first. No one administered the host to him, since he represented Christ, the only redeemer. The deacon gave the chalice to him, since that represented refreshment and should be a matter of human ministry. Then the deacon and subdeacon received the sacrament before the faithful were communicated.[119] Sicard emphasized concomitance in the breaking of the bread. He said of the broken host: "And beware, since, although the body of Christ offered in the sacrament thus is broken and distributed to many, nevertheless, the whole and entire Christ remains in heaven, and He is consumed whole and entire by many in the sacrament. Nor does He pass into food for the body except spiritually."[120] Giving communion to the faithful matched Christ's having eaten not just with a few apostles (*cum paucis apostolorum*) but with a multitude of disciples (*cum multitudine discipulorum*) before ascending. Communion was itself an action of grace received together with the just.[121]

[116] *De sacro altaris mysterio libri sex*, PL 217.843A, "In sacrificio eucharistiae panis unitatis, vinum caritatis, aqua fidelitatis: panis pro corpore, vinum pro anima, et aqua pro populo."

[117] *De sacro altaris mysterio libri sex*, PL 217.867B.

[118] *De sacro altaris mysterio libri sex*, PL 217.879C, "Sicut unus panis ex multis granis conficitur, et unum vinum ex diversis acinis confluit: sic corpus Christi ex multis membris componitur, et unitas ecclesiastica ex diversis constitit; in praedestinatis, vocatis, justificatis et glorificatis."

[119] *Sicardi Cremonensis episcopi... Mitralis de officiis*, ed. Gábor Sarbak and Lorenz Weinrich (Turnhout, 2008), 209.

[120] *Sicardi Cremonensis episcopi Mitralis*, 209, "Et caue, quia, licet oblata aut etiam corpus Christi in sacramento sic frangatur et pluribus distribuatur, tamen totus Christus et integer permanet in cęlo et sumitur a singulis totus et integer in sacramento; nec transit in alimentum corporis nisi spiritualiter." Guillelmus Durantis said the fragment immersed in the chalice showed that Christ's body did not lack blood; see *Guillelmi Duranti rationale divinorum officiorum I–IV*, ed. Anselm Davril and Timothy M. Thibodeau (Turnhout, 1995), 533; William Durand, *Rationale IV: On the Mass and Each Action Pertaining to It*, trans. Thibodeau (Turnhout, 2013), 449–450.

[121] *Sicardi Cremonensis episcopi Mitralis*, 136–137 at 137, "Vel ut cum iustis gratię Dei communicemus. Et est communio gratiarum actio."

Writing about the departure of the Real Presence after communion, Lothar said that the spiritual effect remained: "Therefore, the corporeal presence is not to be sought, but the spiritual is to be retained. Once the rite is complete, Christ passes from the mouth to the heart. It is better that he should enter the mind than descend into the belly."[122] Lothar also said the Real Presence vanished miraculously if a mouse tried to eat a consecrated host.[123]

Later theologians did not cease being concerned with the issue of the departure of the Presence. Thus John Peckham treated it in one of his *quodlibeta*.[124] Later canonists and summists too occasionally discussed the departure of the Real Presence. Hostiensis said the host became flesh and remained such, under the form of bread, until it was received.[125] John of Erfurt said the Presence would cease if too much unconsecrated wine were added to the chalice.[126]

Although the belief in the salvific effects of communion was widely accepted in Christendom, this acceptance of orthodoxy was not complete. Inquisitors reported dissent and doubt about communion, as they did about Christ's presence in the elevated host. Thus Jacques Fournier inquired whether the residents of Montaillou preferred the blessed bread of the Cathars to the sacrament. His register reported that sentiment as well as vituperation of the priests' Eucharist.[127] Fournier also reported that the Waldensians pretended to receive communion at Easter.[128] As noted below, the Lollards criticized existing practices; but they occasionally accepted communion in a parish church, thinking they might still benefit spiritually.

Preparation for communion and proper reception

With a heightened sensitivity to the Real Presence came an emphasis on adequate preparation for communion, especially through confession,

122 *De sacro altaris mysterio libri sex*, PL 217.867B, "Deinceps non est quaerenda corporalis praesentia, sed spiritualis est retinenda. Dispensatione completa, Christus de ore transit ad cor. Melius est enim ut procedat in mentem, quam ut descendat in ventrem."

123 *De sacro altaris mysterio libri sex*, PL 217.863A–C.

124 Johannes Peckham, *Quodlibeta quatuor*, ed. Girard Etzkorn and Ferdinand M. Delorme (Grottaferrata, 1989), 136.

125 *Summa domini Henrici cardinalis Hostiensis* ... (Lyon, 1537; Aalen, 1962), fol. 185rb, "Hostia quam vides ante consecrationem panis est in consecratione de pane fit caro et remanet ibi tantum species siue forma panis: et sub illa forma comeditur."

126 *Die Summa confessorum des Johannes von Erfurt*, 3.875.

127 *Regestre d'inquisition de Jacques Fournier (éveque de Pamiers) 1318–1325*, ed. Jean Duvernay, 3 vols. (Paris, 1978), 1.12–13, 18–21, 24–25, 28–29, 2.628.

128 *Regestre d'inquisition de Jacques Fournier*, 1.80–81.

which cleansed and sanctified.[129] One *exemplum* said that a man died vomiting after receiving communion without first confessing.[130] Additional preparation, as was noted above, involved fasting and sexual abstinence. This idea of preparation was not new. The early penitentials, reflecting older practices, included requirements of refraining from sex before communion. Theodore's penitential, like the early canons, specified three days of abstinence.[131] Penance was required if a person ate before receiving communion.[132] The same was true of anyone who ate meat during Lent. This was punished with denial of Easter communion.[133] One of Aelfric's letters raised the question why Christians fasted before receiving although Jesus dined before instituting the sacrament. He replied that Jesus was fulfilling the "old Passover" (*vetus pascha*) before instituting the "new sacraments" (*nova sacramenta*).[134] The contemporaneous Canons of Edgar specified reception of communion after fasting except in a case of illness.[135]

By the twelfth century, Peter the Chanter treated this need for preparation in devotional terms, linking adoration to sacramental eating: "Unless they adore first, the Eucharist is not to be given to them".[136] Other writers emphasized actual acts of preparation. Thus Hildebert of Lavardin devoted a chapter in his exposition of the mass to preparation for communion. He too emphasized fasting. This practice would please the Holy Spirit, he said, since it was fitting to honor the sacrament by having the Lord's body enter the mouth before any other food. This explained the universal practice of the Eucharistic fast.[137] Much later, Guillelmus Durantis limited his discussion of communion received by the faithful to a requirement that they "fast and abstain from earthly foods."[138]

The fast became part of the canon law as taught and enforced, binding both the priest who celebrated and the lay folk who received. An example is offered by Huguccio, who said that the Eucharist "cannot be confected or consecrated unless by one who has fasted."[139] The practical questions

[129] See the first Salisbury statutes in *Councils & Synods*, 2/1.78.

[130] *Friars' Tales: Thirteenth-Century Exempla from the British Isles*, ed. David Jones (Manchester, 2011), 35.

[131] *Medieval Handbooks of Penance*, 208. [132] *Medieval Handbooks of Penance*, 272.

[133] *Medieval Handbooks of Penance*, 366.

[134] *Councils & Synods*, 1/1.250. He also said the priest should offer the Eucharist "with chastity of body and mind"; see *Councils & Synods*, 1/1.269, 277.

[135] *Councils & Synods*, 1/1.325.

[136] *Petri Cantoris verbum abbreviatum*, ed. Monique Boutry (Turnhout, 2004), 206. This is part of the chapter on receiving the Eucharist unworthily.

[137] *Hildeberti liber de expositione missae*, PL 171.1174D.

[138] *Guillelmi Duranti rationale*, 553; William Durand, *Rationale IV*, 474.

[139] Huguccio, *Summa decretorum*, fol. 431va: De cons. D. 2 c. 54, "confici non potest uel consecrari nisi a ieiuno."

this raised abounded for priestly practice, including questions about whether the wine used to cleanse the chalice could be drunk by the priest without breaking his fast. Antonius de Butrio, for one, said the priest could drink unless he was to celebrate a second mass.[140] He emphasized reverence for "so great a sacrament" (*tanti sacramenti*), but he permitted taking medicine. In his opinion, it did not break the fast.[141] In the thirteenth century, Johannes Teutonicus already had denied that medicine was to be classed as food.[142] Godfrey of Trani, however, thought it was much safer to avoid taking medicine before receiving the Eucharist.[143] In general, reverence demanded that any meal be digested before reception of the sacrament. Huguccio said: "And before food has been digested, the body of Christ should not be received."[144] Huguccio dictated penances for those who violated this rule. Leaving aside communion received by the sick on a full stomach, he imposed three days of penance on children, seven on adults, and fifteen on clergy. Throughout his discussion of fasting, the canonist required that greater reverence be shown to the Eucharist than the other sacraments.[145]

Synodal statutes occasionally addressed issues of fasting and proper reception. Communion itself required proper consumption of the host even by those who had prepared adequately. A 1310 synod of Cologne specified teaching clergy how to administer the sacraments reverently so that they could teach the faithful how to receive them.[146] Likewise the 1287 statutes of Liège said the priest should teach the faithful to receive after they had confessed, while devout and fasting. Nor were strangers to communicate, except pilgrims and other travelers; and even they needed the priest's permission.[147] The priest was to provide communicants on

[140] *Excellentissimi Antonii de Butrio ... In librum tertium decretalium commentarii ...* (Venezia, 1578; Torino, 1967), fol. 191ra.

[141] *Excellentissimi Antonii de Butrio ... In librum tertium decretalium commentari*, fol. 191rb, "non frangitur per medicinam." Antonius, however, preferred the sick person not to eat along with receiving medication.

[142] *Apparatus glossatorum in compilationem tertiam* ad 3 Comp. 3.33.4, ed. Kenneth Pennington, work in progress found at http.//faculty.cua.edu/pennington.

[143] *Summa perutilis et valde necessaria do. Goffredi de Trano super titulis decretalium ...* (Lyon, 1519; Aalen, 1968), fol. 162va.

[144] *Excellentissimi Antonii de Butrio ... In librum tertium decretalium commentarii*, fol. 191rb, "Et antequam cibus digestus sit, corpus Christi sumi non debet. de conse. d. 2."

[145] Huguccio, *Summa decretorum*, fol. 431va: De cons. D. 2 c. 54, "quia maior reuerentia est exhibenda huic sacramento quam aliis ... puer tribus diebus maior vii. Clericus xv diebus penitentie subiciatur."

[146] Mansi 25.243–244. Similarly see a text from Trier in 1310 at Mansi 25.328.

[147] Mansi 24.899. A long-time absentee might need a special permission to confess and receive; see *Repertorium Poenitentiariae Germanicum*, 9 no. 1923, the case of a layman absent on account of poverty for sixteen years.

Easter and other solemnities with whole round hosts, not broken ones.[148] Cambrai's statutes said the same thing,[149] while the 1302 statutes of Toledo required being contrite when receiving communion.[150] The Eucharist was received by all Christians, but more ritual attended communion in the papal chapel. If the pope celebrated, as he did at Easter mass, he took communion himself and gave the sacrament to the deacon and subdeacon. Then the deacon who had read the gospel, having removed his miter in honor of the sacrament, led the congregation in the *Confiteor*. An indulgence was conferred together with absolution. The deacon gave communion to the people with a chalice of consecrated hosts. The pope himself could give communion to some select persons saying, "The body of our Lord Jesus Christ keep your soul to everlasting life." Then the Greek deacon gave them a drink of unconsecrated wine, and they could cleanse their lips with a clean white cloth. The pope finished by reverencing the sacrament before the subdeacon placed the remaining consecrated hosts on the altar[151] Special attention was given to an emperor or king present at Easter, who received communion at the hand of the pope from a paten containing only one host.[152]

Local statutes occasionally set down rules for communicants at the much more humble level of the parish church. Thus the Salisbury statutes wanted communicants reminded "in no way to doubt the truth of the body and blood" (*quod de veritate corporis et sanguinis Christi nullo modo dubitent*). The statutes say to teach "What is consumed with the mouth is what is believed by faith."[153] The statute concluded with the injunction, based on Augustine, that the faithful should believe the bread becomes the body that hung on the cross and the wine in the chalice becomes the blood that flowed from Christ's side.[154] A later version of the Salisbury statutes wanted the priest to examine the life of a parishioner who was to receive communion: "The priest should examine diligently the ways of his life before he approaches such a sublime ministry."[155] The communicant was to keep in mind Paul's injunction against receiving unworthily, as well

[148] Mansi 24.899. [149] Avril, *Les statuts synodaux*, 4.44. [150] Mansi 25,102.

[151] Agostino Patrizzi, *Caeremoniale Romanum* (Paris, 1689; Ridgewood, N.J., 1965), fol. CIV–CX^{r}.

[152] Patrizzi, *Caeremoniale Romanum*, fol. CX^{v}.

[153] *Council & Synods*, 2/1.77, "Hoc enim ore sumitur quod fide creditur." The second Exeter statutes warned against letting the devil raise doubts just before reception of communion; see *Council & Synods*, 2/2.991.

[154] *Council & Synods*, 2/1.77–78, "Nam hoc accipiunt proculdubio sub panis specie quod pro nobis pependit in cruce, hoc accipiunt in calice quod effusum est de Christi latere; hoc bibiunt, ut dicit Augustinus, credentes quod prius fuderunt sevientes."

[155] *Councils & Synods*, 2/1.271, "vias vite sue diligenter examinet sacerdos priusquam accedat ad ministerium tam sublime."

as the morsel Christ gave to Judas at the Last Supper.[156] Anyone who received while well aware of being unable to repent or while excommunicated under his own name (*nominatim*) was threatened with being denied deathbed communion.[157]

The 1281 Council of Lambeth told priests to offer instruction to those about to receive Easter communion or at any other time (*paschali tempore vel alio*) that they received the body and blood of Christ, "whole, live and true" (*integrum, vivum et verum*). The instruction included the doctrine of concomitance, that he was "entirely under the species of the sacrament" (*qui totus est sub specie sacramenti*). The wine given afterward, the statute said, must be explained as only "pure wine" (*vinum purum*) unconsecrated.[158] The parishioners were to be warned to confess and receive permission from the priest (*ipsius licentia*) before receiving.[159] The Lambeth synod gave very careful instructions about how the host was to be received: "[Priests] are to instruct them, having received the sacrament in the mouth, not to break it up too much with their teeth, but to duly absorb the whole thing perfectly, so that no particle remains in the gaps between the teeth or elsewhere."[160]

Spanish statutes occasionally addressed proper reception. The statutes of Orense required that the communicant should say three times "Señor, no soy digno . . .," a translation of the biblical words *Domine non sum dignus* . . . (Luke 7:6–7). The same instruction told the priest how to hold the host over the paten and ended with a requirement that he quiz communicants to be sure they did not carry the host away to use in enchantment (*acantamiento*).[161] Orense also set fourteen years as an age for reception.[162] Mondoñedo's statutes set the age of ten for confession but fourteen for communion.[163] A synod of Bayeux said not to give hosts to children younger than seven.[164]

[156] *Councils & Synods*, 2/1.271–272.

[157] *Councils & Synods*, 2/1.272. The second statutes of Exeter also reminded the faithful about the morsel given to Judas; see *Council & Synods*, 2/2.989.

[158] *Councils & Synods*, 2/2.985. The statute adds that only the priest receives *sub specie vini consecrati*. A 1279 statute from Münster specified using watered wine; see Mansi 24,316. So did a 1280 statute from Cologne; see Mansi 24.352. The statutes of Nîmes only mentioned wine; see Mansi 24.535.

[159] The statute exempts pilgrims from this need for permission; see *Councils & Synods*, 2/2.985.

[160] *Councils & Synods*, 2/2.985, "Instruant etiam eosdem sumptum ore sacramentum non nimis dentibus comminuere, sed *totum* modice sorbere perfecte, ne particulam aliquam eveniat in dentium interstitis vel alibi remanere." John of Erfurt identified chewing with faith, saying those lacking reason could not really "chew" the sacrament; see *Die Summa confessorum des Johannes von Erfurt*, 2.143.

[161] *Synodicon Hispanum*, 1.156–157. [162] *Synodicon Hispanum*, 1.156.

[163] *Synodicon Hispanum*, 1.60. [164] Mansi 25.63.

Beginning with the penitentials, churchmen at the local level worried about persons who vomited up the sacrament. Food, drink, or medicine might cause this regurgitation. So could an imbalance of bodily humors. The penitentials punished vomiting up the host, especially as a result of excessive eating or drinking.[165] A priest, more than a lay person, was punished heavily for vomiting the Eucharist.[166] The Decretists inherited past concerns about vomiting the Eucharist, especially because of drunkenness. Simon of Bisignano was among those who prescribed penances for vomiting after reception of communion.[167] A similar rule appears in the *Summa* of Hostiensis.[168] Likewise, a statute of Nîmes imposed penances for vomiting up the host because of drunkenness. Priests and other clerics were given stiffer penances than were lay persons, but even a sick person was to undergo seven days of penance.[169] The worry about vomiting out of drunkenness entered the tradition of pastoral manuals, like that by John of Erfurt.[170] Antoninus of Florence said clerics should be asked in confession about vomiting the Eucharist, along with ignorance of sacramental forms, negligence in custody of the host, failing to take viaticum to the sick properly and dropping the chalice from negligence.[171] Nicholas of Ausimo added that, when in doubt, a vomited host should be treated as if still consecrated.[172]

Worry about accidentally upsetting communicants through negligent care of the sacraments was common, alongside worries about failures of communicants to prepare adequately. The Paris statutes warned against a fly or spider falling into the chalice, in part because there was a threat of vomit or even poisoning.[173] The statutes of Tournai too warned against that threat.[174] The Cambrai statutes were more concerned with finding any fragments of the host on the altar and having a priest or even one of the faithful consume them with wine.[175]

Looking at the mass, Innocent III wrote that vomit might arise from a problem between the humors and the accidents of the consecrated bread.[176] He said nothing about disciplinary measures for preventing this, but he did warn, yet again, about not being too curious about the coming and departure

[165] *Medieval Handbooks of Penance*, 102, 154, 176, 184, 250, 309.
[166] *Medieval Handbooks of Penance*, 286.
[167] *Summa in decretum Simonis Bisianensis*, 519: De cons. 2 c. 28.
[168] Hostiensis, *Summa*, col. 1199. [169] Pontal, *Les statuts synodaux*, 2.328.
[170] *Die Summa confessorum des Johannes von Erfurt*, 2.121.
[171] Antoninus, *Confessionale "Defecerunt scrutantes scrutinio," Circa clericos in commune*.
[172] Nicholas of Ausimo, *Supplementum Summae Pisanellae* (Venezia, 1489), fol. I-2[ra]. For the penances imposed, see Nicholas, *Supplementum*, fol. I-5[ra].
[173] Mansi 22.682; Pontal, *Les statuts synodaux*, 1.80.
[174] Avril, *Les statuts synodaux*, 4.329. [175] Avril, *Les statuts synodaux*, 4.43.
[176] *De sacro altaris mysterio libri sex*, PL 217.867C.

of the Real Presence: "I do not know how Christ comes, and I am ignorant of how He goes. Only He who is not ignorant of anything knows."[177]

Sicard of Cremona said the chalice had to be of gold, silver, or tin. Bronze or brass might cause vomit when it interacted with the wine. Glass could break; and wood, being porous, might retain the sacrament.[178]

The Decretalists occasionally addressed issues of communion, in theory and practice, although not as frequently as did the Decretists. This was because the *Liber extra* contains texts on the celebration of mass (X 3.41), but little on communion in practice. Bernard of Pavia, one of the earliest Decretalists, defended the rights of parish priests in sacramental matters. He cited texts from Gratian upholding a curate's right to administer the sacraments to the people, as well as to receive offerings. The people in his charge were to go to him for their needs, but he was not to minister to another's parishioners.[179] Hostiensis said reception of part of a host meant reception of Christ, affirming concomitance.[180] The Cardinal of Ostia, commenting on c. *Ex parte vestra* (X 3.41.5), said a priest who drank anything cannot celebrate mass; but he permitted giving consecrated wine to the sick "in a case of necessity" (*in causa necessitatis*).[181] Johannes Andreae too, quoting Hostiensis, affirmed concomitance in the giving of the host.[182] Antonius de Butrio said the two species were friendly to human nature because the body was fed by bread and wine.[183]

Writers on pastoral care gave more attention to the act of communion. Thus William of Pagula, said parish priests were to teach the faithful about what they received and how to receive. Writing about communion "at Easter or some other time," William said to teach the laity that "They receive both Christ's body and blood under the appearance of bread, and that it is Christ, fully and truly man, who is contained in the sacrament." William also referred to teaching the faithful not to believe the drink of wine given to them later to help them swallow the host was

177 *De sacro altaris mysterio libri sex*, PL 217.868A, "Ego nescio quomodo Christus accedit, sed et quomodo recedit ignoro, novit ille qui nihil ignorat."

178 *Sicardi Cremonensis episcopi Mitralis*, 68, "Debet autem esse calix de auro uel argento uel stagno, non de ęre uel auricalco, quoniam ob uini uirtutem ęrucinem et uomitum prouocaret; non de uitro, quia cum sit frangibile, effusionis periculum immineret; non de ligno, quia cum sit porosum corpus et spongiosum, sanguinem absorberet."

179 Bernardus Papiensis, *Summa decretalium*, ed. Ernst Adolph Theodor Laspeyres (Ratisbon, 1861; Graz, 1956), 103–104.

180 *Henrici de Segusio Cardinalis Hostiensis Decretalium commentaria*, 6 vols. (Venezia, 1581; Turin, 1965), 3, fol. 162ra, which makes mention of the practices in a papal mass.

181 *Hostiensis Decretalium commentaria*, 3, fol. 162rb–va.

182 Johannes Andreae, *In decretalium libros novella commentaria* ... (Venezia, 1581; Torino, 1966), 3, fol. 218vb. His commentary also said taking medicine did not violate the Eucharistic fast; see *Novella commentaria*, 3, fol. 219rb.

183 *Excellentissimi Antonii de Butrio ... Super prima parte primi decretalium commentarii* (Venezia, 1578; Torino, 1967), fol. 7va.

sacramental.[184] The faithful were to be taught the way of reception too. They were not to crush the host but chew it, swallowing every particle. William also promised the faithful that they would not grow older during mass or die suddenly that day.[185]

Canon law did not often address the posture to be adopted in receiving communion. William of Pagula did say the communicant should not just kneel to receive but bow the head to show humility.[186] Here, however, art gives us more evidence, showing a devout person on his or her knees while the host is placed directly into the mouth. For example, a depiction of a woman receiving communion can be found in a manuscript in the British Library (Additional 18492). She kneels with her hands together while the priest places a host in her mouth.[187] Similarly, a missal from Beauvais shows the priest putting the host into the mouth of a kneeling man.[188] The priest can be shown holding the paten in his left hand while giving communion with his right.[189] The Smithfield Decretals includes an image of communion in which a "houseling cloth" is held under the chins of three boys, one a Jew, by two acolytes to catch crumbs falling during reception.[190] Deathbed communions, however, are depicted with the dying person lying in bed. For example, Saint Lucy of Syracuse, in a fresco from Padua, is shown lying down while receiving viaticum.[191]

How "average" lay persons felt receiving communion is not always easy to track. The hunger for the host of devout women has received the most attention.[192] Ida of Nivelles, for example, hungered so much for communion that she resorted to subterfuge, pretending to be afflicted with acedia or spiritual weariness.[193] Men's reactions are now receiving some attention too. Here we must distinguish priests, whose unique powers and access to

[184] *Pastors and the Care of Souls*, 146. Note the phrasing in terms of concomitance.

[185] *Pastors and the Care of Souls*, 147.

[186] William of Pagula, *Oculus sacerdotis*, fol. 17va.

[187] Janet Backhouse, *Books of Hours* (London, 1985), pl. 61.

[188] *Index of Christian Art*, record 000195742, accessed on December 28, 2013.

[189] *Index of Christian Art*, record 000082500. The chalice apparently shown in the priest's left hand in some pictures may instead be a ciborium; see, for example, Wieck, *Illuminating Faith*, 34.

[190] Alixe Bovey, "Communion and Community: Eucharistic Narratives and Their Audience in the Smithfield Decretals," in *The Social Life of Illumination: Manuscripts, Images and Communities in the Late Middle Ages*, ed. Joyce Coleman, Mark Cruse, and Kathryn A. Smith (Turnhout, 2013), 53–82 at 70, figure 13, 71. Similarly see Wieck, *Illuminating Faith*, 33.

[191] *Index of Christian Art*, record 000117655.

[192] See especially Carolyn W. Bynum, *Holy Feast and Holy Fast: The Religious Significance of Food to Medieval Women* (Berkeley, 1987).

[193] *Send Me God: The Lives of Ida the Compassionate of Nivelles, Nun of La Ramée, Arnulf, Lay Brothedr of Villers, and Abundus, Monk of Villers, by Goswin of Bossut*, trans. Martinus Cawley (Turnhout, 2003), 36. On Ida's preparation for communion, including use of "the hoe of confession," see ibid, 116–118.

the consecrated wine are underlined by the placing of the chalice on many of their tomb brasses, from lay men, whose piety may not have been similar to women's Eucharistic devotion.[194] We do know that texts of the Devotio Moderna included instructions on preparation not just for spiritual communion but for actual reception, including the possibility of devout communication on several feast days in the liturgical year or even weekly.[195]

Communion under one species or both

Medieval theologians and canonists had a sense of change over time. The Primitive Church, in their minds, had been small but zealous. With increased numbers came cooler zeal and lessened charity. Sacramental practices had been altered to deal with these changes, restricting consumption of the Eucharist by the laity to the bread alone and reducing frequency of communion. Canonists and writers on pastoral care dealt with these changes by emphasizing concomitance (discussed already) and the greater significance of communion received less frequently. Thus Huguccio of Pisa wrote that communion except on Sunday ceased because of increased numbers of Christians, a growth accompanied by cooling charity and unworthy reception. Communion on major feasts continued, however.[196] John of Erfurt offered a similar perspective on changed practices.[197] Nicholas of Cusa too offered this type of overview of liturgical history. He was able to treat different rites as praiseworthy in order to defend the practice then in place and argue for unity in the administration of communion.[198]

The restriction of lay communion to one species was not controversial at first in our surviving sources. Concomitance, of course, entered into the explanation of this change offered by writers on pastoral care. One of these writers, Thomas of Chobham, said that "Likewise it should be known that neither is the bread converted into blood, nor the wine into the body of Christ; but there never is a body without blood or the contrary, and, therefore, the whole Christ is in the chalice and the whole Christ in the form of bread."[199]

[194] P. H. Cullum, "Feasting Not Fasting: Men's Devotion to the Eucharist in the Later Middle Ages," in *Religious Men and Masculine Identity in the Middle Ages*, ed. Cullum and Katherine J. Lewis (Woodbridge, 2013), 184–200.

[195] *Devotio Moderna: Basic Writings*, ed. John Van Engen (Mahwah, 1988), 158, 174, 201, 231–234, 278–280.

[196] Huguccio, *Summa decretorum*, fol. 424rb: De cons. D. 2 c. 10, "Sed quia nec obseruari potuit. quia refrigitur caritas multorum. et ideo communicabant indigne."

[197] *Die Summa confessorum des Johannes von Erfurt*, 3.873–874.

[198] Nicholas of Cusa, *Writings on Church and Reform*, 58–59.

[199] *Thomae de Chobham summa confessorum*, 104, "Item, sciendum quod nec panis convertitur in sanguinem nec vinim in corpus Christi, sed nunquam est corpus sine sanguine nec e contrario, et ideo in calice est totus Christus, et in forma panis totus Christus."

John of Freiburg, looking at the difference between celebrant and congregation, described reception in both kinds as belonging only to the *maiores* (priests and ministers). His *Summa* said the Greeks did well (*bene faciant*) by following their custom of receiving in both kinds, but he still made no concessions to the laity.[200] Nicholas of Ausimo was typical in saying the priest's communion under both species signified completeness, but the laity did not need to do the same.[201]

The issue became crucial, however, in the fifteenth century. The demand for communion under both species, usually identified with the Bohemians, emerged at the Council of Constance. The council, hearing an accusation against Jacoubek of Stříbro (Jacob of Mies) that he demanded the chalice for the laity, issued a condemnation of communion under both species in Session 13 (June 15, 1415).[202] The council did not condemn Wyclif or Hus on this charge. However, Pope Martin V in 1417 in his bull *Inter cunctas* said a suspected follower of Wyclif and Hus was to be asked by inquisitors:

> Likewise, whether he believes the custom of giving communion to lay persons only under the species of bread, observed by the universal Church and approved by the sacred Council of Constance, should be observed thus, that is not licit to reprove it or change it at will without the Church's authority, and that those pertinaciously saying the opposite of the aforesaid must be confined and punished as heretics or understanding heretically.[203]

The condemnation of Hus only made religious strife in Bohemia worse. The result was a series of failed crusades against the Hussites, with Bohemian armies retaliating with campaigns of their own.[204] Jan Hus

200 Johannes de Friburgo, *Summa confessorum* (Paris, 1519), fol. cxxv^{vb} (q. cx).
201 Nicholas of Ausimo, *Supplementum Summae Pisanellae*, fol. I-3^{va-b}.
202 *Decrees of the Ecumenical Councils*, 419, "Et, sicut haec consuetudo ad vitanda aliqua pericula et scandala rationabiliter introducta est, sic potuit simili aut maiori ratione introduci et rationabiliter observari, quod, licet in primitiva ecclesia huiusmodi sacramentum reciperetur a fidelibus sub utraque specie, tamen postea a conficientibus sub utraque et a laicis tantummodo sub specie panis suscipiatur, cum firmissime credendum sit, et nullatenus dubitandum, integrum Christi corpus et sanguinem tam sub specie panis, quam sub specie vini veraciter contineri." See also Heinrich Denzinger, *The Sources of Catholic Dogma*, trans. Roy J. Deferrari (Fitzwilliam, N. H., 2002), 211–212.
203 Mansi 27.1211, "18. Item, utrum credat, quod consuetudo communicandi personas laicales sub specie panis tantum, ab Ecclesia universali observata, et per sacrum Concilium Constantiae approbata, sit servanda sic, quod non liceat eam reprobare aut sine Ecclesiae auctoritate pro libito immutare. Et quod dicentes pertinaciter oppositum praemissorum, tamquam haeretici vel sapientes haeresim, sint arcendi et puniendi." See also Denzinger, *The Sources of Catholic Dogma*, 215; Thomas A. Fudge, *The Crusade against Heretics in Bohemia, 1418–1437: Sources and Documents for the Hussite Crusades* (Aldershot, 2002), 45–49.
204 For the bull proclaiming the first of these crusades, issued in 1420, see Fudge, *The Crusade against Heretics in Bohemia, 1418–1437*, 49–52.

himself was not an Utraquist, but Hussite propaganda annexed his reputation as a martyr to the cause of the chalice.[205] The chalice itself became emblematic of the movement, appearing on shields and in visual propaganda.[206] The army of John Žižka even went into battle preceded by a priest with a monstrance.[207] The altar cup also was used in Catholic art, including in the image of the Man of Sorrows with a chalice.[208] Utraquist verses claiming that those who drank from the cup received the entire sacrament were distributed.[209] In a more practical way, the Hussite-dominated synod of Prague in 1421 claimed the right for any Christian to receive "under both species, wine and bread" (*sub utraque specie vini & panis*).[210]

Unable to defeat the Hussites in war, the Council of Basel negotiated with the Hussites. Envoys from Bohemia were invited to Basel to dispute the issues dividing Catholic from Hussite, including the necessity of communion under both species. These discussions were to be held under terms reached at Cheb in 1432. Among the rules of the "Cheb Judge" was suspension of "the rules of canon law" against doctrinal dissenters. The issues were to be judged under the norms of "the law of God, the practice of Christ, the apostles and the primitive church, with the councils and doctors truly established in it."[211] At Basel in 1433 John Rockycana, archbishop of Prague, debated Eucharistic issues with the Dominican theologian John of Ragusa.[212] Ragusa's case did not rest only on sources listed in the Cheb Judge. He had recourse to the writings of

205 Thomas A. Fudge, *The Memory and Motivation of Jan Hus, Medieval Priest and Martyr* (Turnhout, 2013), 139.

206 Thomas A. Fudge, "Art and Propaganda in Hussite Bohemia," *Religio* 1 (1993), 135–152 at 139; Fudge, "The 'Law of God': Reform and Religious Practice in Late Medieval Bohemia," in *The Bohemian Reformation and Religious Practice*, ed. David R. Holeton, 2 vols. (Praha, 1996), 49–72 at 66.

207 Žižka executed a priest who led the army of Prague against him carrying a monstrance; see Thomas A. Fudge, "Žižka's Drum: The Political Uses of Popular Religion," *Central European History* 36 (2003), 546–569 at 554, 556, 558, 560, figures 1 & 2.

208 Dóra Sallay, "The Eucharistic Man of Sorrows in Late Medieval Art," *Annual of Medieval Studies at CEU* 6 (2000), 45–80 at 64–65, figure 3.

209 Luci Doležalová, "Verses on the Effects of the Eucharist: Memory and Material Text in Utraquist Miscellanies," in *Religious Controversy in Europe, 1378–1536: Textual Transmission and Networks of Readership*, ed. Michael Van Dussen and Pavel Soukup (Turnhout, 2013), 105–136 at 107.

210 *Concilia Germaniae*, ed. Johann Friedrich Schannat and Joseph Hartzheim, 5 (Köln, 1763), 199B (Strasburg, 1432).

211 Fudge, *The Crusade against Heretics in Bohemia, 1418–1437*, 344–346.

212 Mansi 30.269–306 (Rockycana), 699–868 (Ragusa), 1105–1168 (Rockycana). Thomas Kaeppeli, *Scriptores Ordinis Praedicatorum medii aevi*, 4 vols. (Rome, 1970–1993), 2.533. E. F. Jacob, "The Bohemians at the Council of Basel, 1433," in *Prague Essays*, ed., R. W. Seton-Watson (Oxford, 1949), 81–123; Paul De Vooght, "La confrontation des thèses hussites et romaines au concile de Bâle," *Recherches de théologie ancienne et médiévale* 37 (1970), 97–137, 254–291.

Scholastic theologians, especially Thomas Aquinas, to defend Catholic practices. At some places Ragusa also had recourse to canon law, citing passages from the *De consecratione*. In addition he cited the Ordinary Gloss, John of Freiburg, and Hostiensis.[213] At Basel, a few years later, Juan de Torquemada, also a Dominican, wrote his own rejoinder to the Hussites on the Eucharist. His tract made less use of the *Decretum*, three direct references; but it also listed ancient councils that supposedly supported communion under only one species.[214]

Eventually, the envoys of the council negotiated Compacts with the Utraquist factor of the Hussite movement. These agreements, concluded in 1436, granted communion under both species to the Utraquists of Bohemia. Those who wanted the chalice and believed in the Real Presence were (grudgingly) granted that form of communion.[215] In fact, the council never ratified the Compacts in a public session. Instead, in Session 30, in a decree issued after Basel broke with Eugenius IV, the assembly reaffirmed as valid the practice of giving the laity communion under the form of consecrated bread alone.[216] The issue of conformity to the Church arose in a different form later, as the popes tried to force the king of Bohemia to renounce the Compacts. This effort culminated in their revocation by Pius II in 1462.[217] While that issue still was in doubt, a Catholic resident of Prague asked Pope Nicholas V through the Penitentiary to receive communion under the Roman rite, not the Utraquist rite.[218] The cases of Wyclif and Hus had a distant echo in Francisco Peña's edition of Nicholas Eimeric's handbook for inquisitors. He cited Aeneas Sylvius Piccolomini, Pius II, on the problems of

[213] Mansi 30.747–748, 751, 752, 753, 760–761. Ragusa also cited *Ego Berengarius* in an attack on Wyclif's theology of the sacrament; see Mansi 30.849.

[214] *Tractatus de venerabili sacramento* (Delft, ca. 1480), c. 2 & c. 9, cited from Early European Books. Kaeppeli, *Scriptores Ordinis Praedicatorum medii aevi*, 3.29–30, 4.170.

[215] Anton Frind, *Kirchengeschite Böhmens im Allgemeinen und in ihrer besonderen Beziehung auf die jetzige Leitmeritzer Diöcese in der Zeit vor dem erblichen Königthume: nach den zuverlässigsten, grossentheils handschriftlichen Quellen bearbeitet*, 4 vols. (Prague, 1864–1872), 3.354–358. For related documents by King Sigismund and the envoys of Basel, see Frind, *Kirchengeschite Böhmens*, 3.358–365. See also Fudge, *The Crusade against Heretics in Bohemia, 1418–1437*, 368–372. Although a participant in the negotiations with the Hussites, Nicholas of Cusa still argued in his *De usu communionis* for there being no less grace from receiving under one species than under both; see *Writings on Church and Reform*, 50–51.

[216] Mansi 29.158–159. King Sigismund tried to restrict communion under both species to places in which communion *sub utraque specie* "was served in former years"; see Fudge, *The Crusade against Heretics in Bohemia, 1418–1437*, 385–387.

[217] Otakar Odložilík. *The Hussite King. Bohemia in European Affairs 1440–1471* (New Brunswick, N.J., 1965), 135–160. Nicholas of Cusa argued for liturgical conformity in a letter to the Bohemians written during his German legation; see *Writings on Church and Reform*, 356–429.

[218] *Repertorium Poenitentiariae Germanicum*, 2 no. 363.

Bohemia; and he treated the condemnation of Wyclif at Constance to show that inquisitors could proceed against dead heretics.[219]

Communion under both species once took a different form, intinction, dipping the bread into the wine before giving it to the communicant. As noted elsewhere, this practice had an ancient history; but it had fallen into disfavor. As we have seen, the decree of "Pope Julius" was seen as crucial evidence of the move away from intinction. On the local level, the 1175 Council of Westminster forbade "intinction of the body into Christ's blood."[220] By the fifteenth century, the practice was so thoroughly obsolete that Nicholas of Cusa was able to use its abandonment to demonstrate the changeability of Eucharistic practices. Nicholas was able to argue that "The rite of preparing the Eucharist is different from what it once was."[221]

Frequency of communion

The issue of frequent communion appears in the medieval liturgical treatises, as well as canon law. The treatises came to emphasize worthy communion without absolutely prohibiting frequent reception. Thus Johannes Beleth recounted of daily communion giving way, with rising numbers, to reception only on Sunday. Then it was restricted to required communion three times a year: Christmas, Easter, and Pentecost. The kiss of peace and eulogium, blessed bread, sufficed at other times.[222] The mass, however, closed with giving thanks for participation in communion.[223] Hildebert of Lavardin gave advice that was somewhat ambiguous, saying the faithful person should not dare to receive daily but not omit any particular feast day. He did think that Paul did not want anyone who could not distinguish the sacrament "from other foods" (*a caeteris cibis*) to receive.[224] Hildebert also said to choose days for communion "on which a person lived most purely and continently" (*eligendi sunt dies in quibus homo purius continentiusque vivat*).[225]

The *Decretum* included a text attributed to "Hilarius Episcopus" (c. *Si non*, De cons. D. 2 c. 15), which said no one should abstain from receiving

[219] Nicholas Eimeric, *Directorium inquisitorum …*, ed. Francisco Peña (Rome, 1587), 280, 574–575.

[220] *Councils & Synods*, 1/2.980, "Non fiat intinctio corporis in sanguine Christi." See also *Councils & Synods*, 1/2.990, quoting the prohibition attributed to Julius I.

[221] Nicholas of Cusa, *Writings on Church and Reform*, 52–55 at 55. Nicholas cited "Pope Julius" to support this argument.

[222] *Iohannis Beleth summa de ecclesiasticis officiis*, ed. Heribert Douteil (Turnhout, 1976), 85.

[223] *Iohannis Beleth summa de ecclesiasticis officiis*, 86.

[224] *Hildeberti liber de expositione missae*, PL 171.1176B.

[225] *Hildeberti liber de expositione missae*, PL 171.1175B.

the body of Christ unless excommunicated. Only then should he or she not accept the "medicine of the body of the Lord" (*medicina corporis Christi*). A Pseudo-Isidorean text, attributed to "Pope Fabian," follows (c. *Etsi non frequentius*, De cons. D. 2 c. 16). That "decree," already known to earlier canonists like Burchard, required that the faithful receive at least three times in a year, on Easter, Pentecost, and Christmas unless impeded by mortal sins. This became, as we have seen, the standard for frequency of communion applied by the ecclesiastical authorities until the Fourth Lateran Council met in 1215. A conciliar canon (c. *Si quis*, De cons. D. 2 c. 19), said those who did not receive on those occasions should not be regarded as Catholics.

Decretists had to address the issue of frequency of communion. Thus Simon of Bisignano said, as others did, that "all are obliged to communicate" (*omnes communicare teneantur*) three times a year, on Christmas, Easter, and Pentecost, otherwise they could not be regarded as among the faithful (*inter catholicos haberi*).[226] Simon was among those who excepted those guilty of mortal sins from receiving communion.[227] Likewise, those who were doing solemn penances were to refrain from communicating.[228] Sicard of Cremona repeated this teaching.[229] Huguccio made passing reference to the rule of communion three times in a year when discussing worthy and unworthy communion.[230] Glossing *Etsi non frequentius*, Huguccio, usually concerned with ecclesiastical unity in the sacrament, ignored the possibility of punishment for those who failed to receive. He only discussed the necessity of refraining, even on major feasts, if guilty of mortal sins or unable to communicate on account of an imposed penance.[231]

When *Omnis utriusque sexus* appeared in the *Liber Extra*, it immediately attracted commentary. The Decretalists rapidly came to focus on annual confession, including the role of the parish priest as confessor. This may be because *Omnis utriusque* appeared under the title "On Penances and Remissions" (*De poenitentiis et remissionibus*, X 5.38.12). Nonetheless, there were some references to communion in the earlier writings on the *extra*. The *Casus Fuldenses* gave communion the most attention. The author wrote, "*Omnis*. At least once in a year anyone should confess his

226 *Summa in decretum Simonis Bisianensis*, 512: De cons. D. 2 c. 1.
227 *Summa in decretum Simonis Bisianensis*, 516: De cons. D. 2 c. 7.
228 *Summa in decretum Simonis Bisianensis*, 515–516: De cons. D. 2 c. 17.
229 Sicardus Cremonensis, *Summa decretorum*, 100B: De cons. D. 2 c. 17.
230 Huguccio, *Summa decretorum*, fol. 423vb: De cons. D. 2 c. 8, "si in pascha pentecoste et natiuitate communicare non debent."
231 Huguccio, *Summa decretorum*, fol. 425ra: De cons. D. 2 c. 16, "*Etsi non*. uer. maioribus. idest. mortalibus uel nisi ratione iniuncta penitentie etiam in illis diebus a communione cessare teneatur."

sins and receive the Eucharist, unless prohibited by the priest."[232] The *Casus Parisienses* repeated instead the threat, found in the decretal, that anyone who failed to conform could be denied Christian burial (*alias ecclesiastica careat sepultura*).[233] Johannes Teutonicus, Damasus, and Vincentius Hispanus pointed the reader to the canon *Etsi non frequentius* (De cons. D. 2 c. 16). Both Vincentius and Damasus said the faithful person should receive more often (*quia pluries debet*) than once in a year.[234] The *casus* to this text in the Ordinary Gloss combined these sentiments and added further details:

> The general council decreed that any faithful person of either sex after attaining the age of discretion should at least once in a year confess his sins to the proper priest and, at least on Easter, receive the sacrament of the Eucharist reverently, unless the counsel of a priest should lead him to abstain.[235]

The Gloss, focusing on confession, identified the age of discretion with the ability to deceive (*doli capax*).[236] Like other early commentaries, the Gloss refers the reader to c. *Etsi non frequentius*.[237]

Hostiensis, in his *Summa*, tried to combine the increased emphasis on strict preparation for communion noted above and older ideas of reception more often than once a year. He said communion should be received three times a year, as the older canons had required, unless serious crimes impeded this; and he cited the *Decretum* as evidence. Then he stated, following *Omnis utriusque sexus*, that reception should occur at minimum on Holy Thursday or Easter. Once more he permitted abstention on account of sin or crime with a proviso that the lay person should seek the advice of the parish priest. Anyone else who abstained otherwise was in peril of being denied Christian burial as a dissident.[238] The cardinal also required that the faithful hear mass every

232 *Constitutiones Concilii Quarti Lateranensis*, 486, "*Omnis*: Ad minus semel in anno unusquisque debet confiteri peccata sua et sumere Eucharistiam, nisi a sacerdote prohibeatur."

233 *Constitutiones Concilii Quarti Lateranensis*, 469.

234 *Constitutiones Concilii Quarti Lateranensis*, 208, 315, 429.

235 *Glossa ordinaria* ad X 5.38.12, "Statuit concilium generale, quod quilibet fidelis utriusque sexus postquam discretionem habuerit, saltem semel in anno sua solus confiteatur peccata proprio sacerdoti, & ad minus in Pascha sacramentum Eucharistiae suscipere reuerenter, nisi de consilio sacerdotis duxerit abstinendum." The threat of denial of burial follows.

236 *Glossa ordinaria* ad X 5.38.12 v. Discretionis.

237 *Glossa ordinaria* ad X 5.38.12 v. Ad minus.

238 Hostiensis, *Summa*, fol. 185rb, "Ter in anno homines communicare debent nisi pro grauibus criminibus impediantur. scilicet. in pascha pentecoste et natali domini. de con. di. ii. c. et si non frequentius. in cena vel saltem in pascha nisi de consilio proprii sacerdotis aliquis abstineat propter crimen. vt no. supra. et no. infra de peni. et re. omnis. Alius uiuens ab ingress. ec. abstineat et moriens Christiana careat sepultura vt ibi."

Sunday through to the final blessing even if no one but the priest communicated.[239]

Local bishops and synods occasionally legislated about the reception of communion, including by restating the Easter Duty of confession and communion.[240] On the Continent, Federico Visconti, archbishop of Pisa, decreed, paraphrasing *Omnis utriusque*, that anyone having cure of souls should warn his parishioners to confess to his own priest and receive communion once in a year (*semel in anno*). Anyone who did not do so, the Pisan statute said, could be denied Christian burial.[241] A French statute said parish priests should warn everyone over the age of seven to confess and receive at Easter.[242] A canon from Nîmes connected communion of both the sick and the well, requiring that confession precede reception in both cases.[243] As late as 1517, the statutes of Florence required priests to memorize *Omnis utriusque* to be able to explain Easter duty to their flocks.[244] A Council of the diocese of Apt in southern France added censures to the requirement for Easter confession and communion, comparing those who failed in their duty to sick sheep (*oves morbidae*), who were to be separated from the flock for its own good.[245] By 1490 a German version of the Lateran decree appeared in a set of Salzburg canons.[246]

On the Iberian Peninsula, synods continued to remind clergy and people of their Easter Duty, as a 1528 statute of the diocese of Tuy did.[247] The 1543 statutes of Orense reminded priests not to give communion to another priest's parishioners.[248] The same statutes hedged on Easter Duty, saying, as Visconti had, to receive "at least" (*a lo menos*) once in a year. Elsewhere, there is an echo of older practice, urging communication three times in a year but especially on Easter.[249] The statutes of Santiago de Compostella changed from an injunction to receive three times a year, issued in 1289, to one from 1309 that repeats the language of *Omnis*

[239] Hostiensis, *Summa*, fol. 185ra.

[240] See, for example, the Council of Albi (1254) in Mansi 23.840. A 1329 synod of Tarragona specifically said to observe *Omnis utriusque*; see Mansi 25.870.

[241] *Les sermons et la visite pastorale de Federico Visconti archevêque de Pise (1253–1277)*, ed. Nicole Bériou, Isabelle le Masne de Chermont, Pascale Bourgain, and Marina Innocenti (Roma, 2001), 1080.

[242] Pontal, *Les statuts synodaux*, 2.192.

[243] Pontal, *Les statuts synodaux*, 2.322. The same set of statutes allowed a priest to warn a parishioner against receiving; see Pontal, *Les statuts synodaux*, 2.324.

[244] Richard Trexler, *Synodal Law in Florence and Fiesole, 1306–1518* (Città del Vaticano, 1971), 76.

[245] Mansi 26.451. [246] *Concilia Germaniae*, 5.587A–B (Strasburg, 1432).

[247] *Synodicon Hispanum*, 1.404.

[248] *Synodicon Hispanum*, 1.151. See also the 1528 statutes of Tuy in *Synodicon Hispanum*, 1.474–475, and the Prague statutes of 1355 in Mansi 26.394.

[249] *Synodicon Hispanum*, 1.156, 152.

utriusque about annual reception. However, the text does not mention Easter.[250] The statutes of Granada brought canonistic norms to a populace once ruled by Muslim princes. The 1565 provincial council established rules for first communion, with confession preceding reception. More specific to the region, the council required that converts get permission from a confessor or curate before receiving.[251]

In England the Canterbury statutes of the early thirteenth century warned a priest against giving communion to another's parishioners, especially at Easter.[252] The same statutes also required confession at least once a year and communion at Christmas, Easter, and Pentecost. Exceptions from reception were permitted on the advice of the priest, as *Omnis utriusque* permitted.[253] The Salisbury statutes said the same thing, but a threat was added: anyone who did not confess and receive at least once a year, unless on a priest's advice, would be shut out of the church and later denied Christian burial.[254] The Worcester statutes of 1229 simply specified confession and communion once a year near Easter.[255] The 1289 statutes of Chichester took a more positive approach, saying communion should be given liberally (*liberaliter*) on Easter.[256] Denunciation for failure to receive communion continued in the Elizabethan church.[257]

The authors of pastoral manuals had to deal with both Easter Duty and the effects of refusing to receive the sacraments. Thus Thomas of Chobham said the laity should receive at least once in a year (*semel saltem in anno*). Those who did not receive, unless advised by a priest to abstain, could be excommunicated. An unworthy sinner might be denied communion until a penance had been completed.[258] Thomas addressed the question whether children should be given communion, at least as part of Easter Duty. He

250 *Synodicon Hispanum*, 1.276, 285.

251 *El concilio provincial de Granada en 1565: Edición crítica del malgrado Concilio del Arzobispo Guerrero*, ed. Ignacio Pérez de Heredia y Valle (Roma, 1990), 395. These statutes also recited the requirements for reservation of the sacrament and viaticum processions; see *El concilio provincial de Granada*, 395–397.

252 *Council & Synods*, 2/1.30. Similarly see Trexler, *Synodal Law in Florence and Fiesole*, 259–260. The statutes of Avignon (1337) threatened priests who heard the confessions and gave the Eucharist to another's parishioners not just on Easter but for eight days before and after with excommunication; see Mansi 25.1089. See also the Padua statute of 1351 in Mansi 26.243.

253 *Council & Synods*, 2/1.32, 236–237.

254 *Council & Synods*, 2/1.72–73. These statutes also said a priest could warn against reception if he was not yet absolved from sins; see *Council & Synods*, 2/1.74–75. The statutes of London (1245–1259) said the same things about confession and communion as did those of Salisbury; see *Council & Synods*, 2/1.639.

255 *Council & Synods*, 2/1.173. 256 Mansi 24.1060.

257 Caroline Litzenberger, "St. Michael's, Gloucester, 1540–80: The Cost of Conformity in Sixteenth-Century England," in *The Parish in English Life 1400–1600*, ed. Katherine L. French, Gary G. Gibbs, and Beat A. Kümin (Manchester, 1997), 230–249 at 247–248.

258 *Thomae de Chobham summa confessorum*, 106.

decided, after considering the arguments pro and con, that it was a pious thing to do: "Therefore, it would be pious to give the Eucharist to every child." He added, however, the caution that the child might reject the host on account of the taste. In that case, it was to be picked up and burned later.[259] In all cases, communion only could be received from the celebrant of that day's mass.[260] The French *Libellus* for the instruction of archdeacons also required communion on the three major feasts, reception following confession.[261]

John of Freiburg said the Church required receiving "once in a year" (*semel in anno*) except if a confessor counseled abstaining.[262] His *Summa* dealt with the possibility that someone who was obligated might be forced to face receiving when in mortal sin. Accidentally receiving when unaware of the sin was acceptable. However, John's advice was it was better to face excommunication for abstaining than to communicate when knowingly in a state of sin.[263] The communicant was to seek a chance to confess but also had to be wary of giving scandal to the people (*scandalum populi*).[264] Communion could purge venial, but not mortal, sin, especially if reception was moved by charity.[265] Proper preparation required fasting, except by the sick. The fast by the healthy was to last from midnight to allow food to pass out of the body. The communicant was also forbidden to eat quickly after receiving. All this was to be done out of reverence for the sacrament that united the individual who received spiritually (*spiritualiter*) with Christ and the Church.[266] The usual rule of abstaining from marital sex was applied in the *Summa*, and regulations about the effects of nocturnal pollution also were added.[267] Children might receive once "beginning to have discretion" (*incipientibus habere discretionem*). His *Summa* accepted giving communion to children as young as ten years of

[259] *Thomae de Chobham summa confessorum*, 105, "unde pium esset dare omni parvulo eucharistiam cum tali cautela quod si post gustum parvulis reiceret, recolligeretur illa eiectio et igni combureretur ..." Thomas considered the possibility of giving only consecrated wine to children; see *Thomae de Chobham summa confessorum*, 104.

[260] *Thomae de Chobham summa confessorum*, 106.

[261] Elizabeth Kay Todd, "*Libellus pastoralis de cura et officio archidiaconi*: A Thirteenth-Century Handbook for Archdeacons; a Critical Edition and Introduction," PhD Dissertation, Ohio State University, 1993, 77. This text also warned against giving communion to children not yet worthy of the sacrament.

[262] Johannes de Friburgo, *Summa confessorum*, fol. cxxiii^{ra} (q. lxviii).

[263] Johannes de Friburgo, *Summa confessorum*, fol. cxxiii^{ra-b} (q. lxviiii), "Unde etiam potius deberet excommunicationem sustinere quam in peccato communicare."

[264] Johannes de Friburgo, *Summa confessorum*, fol. cxxiii^{rb} (q. lxx).

[265] Johannes de Friburgo, *Summa confessorum*, fol. cxxvi^{ra-b} (qq. cxiii–cxviii). Nicholas of Ausimo, in his *Supplementum Summae Pisanellae*, fol. I-5^{ra-b}.

[266] Johannes de Friburgo, *Summa confessorum*, fol. cxxii^{vb}–cxxiii^{ra} (qq. lxiii–lxvii).

[267] Johannes de Friburgo, *Summa confessorum*, fol. cxxii^{rb}–cxxiii^{ra} (qq. lxxiii–lxxv).

age if they gave "signs of discretion and devotion" (*signa discretionis appareant et deuotionis*).[268]

John of Erfurt said communion was to be received on Easter "of necessity" (*de necessitate*). He added the usual exception for a person advised by the priest against reception, citing *Omnis utriusque* in this context. John thought everyone should communicate on Holy Thursday (*in cena domini*). Here, too, he made exceptions for those guilty of serious crimes. Even penitents at the end of their penitential period were to receive. John permitted reception on other Sundays for those who prepared properly "in devotion and purity of conscience" (*in devotione et conscientiae puritate*).[269] William of Pagula said that those who reached the age of reason (*postquam ad annum discretionis peruenerit*) should receive at least once a year unless advised otherwise by their proper priest. William made reference to *Omnis utriusque*, including its threat that those who did not conform might be denied Christian burial.[270]

Antoninus of Florence treated this issue more than once in his Latin *Confessionale*. A title was devoted to negligence about communion, especially failure of those who had reached the age of reason to confess and receive at least at Easter. If impeded legitimately by a stomach illness or excommunication, the parishioner was obligated to make up for this defect as soon as possible.[271] The archbishop wanted confessors to ask boys and girls whether they had gone to confession and taken communion at least once in a year.[272] Antoninus instructed the faithful to receive communion while fasting, except when gravely ill (*graviter infirmus*).[273] The archbishop believed there could be perils in receiving if the communicant had refrained from confessing a sin out of shame, ignorance, or other causes. A more subtle passage said it was a grave matter to receive while intending to commit a mortally sinful act.[274] Antoninus's vernacular

[268] Johannes de Friburgo, *Summa confessorum*, fol. cxxiii^{rb-va} (q. lxxxiiii).

[269] *Die Summa confessorum des Johannes von Erfurt*, 3.873.

[270] William of Pagula, *Oculus sacerdotis*, University of Pennsylvania MS Codex 721, fol. 7va.

[271] Antoninus, *Confessionale "Defecerunt scrutantes scrutinio"* (Köln, 1470), *De negligentia communionis*, "De negligentia communionis. Si omisit communicare semel in anno. scilicet. in pasca et hoc post annos discrecionis: peccauit mortaliter. nisi fuisset legittime impeditus ut quia alteratur stomacho vel excommunicatus. Querens tamen absolucionem. vel de licentia proprii sacerdotis vel confessoris per aliquod dies differret. In huiusmodi tamen casibus debet supplere defectus quam cito poterit." Antoninus also used the term *indispositus*.

[272] Antoninus, *Confessionale "Defecerunt scrutantes scrutinio," A pueris et puellis*, "De confessione et communione semel in anno fienda."

[273] Antoninus, *Confessionale "Defecerunt scrutantes scrutinio," De negligentia communionis*.

[274] Antoninus, *Confessionale "Defecerunt scrutantes scrutinio," De negligentia communionis*, "Si communionem sumpsit. Cum staret in proposito perpetrandi aliquod mortale. quia mortaliter peccauit."

Confessionale "Omnis mortalium cura" briefly summarized much of this material for those not learned in Latin.[275]

Easter Duty could be understood as defining a parish, including its membership. Even the servants of the Franciscan nuns of Waterbeach were required to communicate in the parish church of that village on Easter.[276] The Apostolic Penitentiary, especially in the late fifteenth century, often was asked by lay persons, including married couples, to grant exceptions to receiving the sacraments from the parish priest. These might be granted, permitting receiving communion from any fitting (*idoneus*) priest. However, the Penitentiary regularly rarely made an exception for Easter communion, which had to occur in the parish.[277] Many individuals understood this, specifying in their petitions receipt of communion on Easter in the parish church.[278] Nobles and other lay persons occasionally asked to substitute a chapel, even one in a castle, for the parish church.[279] An entire village might ask for the sacraments to be offered in a chapel or in a nearby parish because their own parish church was hard to reach, especially in bad weather, or at the end of a dangerous road.[280]

Nonetheless, a priest who administered the sacraments without permission might need absolution from irregularity. In one case, an Augustinian from Krakow had to ask Calixtus III's Penitentiary for absolution after he gave the Eucharist to a local couple.[281] In another way, there might be persons resident in a hospital in need of the sacraments. The patrons of the hospital might ask for service of a priest, even if

[275] Antoninus, *Confessionale "Omnis mortalium cura"* (Milan, 1470), fol. 29r, cited from Europeana [http://www.europeana.eu/portal/record/09428/urn_nbn_de_bsz_24_digibib_bsz3471291104.html?start=1&query=omnis+mortalium&startPage=1&rows=12], accessed on February 5, 2014.

[276] Elizabeth Makowski, *English Nuns and the Law in the Middle Ages* (Woodbridge, 2011), 121.

[277] *Repertorium poenitentiariae Germanicum*, 2 no. 879, 1051, 6 no. 2182, 2185, 3172, 3235, 3237, 7 no. 1519, 2069, 6551. The Margrave of Baden asked this for his whole household in the reign of Sixtus IV; see *Repertorium poenitentiariae Germanicum*, 6 no. 3254. A layman of Liège asked Eugenius IV for this privilege even for Easter communion; see *Repertorium poenitentiariae Germanicum*, 1 no. 553. A cleric asked Alexander VI for the same privilege; see *Repertorium poenitentiariae Germanicum*, 8 no. 6550.

[278] *Repertorium Poenitentiariae Germanicum*, 3 no. 318, 485, 579, 5 no. 1714, 1922, 6 no. 7436, 7 no. 1877, 2144, 2408–2409, 8 no. 2203, 2932, 2959, 5932, 5981, 6051, 6141–6142.

[279] E.g. *Repertorium Poenitentiariae Germanicum*, 7 no. 2137, 2513, 8 no. 2125, 3153.

[280] *Repertorium Poenitentiariae Germanicum*, 4 no. 961, 7 no. 1991, 2113, 2116, 2340, 8 no. 2642.

[281] *Repertorium Poenitentiariae Germanicum*, 3 no. 540. Similarly a priest who gave the sacraments to a pregnant woman had to fast as his penance; see *Repertorium poenitentiariae Germanicum*, 5 no. 1332.

administration of Easter communion was excepted from such a request to the Penitentiary for his ministry.[282]

The extent of lay participation in Easter confession and communion at Easter is hard to document. A welcome insight is offered by the visitations of parishes in the archdeaconry of Josas near Paris in the 1460s and 1470s. The visitors frequently said simply that all of the parishioners received at Easter.[283] Exceptions were noted. Men might be away at Easter; or someone might go elsewhere, especially if newly arrived in the parish.[284] Internal squabbles in a parish might also be reflected in a refusal to receive. A couple and their unmarried children were reported as avoiding communion because they hated another parishioner.[285] A person who failed to receive might be cited by the visitors.[286] One statute from Ferrara, dated to 1332, said the priest was to send the bishop the names of those who failed in their Easter Duty.[287] Parishioners too might be upset by a neighbor's failure to receive together with them. One person who failed in this act of parish solidarity was denounced by the people of a local church to the visitors acting for the archdeacon of Josas.[288]

Similar complaints are found in the 1397 Hereford visitations. Two men from Lanwaran received neither there nor in another church.[289] John Alayn of Wesbury failed his Easter Duty for three consecutive years. He had to swear to mend his ways.[290] Henry Merekote of Minsterworth was reported for neither confessing nor receiving.[291] In the archdeaconry of Prague, a woman professed ignorance whether her husband had ever confessed or received. Other men were reported to perform their Easter Duty only when compelled to do so.[292]

In addition to the reception of communion at Eastertide, the faithful were expected to make an offering. A set of questions for English bishops to use in visitations included one asking whether parishioners had been ordered by the priest not just to receive communion on Easter but to make

282 E.g. *Repertorium Poenitentiariae Germanicum*, 7 no. 1922.

283 E.g. *Visites archdidiaconales de Josas*, ed. J.-M. Alliot (Paris, 1902), 359, 369, 372, 377–378, 380.

284 *Visites archdidiaconales de Josas*, 113, 201, 228, 287.

285 *Visites archdidiaconales de Josas*, 165. An *exemplum* had the devil stranging a woman who pretended to reconcile with an enemy to appear better than she was at Easter communion; see Katherine L. French, *The Good Women of the Parish: Gender and Religion after the Black Death* (Philadelphia, 2008), 201–202.

286 *Visites archdidiaconales de Josas*, 23.

287 Mansi 25.971–972.

288 *Visites archdidiaconales de Josas*, 191.

289 A. T. Bannister, "Visitation Returns of the Diocese of Hereford in 1397," *The English Historical Review* 44 (1929), 279–289, 444–453, 45 (1930), 92–101, 444–463 at 29.287.

290 Bannister, "Visitation Returns," 29.451.

291 Bannister, "Visitation Returns," 29.452.

292 *Visitační protokol Pražského arcijáhna pavla z janovic z let 1379–1382*, ed. Iavan Hlaváček and Zdeňka Hledíková (Praha, 1973), 296, 333, 358.

an offering then.[293] This matches the fact that the churchwardens of St. Mary's at Hill, London, in the period 1493–1494, recorded an Easter offering of 10 shillings and 5 pence.[294] The diocese of Salisbury required offerings by the laity for Christmas, Easter, the patronal festival, and the anniversary of the dedication of the parish church.[295] This obligatory offering was resented on occasion. Thus the Lollard Richard Wyche was accused of asserting that no offering should be received for communion.[296] Another Lollard complained that a priest bought 30 hosts for 1 pence and sold them to communicants for 2 pence each.[297] Nonetheless, some Lollards were reported to receive communion in their parishes, apparently confident that they might receive spiritual benefits from devoutly receiving.[298]

The Lollards were not alone in seeing requirement of Easter offerings as potentially scandalous. In England a legatine Council at Westminster (1125) forbade requiring a payment for the Eucharist or other holy things.[299] The 1175 Council of Westminster indicated that the offering of a penny (*denarius*) might be expected,[300] but the same council restated a canon of the Council of Tours decrying requiring payment as simony.[301] The Lincoln statutes of ca. 1239 prohibited priests from receiving offerings just after Easter communion to avoid showing cupidity and thus undermining the good effects of the congregation's reception of the sacrament.[302] The Durham statutes of ca. 1241–1249 threatened excommunication for exacting offerings at Easter or other occasions on which the Eucharist was received.[303]

On the Continent, the statutes of Le Mans, among others, denounced selling the sacraments as avarice and simony.[304] The diocese of Tournai had a slightly different statute requiring that the sacraments be distributed gratis.[305] By 1461 the statutes of Olomouc in Moravia prohibited exactions for ecclesiastical rites on account of avarice or simony.[306]

293 *Pastors and the Care of Souls*, 288–291. 294 *Pastors and the Care of Souls*, 228.

295 *Pastors and the Care of Souls*, 223–224.

296 Henry Ansgar Kelly, "Inquisition, Public Fame and Confession: General Rules and English Practice," in *The Culture of Inquisition in Medieval England*, ed. Mary C. Flannery and Katie L. Walter (Woodbridge, 2013), 1–29 at 25.

297 John A. F. Thomson, *The Later Lollards 1414–1520* (Oxford, 1965), 247.

298 Thomson, *The Later Lollards 1414–1520*, 246–247.

299 *Councils & Synods*, 1/2.738. This decree was reenacted in 1138; see *Councils & Synods*, 1/2.774.

300 *Councils & Synods*, 1/2.979. 301 *Councils & Synods*, 1/2.986.

302 *Councils & Synods*, 2/1.271. 303 *Councils & Synods*, 2/1.430–431.

304 Pontal, *Les statuts synodaux*, 2.166. Similarly see Mansi 25.74 (Bayeux); *Concilia Germaniae*, 5.245B (Strasburg, 1432).

305 Avril, *Les statuts synodaux*, 4.330.

306 *Synody a statuta Olomoucké diecéze období středověku*, ed. Pavel Krafl (Praha, 2003), 220.

The visitations of the archdeaconry of Prague in the late fourteenth century included one case of a priest collecting the offering and then leaving for another church without completing the mass. In another case a priest was accused of refusing to give communion until a layman put money on the altar.[307]

Nonetheless, Easter offerings were important enough for them to enter into a long-running lawsuit between a parish priest and the patrons of a neighboring parish, a Franciscan women's monastery in London.[308] Moreover, a case of a priest's procurator not permitting communion without an offering was reported at Leomestre in the diocese of Hereford in 1392. The visitor forbade his doing that in the future.[309] In a German city, a priest was reported to the council, a lay body, for trying to deny communion to a layman in a dispute about tithes.[310]

The emphasis on Easter Duty presented dissidents with another challenge. Were they to confess and receive in their parishes? Bernard Gui prepared questions for suspected Waldensians, asking whether they had confessed to their proper priest "in Lent or before Easter" (*in quadragesima vel ante pascha*). They also were to be asked if they had communicated at Easter, since neither they nor their sympathizers received except to dissimulate (*nisi hoc facerent ad dissimulandum*).[311]

Heresy was not the only challenge to the authorities. Lay people might want communion more frequently than a few times in a year. Sixtus IV denied a priest the right to give communion to anyone who asked for it and even to give it to anyone more than once a day.[312] In the same pontificate, a priest complained to Rome about an inquisitor who regarded as heretical parishioners who wanted daily communion, even after confession.[313] Parish priests probably expected their flock to be content outside Eastertide with spiritual communion or kissing the wooden pax, with its image of a host, which the celebrant had kissed before his own communion.[314]

307 *Visitační protokol Pražského*, 243, 319–320.
308 Makowski, *English Nuns and the Law in the Middle Ages*, 143–148.
309 Bannister, "Visitation Returns," 30.99.
310 John Van Engen, "Multiple Options: The World of the Fifteenth-Century Church," *Church History* 77 (2008), 257–284 at 268.
311 Bernard Gui, *Manuel de l'inquisietur*, ed. Guillaume Mollat, 2 vols. (Paris, 1964), 1.80; Gui, *The Inquisitor's Guide: A Medieval Manual on Heretics*, trans. Janet Shirley (Welwyn Garden City, 2006), 75.
312 *Repertorium Poenitentiariae Germanicum*, 6 no. 3222.
313 *Repertorium Poenitentiariae Germanicum*, 6 no. 3713.
314 Katherine A. Smith, *The Taymouth Hours: Stories and the Construction of Self in Late Medieval England* (London, 2012), 65–66, 158.

Denial of communion

Communion cannot be divorced from serious penances and spiritual censures. Thus the early penitentials abound in references to denying the Eucharist to penitents during a term of solemn repentance as well as to excommunicates. Reconciliation with the Church after public penance meant readmission to communion in fellowship with the rest of a parish community.[315] A nun who gave up her habit and married was to be denied the sacrament, as was a cleric who returned to secular garb or wed.[316] Heretics inevitably were to be denied the Eucharist, although some apparently received anyway.[317] Nor were the possessed (mentally ill) to receive communion.[318] Penalties might be changed. Thus the penance for abortion, once a reason for banning communion for life, was reduced to a ten-year term.[319] Anyone who refused to do penance before communion because of the hardships involved was to be "cast out of the Church, or from the communion or the society of the faithful."[320]

On the local level, Hubert Walter's statutes said communion should be denied to the impenitent.[321] So did the first statutes of Salisbury.[322] The 1284 statutes of Nîmes tried to deal with this issue by having the priest warn the congregation against the dangers of receiving without penitence and confession.[323] The statutes of Bordeaux associated this denial of the sacrament with the biblical warning of the ill effects of eating unworthily, eating a judgment on one's self.[324] The 1287 statutes of Liège said no one was to be denied communion except those suffering from excommunication or interdict, guilty of notorious sin or disreputable, as were prostitutes, mimes, actors, and notorious usurers.[325] So did the statutes of Cambrai, which added exclusion of anyone who made chaplets of flowers to sell as love charms.[326] Other pressures were applied using denial of communion. One woman in the diocese of Brixen reported to the Apostolic Penitentiary during the reign of Innocent VIII being denied the sacrament to force her to reconcile with her husband.[327] A priest of the archdeaconry of Prague was denounced for withholding communion

[315] Times of penance and exclusion from communion varied by offense; see *Medieval Handbooks of Penance: A Translation of the Principal "libri poenitentiales" and Selections from Related Documents*, ed. John T. McNeill and Helena M. Gamer (New York, 1938), 81, 94, 111, 113, 160, 217, 239, 252–253, 329, 384. Excommunicates could be given deathbed communion anyway; see *Medieval Handbooks of Penance*, 287.

[316] *Medieval Handbooks of Penance*, 292, 303.

[317] *Medieval Handbooks of Penance*, 188. [318] *Medieval Handbooks of Penance*, 289.

[319] *Medieval Handbooks of Penance*, 304. [320] *Medieval Handbooks of Penance*, 395.

[321] *Councils & Synods*, 1 /2.1061. [322] *Councils & Synods*, 2/1.80. [323] Mansi 24.535.

[324] Pontal, *Les statuts synodaux*, 2.60. [325] Mansi 24.899.

[326] Avril, *Les statuts synodaux*, 4.44–45.

[327] *Repertorium poenitentiariae Germanicum*, 7 no. 2210.

from his parishioners on the grounds that they had not done the penance he had imposed.[328] Bishops used this refusal of the Eucharist in an attempt to keep their subjects away from the competing pastoral services of the friars following the reforming efforts of the Fifth Lateran Council (1512–1517). Pope Leo X had to issue bulls clarifying the Lateran decrees in an effort to soften these harsh measures.[329]

A different obstacle was created by ecclesiastical censures. Excommunicated persons were to be denied communion, and the mass was not supposed to be celebrated in an area under interdict.[330] The threat of being denied the sacraments in a place under censure was a sufficient concern for some persons to petition the Apostolic Penitentiary for the right to receive the Eucharist even in a place under interdict.[331] Moreover, priests who gave communion to the excommunicated, even in ignorance of that fact, or administered the sacraments in an area under interdict, even behind closed doors, sometimes petitioned the Penitentiary for absolution from censures.[332] The 1255 statutes of Valencia described giving communion to those under censure as potentially scandalizing the faithful, but the same statutes said those same persons could still adore the consecrated elements.[333] Nicholas of Cusa said a person unjustly excommunicated should refrain from communicating, obtaining grace through obedience instead.[334]

Even ignorance could be an obstacle to communion. Thus one statute from Toledo in the Spanish Golden Age required that the lay recipient know the *Pater noster, Ave Maria*, Creed, and *Salve Regina*. Another Toledan statute required knowing the Decalogue and the commandments of the Church too.[335]

328 *Visitační protokol Pražského*, 157.

329 Nelson H. Minnich, "Egidio Antonini da Viterbo, the Reform of Religious Orders and the Fifth Lateran Council (1512–1517)," in *Egidio da Viterbo: Cardinal Agostiniano tra Roma e l'Europa del Rinascimento: Atti del Convegno. Viterbo, 22–23 settembre 2012 – Roma, 26–28 settembre 2012*, ed. Myriam Chiabò, Rocco Ronzani, and Angelo Maria Vitale (Roma, 2014), 217–267 at 264–265.

330 Elisabeth Vodola, *Excommunication in the Middle Ages* (Berkeley, 1986), 54–58; Peter D. Clarke, *The Interdict in the Thirteenth Century: A Question of Collectve Guilt* (Oxford, 2007), 18, 77, 149–152.

331 *Repertorium poenitentiariae Germanicum*, 3 no. 127, 137, 288, 866, 6 no. 3183, 8 no. 6373–6374, 6533. A priest petitioned the Penitentiary during the reign of Alexander VI to celebrate mass anywhere even in a place under interdict; see *Repertorium poenitentiariae Germanicum*, 8 no. 5920.

332 *Repertorium poenitentiariae Germanicum*, 1 no. 585, 2 no. 356, 769, 3 no. 125, 4 no. 1232, 5 no. 1214, 7 no. 1741, 7 no. 2181.

333 Mansi 23.1890–1891.

334 Nicholas of Cusa, *Writings on Church and Reform*, 50–51.

335 Patrick J. O'Banion, *The Sacrament of Penance in Golden Age Spain* (University Park, Pa., 2013), 74–76.

Local statutes could, as we have seen, indicate to whom communion should be denied. However, they did not allow public denial of the Eucharist when a priest knew of a parishioner's secret sin. The Canterbury statutes prohibited a priest denying communion under those circumstances.[336] The 1277 Council of Trier issued a similar prohibition.[337] A statute of Nîmes allowed the priest to draw the sinner apart (*trahant ipsum ad partem*) to warn secretly against reception. This warning could include the threat of damnation.[338] Likewise, the York statutes of ca. 1241–1255 prohibited denying communion to anyone on account of a debt.[339] Ivo of Chartres' *Decretum* took a permissive attitude about another matter, saying, in the words of a Council of Carthage, that a woman who had given birth could receive communion if she wished.[340]

Pastoral manuals conveyed precepts about denial of communion to pastors and confessors. Thomas of Chobham said not to communicate impenitent adults. He also repeated that communion could not be denied to one whose secret sins the priest alone knew. If the sinner once divulged the sin to another, he could be denied communion.[341] John of Erfurt said all the faithful theoretically could receive communion. However, communion was to be denied to the impenitent, as well as the excommunicated. Others to be denied communion were actors, the mad, very young children, and others lacking the use of reason (*usu rationis*), as well as outsiders unknown to the priest. Married persons who had just demanded or complied with a demand for the marital debt were expected to refrain, as were those men who suffered nocturnal pollution.[342] William of Pagula said to abstain from marital intercourse for as many as six days. He cited *Omnis utriusque* as saying this was not a command (*praeceptum*) but a counsel (*consilium*). The husband still was required to comply with his wife's demand at any time. William also said that one who was deranged (*amens*) could receive during a lucid interval.[343] Antoninus of Florence expected a confessor to ask a parish priest if he had given communion to the impenitent or publicly denied it to someone whose secret sins he knew.[344]

John of Freiburg summarized these issues. John too said communion could be denied to a public sinner, but not to someone whose secret sin the priest knew. In a case of a secret sin, however, the priest could warn

336 *Council & Synods*, 2/80, 1.33. 337 Mansi 24.194.
338 Pontal, *Les statuts synodaux*, 2.324, 326. 339 *Councils & Synods*, 2/1.489.
340 Ivo Carnotensis, *Decretum*, PL 161.174A.
341 *Thomae de Chobham summa confessorum*, 105–106.
342 *Die Summa confessorum des Johannes von Erfurt*, 3.871–873.
343 William of Pagula, *Oculus sacerdotis*, fol. 7va. Similarly see Johannes de Friburgo, *Summa confessorum*, fol. cxxiii[rb] (q. lxxxiii).
344 Antoninus, *Confessionale "Defecerunt scrutantes scrutinio," Circa clericos in commune.*

the sinner privately not to receive. The same rules applied to those guilty of crimes, hidden or public.[345] John said, however, that menstruating women and those with bodily afflictions like leprosy could receive communion if they so desired.[346] His *Summa* said a person unjustly excommunicated should refrain from communicating, because otherwise there would be a defect in signifying the unity of Christ's Mystical Body. This was more virtuous than defiance.[347]

[345] Johannes de Friburgo, *Summa confessorum*, fol. cxxviii^{ra-b} (qq. lxxviii–lxxx).

[346] Johannes de Friburgo, *Summa confessorum*, fol. cxxviii^{ra} (q. lxxvii).

[347] Johannes de Friburgo, *Summa confessorum*, fol. cxxii^{vb} (q. lxxiii), "quia in talibus defectus rei significate scilicet unitatis corporis mystici."

4 Custody of the Eucharist and communion of the sick

Custody of the reserved Eucharist

Among the decrees of the Fourth Lateran Council was the canon *Statuimus*, number 20 in the traditional order of the Lateran canons. It was concerned with keeping the Eucharist and holy oils secure under lock and key. The text reads,

> We decree that the chrism and the Eucharist are to be kept locked away in a safe place in all churches, so that no audacious hand can reach them to do anything horrible or impious. If he who is responsible for their safe-keeping leaves them around carelessly, let him be suspended from office for three months; if anything unspeakable happens on account of his carelessness, let him be subject to graver punishment.

The council presumed that the Eucharist was to be reserved, at least in the form of consecrated bread, for communion of the sick. It was vague, however, about what an "audacious hand" might do, especially something "unspeakable," to the reserved host. The rationale for this decree, as it was explained by the Decretalists, especially by Hostiensis, was prevention of abuse of the reserved sacrament by practitioners of forbidden magic.[1]

The decree *Statuimus* was not without precedent, although the focus of earlier texts was more on the sick than on malefactors. In the tenth century, Regino of Prüm, summarizing a canon ascribed to a Council of Tours, had required priests to have a fitting vessel for the reserved hosts "Inquiry must be made if the pyx always is over the altar with the sacred offering for viaticum for the sick."[2] Regino backed this requirement with a text

[1] *Decrees of the Ecumenical Councils*, 1.244; *Constitutiones Concilii quarti Lateranensis una cum Commentariis glossatorum*, ed. Antonio García García (Città del Vaticano, 1981), 67. The various rubrics to the text can see found at 148. Most mention keeping the Eucharist and chrism *sub clave* or *sub clavibus*. On the purpose of the decree, see Thomas M. Izbicki, "*Manus temeraria*: Custody of the Eucharist in Medieval Canon Law," in *Proceedings of the Thirteenth International Congress of Medieval Canon Law: Esztergom, 3–8 August 2008*, ed. Peter Erdö and Szabolcs Anzelm Szuromi (Città del Vaticano, 2010), 539–552.

[2] *Das Sendhandbuch des Regino von Prüm*, ed. F. W. H. Wasserschleben and Wilfried Hartmann (Darmstadt, 2004), 26–27, "Inquirendum, si pixida semper sit super altare

Ex capitulis synodalibus and the text from Tours.[3] He also required locking up the holy oils so that they would not be touched by "any infidel or unclean person" (*aliquis infidelis aut immundus tangat*).[4] The Canons of Edgar said that the sacrament was to be kept ready, clean, and undecayed. They also included giving the sacrament to the sick among every priest's duties.[5]

Burchard of Worms used the text from the Council of Tours about keeping the Lord's body in a fitting pyx "for the viaticum of those passing out of the world" (*ad viaticum recedentibus a saeculo*). He followed it with another, from a Council of Worms, for communion of the sick or of infants in danger of death "lest he die without communion" (*ne sine communione moriatur*).[6] Burchard quoted the penances a Council of Orléans imposed on a priest who let a mouse or other animal consume the reserved sacrament or allowed it to become polluted with worms. Penance also was imposed on a priest who lost the Eucharist in his church and was unable to find it.[7] The Gregorian Reform made no changes to these rules. Thus Ivo of Chartres repeated in his *Decretum* the same texts Burchard had employed concerning the proper keeping of the reserved sacrament.[8] The *Panormia* gave a brief version of the regulation of the Council of Orléans assigning a penance for letting a mouse or other animal eat the reserved "sacrifice" (*sacrificium*).[9] These and other texts from earlier collections entered Gratian's *Decretum* in the *De consecratione*, forming the canon law of the sacraments as it was taught at the universities.[10]

The canon law, as taught, was not separate from the liturgical practices of the medieval Church. Increased reverence for the consecrated bread, in the eleventh century and thereafter, led to the creation of special housing for reserved hosts, some of it modeled on reliquaries, and the burning of perpetual lights before that housing. The terminology for this housing did not often include the term "tabernacle" until late in the medieval period.[11] When it was used, the word "tabernacle" was used alongside or

cum sacra oblatione ad viaticum infirmis." Peter Browe, "Die Eucharistie als Zaubermittel im Mittelalter," *Archiv für Kulturgeschichte* 20 (1930), 134–154.

3 *Das Sendhandbuch des Regino von Prüm*, 68, 70.

4 *Das Sendhandbuch des Regino von Prüm*, 70.

5 *Councils & Synods*, 1/1.326, 335–336. Any host kept too long was to be burned and its ashes put under the altar; see *Councils & Synods*, 1/1.326.

6 Burchardus Wormaciensis, *Decretum*, PL 140.754.

7 Burchardus Wormaciensis, *Decretum*, PL 140.762.

8 Ivo Carnotensis, *Decretum*, PL 161.165.

9 *Panormia Project*, 95.

10 Thus the Orléans canon became De cons. D. 2 c. 94.

11 An example of the use of this term is found in the visitation records of Henri de Vezelai; see Léopold Delisle, "Visites pastorales de maître Henri de Vezelai, archidiacre d'Hiémois, en 1267 et 1268," *Bibliothèque de l'École de Chartes* 54 (1893), 457–467 at

interchangeably with other terms like "repository" and shrine (*sacrarium*).[12] A few French churches are described as reserving the sacrament inside a "window" by the high altar.[13] The term "pyx" was used more frequently, at least from Regino's time onward; but it could have various meanings: the housing used in a church to reserve the sacrament, the vessel used to take communion to the sick or both. This chapter will treat any housing used for the reserved Eucharist – and the holy oils used in rites of anointing – according to its function, not according to terminology.[14] Although some Italian churches housed reserved hosts and chrism in the sacristy, most churches elsewhere placed a receptacle on, near, or above the high altar.[15] Castle chapels too might reserve the sacrament for viaticum.[16] Eventually elaborately decorated tabernacles and sacrament houses were built to both protect the reserved sacrament and highlight the ties of the Eucharist to the Incarnation and the Passion.[17]

The issue of custody of the Eucharist was never separable from the original purpose of reserving the sacrament, communion of the sick and dying. This was a matter not just of protection, the issue the Lateran Council underlined, but the readiness of the elements, refreshed on a regular schedule, at the moment of need. Parish churches usually reserved the sacrament and were faced with the need to refresh it frequently. Spoilage, filth, and pests (mice and spiders) might render the reserved sacrament offensive to the sick. Aelfric reported a custom of

466. The term "armoire" appears in the same records; see "Visites pastorales de maître Henri de Vezelai," 464, 466.

12 This terminology is inconsistent in *Visites archdidiaconales de Josas*, ed. J.-M. Alliot (Paris: Picard, 1902), e.g. 16, 25, 27, 267. One record cites the lack of a coffer inside the great ark; see *Visites Josas*, 54. Another church was told to repair the glass of its sacrarium; see *Visites Josas*, 336.

13 *Visites Josas*, e.g. 264–265, 293.

14 The 1287 Council at Liège specifically applied the term "pyx" to vessels for both purposes; see Mansi 24.897. The 1224 Council of Winchester, however, distinguished a pyx for communicating the sick from the vessel used for reserved hosts in a church; see *Councils & Synods*, 2/1.126, 135 n. 1. G. J. C. Snoek, *Medieval Piety from Relics to the Eucharist: A Process of Mutual Interaction* (Leiden, 1995), 227–307; Elizabeth Saxon, *the Eucharist in Medieval France: Iconography and Theology* (Woodbridge, 2006), 32, 243.

15 Archdale King, *Eucharistic Reservation in the Western Church* (London, 1965), 71–95. Chrism and oil might be kept in a separate locked chrismatory (*chrismatorium*) distinct from the pyx or tabernacle used for the reserved Eucharist; see *Visitations of Churches Belonging to St. Paul's Cathedral in 1297 and in 1458*, ed. W. Sparrow Simpson (Westminster, 1895; New York, 1966), xxxii–xxxiii.

16 E.g. *Repertorium poenitentiariae Germanicum*, 6 no. 3251.

17 Kristen Van Ausdall, "Art and Eucharist in the Late Middle Ages," in *A Companion to the Eucharist in the Middle Ages*, ed. Ian Christopher Levy, Gary Macy, and Van Ausdall (Leiden, 2012), 541–617 at 605–615; Van Ausdall, "Communicating with the Host: Imagery and Eucharistic Contact in Late Medieval and Renaissance Italy," in *Push Me, Pull You: Imaginative and Emotional Interaction in Late Medieval and Renaissance Art*, ed. Sarah Blick and Laura D. Gelfand, 1 (Leiden, 2011), 447–486.

keeping the Eucharist consecrated on Easter throughout the year for the sick. He decried the possibility of its becoming moldy and said the sacrament consecrated on any day was just as holy. Aelfric required refreshing the reserved Eucharist every seven or fourteen days.[18]

Gratian's *Decretum*, as noted above, reused existing canons concerned with the reserved sacrament. Distinction 2 of the *De consecratione* cited the decree of the Council of Worms saying the Eucharist always was to be kept ready for the sick, so that they would not die without communion (c. *Presbiter eucharistiam*, De con. D. 2 c. 93), and the one from a Council of Orléans prescribing penance for anyone who did not keep the Eucharist well, so that an animal ate it, or who lost the Eucharist in a church and could not find it (c. *Qui bene*, De cons. D. 2 c. 94).[19] The Ordinary Gloss of Johannes Teutonicus focused not on the discipline of reservation but on the theoretical question of whether a mouse could eat the Body of Christ in the host. The Gloss argued that it ceased to be the body, although mere passage across the host of a mouse or spider did not cause that change. Johannes did admit that this cessation was not absolutely necessary. After all, bad men received the Eucharist daily.[20] This last was not a new sentiment among Decretists. One commentary on the *De consecratione*, *Fecit Moyses tabernaculum*, said that both good and bad persons ate, but only the former to their salvation.[21]

Statuimus, like the other Lateran decrees, soon made its way into medieval canon law. This text was included in *Compilatio quarta* under the title "On Baptism and Its Effect" (*De baptismo et eius effectu*; 4 Comp. 3.16.2).[22] Raymond of Peñafort included the canon in the *Liber extra* as the Chapter 1 of the title "On the Custody of the Eucharist, Chrism and Other Sacraments" (*De custodia eucharistiae, chrismatis et aliorum sacramentorum*, X 3.44.1).[23] The other chapter under this title is *Relinqui* (X 3.41.2), canon 19 of the same Lateran Council, which required that

[18] *Councils & Synods* 1/1.222. [19] *Corpus Iuris Canonici*, 1.1351–1352.

[20] *Decretum divi Gratiani*... (Lyon, 1554), 1294 v. Comederti. On the controversies that the presence of vermin could cause, see Anne Hudson, "The Mouse in the Pyx: Popular Heresy and the Eucharist," *Trivium* 26 (1991), 40–53.

[21] Printed in *Die Summa über das decretum Gratiani*, ed. Johann Friedrich von Schulte (Giessen, 1891; Aalen, 1965), 276: De cons. D. 2 c. 92, "quia veram Christi carnem etiam mali et reprobi comedunt." Peter Landau, "Die Dekretsumme *Fecit Moyses tabernaculum* – ein weiteres Werk der Kölner Kanonistik," *Zeitschrift der Savigny-Stiftung für Rechtsgeschichte, Kanonistische Abteilung* 127 (2010), 602–608.

[22] *Quinque compilationes antiquae nec non Collectio canonum Lipsiensis*, ed. Emil Friedberg (Leipzig, 1882; Graz, 1956), 144. *Compilatio quarta* was assembled by Johannes Teutonicus; see James A. Brundage, *Medieval Canon Law* (London, 1995), 195, 219–220.

[23] *Corpus Iuris Canonici*, 2.649. Honorius III, in the decretal *Sane*, required that the Eucharistic be kept "devoutly and faithfully"; see *Corpus Iuris Canonici*, 2.642: X. 3.41.10, discussed further below. Brundage, *Medieval Canon Law*, 196–197.

churches not become storehouses of furniture, as well as that liturgical vessels and cloths be kept "neat and clean."[24] Both of these texts were intended to make churches fit places for worship, not facsimiles of the homes of the laity. There were complaints enough from bishops and local councils to justify such legislation, including concerns about hosts being allowed to decay without being consumed and replaced with new ones, to justify the Lateran Council's actions.[25] Nonetheless, the reference to an "audacious hand" remained unexplained, especially since there seem to be few complaints outside of polemical texts that heretics such as the Cathars actually violated the reserved sacrament.[26] As noted above, accusations focused instead on mocking the elevation and the sacramental bread.

A possible explanation for locking away the sacrament was that Jews might suborn Christians to steal consecrated hosts to torture them in imitation of Christ's Passion. Bleeding host miracles, however, were not reported until well after the Fourth Lateran Council had adjourned. The earliest of these miracle stories derives from Paris in 1290, a tale which set a pattern for blaming Jews for assaults on the sacrament. They proliferated thereafter, complete with tales of divine or human vengeance on the malefactors; but they arose too late to explain the Lateran decree.[27] A rare concern that either Jews or bad Christians might use hosts for nefarious purposes is found in the statutes of Coventry issued by Alexander of Stavensby (1224–1238).[28] More often the canonists and the authors of synodal decrees were concerned that Christians might attempt to work

[24] *Decrees of the Ecumenical Councils*, 1.244; *Corpus Iuris Canonici*, 2.649–650.

[25] Miri Rubin, *Corpus Christi: The Eucharist in Late Medieval Culture* (Cambridge, 1991), 43–45.

[26] Eucharistic theology did react to these heresies; but reports of Eucharistic wonders before Lateran IV usually are related to the devotion of the faithful, who wanted to see Christ in the sacrament; see Gary Macy, *The Theologies of the Eucharist in the Early Scholastic Period: A Study of the Salvific Function of the Sacrament according to the Theologians, c. 1080–c. 1220* (Oxford, 1984), 86–93. For the polemicists' concerns with this issue, see Jessalyn Bird, "The Construction of Orthodoxy and the (De)construction of Heretical Attacks on the Eucharist in *Pastoralia* from Peter the Chanter's Circle in Paris," in *Texts and the Repression of Medieval Heresy*, ed. Caterina Bruschi and Peter Biller (York, 2003), 45–61.

[27] Other tales involving supposed atrocities by Jews predated the bleeding hosts, but they were focused on other matters; see Miri Rubin, *Gentile Tales: The Narrative Assault on Late Medieval Jews* (Philadelphia, 1999). On the devotional context of the bleeding host phenomenon, see, most recently, Caroline Walker Bynum, *Wonderful Blood: Theology and Practice in Late Medieval Northern Germany and Beyond* (Philadelphia, 2007).

[28] *Councils & Synods*, 2/1, 210, "Quia ergo solent quidam propter obprobria Christi ut increduli, quidam qui propter nimium contemptum descendunt in profundum abyssi, quidam autem propter veneficia, ut mali christiani et iudei, aliqua turpia circa eucharistiam et chrisma et oleum sanctum ausu temerario, immo nimis ausi, presumere, praecipimus ut sub optima clausura clavium reponantur in diversis vasis prout decet honestas."

magic by misusing the Eucharist and holy oils, even baptismal water.[29] Magical practices requiring some form of literacy are missing from the earlier penitentials, although some misuses of hosts for practical purposes are recorded. Complaints that chrism or a host was stolen for magical use were recorded in early synodal decrees.[30] (The penitentials also required elaborate precautions against accidentally profaning the Eucharistic elements during mass.[31]) By the twelfth century, however, growing devotion to the Eucharist was accompanied by continued complaints that the host was being stolen for low-level magical uses ranging from love spells to the protection of livestock.[32] (Similar fears were expressed about misuse of chrism and even of baptismal water.[33]) Denunciations by later witch-hunters included stealing hosts, usually by not swallowing communion, especially Easter communion. Among the practices denounced was writing in blood on a stolen host, a form of learned magic more common late in the Middle Ages.[34] (To the contrary of these accusations, Arnald of Villanova thought confession and communion could undo harmful magic that caused impotence.[35])

The medieval canonists varied in their interest in the Lateran decree, especially in the issues they thought worthy of comment. Few were interested in explaining the rationale for issuing the decree *Statuimus*. When canonists confronted the text of the canon, it usually was in the context of canonistic collections, the collected canons of the Lateran Council, *Compilatio quarta* or, most often, in the *Gregorian Decretals*. The Lateran canons, however, had their own tradition of diffusion and commentary, starting with their proclamation to the church at large, even

[29] See, for example, a statute of Edmund of Abingdon in Lyndwood, *Provinciale seu Constitutiones*, 247. *Lyndwood's Provinciale*, 103, says "for fear of witchcrafts," but the Latin is *sortilegis*, divination or sorcery.

[30] Valerie I. Flint, *The Rise of Magic in Early Medieval Europe* (Princeton, 1991), 214, 285, 298. Taking the host to prove innocence or guilt also was practiced; see Flint, *Rise of Magic*, 283.

[31] See *Medieval Handbooks of Penance: A Translation of the Principal "libri poenitentiales" and Selections from Related Documents*, ed. John T. McNeill and Helena M. Gamer (New York, 1938). Misuse of holy oil is mentioned, however, by Burchard of Worms; see *Medieval Handbooks of Penance*, 339.

[32] Richard Kieckhefer, *Magic in the Middle Ages* (Cambridge, 1989), 79–80, 82–83, 190; Browe, "Die Eucharistie als Zaubermittel im Mittelalter," 135–136.

[33] Some English statutes required locking the baptismal font *propter sortilegia;* see Christopher Cheney, *English Synodalia of the Thirteenth Century* (Oxford, 1968), 82.

[34] Waldensians were among those accused of misusing the sacrament; see *Witch Beliefs and Witch Trials in the Middle Ages: Documents and Readings*, ed. P. G. Maxwell-Stuart (London, 2011), 23, 49, 56, 88, 96, 113, 198–200. Even a monk could be accused of misusing the host; see *Witch Beliefs and Witch Trials*, 151–152.

[35] *Witch Beliefs and Witch Trials in the Middle Ages*, 53–54. Heinrich von Gorkum, however, dismissed as superstitious showing a host to the godparents after baptism; see *Witch Beliefs and Witch Trials*, 59.

before they were deployed in larger canonistic collections. The available *casus* or summaries of the Lateran Council's decrees, however, omit *Statuimus* entirely.[36] The apparatus of Johannes Teutonicus on these decrees makes reference to the relevant text in Gratian's *Decretum*, c. *Pervenit* (De cons. D. 2 c. 29), which was derived from a Council of Rheims. (The text had been added to the canon law at least as early as the time of Regino of Prüm.[37]) That canon decried any priest permitting a layman or a woman to carry viaticum to the sick. These persons also were forbidden to enter the sacristy or approach the altar. Otherwise the canon was concerned with the degree of culpability of a priest negligent in custody of the Eucharist and holy oils.[38] The Ordinary Gloss on c. *Pervenit* made a reference to the text, but it quoted other canons saying a deacon could deliver communion in case of necessity, and it even permitted employment of a Catholic layman in an emergency.[39]

Vincentius Hispanus said *Pervenit* was relevant to the safe custody of the Eucharist. He went on to cite, in this context, a decree of Alexander III, c. *Plene* (1 Comp. 3.26.30), which treated possession by a certain canon of a host that seemed to display, in part, the flesh of Christ. The issue in that decretal was the receipt of offerings made to the canon once possession of the wonder host had passed from the parish church to the cathedral of Arras.[40] Otherwise Vincentius concerned himself with false testimony, discussing punishment of a lying witness.[41] Damasus too cited *Pervenit*. Only he, however, among the commentators on the collected Lateran decrees, made a specific connection between the Lateran decree and the practice of magic. Damasus cited a decretal of Clement III that imposed penance on a woman who kept the host she received in her mouth to use it magically, to reawaken her husband's passion by kissing him while she still had the Eucharist back between her molars.[42] Both

[36] *Constitutiones Concilii quarti Lateranensis*, 469, 486.

[37] *Das Sendhandbuch des Regino von Prüm*, 86.

[38] *Constitutiones Concilii quarti Lateranensis*, 208. For the reference to the *Decretum*, see also 67: c. 20 n. 1. *Pervenit* required a priest to give communion to the sick and threatened a cleric with degradation from his order; see *Corpus Iuris Canonici*, 1.1323–1324. The Ordinary Gloss permitted a deacon to carry viaticum if necessary, and it even granted the possibility that a layman might be thus employed; see *Decretum divini Gratiani* . . ., 1270 at De cons. D. 2 c. 29 v. Per semetipsum.

[39] Ordinary Gloss at De cons. D. 2 c. 28 v. Per semetipsum, "Per semetipsum. vel per diaconum, si necesse est: vt xciii. distin. pręsente. vel per laicum catholicum. xxiiii. q. i. coepit."

[40] *Quinque compilationes antiquae nec non Collectio canonum Lipsiensis*, 38.

[41] *Constitutiones Concilii quarti Lateranensis*, 314.

[42] *Constitutiones Concilii quarti Lateranensis*, 428. Damasus cited 2 Comp. 5.17.2; see *Quinque compilationes antiquae nec non Collectio canonum Lipsiensis*, 102.

Vincentius and Damasus referenced the sacristan as the official responsible for keeping the host and the chrism safe.[43]

Most of the major canonists of the thirteenth and early fourteenth centuries, however, treated *Statuimus* when they commented on decretal collections, especially the *Liber extra*. At the beginning of the Ordinary Gloss, in an addition made in the age of printing, a connection is drawn between discussions of the mass and baptism and the custody of the Eucharist and chrism.[44] The *casus* by Bernardus Parmensis to *Statuimus* summarized the text, noting that, if anything nefarious (*nefandum*) happened to reserved hosts or chrism, the one entrusted with their care was to be punished as if guilty of the offense.[45] The Ordinary Gloss to the text, also by Bernardus Parmensis, was more concerned with preventing lay folk from taking communion to the sick than with the rationale for the decree's requirement that reserved hosts be protected. The Gloss said that the negligent custodian was held responsible for whatever followed from his negligence.[46] The Gloss concluded with a discussion, based on the text by Vincentius, of false witnesses, including whether they were responsible for all the evils that followed. Only a deliberately false witness was to be punished, but the evils that had been done might cause the judge to regard a case in a more serious light than otherwise.[47]

Another early discussion of custody of the Eucharist can be found in the *Summa super titulis decretalium* of Geoffrey of Trani. This *Summa* inevitably discussed keeping the Eucharist in a place that was both clean and safe, conserved "honorably and devoutly."[48] Geoffrey devoted more space to denying that a woman or a layman could take communion to the sick. Only a deacon, he said, in line with contemporary opinions, could substitute for a priest. This opinion was stricter than that of Rufinus, who said that, if the priest was sick, even a boy could give communion to the sick.[49] Geoffrey

[43] *Constitutiones Concilii quarti Lateranensis*, 314, 428.

[44] *Decretales Gregorii noni pontificis* ... (Lyon, 1556), col. 1277A, citing Panormitanus, "Abb. Sicu."

[45] *Decretales Gregorii noni pontificis*, col. 1277A. Similarly see a Bamberg canon of 1490 in *Concilia Germaniae*, ed. Johann Friedrich Schannat and Joseph Hartzheim, 5 (Köln, 1763), 618B–619A. Brundage, *Medieval Canon Law*, 210.

[46] *Decretales Gregorii noni pontificis*, col. 1277A–B.

[47] *Decretales Gregorii noni pontificis*, col. 1277C.

[48] *Summa perutilis et valde necessaria do. Goffredi de Trano super titulis decretalium* ... (Lyon, 1519; Aalen, 1968), fol. 165vb. Geoffrey quoted c. *Sane* in this place. Geoffrey composed his *Summa* ca. 1241–1243, according to Martin Bertram, "Goffredo da Trani," in *Dizionario biografico degli italiani*, 57 (Roma, 2001), 545–549.

[49] Rufinus cited the *Decretum* of Burchard of Worms, Bk. 17 c. 15, to support his opinion; see *Summa decretorum*, ed. Heinrich Singer (Paderborn, 1902; Aalen, 1963), 554: De cons. D. 2 c. 26.

also noted, baldly, that chrism was to be kept in the same safe place with the Eucharist.[50]

The period following the composition of the Ordinary Gloss and Geoffrey's *Summa* saw the writing of some of the most important commentaries on the *Liber extra*. Pope Innocent IV (1243–1254) composed an apparatus on the *Gregorian Decretals* that he published as a private doctor. It was widely read and quoted.[51] Innocent was uninterested in the contents of *Statuimus*. He limited himself to pointing the reader to texts in the *Decretum* that addressed measures to be taken if the consecrated elements fell to the ground or if someone vomited after receiving communion.[52]

Much more significant discussions were penned by Hostiensis in his *Summa super titulis decretalium*, and in the extensive commentary on the *Extra*.[53] The Cardinal of Ostia showed considerable interest in Eucharistic reservation, much more than had Innocent IV.[54] In the *Summa*, Hostiensis connected his discussion of custody of the Eucharist and chrism with his preceding expositions of the canon law governing the celebration of mass and the administration of baptism. He summarized *Statuimus* and then commented succinctly: "This, however, was enacted on account of those who commit sorceries thereupon."[55] Hostiensis went on to discuss, as his predecessors had, the proper persons and processes for carrying communion to the sick.[56] His discussion of the title *De custodia* concluded with a review of the penalties inflicted on negligent guardians of the Eucharist and chrism, plus the penances imposed on those, clerical or lay, who vomited up communion because of drunkenness.[57]

In the final version of his *Commentary*, Hostiensis addressed these issues again. There his concern about magical practices using sacred things is made clearer and more personal. At the word *manus*, the cardinal commented, "Sorcery, those who commit thereupon many horrible and nefarious things, as follows; and we have heard many things about this in

[50] *Summa ... Goffredi ...*, fol. 165vb. Geoffrey quoted c. *Pervenit*, as does the Ordinary Gloss, when denying a role to the laity in taking communion to the sick.

[51] Alberto Melloni, *Innocenzo IV: la concezione e l'esperienza della cristianità come regimen unius personae* (Genova, 1990).

[52] Innocentius IV, *Commentaria apparatus in V libros decretalium* (Frankfurt, 1570; Frankfurt, 1968), fol. 457ra.

[53] Brundage, *Medieval Canon Law*, 214; Kenneth Pennington, "Henricus de Segusio (Hostiensis)," in Pennington, *Popes, Canonists and Texts, 1150–1550* (Aldershot, 1993), XVI, 1–12.

[54] Kenneth Pennington, *The Prince and the Law, 1200–1600: Sovereignty and Rights in the Western Legal Tradition* (Berkeley, 1993), 48–51.

[55] *Summa domini Henrici cardinalis Hostiensis ...* (Lyon, 1537, 1962), fol. 187va, "Hoc autem statutum est propter illos qui inde sortilegia committunt."

[56] *Summa domini Henrici cardinalis Hostiensis*, fol. 187va, with a discussion of the care of churches, vessels, and vestments following.

[57] *Summa domini Henrici cardinalis Hostiensis*, fol. 187va–b.

hearing confessions and which we experience daily, about which it is safer to keep silence."[58] Hostiensis stated that a negligent custodian was to be punished even if nothing nefarious happened. Negligence was a grave sin that deserved severe correction.[59] The commentary on *Statuimus* ends with a discussion, as in the commentary of Innocent IV, of dropping hosts or vomiting up communion.

Hostiensis's opinion in the *Commentary* was restated in an abbreviated form by Johannes Andreae in his *Novella commentaria* on the Decretals. Thus he said, at v. Manus: "Sorcery, which is done with these things, about which it is more discrete to be silent."[60]

Johannes Andreae also agreed with Hostiensis that negligence was to be punished even if nothing nefarious resulted from it. (Being a layman, apparently he had nothing to add from his own experience to the discussion of magical practices.)[61] Johannes concluded his discussion of the canon *Statuimus* by briefly discussing the law governing the dropping of a host or its having been eaten by a mouse, a topic closer to what the canon *Qui bene* in the *Decretum* had said.[62] Antonius de Butrio closely paraphrased *Statuimus* concerning a rash or audacious hand reaching for the Eucharist to do horrible and nefarious deeds.[63] Antonius also recited existing opinions about topics like a mouse eating the Eucharist and the need for a priest or deacon, not a lay person, taking communion to the sick.[64] Antonius also said that the Eucharist was reserved only for sick communion, not for other needs.[65]

The provisions of *Statuimus* entered into the local body of canon law through synodal enactments, especially those from the century following the Fourth Lateran Council, and other, more local provisions, were

[58] *Hostiensis Decretalium commentaria*, 6 vols. (Venezia, 1581; Torino, 1965), 3, fol. 172ra, "[*Manus*]. Sortilegium, qui inde multa horribilia & nepharia committunt, ut sequitur, & in confessionibus. Multa circa hoc audiuimus, & quotidie experimur, quae tutius est tacere." This is the later version and should be checked against manuscripts; see Kenneth Pennington, "An Earlier Recension of Hostiensis's *Lectura* on the Decretals," *Bulletin of Medieval Canon Law* 17 (1987), 77–90.

[59] *Hostiensis Decretalium commentaria*, 3, fol. 172ra.

[60] Johannes Andreae, *In quinque decretalium libros novella commentaria* ... (Venezia: 1581; Torino, 1963), 3, fol. 229va, "[*Ne posit*] ratio [*Manus*] sortilegiarum, quae operantur ex his, quod discretius tacere. 41 dist. sit rector. Hostien." The *Novella* was completed by 1338; see Kenneth Pennington, "Johannes Andreae's *Additiones* to the Decretals of Gregory IX," *Zeitschrift der Savigny-Stiftung für Rechtsgeschichte, Kanonistische Abteilung* 74 (1988), 328–347.

[61] Johannes Andreae, *In quinque decretalium libros novella commentaria*, 3, fol. 229va.

[62] Johannes Andreae, *In quinque decretalium libros novella commentaria*, 3, fol. 229va.

[63] *Excellentissimi Antonii de Butrio* ... *In librum tertium decretalium commentaria* ... (Venezia, 1578; Torino, 1967), fol. 198rb.

[64] *Excellentissimi Antonii de Butrio* ... *In tertium librum decretalium commentaria*, fol. 198rb.

[65] *Excellentissimi Antonii de Butrio* ... *Super secunda parte primi decretalium commentarii* (Venezia, 1578; Torino, 1967), fol. 19va.

added to those rules. Enactments concerning the Eucharist abounded, but fewer addressed custody of reserved hosts or chrism. Notably, for the reservation of the Eucharist, the synodal legislation of Paris treated related topics, including reverencing altars, especially one on which the Eucharist was reserved and mass celebrated, and having a priest or deacon carry communion to the sick, as well as having the laity genuflect whenever they saw the sacrament being carried.[66] Particularly, a Paris statute decreed that "The most holy body of the Lord should be kept locked with a key on the most beautiful part of the altar, with greatest diligence and respect."[67] One notes here a greater concern for decorum than for security.

Elsewhere on the Continent, local canons also addressed the renewal of the reserved sacrament. A late twelfth-century council required renewal within eight days, usually by the celebrant of the main mass on Sunday.[68] After the influential Paris statutes required weekly renewal of the reserved Eucharist, the Arras statutes restated that requirement.[69] The statutes of Cambrai simply required weekly renewal before briefly addressing the place in which the sacrament was to be reserved.[70] An advice (*consilium*) of the statutes of Soissons required not retaining the reserved sacrament longer than fifteen days before replacing it.[71] The statutes of Rouen required weekly renewal of the reserved sacrament, the font, and holy water.[72] The 1284 synod of Nîmes indicated how reservation was to begin. A priest was to consecrate several hosts during the mass, consuming one and setting the others aside before receiving the consecrated wine.[73] In thirteenth-century Italy, Federico Visconti, archbishop of Pisa, took a slightly different tack. He forbade giving the body of Christ to anyone "for committing any sorcery or outrage" (*pro aliquo maleficio vel facinore commitendo*).[74]

The texts about the reserved sacrament and its renewal issued in Paris had a strong impact in England. An undated English council of the same

[66] Mansi 22.677–678. Odette Pontal, *Les statuts synodaux francais du XIIIe siècle*, 1 (Paris, 1971), 58–61. For Odo's influence in England, see Cheney, *English Synodalia*, 83, 88.

[67] Mansi 22.678, "7. In pulcriore parte altaris cum summa diligentia & honestate sub clave sacrosanctum corpus Domini custodiatur." Browe, *Die Verehrung der Eucharistie im Mittelalter* (Roma, 1967), 18.

[68] Mansi 22.725.

[69] Pontal, *Les status synodaux*, 1.78; Joseph Avril, *Les statuts synodaux francais du XIIIe siècle*, 4 (Paris, 1975), 192. See also the 1274 statutes of Girona in Mansi 23.937.

[70] Avril, *Les statuts synodaux francais du XIIIe siècle*, 4.43.

[71] Avril, *Les statuts synodaux francais du XIIIe siècle*, 4.294.

[72] Mansi 23.375.

[73] Mansi 24.534–535.

[74] *Les sermons et la visite pastorale de Federico Visconti archevêque de Pise (1253–1277)*, ed. Nicole Bériou, Isabelle le Masne de Chermont, Pascale Bourgain, and Marina Innocenti (Roma, 2001), 1080.

period restated the Parisian enactments on custody of the Eucharist, reverence for the altar, and taking communion to the sick. It also required that the reserved elements be kept in a clean pyx (*in munda pyxide conservetur*) and that they be renewed weekly. The previously reserved host was to be consumed during the mass after reception of the one consecrated for that rite.[75] This last Parisian provision was repeated almost verbatim by Richard Poore, bishop of Salisbury, in his widely influential statutes of 1217. So was the provision about using a clean pyx. Most English statutes of the early thirteenth century made some use of Poore's enactments.[76] This language about the placing of the reserved Eucharist was repeated in a statute of Fulk Basset (1245–1259) for the diocese of London.[77] The second statutes of Winchester specified using a glass container for the reserved sacrament so that it should not become spoiled and disgusting to the recipient, as well as its weekly renewal.[78] Such concerns continued into the sixteenth century when a 1526 synod of Léon required reservation of small hosts for communion of the sick.[79]

A concern for placement of the reserved Eucharist can be found in a 1255 canon from Valencia, issued well after the *Gregorian Decretals* had been published. The Eucharist was to be kept, it said, "in the middle part of the altar" under lock and key, if at all possible.[80] Synodal statutes from Girona, dated 1274, combined a concern for the placing of the reserved hosts, oil, and chrism on a consecrated altar with a concern for security. The Lateran decree's warning against an "audacious hand" reaching out for nefarious purposes was repeated in the council's own words.[81] The 1279 Council of Buda also required placement of the reserved Eucharist

[75] Mansi, 22.725, 731–732; *Councils & Synods*, 2/1.184. Statutes attributed to Stephen Langton used similar language about refreshing the reserved sacrament; see Mansi 22.1175. This idea was not entirely new in England, as the legatine statutes of 1138 show; see *Councils & Synods*, 1/2.774.

[76] Mansi 22.1118–1119; *Councils & Synods*, 2/1.78–79. Poore warned against consuming unconsecrated hosts in the mistaken belief that they had been consecrated. Cheney, *English* Synodalia, 51–62, notes that Poore was at Lateran IV and knew its decrees first hand. The provisions about a "clean pyx" and replenishment of the reserved species were repeated at a Scottish Council of 1225 (Mansi 22.1239) and the statutes were attributed to a 1230 Council of Edmund, archbishop of Canterbury (Mansi 23.373); see Cheney, *English Synodalia*, 65–67. Similar provisions are found in the 1235 *Praecepta antiqua* of the archdiocese of Rouen; see Mansi 23.374.

[77] *Councils & Synods*, 2/1.639–640. [78] *Councils & Synods*, 2/1.404.

[79] *Synodicon Hispanum*, 5.XXVII no. 2.

[80] Mansi 23.1890, "& in media parte altaris cum summa diligentia & honestate sub claue, si fiery potest, Corpus Christi custodiatur."

[81] Mansi 23.936–937, "Chrisma, oleum & eucharistia caute seruentur, clauibus adhibitis, necnon & altare consecratum diligent seruetur custodia, ne ad aliquod praedictorum manus temeraria se extendat pro aliquibus nefariis exercendis." See also see *Councils & Synod*, 2/1.115.

on the altar under lock and key.[82] The 1280 Council of Cologne used exactly the same words about reservation on an altar.[83] A 1284 synod of Passau specified, atop the Lateran decree on custody, the use of lights (*lampadibus*). In that context, this decree seems more motivated by security of the reserved sacrament, making theft less likely, than honoring the Real Presence.[84] By the end of the fifteenth century, statutes on keeping lamps lit before the reserved sacrament as a matter of reverence had become common.[85]

Following in the wake of the Lateran Council, we find distinct echoes of *Statuimus* in local enactments, probably derived directly from a collection of the council's canons. Thus a statute of Stephen Langton's 1222 Council of Oxford dealt with enforcement of the rules of custody. It entrusted archdeacons with the duty of seeing that oil and chrism were kept locked up "according to the form of the general council." The Eucharist too was to be entrusted to a "faithful custodian." (As a former cardinal, Langton may have been unusually quick to enact legislation based on the Lateran canons.)[86] A set of statutes, frequently described as prepared by Archbishop Langton for the same council, includes a statute *De sacramento altaris*. It provided, in language drawn almost verbatim from the Paris statutes, that altars should be reverenced, especially those on which the Lord's body was reserved and mass celebrated.[87] This Langton text also repeated the phrasing about a "clean pyx," adding that it should be of "ivory or some other material fitting and worthy of so great a sacrament."[88] Similar additions were made by later bishops. The statutes attributed to Edmund of Abingdon, archbishop of Canterbury, specify a pyx of silver or tin (*stanneum*).[89] Similarly, a 1280 Council of Cologne required that a pyx be made of "gold, silver, ivory, or at least well-polished copper" (*aurea,*

[82] Mansi 24.316. [83] Mansi 24.352.

[84] Mansi 24.504. The same canon forbade committing custody to lay persons (*numquam laicis committatur*).

[85] *Synodicon Hispanum*, 6, 67–68 (Avila, 1481); 465–466 (Segovia); *Synodicon Hispanum*, 9.626–627 (Jaén).

[86] Mansi 22.1159, "XXIV: Quod oleum & Eucharistia custodiantur sub sera, & similiter chrisma. Prouideant utique archidiaconi, quod diligenter, juxta formam concilii generalis, Eucharistia, chrisma, & oleum sanctum, salua sub clauibus recondantur, fideli custodiae deputata." A 1280 synod of the diocese of Saintes made separate provision for putting holy oils in fitting vessels; see Mansi 24.378. Archdeacons were key players in enforcing ecclesiastical discipline at the local level; see Cheney, *English Synodalia*, 22.

[87] Mansi 22.1175. Cheney, *English Synodalia*, 62–65.

[88] Mansi 22.1175, "Eucharistia in munda pixide argentea, aut eburnea, aut alia tanto sacramento digna & idonea conseruetur. " The same phrasing is found in the "synodal statutes for an English diocese" (ca. 1225); see *Councils and Synod*, 2/1.142. Langton also required a "clean pyx" in his statutes for the diocese of Canterbury; see *Councils & Synods*, 2/1. 27.

[89] *Visitations of Churches Belonging to St. Paul's Cathedral*, xxxviii–xxxix.

argenta, eburnean, uel ad minus cuprea bene eminata).[90] A 1287 synod at Exeter specified silver or ivory.[91] The statutes of William de Blois for the diocese of Worcester (1229) specified two pyxes, one of silver, ivory, or *de opere Lemovitico* (Limoges work) for communicating the sick, and another for reserving the host *sub fideli custodia clavi . . . secundum tenorem Concilii*.[92] The statutes of Cambrai reused the language of the Paris texts when addressing reservation and the vessels to be set aside for communion of the sick.[93] As late as 1553, a synod of Astorga said a chalice and paten could be used if no pyx was available.[94]

Atop direct transmission of the Lateran decrees to local bishops, *Statuimus* also entered local canon law via the *Gregorian Decretals* once they had been diffused throughout Latin Christendom. These were not just read in private or taught in schools; decretal texts were read aloud to synods in England and on the Continent. In those gatherings authoritative text and local practice met, as did pastoral care and the enforcement of statutes. Parish priests with minimal education could be taught at a synod in ways that handing them compendious books of canon law would not have achieved.[95] By 1240, six years after the *Gregorian Decretals* were sent to the major universities, the Council of Worcester addressed custody of the Eucharist, oil, and chrism in terms derived from the Lateran canon. Walter de Cantilupe and his clergy expressed concerns that mice or damp might make hosts vile to taste or sight, needing, therefore, to be refreshed regularly. The provisions of the Lateran Council about locking up the Eucharist, oil, and chrism "in a sufficient enclosure" (*sub competente clausura*) were repeated. If archdeacons or other visitors found these things "blasphemed" by sacrilegious persons, the rectors and resident vicars in charge of parishes were threatened with punishment for their negligence.[96]

[90] Mansi 24.351. A 1287 Council of Liège provided for a pyx of "ivory, or silver, or at least well-polished copper"; see Mansi 24.897.

[91] Mansi 24.789. [92] *Councils & Synods*, 2/1.171.

[93] Avril, *Les statuts synodaux*, 4.41. [94] *Synodicon Hispanum*, 5.136–137.

[95] Cheney, *English Synodalia*, 31–33; Christopher Cheney, "Some Aspects of Diocesan Legislation during the Thirteenth Century," in Cheney, *Medieval Texts and Studies* (Oxford, 1973), 185–202.

[96] Mansi 23.528, "secundum statute Concilii generalis, Eucharistia simul cum oleo & chrismate, sub competente clausura seruetur: ne, quod absit, contingat in ipsis per sacrilegos nomen Domini blasphemari. Quod si neglectum fuerit, ad archidiaconi uel uisitantis arbitrium, rectoris uel uicarii residentis negligentia puniatur." The same council decreed that "lamps" should burn day and night before the receptacle in which the Eucharist was reserved; see Mansi 23.528–529. See also *Councils & Synods*, 2/1.299–300. The same language about damp and mice can be found in Robert Grosseteste, *Letter 52bis*, in *The Electronic Grosseteste* [www.grosseteste.com/], "Observent etiam sacerdotes cum omni diligentia ne sacra Eucharistia per vitium aut diutinam conservationem contraheret humiditatem seu mucorem, unde reddatur vel turpis aspectu vel gustui abominabilis." Cantilupe probably used Grosseteste's statutes as his source; see Cheney, *English*

A 1246 Council at Fritzlar decreed, in language drawn from the Decretals, that the baptismal font, chrism, and Eucharist be kept "in faithful custody" (*sub Fideli custodia*) lest an "audacious hand" be extended to it.[97] A statute issued in the diocese of Le Mans one year later simply restated *Statuimus*.[98] So did a synod of the diocese of Passau in 1284.[99] A Council of the province of Tours in 1253 reorganized the Lateran text. It said the Eucharist was to be kept "in faithful custody"; but it specified that baptismal water, oils, and chrism were to be kept under lock and key as well. Archdeacons, archpriests, and rural deans were charged with enforcing these regulations.[100] A synod at Nîmes in 1284 said a priest was not supposed to be found negligent or careless in his treatment of the sacraments. It listed keeping the Eucharist in a clean, locked place, honorably located, among a parish priest's duties.[101]

A few synods and councils enacted regulations phrased somewhat differently, although not dissimilar in meaning to the canon of the Lateran Council. Thus the 1281 Lambeth Council of John Peccham, archbishop of Canterbury, required each parish to have a "decent and fitting" tabernacle, able to be locked; but it was to be fitting to the size and resources of the church.[102] The 1287 Council at Liège permitted reservation either in a fitting place *sub altari* or in a small chest (*armariolo*), in either case under lock and key. The council was specific that the area around the altar be kept clean and free of spider webs.[103] The statutes of Bordeaux warned against reserving the sacrament in a receptacle of worm-ridden wood, but they also said the reserved hosts should be

Synodalia, 90–96. The same language was used in the statutes of Ely (1229–1256); see *Councils & Synods*, 2/1.518.

97 Mansi 23.725. The language, "ne posit ad illa temeraria manus extendi," is a direct quotation from c. *Statuimus*.

98 Mansi 23.75. A reference to a Lateran canon against displaying relics for venal purposes follows without a rubric separating the texts.

99 Mansi 24.504, with the added words, "secundum constitutionem Lateranensis Concilii."

100 Mansi 23.809.

101 Mansi 24.534, "discrete praecipimus, quatenus a sacerdotibus Eucharistia in loco singulari mundo, & clavi firmato, simper honorifice collocate, devote ac fideliter conservetur."

102 Mansi 24.406, "& in qualibet ecclesia parochiali fiat tabernaculum cum clausura, decens & honestum, secundum magnitudinem & ecclesiae facultates." See also *Councils & Synods*, 2/2.894; Lyndwood, *Provinciale seu Constitutiones*, 248. For a translation, see Lyndwood, William, *Lyndwood's Provinciale: The Text of the Canons Therein Contained, Reprinted from the Translation Made in 1534*, ed. J. V. Bullard and H. Chalmer Bell (London, 1929), 103–104.

103 Mansi 24.899, "XLII. Corpus domini in honesto loco sub altari vel in armariolo sub clave sollicite custodiatur. Similiter chrisma & oleum in alio loco." On cleanliness of altar area, see 24.895 IX.

whole and recently consecrated.[104] The Latins imposed their practice of reservation in the East, when the authorities on Cyprus required the use of a clean pyx to avoid invasion of the sacrament by worms.[105]

A different concern for decorum emerged at least once, looking not only at security or cleanliness but at honoring God in the reserved sacrament. The 1240 Council of Worcester required that lamps burn night and day before the "pledge of redemption" (*pignus redemptionis*). It was a step toward requiring a vigil light to burn before the tabernacle.[106] This concern, however, was not separable from that with security of the sacrament. A 1284 synod of the diocese of Passau combined a requirement that the Eucharist be kept faithfully with one that required employing lamps (*& lampadibus adhibitis*) before the repository.[107] John de Burough's *Pupilla oculi* identified the *hostiarius* or porter, the lowest ranking of the minor orders, as deputized (*deputatum*) to see to the custody of the Eucharist.[108]

More typically, in the year 1310, Antonio d'Orso Biliotti, bishop of Florence, adapted the Lateran decree's provisions about the use of a clean pyx and ideas of reservation on or near an altar into a single canon. The sacraments, he said, were to be revered by all Christians. No one, priest, cleric, or lay person, was to furnish any man or woman with the Body of Christ, chrism, or oil except in a pastoral context. Nor were they to receive any of those things, except in a sacramental rite. Such offenses merited excommunication. The Eucharist was to be kept in a clean pyx. Together with chrism and oils, it was to be kept under lock and key. These things were to be kept on an altar or in a place specially chosen and located nearby. Nor were they to be touched by anyone without the priest's knowledge lest they be used for sacrilegious purposes. The canon blended this concern for security with the proper process for taking the Eucharist, with due reverence, to the sick.[109]

104 Odette Pontal, *Les statuts synodaux francais du XIIIe siècle*, 2 (Paris, 1985), 56, "cum integre esse debeant et decenter." Another French statute combined the emphasis on a newly consecrated host with the fear a person might die without confession and communion; see Pontal, *Les statuts synodaux francais du XIIIe siècle*, 2.322.

105 *The Synodicum Nicosiense and Other Documents of the Latin Church of Cyprus, 1196–1373*, ed. Christopher David Schabel (Nicosia, 2001), 196–197.

106 Mansi 23.528–529. *Harper-Collins Encyclopedia of Catholicism*, ed. Richard P. McBrien (San Francisco, 1995), 1312.

107 Mansi 24.504. The council also warned against giving lay people responsibility for custody of the sacrament.

108 *Pupilla oculi omnibus presbyteris precipue Anglicanis summe necessaria* . . . (London, 1510), fol. lxxii^{ra}.

109 Richard Trexler, *Synodal Law in Florence and Fiesole, 1306–1518* (Città del Vaticano, 1971), 267–268.

Biliotti's decree brings us back to the purpose of the Lateran decree. What is the evidence of the local canon law? Many synods and councils simply reenacted the decree *Statuimus* or adapted it slightly. The specific language of the decree, including the concern for "rash" use of the Eucharist, seems not to have been given much thought. Among the few exceptions are the statute of Alexander of Stavensby cited earlier and one by Richard Wyche, bishop of Chichester, who said that Eucharist, oil, and chrism were kept locked up *propter sortilegia.*[110] Bishop Biliotti, however, did reflect the concern, expressed mostly clearly by Damasus and Hostiensis, that the reserved Eucharist and holy oils might be used in magical practices. This is a concern that would become very significant later, as the hunting out of witches became common and misuse of hosts by Jews and workers of magic often was suspected.[111] A statute from Lucca (1308) combined protection from would-be magicians with keeping the sacrament away from animals *(ab indiscretis vel bestiis)*.[112]

The same concern felt by Biliotti, Stavensby, and Wyche for potential misuses of holy things in magic can be found expressed at Olomouc in Moravia. A 1413 statute, issued by Wenceslaus, patriarch of Antioch and commendatory bishop of the see, expressed concern that chrism might fall into the hands of irreverent lay people who might sell it or work magic with it. The statute specifically phrases its concerns in the language of *Statuimus*, requiring faithful custody to avoid an "audacious hand" reaching out to sacred things for nefarious purposes. Enforcement of this statute was entrusted to the rural deans.[113] The 1461 diocesan statutes from Brno in Moravia required that only the parish priest have keys to the repository of reserved hosts, chrism, and oil. This statute too reiterated most of the language of *Statuimus*, including the worry that an "audacious hand" might reach out to these things.[114] The 1446 statutes of Eichstät said not to leave the keys "in the hands of bell ringers and other secular persons" *(in manibus campanatorum, & aliarum saecularium personarum)*.[115] A 1470 canon from Passau forbade giving the keys to bell ringers or nuns.[116]

110 For Stavensby, see n. 28; for Wyche, see *Councils & Synods*, 2/1.453.

111 Walter Stephens, *Demon Lovers: Witchcraft, Sex and the Crisis of Belief* (Chicago, 2002), 209–218, 235–238.

112 Mansi 25.177.

113 *Synody a statute Olomoucké diecéze období středověku*, ed. Pavel Krafl (Praha, 2003), 179.

114 *Synody a statute Olomoucké diecéze*, 222. A Ravenna statute of 1311 used the term *manus nefaria*; see Mansi 25.453–454.

115 *Concilia Germaniae*, 367B. See also the same wording in a 1463 text from Constance in *Concilia Germaniae*, 5.464B–465A.

116 *Concilia Germaniae*, 5.486B. The same text said not to carry the host through the fields not just because devotion might be diminished but because there was a danger of idolatry.

Although the councils and the canonists relentlessly required protection of the reserved sacrament and other sacred materials, as we have seen, pastoral concerns were not ignored. The reserved hosts, with or without consecrated wine, did not last long; and a series of enactments required refreshing the sacrament weekly. For example, a statute from Buda (1279) required weekly renewal of the reserved host.[117] Canterbury statutes warned the priest to be sure the reserved hosts were consecrated before consuming them during a mass.[118] How well the practice of reservation matched the Lateran Council's legal norms or those of synods – whatever the explanation – is difficult to determine for much of this period. Reservation was not a new practice even before it became universal and a subject for legal enforcement. Juliana of Mont Cornillon, when visiting the recluse Eve, although she could detect the absence of the reserved sacrament in the church of Saint Martin, was unsure whether this simply was the custom of that place.[119]

Visitation instructions occasionally focused on the issue of reservation. For example, the archdeacons of the diocese of Lincoln were told in 1233 to inquire whether the Eucharist was borne fittingly to the sick and whether it was housed as was fitting.[120] The visitation records of Eudes Rigaud, archbishop of Rouen, for 1249 show that he required the monks of St. Ouen de Rouen to see to the proper care of the sacrament reserved in their church. He also required that the monks provide "clean and decent" cloths for the celebration of the mass.[121] John Waltham, bishop of Salisbury (1388–1395), is known to have inquired during visitations on how parishes kept "pyx, font and chrismatory" secured.[122] The 1301 visitation of Clyton in the diocese of Exeter noted that the parish had a pyx of ivory "securely" hanging but not locked. Nor was the "lead chrismatory" locked.[123] Visitation records reveal similar provisions made to

[117] Mansi 24.352. [118] *Councils & Synods*, 2/1.27.

[119] *The Life of Juliana of Mont-Cornillon*, trans. Barbara Newman (Toronto, 2002), 55. See also Barbara R. Walters, "The Feast and its Founder," in *The Feast of Corpus Christi*, ed. Walters, Vincent Corrigan, and Peter T. Ricketts (University Park, Pa., 2006), 3–54 at 18.

[120] Mansi 23.327. Ross William Collins, "The Parish Priest and His Flock as Depicted by the Councils of the Twelfth and Thirteenth Centuries," *The Journal of Religion* 10 (1930), 313–332.

[121] *The Register of Eudes of Rouen*, trans. Jeremiah F. O'Sullivan (New York, 1964), 62–63. For Eudes's relations with the monastery; see Adam J. Davis, *The Holy Bureaucrat: Eudes Rigaud and Religious Reform in Thirteenth-Century Normandy* (Ithaca, 2006), 68, 81, 84, 88–89, 101–102, 138, especially 88.

[122] King, *Eucharistic Reservation*, 69. This was not a new practice in the diocese. Salisbury visitations from 1220 also twice mention the type of pyx used at a particular church; see Peter Browe, *Die Verehrung der Eucharistie im Mittelalter* (Roma, 1967), 18 n. 119.

[123] *Pastors and the Care of Souls*, 301. Two complaints from the diocese of Hereford arising from visitations note the removal of the lock from one baptismal font and the lack of one on another; see *Pastors and the Care of Souls*, 293, 295.

remedy lax practices. One notes in this context that a substantial tabernacle or pyx able to be locked could not be borrowed easily to show the visitor, as a synod of Exeter (1287) complained parishes did with other ornaments, possibly including an acceptable pyx for carrying communion to the sick.[124] Shortly after 1400, visitations by the dean of Salisbury pointed out failures to lock the pyx, occasionally to lock font and chrismatory too. These failings often were blamed on the parishioners, and the church wardens were threatened with fines if they did not remedy defects in the custody of the Eucharist.[125] Lack of a pyx or its poor shape was a concern in Lincoln visitations in the reign of Henry VIII.[126] (A matter worth further exploration is the provision made by religious orders for custody of the Eucharist in their own chapels.[127])

Concern for observance of norms for reservation of the Eucharist remained an issue in practice on the Continent, and it did not evaporate over time. The 1408 visitation instructions for Reims included questions about issues like spilled wine and worms in the reserved sacrament.[128] In the mid-fifteenth century, Cardinal Niccolò Albergati instructed his visitors for the cathedral of Bologna to ask, first of all, about the handling of the Lord's body, the holy oils, and relics.[129] Nicholas of Cusa, later in the same century, in his instructions for visitations in the diocese of Brixen, still was asking about custody of the Eucharist, oils, and sacred vessels. The records for a visitation of the parish of Albeins in that diocese in 1455 required that only the priest have keys to the receptacle of the reserved sacrament and oils, except where trustworthy persons could keep secondary stores for the care of sick persons living far from the parish church.[130]

[124] Mansi 24.801; *Councils & Synods*, 2/2.1006. The same synod also required that clergy, not the laity of the parish, have custody of church ornaments; and it apportioned blame for a theft to the priest if something was stolen from the chancel, but to the laity if the theft occurred in the nave of the church.

[125] *The Register of John Chandler Dean of Salisbury 1404–1417*, ed. T. C. B. Timmins (Devizes, 1984), 18 no. 31, 22 no. 38, 27 no. 52, 113 no. 315, 116 no. 336, 117 no. 344.

[126] *Visitations in the Diocese of Lincoln 1517–1531*, 1.13, 22, 24, 138. One parish had a pyx but lacked a cloth in which to wrap it; see *Visitations in the Diocese of Lincoln*, 16.

[127] Cistercian enactments from the thirteenth century are mentioned by Archdale King in *Eucharistic Reservation*, 68. Visitations of priory churches are mentioned in *Visites Josas*, ed. J.-M. Alliot (Paris, 1902), e.g., 9, 58.

[128] Mansi 26.1070.

[129] Riccardo Parmegiani, *Il vescovo e il capitlo: Il cardinale Niccolò Albergati e i canonici di S. Pietro di Bologna (1417–1443), Un' inedita visita pastorale alla cattedrale (1437)* (Bologna, 2009), 117.

[130] *Akten zur Reform des Bistums Brixen*, ed. Heinz Hürten, Cusanus-Texte 5, fasc. 1) (Heidelberg, 1960), 28, 35.

The visitations done for Jean de Courselles, archdeacon of Josas, in the 1460s and 1470s are unusually detailed about all these matters. Unlike many visitation records, they comment on good things, not just errors needing correction. Thus the records say parishes keep the sacraments "well" (*bene*), "worthily" (*honeste*), "honorably" (*honorifice*), in a good state (*in bono statu*) or at least "fittingly" (*competenter*).[131] Faults were found, of course; and remedies were imposed, often *sub pena*. A parish might be told to create a tabernacle, repair the door, have it locked, make a key, or be more careful where the keys were left, not "in a public place" (*in loco publico*) or on the altar. All of these measures were intended "to avoid perils" (*ad obviandum periculis*), almost certainly abuse of the sacrament.[132] A variety of complaints were written down about the vessels kept in the tabernacle, usually the need for a *cuppa* to hold hosts or a pyx for carrying them to the sick. One priest was threatened with suspension for having the reserved sacrament only kept in a cloth (*in quodam drapello*).[133] The number of reserved hosts and whether they had been renewed recently also was recorded, including instructions to refresh the reserved sacrament more frequently.[134] One can only imagine the reaction of the visitors when they found a mouse or worms in the reserved sacrament.[135]

A bishop who showed particular concern for the care of the reserved sacrament was the Dominican Antoninus of Florence. His visitations began with the high altar or other place of reservation with comments whether this was well or ill handled. In the latter case, repairs might be ordered on pain of a fine. In two cases at least, Antoninus ordered creation of a tabernacle together "with some devout picture" (*cum quadam pictura devota*).[136]

John of Erfurt included in his pastoral manual a title about negligence concerning the Eucharist. He wanted the clergy asked about failing in custody of the sacrament. Noting the penance imposed in the *Decretum* for letting a mouse or other animal eat the Eucharist, he said that "today" (*hodie*) the law punished this failure more harshly, threatening suspension from office. John then said that only crass negligence should be punished thus.[137] His text also quoted the *Decretum* on not letting anyone die without the sacrament with an eye toward the priest being sure he has

[131] *Visites Josas*, e.g. 4, 13, 17, 23, 25, 47, 267, 268, 280. One parish was recorded as keeping the sacraments *optime*; see *Visites Josas*, 183.

[132] *Visites Josas*, e.g. 18, 25, 27, 38, 41, 72, 96, 100, 126, 155, 196, 322.

[133] *Visites Josas*, e.g. 48, 79, 108, 277, 378.

[134] *Visites Josas*, e.g. 65, 73, 76, 151, 238, 356, 359, 382. One curate said he had kept a broken host after giving part of it to a sick woman; see *Visites Josas*, 131.

[135] *Visites Josas*, 102, 230, 362.

[136] Stefano Orlandi, *S. Antonino*, 1: *Studi bibliografici* (Firenze, 1959), 139 (repair), 147 & 148 (pictures).

[137] Johannes de Erfordia, *Die Summa confessorum*, 2.119.

consecrated the available hosts.[138] A set of Norwich synodal statutes expanded on this sentiment. It said priests should be ready day and night to go to the sick, "lest from their negligence – far be it! – a sick person might die without confession or communion with the Lord's body or extreme unction."[139] Antonius de Butrio said it was the principal task of the archpriest to see that the sick would not lack the Eucharist.[140]

This concern for the dying was real enough in the minds of English prelates for visitation questions, formulated in 1253, to include an inquiry whether clerical negligence caused lay persons to die "intestate or without the sacraments."[141] A French manual for archdeacons made this concern part of a visitation, expressing a belief that the sick frequently (*frequenter*) died without viaticum.[142] The 1408 visitation instructions from Reims included a question whether a priest let anyone die without the sacraments because of negligence.[143] A 1440 synod of Segovia ordered any priest who allowed a parishioner to die without the sacraments deposed from his benefice.[144]

Although his synodal statutes did not address this issue, Antoninus of Florence prepared interrogatories to be used in hearing confessions that addressed both magical practices and clerical negligence. The archbishop wanted inquiries made about the grave sin of using sacraments and sacramentals in magical acts.[145] Antoninus, however, was suspicious of more extreme ideas about witchcraft, like believing women could take animal shapes in order to go out by night sucking the blood of children. Similarly he dismissed the idea that witches could fly. This was impossible for them.[146]

138 Johannes de Erfordia, *Die Summa confessorum*, 2.119–120.

139 Synodal Statutes, Cambridge Corpus Christi College Manuscript 255, fol. 209vb–210ra, "ne eorum negligentia quod absit moriatur infirmus sine confessione aut dominici corporis communion aut unction extrema."

140 *Excellentissimi Antonii de Butrio ... Super secunda parte primi decretalium commentarii* (Venezia, 1578; Torino, 1967), fol. 19va, "Nota quod eius officium principale est, quod non deficiat infirmis sacramentum eucharistiae."

141 *Pastors and the Care of Souls*, 289.

142 Elizabeth Kay Todd, "*Libellus pastoralis de cura et officio archidiaconi*: A Thirteenth-Century Handbook for Archdeacons; a Critical Edition and Introduction," PhD Dissertation, Ohio State University, 1993, 76.

143 Mansi 26.1071.

144 Synodicon Hispanum, 6.413.

145 Antoninus, *Confessionale "Defecerunt scrutantes scrutinio"* (Köln, 1470), *De decem preceptis, Quo ad aquam*. "Si fecit. vel fieri procuravit. aut docuit aliquam incantacionem cum sacramentis vel sacramentalibus ecclesie ut oleo sancto. vel aqua baptismali et huiusmodi ob sanitatem vel aliam causam: quod gravissimum est peccatum." Similarly see the Reims visitation instructions from 1408 in Mansi 26.1073–1074, "Sortilegia in sacramentis, vid. in Eucharistia."

146 Antoninus, *Confessionale "Defecerunt scrutantes scrutinio"*, *De terra*, "Si estimauit mulieres conuersas in cattos vel simeas vel alia animalia et nocte ambulare ac sugere sanguinem puerorum. Et exire et intrare domum ostiis clausis et volare per longam terrarum spatia. Et huiusmodi que impossibilia sunt talibus. et ideo falsa." Also at *De terra*, he added an inquiry about writing on a host when seeking a cure for worms or fever. Thomas

The section of the interrogatories addressed to clergy included whether the reserved sacrament was kept safe from theft and contamination with worms. The archbishop also wanted the clergy asked how often they renewed the reserved Eucharist to keep it fresh for communion of the sick. The next question focused on taking communion to the sick in the proper way.[147]

The clergy occasionally were threatened by bishops and their synods with penalties for failing to observe these norms, as they already were threatened by general canon law. Thus the statutes of York (ca. 1241–1245) mandated three-month suspension for careless custody of the Eucharist.[148] Norms were communicated to local clergy through written texts that were supposed to be used by pastors in briefing their congregations, almost certainly in the vernacular.[149] The archdeacon was to look into such matters when even local norms, communicated in writing, seemed too abstract to a parish priest.[150] The compliers of the customs of the diocese of Salisbury tried a slightly different tack, requiring the parson to provide a lockable "chrismatory" as one of a list of duties involved in care of the chancel. The duties of the laity to provide for other parts of the church also were listed.[151] Providing fit housing for the reserved sacrament and holy oils, however, was an obligation of church wardens in other parts of England. Complete conformity, however, seems never to have been achieved.[152] Not even the appearance of conformity could be trusted, as the statutes of Exeter show, with their concern about parishes borrowing ornaments to delude visiting archdeacons.[153] Where limited evidence of actual practice exists, as in the case of the 1297 visitation of the churches dependent on St. Paul's Cathedral, London, the enclosures used in reservation varied in material from wood to enamel, where a proper receptacle was not lacking entirely. Four of the sixteen churches visited were found deficient in the quality of the housing or its lack of an adequate lock.[154] Wooden enclosures also were found in

M. Izbicki, "Antoninus of Florence and the Dominican Witch Theorists," *Memorie Domenicane* 42 (2012), 347–362.

147 Antoninus, *Confessionale "Defecerunt scrutantes scrutinio"*, Circa clericos in commune.

148 *Councils & Synods*, 2/1.491. See also the statutes of Chichester of 1289 in *Councils & Synods*, 2/2.1087. Visitors to the churches under the jurisdiction of St. Paul's London in 1297 found, however, that 7 or 16 parishes lacked the appropriate statutes; see Cheney, *English Synodalia*, 143.

149 Cheney, *English Synodalia*, 45–48 notes that updating these written texts could cause confusion, as addenda crowded the pages.

150 Fulk Basset's statutes for London in *Councils & Synods*, 2/1.649.

151 *Councils & Synods*, 2/1.512.

152 Rubin, *Corpus Christi*, 45–47.

153 See above n. 124.

154 *Visitations of Churches Belonging to St. Paul's Cathedral*, xxx–xxxi, 8.

the archdeaconry of Prague, with commands that a gate be put in front of any receptacle recorded frequently in the visitation records.[155]

What is harder to document is actual misuse of chrism or the host. Local church courts might mention inquiries into cases of sorcery, but the records are few in number – especially compared to proceedings for crimes like fornication – and even cryptic.[156] Other cases may have been handled not in the external forum of church courts but in the internal forum of penance. Thus William of Rennes, in his gloss to the *Summa* of Raymond of Peñafort, asked whether clerics who worked magic with the sacraments, especially the Eucharist, chrism, blessed oil, or baptismal water, incurred canonical irregularity. He noted differing opinions but recommended getting a dispensation from the effects of such illegal practices.[157] This suggests that cases of misuse of Eucharist and chrism might lie concealed from researchers under the seal of confession. The Apostolic Penitentiary did absolve, during the reign of Nicholas V, a priest of the diocese of Salzburg who took "the sacrament," chrism, and holy water from another church in order to conduct a secret baptismal ceremony.[158] Under Paul II, a woman from the diocese of Cologne received absolution for baptizing and anointing a stone with chrism in an effort to get her husband to be faithful.[159] These offenses are few compared with the numerous petitions about remedying the effects of illegitimacy or granting marital dispensations, but they point to practical reasons – apart from rote repetition of visitation questions – why enforcing the canon law of reservation might be a real concern of pastors and prelates.

Evidence of belief in the misuse of hosts may be sparse in the law, but not in other sources. The Eucharist might be invoked even in its absence, as in a fifteenth-century necromancer's manual edited by Richard Kieckhefer.[160] Actual use or misuse of the sacrament, however,

[155] *Visitační protokol Pražského arcijáhna pavla z janovic z let 1379–1382*, ed. Iavan Hlaváček and Zdeňka Hledíková (Praha, 1973), 141, 144, 177, 292, 302.

[156] See, for example, *Lower Ecclesiastical Jurisdiction in Late-Medieval England: The Courts of the Dean and Chapter of Lincoln, 1336–1349, and the Deanery of Wisbech, 1458–1484*, ed. L. R. Poos (Oxford, 2001), 26, 64, 106, 352–353, 463, 553.

[157] *Summa Sancti Raymundi de Peniafort ... de Poenitentia, et Matrimonio ...* (Roma, 1602; Farnborough, 1967), 105–106, "aut qui de sacramentis Ecclesiae, Eucharistia scilicet, vel Chrismate, vel oleo benedicto, aut aqua fontium facit sortilegium, vel baptizat imagine ... Unde in hoc consulendum est talibus, quod petant dispensationem."

[158] *Repertorium Poenitentiariae Germanicum*, 2 no. 68.

[159] *Repertorium Poenitentiariae Germanicum*, 5 no. 1572. Absolution was given for theft of a monstrance, apparently containing a host, in the diocese of Halberstadt during the same pontificate; see *Repertorium Poenitentiariae Germanicum*, 5 no. 1193.

[160] Richard Kieckhefer, *Forbidden Rites: A Necromancer's Manual of the Fifteenth Century* (University Park, Penna., 1998), 137, 226, 331, 338.

usually was believed to require physical access. Tales of stolen hosts abounded in the literature of witchcraft as did allegations of the Eucharist by Jews. There is written evidence of how the hosts supposedly were obtained. Most often Christians, particularly servants, were suspected of obtaining hosts for Jews. These thefts are said to have been done while receiving communion, rather than by breaking into a tabernacle or pyx to steal hosts.[161] The fear of misuse of the Eucharist and other sacred things was among the questions inquisitors were to ask at least as early as 1270.[162] In his manual for inquisitors Bernard Gui provided an interrogatory about magic done using the body of Christ and a formula of abjuration for those who did such irreverent things.[163] Backing by the papacy can be found in instructions a cardinal sent an inquisitor on behalf of Pope John XXII in 1320, warning against abuse of the Eucharist or other sacraments.[164] The same fears were expressed later in witch-hunting manuals like the *Malleus malleficarum*. One of the practices denounced in the *Malleus* was desecration of the host to renounce God and the Church.[165]

Beliefs about theft of the host for magical practices lived on throughout Europe. Sermon *exempla* could focus on tales of women keeping the host in their mouths for use in witchcraft.[166] The great preacher Bernardino of Siena in the fifteenth century warned priests against their performing magical rites with sacred items. He also warned priests to lock up the Eucharist and chrism to prevent old women from taking hold of them for magic.[167] These beliefs endured in Poland into the seventeenth century and even later. Accusations of uses for self-interested purposes like love magic and protection of farm animals coexisted with accusations of efforts to misuse Christ in the consecrated bread.[168]

[161] Stephens, *Demon Lovers*, 221–223; Rubin, *Gentile Tales*, 33, 52, 61, 73, 75.

[162] P. G. Maxwell-Stuart, *Witch Beliefs and Witch Trials in the Middle Ages: Documents and Readings* (London, 2011), 50.

[163] Bernardus Guidonis, *Manuel de l'inquisiteur*, ed. and trans. G. Mollat, 2 vols. (Paris, 1964), 2.22–23, 50–53; Gui, *The Inquisitor's Guide: A Medieval Manual on Heretics*, trans. Janet Shirley (Welwyn Garden City, 2006), 150, 167–168. Rubin, *Corpus Christi*, 341.

[164] Maxwell-Stuart, *Witch Beliefs and Witch Trials in the Middle Ages*, 23.

[165] Henricus Institoris and Jacobus Sprenger, *Malleus maleficarum*, ed. and trans. Christopher S. Mackay, 2 vols. (Cambridge, 2006), 1.425–426, 2.271–272.

[166] E.g., *Friars' Tales: Thirteenth-Century Exempla from the British Isles*, ed. and trans. David Jones (Manchester, 2011), 83–84.

[167] Franco Mormando, *The Preacher's Demons: Bernardino of Siena and the Social Underworld of Early Renaissance Italy* (Chicago, 1999), 96.

[168] Michael Ostling, *Between the Devil and the Host: Imagining Witchcraft in Early Modern Poland* (Oxford, 2011), 140–182.

Viaticum processions

Reservation properly practiced discouraged magical practices while providing a ready supply of hosts, frequently renewed, for communion of the sick and dying. As noted above, when the Decretalists discussed the canon *Statuimus*, some focused less on its provisions for custody of the reserved Eucharist and chrism than on the proper person to take viaticum, communion drawn from this reserve, to the dangerously, possibly mortally ill. Those who died would be comforted on their way (*via*) to the hereafter. The issue of taking communion to the sick had been settled in practice centuries before, forbidding lay persons, especially women, from carrying viaticum.[169] Nevertheless, commentators on the canon law, when they did take cognizance of this rite, still concerned themselves with the identification of the proper minister. Thus the Ordinary Gloss on the *Gregorian Decretals* repeated the denial that a lay person could carry communion to the sick. In the absence of a priest, only a deacon could (with permission) perform this pastoral function. This opinion was shared by Geoffrey of Trani and Hostiensis. The canonists and local councils did become concerned with how communion processions were to be conducted when viaticum was carried outside the church. The priest or deacon had to conduct this rite properly for the edification of the faithful, and it was part of the parish priest's role to visit the sick and hear the confessions of the dying.[170]

One papal decretal directly affected viaticum processions by requiring veneration of the host being carried to the sick person. Pope Honorius III in his decretal *Sane* required the faithful to reverence the Real Presence in the host consecrated at mass, especially, as noted above, at the elevation. Priests were to instruct the faithful to show the same deference when they saw communion being carried to the sick that they displayed at the elevation. Like *Statuimus*, *Sane* required safekeeping of the reserved Eucharist. Honorius threatened those prelates who failed to enforce *Sane*, including its provision for the safekeeping of the reserved Eucharist, with his wrath and that of God. This text appeared in *Compilatio quinta* (5 Comp. 3.24.1), one of the major collections of papal decretals from the early thirteenth century, compiled by Tancred

[169] *Das Sendhandbuch des Regino von Prüm*, 26–29. Snoek, *Medieval Piety from Relics to the Eucharist*, 44–45. On the changes in viaticum practices over the centuries, see Bert Wirix, "The Viaticum: From the Beginning until the Present Day," in *Bread of Heaven: Customs and Practices Surrounding Holy Communion, Essays in the History of Liturgy and Culture*, ed. Charles Caspers, Gerard Lukken, and Gerard Rouwhorst (Kampen, 1995), 247–259.

[170] These are among the parochial duties enumerated in Bernardus Papiensis, *Summa decretalium*, ed. Ernst Adolf Theodore Laspeyres (Ratisbon, 1860; Graz, 1956), 104. Similarly see the statutes of Chichester (1289) in *Councils & Synods*, 2/2.1085.

of Bologna with the approval of Pope Honorius in 1226.[171] Then the text entered the *Gregorian Decretals*, in the title "On the Celebration of Masses, the Sacrament of the Eucharist and Divine Offices" (*De celebratione missarum, et sacramento eucharistiae et divinis officiis*, X. 3.41) when that collection was promulgated in 1234.[172]

Some canonists gave attention to the viaticum provisions of *Sane*. Hostiensis explained that the priest should wear a suitable garment with a stole over it. The priest was to take more than one host, so that he would not be without one when returning to the church. The faithful might otherwise be deceived into venerating a mere creature lacking the sacrament. If he had to expend all these hosts by communicating several sick persons, then the priest was to take measures to prevent the faithful falling into idolatry. A supposition already existed that a light and a bell might be carried before the priest to alert the faithful to his coming. Hostiensis told the priest that he should have the lamp extinguished and the bell silenced as he returned to keep the faithful from thinking he still carried the sacrament.[173]

Johannes Andreae repeated Hostiensis's discussion of the way a priest should dress when carrying viaticum.[174] Johannes also gave detailed instructions for how a priest was to carry the host in its pyx. He was to carry it reverently, neither under his garment nor under his chin, instead of being carried openly on the priest's breast. Johannes also repeated what Hostiensis had said about carrying more than one host or, when returning without one, extinguishing the lamp and silencing the bell.[175] Antonius de Butrio repeated what Johannes Andreae had said about carrying the host in the right clothing in the correct posture and about carrying more than one host.[176] Glossing *Sane*, he gave the lamp carried before the priest a symbolic meaning, saying it represented the "splendor of eternal light" (*candor lucis eternae*).[177]

These canonists agreed with Pope Honorius that the faithful were to be taught to venerate the carried host just as they did the one that was elevated at mass. Hostiensis instructed parish priests to tell their parishioners to send children for instruction in the rudiments of the faith, including the need to reverence the sacrament.[178] Johannes Andreae

[171] *Quinque compilationes antiquae nec non Collectio canonum Lipsiensis*, ed. Emil Friedberg (Leipzig, 1882: Graz, 1956), 178.

[172] *Corpus Iuris Canonici*, 2.642. [173] *Hostiensis Decretalium comentaria*, 2, fol. 166rb.

[174] Johannes Andreae, *In quinque decretalium libros novella commentaria*, 3, fol. 223vb.

[175] Johannes Andreae, *In quinque decretalium libros novella commentaria*, 3, fol. 223vb.

[176] *Excellentissimi Antonii de Butrio . . . In tertium librum decretalium*, fol. 194ra–b.

[177] *Excellentissimi Antonii de Butrio . . . In tetrium librum decretalium*, fol. 194ra–b.

[178] *Hostiensis Decretalium commentaria*, 2, fol. 166ra.

said the faithful were to be instructed by their priest to bow reverently to the carried sacrament.[179]

These generalities in the works of the Decretalists aside, arrangements for delivery of communion to the sick usually were left to local councils and synods.[180] These assemblies almost always presupposed the priest's role as the bearer of viaticum when providing for the right ordering of these processions. A legatine council held at Westminster in 1138 did allow, in the absence of a priest or even a deacon, the carrying of communion by whomever (*per quemlibet*) in a case of necessity (*necessitate instante*).[181] Otherwise, their decrees laid down rules for the conduct of the priest going to an ailing parishioner.[182] Church councils also tried to give guidance, through the parish priest, to those who might see communion being carried to the sick in the form of a consecrated host. (The liturgist Johannes Beleth specified use of bread in communion of the sick because wine was too easily spilled, and because bread represented the New Dispensation replacing the Old.[183])

The basic script for viaticum processions had become established in practice, as well as in theory, by 1238, existing in close relationship to the elevation of the host. In that year Robert Grosseteste, bishop of Lincoln, instructed his clergy about their duties in terms that would have been familiar to the canonists. The faithful, he said, were to be taught to bow their heads at the elevation of the host during mass, because Christ was seen at that moment under the appearance of bread. One or more reserved hosts, renewed weekly, were to be kept in a clean, sealed receptacle for communion of the sick. The priest was to carry viaticum with dignity, properly robed, and with the sacrament properly veiled. The faithful were to adore Christ in the host that was being carried among them. A "light" was to be carried before the sacrament, and a bell was to call the attention of the laity to the procession.[184]

179 Johannes Andreae, *In quinque decretalium libros novella commentaria*, 3, fol. 223vb.

180 One German synod of 1287 also authorized carrying communion to women who had just given birth; see Mansi 24.853–854.

181 *Councils & Synods*, 1/2.774–775.

182 A Strasburg canon from 1432 added *mulieres vicinas partui* to the recipients of communion delivered to the home; see *Concilia Germaniae*, 5.236A.

183 Johannes Beleth, *Summa de ecclesiasticis officiis*, ed. Heribert Douteil (Turnhout, 1976), 182–183. Beleth also noted that a chalice used to reserve wine could not be washed; see *Summa de ecclesiasticis officiis*, 184. *Quinque verba*, a vademecum for priests, also underlined the danger of spilling wine when giving the sacrament to the laity; see *Pastors and the Care of Souls*, 137. Beleth stated another reason for reservation, giving communion during the Triduum, the days between Holy Thursday and Easter; see *Summa de ecclesiasticis officiis*, 182.

184 *Letter 52bis*, cited from *The Electronic Grosseteste* [http://www.grosseteste.com/]. Grosseteste's instructions have been reordered here for clarity. See also *Councils & Synods*, 2/1.268.

Instructions of this sort can be found in conciliar enactments by the end of the twelfth century. Here too one of the most influential texts came from Paris, commanding that the Eucharist be carried with reverence and maturity "enclosed in an ivory pyx." A lamp was to be carried before. The priest and his attendant were to chant the seven penitential psalms and the litany both while going out and returning.[185] The laity were to be taught to kneel "as if to their Lord and Creator," praying with their hands clasped.[186] The Paris statutes also required a parish priest who lacked chaplains (apparently ordinarily tasked with this) to inquire publicly whether anyone was ill and visit them, even if they did not ask for the sacraments.[187]

These instructions too were widely diffused and copied, especially in England.[188] Thus the council Mansi was unable to identify added the Paris text on the carrying of viaticum almost word for word to an injunction to keep a clean and properly decorated chalice for the communion of those too sick to receive the host, so that consecrated wine or a host dissolved in unconsecrated wine could be employed instead.[189] These instructions to the laity were copied, with minor changes, into the statutes prepared on behalf of Stephen Langton for the 1222 Council of Oxford. Lay persons were to reverence the host "like their creator and redeemer," praying humbly. Langton too tied adoration of the host to the reverence given to it at the elevation during the mass.[190] These instructions did not differ in essence from those of Hubert Walter requiring that viaticum be carried by the priest himself in his clerical habit with a light preceding it unless intemperate weather or long distance prohibited the use of light.[191]

Instructions about carrying the host were not limited to any one region, although the details varied by time and place. Thus Eastern European councils required a priest, cleanly and fittingly robed, to carry the Eucharist with a small banner (*cum vexillo parvo*) and a light, or a light

[185] Mansi 22.677–678; Pontal, *Les Odo synodaux*, 1.58–61. The 1279 Council of Münster specified saying the penitential psalms and other prayers; see Mansi 24.315. The 1281 synod of Liège said to start with the penitential psalms but to add other psalms, the litany, and prayers if the way was long; see Mansi 23.897–898. Likewise, see the 1410 *Liber synodalis* of Salamanca in *Synodicon Hispanum*, 4.131.

[186] Mansi 22.678 Pontal, *Les Odo synodaux*, 1.58–59.

[187] Mansi 22.681; Pontal, *Les statuts synodaux*, 1.80.

[188] Cheney, *English Synodalia*, 83, 88.

[189] Mansi 22.731–732. Rubin, *Corpus Christi*, 80. Hostiensis specified using a host dissolved in unconsecrated wine for this purpose; see *Hostiensis Decretalium commentaria*, 3, fol. 162rb–va.

[190] Mansi 22.1175–1176. Langton's canons also mentioned the possibility that a deacon might carry viaticum if a priest were not available; see Mansi 22.1175, which may indicate knowledge of the opinions of early canonists.

[191] *Councils & Synods*, 1/2.1048, 1061.

and a bell, going before. The faithful were enjoined to kneel when they saw the procession pass by.[192] Far to the southwest, in Spain, the 1320 synod of Santiago de Compostella reported it was acting because priests failed to administer the sacrament to the sick. It required a priest to go dressed properly with a cross, bell, and candle (inside or outside a lantern) going before. Priest who failed to do this were fined, and the money went to the fabric of the cathedral.[193] The statutes of Albi instructed to wrap the sacrament in "a clean cloth" (*in syndone munda*), and the priest, or at least a deacon, was to say the penitential psalms when carrying the sacrament to the sick.[194] The Paris instructions for viaticum processions were replicated in Portugal. The synodal decrees of 1240 from Lisbon matched the Paris texts down to the detail of recommending use of an ivory pyx.[195] In the north, a Scottish Council of 1225 ordered a priest to use a clean purse (*bursa*) for carrying the Eucharist. A lamp was to go before, and a bell was to be rung to arouse the devotion of the faithful. An exception to the exact execution of these instructions about the lamp was permitted if the sick person lived far from the church.[196] John Peccham, however, thought a purse or bag might damage the host. He did think the pyx might be draped in satin.[197]

The problem of distance also was addressed, among others, by the provincial council held by Edmund, archbishop of Canterbury, in 1230. The council required a parish to have a vessel of silver or tin set aside for communicating the sick. It also provided that the lamp might be left out of the procession if the sick person were far away, possibly because it might go out during a long walk.[198] The 1247 Council of Le Mans also permitted omission of the light if the weather was unfavorable.[199] Taking a slightly different tack, the synodal statutes of Winchester of circa 1224 specified a

[192] *Synody a statuta Olomoucké diecéze období středověku*, 132, 162, 178, 220. These canons also connected reverencing viaticum with adoration of the elevated host at mass, as is typical of the canon law.

[193] *Synodicon Hispanum*, 1.298. The same thing was said briefly by the 1281 Council of Braga; see *Synodicon Hispanum*, 2.22–23.

[194] Odette Pontal, *Les statuts synodaux francais du XIIIe siècle*, 2.20.

[195] *Synodicon Hispanum*, 2.288.

[196] Mansi 22.1240. The preceding canon required use of a clean pyx for reservation of the Eucharist and the replacement of the reserved Eucharist once a week; see Mansi 22.1239.

[197] Lyndwood, *Provinciale seu Constitutiones*, 248; *Lyndwood's Provinciale*, 103–104.

[198] Mansi 23.373. The council also carefully affirmed that the whole Christ was present in either Eucharistic element; loc. cit. The 1279 Council of Münster specified the use of lamp and bell if the sick person was near, but only a bell was needed if he or she was farther away; see Mansi 24.315. The legatine council held at St. Peter's, York (1195), made allowances for intemperate "air" and the difficulty of the way; see *Councils & Synods*, 1/2.1048.

[199] Mansi 23.746–747. See too the Worcester statutes, which also required that a light burn before the repository of the reserved sacrament; see Mansi 23.528–529.

full ritual only for carrying the Eucharist in cities and towns. These statutes specified that a candle and holy water be carried before the host.[200]

Viaticum processions required that the priest have an assistant, preferably a cleric. Thus occasional efforts were made by bishops and councils to make sure that the priest engaged a deacon or another cleric to help in pastoral care. This included walking before him in a viaticum procession with bell and light. Some pastors failed to hire help. Thus, in a visitation of Eardisley in the diocese of Hereford in 1397, a priest was ordered to hire a cleric to help him.[201] Another parish in the same diocese, Leominster, had a rector who failed for three years to hire a cleric to assist in his duties.[202] If no deacon or parish clerk was available to help deliver communion to the sick, a respectable lay person might grudgingly be permitted to carry the light and ring the bell.[203]

Councils also took into account other potential problems in the delivery of viaticum. A 1307 synod of Lisbon took cognizance of a potential abuse not mentioned elsewhere, the carrying of viaticum on horseback to remote locations. The decree described the practice as possibly scandalous and dangerous to the priest. It permitted the practice only when the cross and other things necessary for communion also were sent out on horseback.[204] On occasion some thought was given to the possibility of other, more dangerous obstacles to communion of the sick. Thus, picking up a discussion begun by Johannes de Lignano, Honoré Bonet presented an argument that a priest carrying communion to the dying could lawfully defend himself if attacked on the way, even if he then could not reach his parishioner in time to "housel" him or her. Bonet noted that many holy men, including John the Baptist, Peter, and Paul, had died without viaticum. Consequently, the salvation of the dying parishioner would not be endangered if the priest took measures to save his own life. Bonet thought this opportunity was not available to a priest who, under similar circumstances, found a dying baby by the roadside. Saving a soul was treated, in this context, as more important than saving the priest's life.[205] This may seem very theoretical; however, a 1216 synod of Segovia told priests that if they were attacked while carrying the Eucharist to the sick, they were to defend it as they would the Church.[206]

[200] *Councils & Synods*, 2/1.126. The statutes of Bordeaux also specified carrying holy water; see Pontal, *Les Statuts Synodaux*, 2.62.
[201] *Pastors and the Care of Souls*, 299. [202] *Pastors and the Care of Souls*, 298.
[203] See the Coventry statutes of 1224i1237 in *Councils & Synods*, 2/1.211. Similarly see a 1339 text from Padua in Mansi 25.1136–1137. Rubin, *Corpus Christi*, 78.
[204] *Synodicon Hispanum*, 2.313–314.
[205] *The Tree of Battles*, trans. G. W. Copland (Liverpool, 1949), 171–173.
[206] *Synodicon Hispanum*, 6.305.

Another problem little discussed by canonists and prelates was making confession and communion available to those about to be executed. Martinus Garratus, an Italian jurist of the fifteenth century, argued briefly that this should be permitted by a prince.[207] There was some sentiment in early canon law and later in the *Clementines* (Clem. 5.9.1) that the clergy and lay members of confraternities should try to save souls by comforting the condemned.[208] Synods seem almost never to have addressed this topic separately, but the 1534 synod of Plasencia did reprove judges who prevented confession and housel of the condemned. These magistrates were threatened with excommunication *latae sententiae*.[209] Nicholas of Cusa's visitation instructions for the diocese of Brixen included an inquiry whether lay judges used torture on feast days and, when they had tortured the accused to the point of death, impeded his or her access to confession and communion. This, he feared, might happen even if access to the sacraments had been requested devoutly.[210] The Apostolic Penitentiary occasionally was asked to permit access to the sacraments for the condemned.[211] Felinus Sandeus said even a heretic condemned to death should be granted confession and communion but not extreme unction before execution.[212] Nicholas Eimeric took the opposite tack, denying the sacraments to relapsed heretics.[213]

A rationale for viaticum was offered by the council held by Walter de Cantilupe, bishop of Worcester, in 1240. Its tone was military in part. Viaticum provided strength to sustain the sick person "for war" (*ad bellum*). More theologically, it could sustain because it was the pledge of redemption, the sweet body and blood Christ left on earth to sustain the faithful. The host was to be kept free from damp so that it would not have a foul taste or a disgraceful appearance. Archdeacons were charged by the bishop with the responsibility to see that the Eucharist was reserved properly for communion of the sick. Negligent priests, whether the parish's rector or his vicar, were threatened with punishment for failing in performance of these

[207] Gigliola Rondini Soldi, *Il Tractatus de principibus di Martino Garati da Lodi* (Milano, 1968), 164 no. 352, citing Clem. 5.9.1.

[208] Adriano Prosperi, "Consolation or Condemnation: The Debates on Withholding Sacraments from Prisoners," in *The Art of Executing Well: Rituals of Execution in Renaissance Italy*, ed. Nicholas Terpstra (Kirksville, Mo., 2008), 98–117.

[209] *Synodicon Hispanum*, 5.471. [210] *Akten zur Reform des Bistums Brixen*, 31.

[211] *Repertorium Poenitentiariae Germanicum*, 7 no. 1847, 1877, 9 no. 1530, 1605.

[212] Felinus Sandeus, *Commentaria ... in V. lib. Decretalium ...*, 3 vols. (Basel, 1567), 3, col. 1098.

[213] Nicholas Eimeric, *Directorium inquisitorum ...*, ed. Francisco Peña (Roma, 1587), 647.

duties.[214] (The Council of Le Mans extended this responsibility to archpriests and rural deans.[215])

Councils and synods ordered that the laity be taught to reverence the Eucharist as it was carried by, wherever they were. Several decrees offered a rationale similar to that found in the statutes of Paris. Thus the 1240 Council of Worcester claimed that adoration of the elevated host would arouse torpid souls and inflame them with charity. The council also thought that the sight of the host being carried, even enclosed in a pyx, was spiritually beneficial. It seems to have ignored the likely spiritual effects of requiring that the laity kneel even if the ground were muddy (*luto non obstante*).[216] In the same year, a synod of Lisbon said the laity were to be admonished frequently to kneel, "as if to their Lord and creator" (*tanquam Domino et creatori suo*), and join their hands.[217] The 1281 statutes of Liège were more accommodating about when the laity had to kneel, urging them to do so if they could do so conveniently (*commode*). They were more demanding of those who were on horseback, who were urged to descend, honoring Christ, Who came down from heaven for their salvation.[218] The statutes of Angers wanted children, not just adults, to be taught to genuflect and pray when they saw their Lord and Creator carried to the sick.[219]

Eventually the spiritual benefits of seeing the procession were augmented with recommendations that the faithful follow along behind. Such devotion was encouraged by granting indulgences, a growing part of late medieval piety, with bishops and popes granting remission of spiritual punishments in the hereafter.[220] The Council of Münster, however, was not evenhanded in offering this opportunity. Women were threatened with censures if they followed the priest. The clergy of that diocese thought women might disrupt the procession.[221] The provincial Council of Trier of 1227 invited the laity to follow the procession but issued a more general warning against making noise.[222] More stringently,

[214] Mansi 23.528; *Councils & Synods*, 2/1.299. See also the first Salisbury statutes of 1217/1218 in *Councils & Synods*, 2/1.148. Walter de Cantilupe also required that a lamp burn before the reserved host; see *Councils & Synods*, 2/1.300.

[215] Mansi 23.753. [216] Mansi 22.528; *Councils & Synods*, 21.299–300.

[217] *Synodicon Hispanum*, 2.288. [218] Mansi 23.789.

[219] Pontal, *Les statuts synodaux*, 1.186–187.

[220] See Mansi 23.406, 24.378, 24.505, 25.291, 26.521, 603–604. Rubin, *Corpus Christ*, 78–80; R. N. Swanson, *Indulgences in Late Medieval England: Passports to Paradise?* (Cambridge, 2007). On the Continent, confraternities became involved in viaticum processions; see Rubin, *Corpus Christi*, 236; "Statutes of the Confraternity of the Most Holy Sacrament in the Church of San Felice, Venice," *Confraternitas*, 22 (2011), 30–40.

[221] Mansi 24.315. Similarly, the 1280 synod of Cologne warned women away; see Mansi 24.351.

[222] Mansi 23.77.

the 1281 synod of Liège threatened anyone who disrupted a procession with excommunication.[223] Although there were many accusations that heretics disrespected the elevated host, similar comments about viaticum processions seem to have been rare.[224]

There occasionally were concerns about wrong messages to the faithful similar to those the canonists had discussed, just as there were problems with the timing of the elevation. Thus the Valencia synodal constitutions of 1255 specified that bells were to be rung and the lamp lighted only if the priest still carried a host when returning to the church. Otherwise the faithful might bow their heads or kneel before a mere creature no longer carrying the Body of Christ.[225] The 1281 synod of Liège also said that the lamp could be lighted and the bell rung before a priest returned to his church only if he still had a consecrated host with him. Otherwise the laity might be led to adore in vain.[226] (This rationale was similar to a warning of the 1287 synod of Liège that elevating an unconsecrated host might lead to the adoration of a material object.[227]) The *Pupilla oculi*, one of the English manuals for priests, recited the usual instructions for carrying the Eucharist, including the use of the bell to arouse devotion in the faithful. The author, John de Burough, also warned against the use of the bell when returning to the parish church without a host. He feared the laity might be led into idolatry.[228] (The Bolognese instructions for comforting condemned prisoners tell how a lay member of a confraternity should behave when first hearing the bell as a priest brought the Eucharist to the prison through the administration of communion.[229])

These enactments also required enforcement, which entered into the instructions by local bishops to their archdeacons for visiting parishes. As Hostiensis said at c. *Perniciosus* (X 3.41.13), archdeacons were to correct scandals.[230] These officers were to inquire, among other things, whether each parish had the means for properly conducting viaticum processions. This was part of their enforcement of regulations about parish buildings, vessels, vestments, and books. Parish priests and church wardens were told that they were to present all liturgical objects for inspection during an

[223] Mansi 23.898.

[224] For instance, see *Regestre d'inquisition de Jacques Fournier (éveque de Pamiers) 1318–1325*, ed. Jean Duvernay, 3 vols. (Paris, 1978), 2.461, 1010.

[225] Mansi 23.889. [226] Mansi 23.898. [227] Mansi 23.1191.

[228] *Pupilla oculi*, Cambridge, Corpus Christi College Manuscript 255, fol. 32r, cited from the *Parker Library on the Web* [http://parkerweb.stanford.edu/parker/], accessed October 30, 2009. This warning is absent from the *Oculus sacerdotis* of William of Pagula; see *Pastors and the Care of Souls*, 146. William did require the priest to punish those who did not venerate the Eucharist on these occasions.

[229] "The Bologna Comforters' Manual," in *The Art of Executing Well*, 183–292 at 264–267.

[230] *Hostiensis Decretalium commentaria*, 3, fol. 166vb.

official visitation. This included inspection of vestments, sacred vessels, and books (*visitatio rerum*).[231] Part of the equipment required in a parish was used for the communion of the sick. This equipment included items that could be used for more than one purpose. Thus the 1287 Council of Exeter ordered parishes to have a bell to ring at the elevation of the host and during viaticum processions.[232] Pyxes were needed for both reservation of the sacrament and its being carried to the sick. Regulations were formulated requiring provision of vessels worthy of the Real Presence and the dignity of divine worship, just as they had to be provided for reservation in church. For example, the 1287 synod of Liège specified that pyxes should be of gold or silver, or at least copper.[233] The laity often made this process an object of benefaction, as when, in 1349, three laymen of Norfolk underwrote providing three good wax candles to go before the priest, not just one poor one.[234]

Records of visitations by archdeacons and other clerical authorities are not always available for the pre-Reformation period, even in England; and the level of detail varies. The 1297 visitation of the parishes belonging to St. Paul's Cathedral provides us with a small sample with which to start. One factor to be noted is that these records often say little or nothing about the actual conduct of rites and ceremonies.[235] They do say a good deal about the condition of a church's fabric and of the cemetery – even of the vicarage – as well as the availability of vestments, sacred vessels, other church equipment, and books. Among the books noted by their presence or absence are synodal and episcopal statutes, as well as the legatine constitutions of Cardinal Ottobono, which provided instructions for priests about their duties.[236] The visitor carefully recorded the presence or lack of equipment that might be used in communication of the sick. These entries in the record indicated of what material the pyx for sick communions was made and with what cloth or other material it was covered. They reflect the instructions for providing an adequate supply of ritual items decreed by bishops and councils.[237] Church wardens' accounts can show purchases of needed items. The wardens of

[231] For example, see the statutes attributed to Robert Winchelsey, archbishop of Canterbury, in *Councils & Synods*, 2/1., 1386–1387.

[232] Mansi 23.801; *Councils & Synods*, 2/2.1006. [233] Mansi 23.897.

[234] Sarah Beckwith, *Christ's Body: Identity, Culture and Society in Late Medieval Writings* (London, 1993), 103.

[235] Visitations instructions can require an inquiry into the conduct of this rite; see, for example, the set of questions from the *Annales de Burton* (1253) in *Pastors and the Care of Souls*, 289.

[236] For example, the parish of Barlinge lacked all of the required texts; see *Visitations of Churches belonging to St. Paul's Cathedral*, 9, whether individually or in a single volume.

[237] Archbishop Peccham, for example, required the parishioners in the province of Canterbury to provide liturgical vessels for the church; see Rubin, *Corpus Christi*, 45.

Morebath in Devon, for example, bought a new "purse" for carrying communion to the sick in the period before the Reformation.[238]

The vessels available in parishes actually varied widely, as archdeacons' records reveal. This was especially true of pyxes for communion of the sick. For example, the visitations of parishes near London dependent on St. Paul's Cathedral mentioned earlier show a wide variety of materials employed, possibly because of the differing economic conditions of those churches.[239] The majority of the parishes visited had some such pyx. Nastoke, for example, had what appears to have been a lockable leather box to take both the Eucharist and the oil used to anoint the sick.[240] West Lee had a pyx wrapped in silk.[241] Tillingham was able to afford a silver pyx, while Walestone only had one made of wood.[242] Only three parishes – Drayton, Chiswick, and Saint Pancras, London – possessed a pyx for reservation of the Eucharist but lacked one for communion of the sick.[243] During the 1458 visitation of these parishes, an intriguing detail was recorded: that two of them had one pyx (probably for communion of the sick) nested inside another (for reservation).[244]

A further problem afflicting parishes was theft of sacred vessels for mercenary reasons. Pyxes and monstrances, especially if made of silver or gold, were among the objects that were under the risk of being stolen and needed replacement before the next visitation. Examples of such thefts can be found in the archdiocese of Prague in the fourteenth century. In one case, a bell ringer was accused of stealing a pyx from the parish.[245] In the reign of Paul II a man who was involved in the theft of a monstrance with a consecrated host in it had to petition the Penitentiary for absolution.[246] In the diocese of Basel, under Sixtus IV, soldiers stole a pyx and discarded it. One eventually asked the Apostolic Penitentiary for absolution.[247] In 1554 Morebath suffered theft of a pyx.[248] Such thefts were regarded as sacrilegious. Antoninus of Florence, in his vernacular

[238] Eamon Duffy, *The Voices of Morebath: Reformation and Rebellion in an English Village* (New Haven, 2001), 66.

[239] *Visitations of Churches belonging to St. Paul's Cathedral, in 1297 and in 1458* (New York, 1966), xxxi–xxxii.

[240] *Visitations of Churches belonging to St. Paul's Cathedral*, 5.

[241] *Visitations of Churches belonging to St. Paul's Cathedral*, 8. For other rich pyxes, see Visites Josas, xxx–xxxii.

[242] *Visitations of Churches belonging to St. Paul's Cathedral*, 14, 22.

[243] *Visitations of Churches belonging to St. Paul's Cathedral*, 56, 58, 62–63.

[244] *Visitations of Churches belonging to St. Paul's Cathedral*, 83, 91.

[245] *Visitační protokol Pražského*, 47. In the same year a monstrance was stolen from another church; see *Visitační protokol Pražského*, 54.

[246] *Repertorium Poenitentiariae Germanicum*, 5 no. 1193.

[247] *Repertorium Poenitentiariae Germanicum*, 6 no. 2547.

[248] Duffy, *Voices of Morebath*, 164.

Confessionale "Omnis mortalium cura", said sacrilege could pertain to stealing from churches as well as misusing sacred things. (Those who used these for magic were to be burned.)[249]

Astesanus, in his *Summa*, said sacrilege was worst when it involved the Eucharist.[250] A negligent cleric could suffer for laxity in care of vessels. A priest of Halberstat was tortured by local lay leaders to account for theft of a monstrance with a *sacramentum miraculosum*. He died, and they had to petition to be absolved from excommunication.[251] English parishes sometimes sought remedies from lay authorities, especially from the English Crown, because of theft of sacred objects.[252]

Even where nothing had been stolen, the prospect of a visitation must have sent parishes scrambling to provide or clean items to present to the archdeacon. To prevent deception by parishes, the third statutes of Winchester, like those of Exeter mentioned earlier, forbade churches from borrowing vestments and ornaments from another nearby.[253] When a strict version of the Reformation was implemented in the reign of Edward VI, we do know that the inventories of Alburye, Chiswick, and Saint Pancras still included pyxes, although two reported that theirs were made only of latten, a copper alloy.[254]

Records of archdeacons' visitations to France are less easily available. Those of Henri de Vezelai, archdeacon of Hiémois in the diocese of Bayeux, give us a glimpse of ecclesiastical discipline in thirteenth-century Normandy. Thus in 1267 Henri required the parish of Folie to buy a lead chalice for viaticum.[255] The next year he told the parish of Bavent to acquire a lantern for viaticum processions.[256] Henri also frequently reported failure in custody of the sacraments, including failure to lock up the reserved Eucharist and the baptismal font.[257] Once he threatened a

249 Antoninus, *Confessionale "Omnis mortalium cura"* (Milan, 1470), fol. 53v–54r at 54r, "Chi adonche fa o usa niente del sacramento del corpo de cristo per incanti o simili comette grauissimo sacrilegio & doueria esser bruxato."

250 Astesanus, *Summa de casibus conscientiae* (Nuremberg, 1482?), Lib. I, tit. xxxiii. Astesanus noted that punishments could well include not just fines and censures but death.

251 *Repertorium Poenitentiariae Germanicum*, 6 no. 2627.

252 Robert C. Palmer, *Selling the Church: The English Parish in Law, Commerce and Religion, 1350–1550* (Chapel Hill, 2002), 69–70.

253 *Councils & Synods*, 2/1.710. See also the first Canterbury statutes (1213–1214) in *Councils & Synods*, 28–29.

254 *Visitations of Churches belonging to St. Paul's Cathedral*, 115, 116, 119. The Crown was looking for objects to confiscate, and these parishes may have hidden or sold some vessels in advance of confiscation; see Eamon Duffy, *The Stripping of the Altars: Traditional Religion in England 1400–1580* (New Haven, 1992), 482–486.

255 Delisle, "Visites pastorales de maître Henri de Vezelai," 463–464.

256 Delisle, "Visites pastorales de maître Henri de Vezelai," 466.

257 Delisle, "Visites pastorales de maître Henri de Vezelai," 463–466.

priest with suspension if he did not see that there was a key for the aumbry.[258] In the fifteenth century, a visitation of the archdeaconry of Josas noted the need to repair the door of a tabernacle.[259] The visitor may have ordered priests and churchwardens to make good any defects, but it is unclear what a French pastor did for his gravely ill parishioners when lacking a pyx for carrying viaticum. He may have used a chalice and paten, as the Spanish councils cited later allowed.

It is hard too to ascertain how many clergy failed in the essential pastoral duty of taking communion to the sick. A few cases can be noted here. In 1397, the vicar of Eardisley in the diocese of Hereford was reported to have allowed parishioners to die without confession, viaticum, or anointing.[260] A vicar of Minster Lovell in the diocese of Lincoln was reputed to arrive only after the sick parishioner had died.[261] In 1458, the vicar of Pelham Arsa, one of the churches subject to St. Paul's Cathedral, was reported to have failed to visit the sick when he was in his most prosperous days.[262] Two such accusations arose in visitations in the diocese of Lincoln before Henry VIII broke formally with Rome.[263] Far away in the archdeaconry of Prague, a priest went to the city overnight. The visitor later heard a complaint that a sick woman had to send to another parish for communion.[264]

The later Middle Ages placed a greater emphasis than ever before on the Real Presence of Christ in the Eucharist, including in viaticum. Believing He was present "hidden in bread" meant that the faithful might expect to experience God by sight if not by taste. Moreover, even when they could not see the host, when it was carried enclosed, the faithful still could believe they were in the very presence of the divinity.[265]

[258] Delisle, "Visites pastorales de maître Henri de Vezelai," 466.

[259] Pierre-Clément Timbal and B. Auzay, "Visites décanales faites dans l'archidiaconé de Paris en 1468–1470," *Revue d'Histoire de l'église de France* 62 (1976), 361–374 at 368.

[260] *Pastors and the Care of Souls*, 299. This is an example of the "spiritual murder" responsible clerics feared might occur when a pastor failed in his cure of souls; see Rubin, *Corpus Christi*, 81–82. For other examples from Hereford, see A. T. Bannister, "Visitation Returns of the Diocese of Hereford in 1397," *The English Historical Review* 44 (1929), 279–289, 444–453, 45 (1930), 92–101, 444–463 at 29.286, 450, 30.95, 97.

[261] Margaret Bowker, *The Secular Clergy in the Diocese of Lincoln 1495–1520* (Cambridge, 1968), 113.

[262] *Visitations of Churches belonging to St. Paul's Cathedral*, 106.

[263] *Visitations in the Diocese of Lincoln 1517–1531*, ed. A. Hamilton Thompson, 3 vols. (Hereford, 1940), 2.13, 50.

[264] *Visitační protokol Pražského*, 262. Other Prague priests were criticized, one who took the host into a tavern and another who left the pyx on the altar unsecured for three days after returning from a visit to the sick; see *Visitační protokol Pražského*, 266, 319.

[265] Margaret R. Miles, *Image as Insight: Visual Understanding in Western Christianity and Secular Culture* (Boston, 1985), 96–97.

We need not wonder that respect and contemplation were expected of the faithful, and that the dying would be comforted by deathbed communion. The English Reformation took these rites seriously enough to forbid the use of lights or bells in taking communion to the sick. Eventually even the processions were suppressed in favor of a reformed rite for comforting the dying that reflected a different idea of the Eucharist.[266]

Viaticum processions continued elsewhere past the end of the Middle Ages. Thus the 1543–1544 synodal statutes of Orense in Spain repeated the usual requirement that communion be carried to the sick with a lamp preceding it.[267] The 1528 synod of Tuy offered even more detailed instructions, including use of a chalice and paten where a pyx (*el relicuario*) was lacking. The synod required that holy water, as well as bell and lantern, be carried with the host. The enactment also required veneration by bystanders on horse or on foot and promised indulgences to those who followed after the priest.[268] A 1510 synod of Segovia ordered any cleric or sacristan not otherwise prevented from doing so to follow along, suitably dressed, after any priest carrying viaticum.[269] Only one major change in process was introduced in Spain after the thirteenth century. The 1403 synod of Lisbon and the 1500 synod of Guarda allowed setting up a temporary altar to celebrate mass for a dying person.[270] Little changed elsewhere until the Reformation caused displacement of traditional rites intended to comfort the dying. Otherwise, the faithful expected the Lord's body to be delivered to their sickbeds, and the priest's duties still included both carrying viaticum and teaching the faithful to reverence the sacrament as he carried it outside the church.

Sickbed communion

Communion of the sick and dying got less attention in medieval canon law than did custody of the sacrament or its carrying in public. The surviving texts treat this practice (if at all) in conjunction with other

266 Duffy, *Stripping of the Altars*, 466–467, 472, 474. The first prayer book of Edward VI allows for continuity between communion in the church and communion of the sick, but the second book does not; see *The First and Second Prayer Books of Edward VI*, ed. Douglas Harrison (London, 1968), 266–268, 422–423.

267 *Synodicon Hispanum*, 1.227. The statures of Orense also forbade monks, women, and other "secular persons" to carry holy oil and chrism under pain of excommunication; see *Synodicon Hispanum*, 1.197.

268 *Synodicon Hispanum*, 1.495–496. Similarly see the 1553 synod of Astorga in *Synodicon Hispanum*, 3.136–137.

269 *Synodicon Hispanum*, 6.510.

270 *Synodicon Hispanum*, 2.232 (Guarda), 333–334 (Lisbon). The same synod of Guarda offered indulgences to those who followed a viaticum procession; see *Synodicon Hispanum*, 2.231–232.

practices, such as anointing of the sick. Thus Regino of Prüm wanted the parish priest to be asked, "If he visits the sick, if he reconciles them, if he anoints them with holy oil according to the apostle [James], if he communicates them with his own hand and not through some lay person."[271] Regino supported these instructions with a canon of the First Council of Nicaea saying a dying person should not be denied viaticum. He added a canon of a Council of Vaison providing proper burial for someone who died suddenly after being absolved but before receiving communion.[272]

In a rare case for a Decretist, Rufinus quoted a canon of the Council of Tours from Burchard's *Decretum*. He then said that communion of a sick person in danger of death could be given by intinction, using the words "The body and blood of Christ accomplish for you etc." Otherwise, intinction had ceased being used in communion. This negative opinion about intinction as a common practice, as has been seen elsewhere, became widespread.[273] The author of *Fecit Moyses tabernaculum*, like Rufinus, limited communion by intinction – or at least with a host in unconsecrated wine – to the sick.[274] The Ordinary Gloss took a permissive attitude toward intinction in sickbed communions, although Huguccio had described the practice as abrogated.[275] What these authors did not discuss, as Johannes Beleth did, was the problem of reserved wine going sour out of negligence, making it difficult to reserve for the sick.[276]

Local councils and synods occasionally gave instructions for communion of the sick. A few expressed concerns that the priest might fail in his duty to the dying. Thus the 1284 synod of Nîmes, using language reflecting the canon of the Council of Worms found in the *Decretum* of

[271] *Das Sendhandbuch des Regino von Prüm*, 26–27, "Si visitet infirmos, si eos reconciliet, si eos unguat oleo sancto iuxta apostolum, si eos propria manu communicet et non per quemlibet laicum, aut si tradat communionem laico aut feminae ad deferendum infirmo quod nefas est?"

[272] *Das Sendhandbuch des Regino von Prüm*, 84. Regino also added a text provided for annointing the dying person who had been reconciled and absolved; see *Das Sendhandbuch des Regino von Prüm*, 86.

[273] Rufinus, *Summa*, 553: De cons. d. 2 c. 7, "que sacra oblatio intincta debet esse sanguine Christi, ut veraciter posit presbiter infirmo dicere: 'Corpus et sanguis Christi proficiat tibi' etc.": The "etc." replaces the words "in remissionem peccatorum et vitam aeternam." In the fifteenth century, when answering the Utraquists, Nicholas of Cusa would refer to intinction as a practice of the past; see Nicholas of Cusa, *Writings on Church and Reform*, trans. Thomas M. Izbicki (Cambridge, Mass, 2008), 52–55.

[274] Stephen of Tournai, *Die Summa über das Decretum Gratiani*, 269–270: De cons. D. 2 c. 1, "et si necessitas urget puta aegrotantis debilitas, etiam in liquore non sanctificato eucharistiam dare inconveniens non est."

[275] Ordinary Gloss at De cons. D. 2 c. 7 v. Intinctam, citing Huguccio, *Summa decretorum*, Admont Stiftsbibliothek MS 7, fol. 423rb–va: De cons. D. 1 c. 7, "prohibetur intinctam dari."

[276] *Iohannis Beleth summa de ecclesiasticis officiis*, ed. Heribert Douteil (Turnhout, 1976), 183.

Burchard, wanted the patient to communicate quickly "lest he die without communion." The text presupposed that the person had indicated a desire for confession and communion.[277] The statutes of Arras required the priest to be ready to perform this duty day or night unless an interdict or excommunication forbade it.[278] The Third Council of Worcester also required the priest to be ready at any time; however, it also threatened negligent priests with punishment if the patient died without confession, communion, or anointing. The priest had to be punished for showing himself pernicious and useless to the faithful.[279] Thomas of Chobham reasoned that priests should stay sober to be able to respond when called to a sickbed. Otherwise someone might die with sins not absolved.[280] (One lawsuit alleged that another reason the sick, infants, or women giving birth might die without the sacraments was the lack of a priest. One Premonstratensian monastery that had gained possession of a large parish church in Lancashire was denounced for appointing only one priest to care for numerous parishioners, causing neglect of the sick.[281])

Local statutes said very little about the actual communion of the sick. The statutes of Cambrai wanted the priest, if possible, to visit the sick person and hear his or her confession before going to the church for the reserved sacrament. Only then would he execute the type of procession described above. Once he reached the patient, the priest was to judge if the Eucharist might be vomited. In that case, spiritual communion (*spiritualier accipiat*), not physical reception, was mandated.[282] The 1287 statutes of Liège wanted the priest to have the ailing penitent profess faith in the Real Presence before giving communion.[283] A 1247 French statute permitted putting a host into a cup with wine for communion of a sick person who might otherwise vomit.[284] Actual vomit containing the Eucharist, according to the Liège statutes, was to be collected. Any evident fragments of the host were to be gathered and consumed with

[277] Mansi 24.535, "Et quando ab infirmo, vel confesso fuerit requisitus, statim eum communicet, ne sine communione moriatur."

[278] Avril, *Les statuts synodaux*, 4.192, "Quacumque hora infirmus communionem petierit, nisi ab hoc quidem interdictus vel excommunicatus fuerit, sacerdos sit paratus accedere, aliis obmissis."

[279] *Councils & Synods*, 2/1.305, "Sacerdos autem qui se pigrum exhibet in visitandis infirmis, ex quo quandoque forsitan accidit quod egrotus absque confessione vel dominici corporis et sanguinis perceptione decedat, espers unctionis extreme, perniciosum se non solum inutilem subditis exhibet et tantam eius incuriam per nos noverit condigna pro viribus animadversione plectandam."

[280] *Pastors and the Care of Souls*, 8.

[281] Geoffrey Barraclough, *Papal Provisions: Aspects of Church History Constitutional, Legal, and Administrative in the Later Middle Ages* (Oxford, 1935), 52–53.

[282] Avril, *Les statuts synodaux*, 4.41–42. The same wording is found in a synodal statute from Liège in 1287; see Mansi 24.898.

[283] Mansi 24.898. [284] Mansi 23.746–747.

wine. The remainder of the vomit was to be burned and the ashes buried near the altar or in another sacred place.[285]

Pastoral manuals touched, some of them lightly, on deathbed communion. Thus Thomas of Chobham discussed this in terms of the ability of the sick person to retain communion. Thomas thought the priest should determine whether a sick person unable to speak was penitent. This was a supposition similar to regarding the desire for baptism as equivalent of receiving the sacrament.[286] He considered the possibility that the penitent would be unable to swallow a consecrated host. Thomas rejected the practice of some who gave the patient an unconsecrated host instead. It was preferable to take the risk; and, in case a host was vomited, the results should be burned and the ashes retained in the sacristy.[287] To illustrate this point, he told the story of Maurice, bishop of Paris, who was twice offered unconsecrated hosts by persons who feared he would vomit up communion. Maurice knew by the inspiration of the Holy Spirit that these hosts were unconsecrated and said so. When they brought him a consecrated host, he knew his Lord was present and received communion.[288] John of Erfurt emphasized the faith of the person unable to receive deathbed communion. Thus the priest could decide if vomiting was probable and devoutly show the host, as Christ had manifested Himself, trusting the sick person to receive in the heart.[289] The author of the *Quinque verba* also worried about the sick person vomiting up a host.[290] John Mirk offered a set of interrogations of the dying, asking about belief and past sins. Mirk allowed the priest to say the words "Into your hands etc." on the dying person's behalf.[291] A curious story about Ida of Nivelles says that she was allowed to receive the host as a proxy for a sick woman unable to swallow the consecrated host, even a fragment of one.[292]

Accounts of actual deathbed communions are not found in canon law, which was concerned with the discipline of the sacrament. To grasp the reality of the practice, recourse must be had to other sources. One, the

285 Mansi 24.898.

286 *Thomae de Chobham summa confessorum*, ed. F. Broomfield (Louvain, 1968), 136.

287 *Thomae de Chobham summa confessorum*, 136–137.

288 *Thomae de Chobham summa confessorum*, 136–137.

289 *Die Summa confessorum des Johannes von Erfurt*, ed. Norbert Brieskorn, 3 vols. (Frankfurt, 1980), 2.121.

290 *Pastors and the Care of Souls*, 137.

291 *Pastors and the Care of Souls*, 195–196.

292 *Send Me God: The Lives of Ida the Compassionate of Nivelles, Nun of La Ramée, Arnulf, Lay Brothedr of Villers, and Abundus, Monk of Villers, by Goswin of Bossut*, trans. Martinus Cawley (Turnhout, 2003), 61. Sara Ritchey, "Affective Medicine: Later Medieval Healing Communities and the Feminization of Health Care Practices in the Thirteenth-Century Low Countries," *The Journal of Medieval Religious Cultures* 40 (2014), 113–143 at 123.

necrology of the nuns of Corpus Domini in Venice, offers some insights into the reactions of witnesses at deathbeds. Some sisters are described as being "rapt" upon receipt of viaticum. One wanted to die on a day when communion was to be distributed. Another experienced remission of a flow of blood once while in danger of death. Later she received the sacraments devoutly before she "passed to her beloved spouse."[293] Even communion under more ordinary circumstances could be recorded. The death notice for Sister Onesta dei Marchesi said she received the Eucharist with tears and sighs.[294] Sister Felcitas Buono had a more unusual experience. On the octave of the feast of Corpus Christi, when the tabernacle was kept open, she saw "a lovely child," the Christ child. She understood this vision to be a promise of everlasting life. Falling terminally ill shortly thereafter, she passed to her "spouse" after a year of illness.[295]

A related concern was whether the dying person was unconscious or delirious. Thus Raymond of Peñafort's *Summa de penitentia*, one of the most important *summae confessorum*, discussed saving dying sinners by hearing their deathbed confessions. Raymond said the priest was permitted to presume that someone who had sent for him but was *non compos mentis* upon his arrival was penitent, especially if others could witness his or her penitence. Then the priest could give communion, if it could be done "without peril" (*sine periculo*), by pouring consecrated wine into the open mouth.[296] William of Rennes added that viaticum was not to be denied to the dying.[297]

The *artes moriendi* promoted the idea of an edifying death. The deathbed would be surrounded by witnesses who would see the dying person receive the sacraments, anointing, confession, and communion, before passing in a devout manner. This ideal endured well into the Early Modern period, being well enough known to be parodied. The pastoral manuals looked at less edifying possibilities, including, as we have seen, vomit and delirium. The priest was expected to deal effectively with these evidences of mortality.[298] The fear that a sick person might even refuse viaticum was expressed in an image in the Taymouth Hours,

[293] Bartolomea Riccoboni, *Life and Death in a Venetian Convent: The Chronicle and Necrology of Corpus Domini, 1395–1436*, trans. Daniel Bornstein (Chicago, 2000), 65, 78, 97.

[294] Riccoboni, *Life and Death in a Venetian Convent*, 93.

[295] Riccoboni, *Life and Death in a Venetian Convent*, 68.

[296] *Summa Sancti Raymundi de Peniafort*, 66–467 at 467, "Eucharistiam ori eius infundendo."

[297] *Summa Sancti Raymundi de Peniafort*, 467.

[298] Philippe Ariès, *The Hour of Our Death: The Classic History of Western Attitudes Toward Death Over the Last Thousand Years*, trans. Helen Weaver (New York, 2000), 18–19, 23–24, 303, 562–563.

which shows a demon turning away a sick merchant from a priest holding ciborium and host.[299]

The widely read *Manipulus curatorum* tied deathbed communion inevitably to penance and absolution. If the dying person was in mortal sin, confession was to be heard before communion was administered. If that person was excommunicated, the priest could absolve him or her even of the most grievous censures.[300] If a formal confession was not physically possible, a sign of penitence could be accepted, permitting absolution and communion.[301] The *York Manual*, in its order for visiting the sick, allowed for the possibility that a dying person (*in articulo mortis*) might have a papal bull allowing for a special absolution of sins.[302] Antoninus of Florence addressed all these issues, even adding a concern that a dying person might be senile, in his interrogatories about care of the sick. His questions began with whether the person was indeed dying, covered many contingencies, and concluded with a reminder to apply any papally conferred indulgence.[303] In the context of the deathbed, Antoninus and other writers on the topic agreed that the salvation of souls trumped all legal concerns.[304]

[299] Kathryn A. Smith, *The Taymouth Hours: Stories and the Construction of the Self in Late Medieval England* (London, 2012), 245, figure 147.

[300] The statutes of Sisteron also permited the priest to absolve persons *in extremis* of all sins and censures; see Pontal, *Les statuts synodaux*, 2.220.

[301] Guido de Monte Rocherii, *Manipulus curatorum* (London, 1508), fol. xxxv^{v}–xxxvi^{r}; Guido, *Handbook for Curates*, trans. Anne T. Thayer (Washington, D.C., 2011), 85–86.

[302] *Manuale et processionale ad usum insignis ecclesiae Eboracensus* (Durham, 1975), 41–49, 129.

[303] Antoninus, *Confessionale "Defecerunt scrutantes scrutinio", Circa infirmos.*

[304] Even a man who died after a relapse and before the priest arrived was granted Christian burial by the papal Penitentiary; see *Repertorium Poenitentiariae Germanicum*, 6 no. 3562.

5 Corpus Christi and wonder hosts

The feast of Corpus Christi

In 1264 Pope Urban IV authorized the celebration of the feast of Corpus Christi, honoring the Real Presence, in his bull *Transiturus*. This bull set the date for the feast as the Thursday after Trinity Sunday, a date parallel with the institution of the sacrament on Holy Thursday. Atop requiring the faithful to honor the Eucharistic Presence devoutly, Pope Urban offered days of pardon for those who confessed and otherwise prepared to receive communion on the feast. The impetus for the celebration came at first from the canoness Juliana of Mont Cornillon of the diocese of Liège, who interpreted her vision of the full moon with dark stain as indicating the need for such a feast.[1] This idea spread from Liège to Rome, apparently via the Dominican theologian Hugh of Saint Cher. Offices and propers for the mass were composed for the feast. They included some of the most important liturgical poetry about the Eucharist (*Pange lingua, O salutaris hostia, Lauda Sion*). The role of Thomas Aquinas in the composition of these texts remains under discussion.[2] Although *Transiturus* was addressed to all prelates, it had no immediate effect in canon law. The feast entered canon law via the Council of Vienne (1311–1312) and the *Constitutiones Clementinae* (1313) as Clement V's decree *Si Dominum*. These decrees were republished by John XXII in 1317. *Si Dominum* appeared in book III under the title "On Relics and the Veneration of Saints" (*De reliquiis et veneratione sanctorum*; Clem. 3.16.un.). It contains the text of *Transiturus* in full, extending the feast it authorized to places where its observance had not yet taken root. The bull also extended indulgences to all who received communion on the feast after proper preparation and remission of sins.[3]

[1] *Life of Juliana of Mont-Cornillon*, trans. Barbara Newman, 2nd ed. (Toronto, 1991).

[2] Barbara R. Walters, "The Feast and Its Founder," in *The Feast of Corpus Christi*, ed. Vincent Corrigan, Walters, and Peter T. Ricketts (University Park, Penna., 2006), 3–54; Peter Browe, "Die Entstehung der Sakramentsandachte," *Jahrbuch für Liturgiewissenschaft* 7 (1927), 83–103.

[3] *Corpus Iuris Canonici*, 2.1174–1177.

The most important commentaries on the *Clementines* appeared shortly after the collection was promulgated. One leading canonist expressed an awareness of the history of the feast. The *casus* to Johannes Andreae's Ordinary Gloss on the *Clementines* summarized the scheduling of the feast on the fourth *feria* (Thursday) after the octave of Pentecost and the granting of indulgences to the faithful who observed it. Then it said that Urban's constitution "was not received by all" (*non fuit recepta ab omnibus*). That was why Clement V renewed it and ordered it "to be observed by all" (*ab omnibus servari*).[4] The Gloss summarized Urban's pontificate briefly, underlining his invitation to Charles of Anjou to supersede Manfred as king of Sicily.[5] Citing both the *Decretum* and c. *Cum Marthae*, Johannes Andreae underlined the role of the priest's words in effecting transubstantiation, "by the power of the Holy Spirit, not by the merits of the priest."[6]

Other canonists gave less attention to the history behind the canon *Si Dominum*. Guillelmus de Monte Lauduno, in one of the earliest commentaries on the *Clementines*, made passing mention of authorization of the feast by the pope, including the existence of heretics who denied Christ's presence in the Eucharist.[7] Perhaps more because of his consciousness of contemporary heresies than because theologians were discussing the ability of a host to contain the Real Presence, Guillelmus wrote at length about how the glorified body of Christ present in heaven related to the body present on the altar, any altar, including many simultaneously. His exposition went well beyond reaffirmation of concomitance to presenting a theology of the sacrament, affirming the complete presence of Christ in a host and in each part when it was broken. This text included too a theology of the priesthood and episcopate as established to provide the people with the sacraments.[8] Having offered this theological discourse, Guillelmus also wrote about the proper preparation for communion on the feast and the indulgences to be gained by participation in the festal mass. This

[4] Ordinary Gloss at Clem. 3.16.un v. Si Dominum.

[5] Ordinary Gloss at Clem. 3.16.un v. Urbano.

[6] Ordinary Gloss at Clem. 3.16.un v. Mirabilia, "fit transubstantiatio uirtute Spiritus sancti, non merito sacerdotis." This gloss emphasized biblical parallels to the blessed sacrament.

[7] Guillelmus de Monte Lauduno, *Apparatus ... super Clementinas ...* (Paris, 1517), fol. cxxxvii[ra], cxl[vb], accessed via Google Books on January 1, 2014.

[8] Guillelmus de Monte Lauduno, *Apparatus ... super Clementinas*, fol. cxxxviii[ra–va], cxxxviii[vb]–cxl[ra]. On the theological issues Guillelmus addressed, see Marilyn McCord Adams, *Some Later Medieval Theologies of the Eucharist: Thomas Aquinas, Giles of Rome, Duns Scotus and William of Ockham* (Oxford, 2012).

preparation included fasting to remove all earthly foods from the stomach before receiving heavenly nourishment.[9]

Paulus de Liazariis summarized the intention of Urban IV's decree (1264), both the celebration of the feast with its octave and the concession of indulgences.[10] Paulus underlined the need to abstain from "servile work" (*ab opere seruili*) on the feast.[11] His commentary accepted use of leavened or unleavened bread at mass; but he noted that Christ would have used unleavened bread when "in the houses of Jews" (*in domibus Iudeorum*), at least on days when no yeast would be found there.[12] After expounding the doctrine of concomitance, Paulus noted how wondrous it was that Christ gave Himself entirely to humanity.[13]

Later canonists made extensive use of the Gloss and Paulus's text. Petrus de Ancharano offered a detailed discussion of the materials of the sacrament, including Paulus's argument that Christ used unleavened bread in the houses of the Jews.[14] Petrus discussed indulgences, arguing that they extended to those unable to get into a crowded church for the festal mass.[15] Francesco Zabarella, summarizing *Si Dominum*, said that, "on the feast of Corpus Christi, we should give thanks to God."[16] On the feast, the memory of the body of Christ should be brought to mind for veneration.[17] Zabarella noted that Clement's decree commanded observance of Urban's original bull.[18] Considering the need for such a feast, he admitted that every mass was a celebration of the memory of Christ's sacrifice. Nonetheless, he argued that the Church should have a special

9 Guillelmus de Monte Lauduno, *Apparatus ... super Clementinas*, fol. cxxxviii^{ra}, cxli^{rb-va}. Guillelmus also considered the possibility that the host might revert to being bread in the stomach, especially that of a mouse; see *Apparatus super Clementinas*, fol. cxl^{va}.

10 Paulus de Liazariis, *Super clementinis*, University of Notre Dame MS Latin e.3, fol. xxxix^{ra}, "et breuiter intendit hoc festum de corpore Christi quinta feria post octauam pentecostem singulis annis debet sollempniter celebrari et diuinis die festi uel infra octauam interessentibus certe indulgentie conceduntur."

11 Paulus de Liazariis, *Super clementinis*. loc. cit.

12 Paulus de Liazariis, *Super clementinis*. loc. cit., "Christum hoc fecisse in azimis cum in domibus iudeorum non esset fermenta."

13 Paulus de Liazariis, *Super clementinis*, fol. xxxix^{rb}, "et inde mirabile quod Christus dedit se totum."

14 Petrus de Ancharano, *Super clementinis facundissima commentaria* (Bologna, 1580), 228A.

15 Petrus de Ancharano, *Super clementinis*, 228B. For indulgences received during the octave of Corpus Christi, see *Super clementinis*, 229A.

16 Franciscus de Zabarellis, *Lectura super clementinis ...* (Venezia, 1481), [162]^{va}, "Septimo no. quod in festo corporis Christi debemus referre gratias deo."

17 Franciscus de Zabarellis, *Lectura super clementinis*, loc. cit., "Sexto no. quod de festiua ueneratione debet coli memoria corporis Christi. ibi festiua uenerationis."

18 Franciscus de Zabarellis, *Lectura super clementinis*, loc. cit., "quia hic precipit constitutionem urbani seruari."

celebration because Christ was to be extolled as superior to all others.[19] This commentary on the *Clementines* provides an extensive discussion of the institution of the Eucharist, transubstantiation, the great dignity of the sacrament, and of its ministers. Zabarella also commented on the materials of the Eucharist, quoting Paulus de Liazariis on Jesus's use of unleavened bread in the homes of the Jews, especially at the Last Supper.[20] Discussing transubstantiation, Zabarella repeated an old comment that creating something from nothing (a reference to the creation of the world) was a greater miracle than transforming a single thing into another one (transubstantiation).[21] Like Guillelmus de Monte Lauduno, Zabarella gave considerable attention to how Christ could be present on many altars not limited by the number of altars or by the dimensions of the individual host. As all canonists did, he also affirmed concomitance, the whole Christ present in each host or fragment of a host.[22] Zabarella's commentary ended with an affirmation of the pope's role as Vicar of Christ, the custodian of the treasury of merits, which allowed him to grant indulgences for those who worthily celebrated the feast of Corpus Christi.[23]

Writing in the next generation after Zabarella, Nicholas de Tudeschis, known as Panormitanus, began with the historical summary from the Ordinary Gloss, stating that Pope Urban's invitation to Charles of Anjou to supersede Manfred as king of Sicily was justified (*ex iusta causa*) because the patrimony of Peter was at stake.[24] Panormitanus then outlined the number of miracles involved in the Eucharist; he said that the priest's voice could open the heavens (*ad vocem sacerdotis aperiuntur celi*) – this was true whether the priest was good or bad, and it happened daily; the elements were transubstantiated; those who ate this food worthily benefited, but the unworthy ate a judgment upon themselves.[25] Like Zabarella, Panormitanus underlined the joyful celebration of the feast.[26] His gloss ended with a brief exposition of the

[19] Franciscus de Zabarellis, *Lectura super clementinis*, fol. [165]^{ra}, "Secundo no. quod festum corporis Christi debet prefulgere celebritate speciali ut sicut christus potior est ceteris ita potius extollatur. de consec. di. ii. nihil." Zabarella also said the feast should be celebrated with joy; see *Lectura super clementinis*, fol. [165]^{rb}.

[20] Franciscus de Zabarellis, *Lectura super clementinis*, fol. [163]$^{ra–va}$. The text cites Thomas Aquinas on the use of natural water and wheat grain in making the bread; see *Lectura super clementinis*, fol. [163]^{rb}.

[21] Franciscus de Zabarellis, *Lectura super clementinis*, fol. [163]^{vb}, "quia maius est de nihilo aliquid facere quam unam rem in aliam transubstantiare."

[22] Franciscus de Zabarellis, *Lectura super clementinis*, fol. [163]^{va}–[164]^{rb}.

[23] Franciscus de Zabarellis, *Lectura super clementinis*, fol. [166]^{ra}.

[24] Nicholas de Tudeschis (Panormitanus), *Apparatus solemnis ... in Clementinas de novo correctus cum additionibus ...* (Lyon, 1513), fol. lxxxi^{v}.

[25] Nicholas de Tudeschis, *Apparatus solemnis ... in Clementinas*, fol. lxxxi^{v}–lxxxii^{r}.

[26] Nicholas de Tudeschis, *Apparatus solemnis ... in Clementinas*, fol. lxxxii^{v}.

concession of indulgences to the truly penitent who had confessed (*vere penitentibus et confessis*). These indulgences, however, required praying in church, not in a private oratory.[27]

John of Imola, writing in the same generation, began his commentary of *Si Dominum* with a series of *notabilia*. These included observations about the spiritual effectiveness of the sacrament.[28] John's text recited much of what Paulus de Liazariis said about the materials of the sacrament and indulgences. Like Petrus, John said the canon extended indulgences to those unable to enter a crowded church.[29] John of Imola also noted the instruction in the original decree that the clergy preach proper preparation for the feast to the laity. This preparation included confession, as well as alms-giving and prayers. In that way they would benefit from receiving communion on the feast.[30]

During the period following the promulgation of the *Clementines*, the feast gradually became universal in practice. Local synods occasionally enacted observance, and the feast was added to official liturgical calendars. One decree predates *Si Dominum*. In 1313 a synod at Nicosia on Cyprus decreed, even before the *Clementines* appeared in the canon law, celebration of the feast of Corpus Christi for the whole province. It referred specifically to the ordinance of Pope Urban.[31] In 1318, just after the *Clementines* were published, the bishop of Bath and Wells introduced the feast in his diocese. His successor made it a *festa ferianda*, on which day no work was to be done.[32] In the same year, the statutes of Leòn ordered observance of the feast on the basis of Pope Clement's constitution (*seguiendo la constituçion del papa Clemente quinto*) as issued at the Council of Vienne (*Viana*). The diocesan statute explained the indulgences to be earned by penitent observance of Corpus Christi.[33] In 1340 the diocese of Florence required keeping the feast as commanded by Pope Urban in *Transiturus* and incorporated in the Clementines, "the seventh

[27] Nicholas de Tudeschis, *Apparatus solemnis . . . in Clementinas*, fol. lxxxiiii^{v}.

[28] Johannes de Imola, *Super clementinis* (Lyon, 1525), fol. 123ra.

[29] Johannes de Imola, *Super clementinis*, fol. 123ra, 123va, 124rb.

[30] Johannes de Imola, *Super clementinis*, fol. 123ra, "No. quod in dominica prima precedenti dictam quartam feriam. Et sic in octaua penthecostes debent clerici predicare festum et exhortari et monere laycos ut se preparent ad ueram et puram confessionem et largitionem elemosynarum et sedulas orationes et ad alias deuotiones et opera pietatis. Et sic possunt illa die corpus domini reuerenter suscipere et eius uirtute consequi augmenta gratiarum."

[31] *The Synodicum Nicosiense and Other Documents of the Latin Church of Cyprus, 1196–1373*, ed. Christopher David Schabel (Nicosia, 2001), 222–223. As late as 1392 a statute of Cartagena still referred to Urban IV as founder of the feast; see *Synodicon Hispanum*, 11.201–202.

[32] Katherine L. French, *The People of the Parish: Community Life in a Late Medieval English Diocese* (Philadelphia, 2001), 181.

[33] *Synodicon Hispanum*, 3.287–288.

book of decretals." Those with cure of souls, both secular clergy and regulars, were to promote observance of the feast to benefit the souls of their subjects.[34] The 1396 statutes of Salamanca and the 1481 statutes of Avila specifically cited *Si Dominum* when mandating the observance of Corpus Christi and its octave.[35] The same Avila statute added Corpus Christi as a day on which, like at Easter, communion should be received. This text added that this rule bound boys from the age of 14 and girls from the age of 12.[36] In the diocese of Granada, a region wrested away from Muslims in the late fifteenth century, the statutes issued c. 1505 required preaching observance of Corpus Christi to the people on the Sunday before the feast.[37] As late as 1565, the provincial Council of Granada still legislated the celebration of the feast "with much solemnity" (*de mucha solemnidad*) in every part of the province.[38] A slightly different approach, in the French province of Sens, was the institution of a fast on the vigil of Corpus Christi.[39]

Like these synodal decrees, the evidence for adoption of the feast in calendars and lists of holy days suggests gradual adoption across Europe. Thus some clerics simply tipped Corpus Christi into existing calendars, as they did in certain copies of the 1287 statutes of Exeter.[40] Other sees issued new lists. In Spain, the diocese of Toledo added Corpus Christi to its calendar by 1338, repeating that listing in 1356.[41] In 1349, the diocese of Olomouc in Moravia listed Corpus Christi among the important feasts to be celebrated.[42] The province of Prague had added Corpus Christi to

[34] Mansi 26.53–54, "in decretali edita per bonae memoriae dominum Urbanum summum pontificem, & inserta in libro VII decretalium per sanctissimum patrem dominum Joannem Papam XXII. quae incipit: Transiturus de mundo ad patrem &c. quam quilibet ecclesiarum Rectores tam saeculares, quam regulares teneantur habere, & eam totaliter debeant observare, ut subditorum animas deo lucrari faciant, & ipsi prȩmium mereantur retributionis aeternae."

[35] *Synodicon Hispanum*, 4.41–42, 6.68–69. Similarly see the 1548 synod of Alcalà la Real in *Synodicon Hispanum*, 9.80.

[36] *Synodicon Hispanum*, 6.71–72.

[37] *Synodicon Hispanum*, 11.587–588. The following statutes establish norms for the treatment of converts; see *Synodicon Hispanum*, 11.588–590, including instruction about the sacraments. For a similar enactment from Plasencia in 1534, specifying preaching the indulgences available on Corpus Christi, see *Synodicon Hispanum*, 5.469–470.

[38] *El concilio provincial de Granada en 1565: Edición crítica del malogrado Concilio del Arzobispo Guerrero*, ed. Ignacio Pérez de Heredia y Valle (Roma, 1990), 388, 397. These decrees make reference to the canons of Trent about the sacraments.

[39] Mansi 25.648–649, 727–728.

[40] *Councils & Synods* 2/2.1022 nn. o and z. Similarly the offices for Corpus Christi often were added to existing liturgical manuscripts; see Barbara R. Walters, "Introduction to the Liturgical Manuscripts," in *The Feast of Corpus Christi*, 58–76 at 58–59.

[41] *Synodicon Hispanum*, 10.552, 573.

[42] *Synody a statuta Olomoucké diecéze období středověku*, ed. Pavel Krafl (Praha, 2003), 152.

its list of major feasts in 1355,[43] but the province of Narbonne did not list the observance officially until 1374.[44] The diocese of Würzburg listed Corpus Christi by 1407.[45] By the end of the fifteenth century, Corpus Christi was a long-established day on the festal calendars of sees like Badajoz, Plasencia, Avila, and Segovia.[46] In 1499 the diocese of Pamplona said that one had to celebrate Corpus Christi or be guilty of a mortal sin.[47] Similarly the sixteenth-century calendar for the diocese of Orense listed Corpus Christi as a feast on which work was to cease to permit offering thanks to God.[48] Areas occupied during the Spanish Reconquista had the observance of Corpus Christi imported together with other sacramental rites. Thus the sees of Cordoba, Cartagena, Malaga, and Granada eventually had Corpus Christi on their liturgical calendars. So did the Canary Islands after the Castilian conquest in the early fifteenth century.[49]

A procession with the consecrated host made visible in a monstrance or ostensory became the hallmark of the feast, as its observance spread across Europe. This ritual probably was based on viaticum processions, while monstrances were patterned after reliquaries. The sacred was made visible to the faithful behind a window of crystal or glass in a metal frame, usually golden or gilded.[50] For example, the *York Manual* eventually included a processional order for the feast of Corpus Christi, marking the integration of the feast into the liturgy of an ecclesiastical province far from Rome. This is an example of the importation of a recently authorized feast into the local liturgy.[51] New mass texts for that feast could be provided in booklets used to supplement the parish missal. Thus some

43 Mansi 26.398. 44 Mansi 26.651.

45 *Concilia Germaniae*, ed. Johann Friedrich Schannat and Joseph Hartzheim, 5 (Köln, 1763), 10B–11A.

46 *Synodicon Hispanum*, 5.28, 6.61, 344, 391, 486. Calahora listed the feast by 1410, repeating that listing in 1553; see *Synodicon Hispanum*, 8.118, 296. See also, among others, the calendars of Astorga and Leòn; see *Synodicon Hispanum*, 3.74, 329, 331.

47 *Synodicon Hispanum*, 8, 593, "so pena de pecado mortal." The same see decided in 1523 to celebrate the feast "with four capes" (*in quattuor cappis*); see *Synodicon Hispanum*, 8.608. The 1388 decree of Bishop Martin had said it was a *festum duarum capparum*; see *Synodicon Hispanum*, 8.487.

48 *Synodicon Hispanum*, 1.243. See also the 1528 statutes of Tuy in *Synodicon Hispanum*, 1.440.

49 *Synodicon Hispanum*, 11.43, 316, 393, 463, 613.

50 Charles Zika, "Hosts, Processions and Pilgrimages: Controlling the Sacred in Fifteenth-Century Germany," *Past and Present* 118 (1988), 25–64 at 38. The most detailed study of the monstrance is Frédéric Tixier and Jean-Pierre Caillet, *La monstrance eucharistique genèse, typologie et fonctions d'un objet d'orfèvrerie, XIIIe–XVIe siècle*. Rennes, 2014.

51 *Manuale et processionale ad usum insignis ecclesiae Eboracensis* (Durham, 1875), 192–193. Eventually the feast also became an anti-Lollard display; see French, *People of the Parish*, 191.

parishes near Paris were reported to have such booklets for Corpus Christi.[52] The same was true of churches in the region of Madrid.[53] (The archdeacon of Prague once listed instead a *missale de specialibus missis.*[54]) Monstrances and Corpus Christi processions eventually appeared in books of hours for the edification of the faithful.[55]

An additional set of papal letters about Corpus Christi appeared in the fifteenth century from the chanceries of Martin V and Eugenius IV. These pontiffs granted additional indulgences for devoutly celebrating the feast of Corpus Christi, including the hours of its festal office. They also permitted the celebration of the feast and its octave even in a place under interdict. Only excommunicates and persons whose faults had caused the imposition of an interdict were excluded. One bull of Eugenius recalled the foundation of the feast by Pope Urban and recited the concessions already made by Pope Martin. These concessions were made known by synodal statutes in Spain, one of which included the complete text of a decree of Eugenius.[56] Concessions by Martin and Eugenius of the public celebration of Corpus Christi even during an interdict found their way into the 1481 statutes of Avila and 1501 statutes of Badajoz.[57] The same bull of Eugenius that mentioned Pope Martin's decree appeared occasionally in German synodal statutes.[58]

A church, whether a parish or a cathedral, celebrated Corpus Christi with full liturgical office, as when Salamanca declared Corpus Christi a feast of nine lessons at Matins. Salamanca, in 1497, also specified the office attributed to Thomas Aquinas.[59] More famously, as noted above, the feast was celebrated with a full public procession. The clergy in some places were required to participate, and money might be given to those who took part in the public observance. Thus the see of Orense had a statute requiring all those who held ecclesiastical dignities, presided over

[52] E.g. *Visites archdidiaconales de Josas*, ed. J.-M. Alliot (Paris, 1902), 74.

[53] Gregorio de Andrés, "Actas de la visita al arcedianazgo de Madrid en 1427," *Hispania Sacra* 38 (1986), 153–245 at 164, 169 177, 183, 218.

[54] *Visitaĉní protokol Pražského arcijáhna pavla z janovic z let 1379–1382*, ed. Ivan Hlaváček and Zdeňka Hledíková (Praha, 1973), 256.

[55] Rogers S. Wieck, *Illuminating Faith: The Eucharist in Medieval Life and Art* (New York, 2014), 61–62, 64–66.

[56] *Synodicon Hispanum*, 9.303–305, followed by a synodal decree on the topic of administering the sacraments during a period of interdict. See also references at *Synodicon Hispanum*, 5.28 (Badajoz), 257 (Coria); *Synodicon Hispanum*, 9.628 (Jaén). Eugenius's bull *Excellentissimum Corporis* (1433) appears in *Bullarium privilegiorum ac diplomatum Romanorum pontificum amplissima collectio*, ed. Charles Cocquelines, 23 (Roma, 1743), 9–10. The Council of Basel ratified this indulgence; see Mansi 29.222–225.

[57] *Synodicon Hispanum*, 5.61 (Badajoz), 6.69 (Avila); 11/499 (Granada).

[58] *Concilia Germanie*, 5.274B–276A (Freising, 1440), 412A–B (Bamberg, 1451), 431A–432B (Würzburg, 1453).

[59] *Synodicon Hispanum*, 4.335, 356.

a religious house, had cure of souls, or served as chaplains not just to celebrate the feast but to participate in its public observances.[60] The 1554 synod of Guadix set out in detail the order of clergy in the procession.[61] As one consequence of required participation, the diocese of Cartagena had to condemn in 1438 any pretense of going in the festal procession to receive money distributed to its participants.[62] A priest at Clunbury in the diocese of Hereford did worse, absenting himself on Corpus Christi and thus denying the parish the festal service.[63] The 1548 synod of Alcalà la Real dictated the route of the procession.[64] A 1446 canon from Würzburg required Jews to close the windows of their houses as soon as they heard a procession coming.[65]

Like Eastertide, Corpus Christi was a social occasion, showing both the solidarity and the divisions of a parish. Many parishes in England shared food and drink at Corpus Christi, provision of which was a role of the "good women" of the parish.[66] Wealthier churches in cities across Europe experienced the feast as a site for display of status by lay persons, whether guilds or individual patrons. Rich or well-born individuals might also provide sumptuous vestments, some decorated with their own coats of arms.[67] Providing the church with a monstrance in which the host would be carried offered another opportunity for the wealthy and powerful to display their social prominence through conspicuous expenditure. These sacred vessels were based on designs for reliquaries, flat-faced or cylindrical, adapted to display the host to the faithful.[68] There was common participation of the leading persons in the community, who often donated the monstrance to the parish church, but they sometimes jockeyed for places close to the priest carrying the monstrance.[69] Consequently, the

[60] *Synodicon Hispanum*, 1.231–232. The statute makes specific reference to a bull of Paul III offering indulgences on the feast day. Similarly see, *Synodicon Hispanum*, 9, 623–624 (Jaén).

[61] *Synodicon Hispanum*, 9.301–302. [62] *Synodicon Hispanum*, 11.217–218.

[63] A. T. Bannister, "Visitation Returns of the Diocese of Hereford in 1397," *The English Historical Review* 44 (1929), 279–289, 444–453, 45 (1930), 92–101, 444–463 at 45.458.

[64] *Synodicon Hispanum*, 9.68. Similarly see the 1554 statutes of Guadix in *Synodicon Hispanum.*, 9.299–300.

[65] *Concilia Germaniae*, 5.344B–345A.

[66] Katherine L. French, *The Good Women of the Parish: Gender and Religion after the Black Death* (Philadelphia, 2008), 22. Baking for parish or home could have a Eucharistic significance for women; see French, *Good Women of the Parish*, 22, 29, 180.

[67] R. N. Swanson, *Church and Society in Late Medieval England* (Oxford, 1989), 258–259.

[68] For a study of monstrance production, see Heather C. McCune Bruhn, "Late Gothic Architectural Monstrances in the Rhineland, c. 1380–1480: Objects in Context," PhD Dissertation, Pennsylvania State University, 2006. There are references to glass monstrances but this may indicate the glass cylinder in a metal framework; see *Repertorium Poenitentiariae Germanicum*, 9 no. 1584, 1818, 1843.

[69] Zika, "Hosts, Processions and Pilgrimages: Controlling the Sacred in Fifteenth-Century Germany," 38–43. In an English city, the mayor often was nearest the host, while

1548 synod of Alcalà la Real warned against scandal, disturbances, and irreverence among those following the host. Those who failed to observe the statute were threatened with a fine payable to the "fabric" of the cathedral or even excommunication.[70] A statute of Braga (1447) required that only clerics carry the "ark of the body of God" (*arca do Corpo de Deus*).[71] Participants in these processions frequently were offered indulgences.[72]

The papal court eventually celebrated the feast in high style. The feast, together with its octave, gained its place on the curia's calendar among the addenda to the books of papal ceremonial, at least by the time of Urban VI (1378–1389).[73] Agostino Patrizzi, writing late in the fifteenth century, listed Corpus Christi among the days on which the cardinals attended the papal chapel (but without a sermon). So too was Holy Thursday with its commemoration of the night on which the Eucharist was instituted (with a sermon).[74] The Corpus Christi observance at the Roman curia was basically a procession with the sacrament. It was made more spectacular, however, by the number and ranks of the participants, including the Roman pontiff, proceeding in a fixed order. The procession began in the Vatican Palace and only went to St. Peter's, but its splendor was notable.[75] The feast often was accompanied by tableaux vivants. Thus, when Pius II celebrated Corpus Christi in Viterbo in 1462, the cardinals arranged splendid tableaux along the route of the procession.[76]

Building on the model of Corpus Christi, the clergy included carrying the host in their processions seeking divine relief from calamities like outbreaks of the plague. Nicholas of Cusa, during his legation to Germany, sought to regulate this practice. Thus he required that the clergy of Utrecht, in such cases, as well as on major festivals, should carry the consecrated host behind crystal or glass "out of greater reverence for it and to incite the people to greater devotion" (*ob maiorem*

churchwardens carried crosses in the procession; see French, *People of the Parish*, 191–192; Andrew Brown, *Church and Society in England, 1000–1500* (Houndsmills, 2003), 6–7, 81.

70 *Synodicon Hispanum*, 9.68–69. See also the 1477 statutes of Braga in *Synodicon Hispanum*, 2.108, 127. See also the Guadix statute of 1505 in *Synodicon Hispanum*, 2.187.

71 *Synodicon Hispanum*, 2.97–98.

72 E.g. *Synodicon Hispanum*, 4.358–359 (Salamanca).

73 Marc Dykmans, *Le cérémonial papal de la fin du Moyen Âge à la Renaissance*, 4 (Bruxelles, 1985), 260–263, 272–274.

74 Agostino Patrizzi, *Caeremoniale Romanum* (Paris, 1689; Ridgewood, N.J., 1965), fol. CXLI^{v}–CXLII^{r}.

75 Patrizzi, *Caeremoniale Romanum*, fol. CXIII^{r}–CXIV^{r}.

76 *Memoirs of a Renaissance Pope: The Commentaries of Pius II, an Abridgement*, trans. Florence A. Gragg, ed. Leona C. Gabel (New York, 1962), 259–269.

reverenciam eiusdem et ad incitamentum maioris devocionis populi).[77] Nicholas's legatine synod for Cologne tried to limit the display of consecrated hosts to placing them "in monstrances" (*in monstranciis*). The principal time for this display was Corpus Christi with its octave. A city, town, or parish might also display the host once a year. In addition, this could be done in an urgent situation, like praying for peace in a time of war, or with the bishop's special permission. In all cases, this was to be done "with greatest reverence and devotion" (*cum summa reverencia atque devocione*) following the customs of the ecclesiastical province.[78]

Carrying the host in procession outside the feast of Corpus Christi and its octave seems to have been unusual at first except in the emergency situations noted above. However, this practice became more common later in the Middle Ages. For example, during the reign of Pope Julius II, the Antonite house in Cologne, wanting to take their procession honoring Saint Anthony through the territories of several parishes, appealed to the Apostolic Penitentiary for permission to carry the host and the saint's image. This permission was granted as a special grace by the regent of the Penitentiary.[79] This is just one example of a large number of petitions received in Rome from various sources. Requests from Germany and Poland became common in the reign of Sixtus IV. Thus a priest of Augsburg asked Sixtus's Penitentiary for permission to hold a procession like those for Corpus Christi and its octave.[80] Similar requests from priests, bishops, hospitals, and lay persons of some prominence multiplied. Even towns and craft guilds made such requests, asserting their pious solidarity.[81] A couple from the diocese of Meissen specified carrying the sacrament on a circuit of the town walls.[82] A chapter of canons from the diocese of Poznań wanted to process around both church and cemetery.[83] A hospital for sailors in Danzig wanted indulgences for its procession. These were to be available whether the procession was held

[77] *Acta Cusana: Quellen zur Lebensgeschichte des Nikolaus von Kues*, ed. Erich Meuthen and Hermann Hallauer, 3b (Hamburg, 1996), 1207.

[78] *Acta Cusana*, 3b.1504.

[79] Kirsi Salonen and Ludwig Schmugge, *A Sip from the 'Well of Grace': Medieval Texts from the Apostolic Penitentiary* (Washington, D.C., 2009), 158–160. Other requests only specified going around the borders of the parish; see *Repertorium Poenitentiariae Germanicum*, 8 no. 2810, 2936, 2949.

[80] *Repertorium Poenitentiariae Germanicum*, 6 no. 3156.

[81] E.g. *Repertorium Poenitentiariae Germanicum*, 6 no. 3398, 3431, 7 no. 1485, 1541, 1573, 1757, 1760, 1765, 1802, 8 no. 2268, 3039.

[82] *Repertorium Poenitentiariae Germanicum*, 8 no. 3004. See also *Repertorium Poenitentiariae Germanicum*, 9 no. 1584 1818. A Carmelite house in the diocese of Leslau specified the town squares near their convent; see *Repertorium Poenitentiariae Germanicum*, 8 no. 3078.

[83] *Repertorium Poenitentiariae Germanicum*, 6 no. 3397.

outdoors or indoors in case of rain.[84] A rector from the diocese of Meissen asked to accompany this procession with a votive mass of Corpus Christi.[85] A duchess from Silesia wanted to display the host on Thursdays, just like on the Thursday of Corpus Christi; and the Premonstratensians of Constance requested the same thing.[86] A priest of Salzburg wanted to hold a procession "with reverence and honor and due ceremonies" (*cum reverentia et honore ac ceremoniis debitis*) on Easter. Hospitallers of the diocese of Pomesanien in northern Poland asked Innocent VIII for a procession once peace was restored in that region.[87] In a different situation, a parish from Krakow asked to have the objections of the cathedral chapter to their procession overruled.[88] A Hospitaller house in the diocese of Prague wanted to have a procession to strengthen the faithful, who were surrounded by Hussite heretics.[89]

Other dramatic displays of the sacrament were subjects of petitions sent to Rome. A priest of Breslau asked to open the repository of the reserved host to let the faithful contemplate it by the light of candles.[90] A layman of the diocese of Lebau asked for confirmation of a privilege granted by a legate for opening the *sacrarium* and displaying the sacrament on the high altar during mass.[91] An inhabitant of Goslar in the diocese of Hildesheim built an altar of Corpus Christi and then asked the Penitentiary for permission to hold mass and a display of the sacrament there.[92] The rector and wardens of a parish of Poznań wanted to display the sacrament on an altar of Saint Catherine.[93] A Count Palatine of the Rhine petitioned to be able to display the Eucharist in his chapel on Corpus Christi and during its octave.[94] A group of female Franciscan tertiaries of the diocese of Constance asked indulgences for those who visited the sacrament reserved in their chapel.[95] A town in Meissen desired holding a special

[84] *Repertorium Poenitentiariae Germanicum*, 8 no. 2521.

[85] *Repertorium Poenitentiariae Germanicum*, 7 no. 1699. Similarly see *Repertorium Poenitentiariae Germanicum*, 7 no. 2054, 8 no. 2342.

[86] *Repertorium Poenitentiariae Germanicum*, 7 no. 1487, 1490. Similarly see a request from a layman of Nuremberg in *Repertorium Poenitentiariae Germanicum*, 7 no. 1512.

[87] *Repertorium Poenitentiariae Germanicum*, 7 no. 1836. One petition from Gnesen specifies lights and hymns; see *Repertorium Poenitentiariae Germanicum*, 8 no. 2138.

[88] *Repertorium Poenitentiariae Germanicum*, 7 no. 1549.

[89] *Repertorium Poenitentiariae Germanicum*, 9 no. 1888.

[90] *Repertorium Poenitentiariae Germanicum*, 6 no. 3417. See also *Repertorium Poenitentiariae Germanicum* 6 no. 3422.

[91] *Repertorium Poenitentiariae Germanicum*, 6 no. 3426. A priest of Poznań asked to be able to do this on Thursdays; see *Repertorium Poenitentiariae Germanicum*, 7 no. 2047.

[92] *Repertorium Poenitentiariae Germanicum*, 8 no. 2627.

[93] *Repertorium Poenitentiariae Germanicum*, 7 no. 1667.

[94] *Repertorium Poenitentiariae Germanicum*, 6 no. 3252.

[95] *Repertorium Poenitentiariae Germanicum*, 6 no, 3370.

mass with an unveiled host present on the altar.[96] Such a display during mass was depicted in the *Hours of Catherine of Cleves*, in the Hours of the Sacrament.[97] All of this was expected to incite devotion, as a priest in the diocese of Pomesanien argued in a petition to expose the host on an altar.[98]

These petitions to Rome may be explained, at least in part, by local worries about excessive display of the sacrament. Thus a 1416 decree from Bratislava expressed worry that, with frequent exposition, "reverence might diminish, charity become cool" (*minoratur reverentia, tepescit charitas*). No consecrated bread was to be retained after mass except for the reserve kept to comfort the sick. Nor was the sacrament to be displayed except on Corpus Christi (*Festo Corporis Domini nostri JESU CHRISTI: & si ejusdem sacramenti singularis fiat memoria, excepto*). Those who failed to follow this ruling were threatened with the penalty for rebellion.[99] Similarly, a decree from Mainz (1451) tried limiting exposition of the sacrament "lest the devotion of the faithful people should grow cold from its frequent sighting." The archbishop and his synod ordered display only on Corpus Christi and its octave, or on other fitting occasions like those authorized by the ordinary for a confraternity or religious guild. Priests who violated this decree were threatened with grave punishment.[100] The Schwerin statutes of 1492 forbade a priest from showing Christ's body by opening closed containers (pyx or tabernacle) at the will of his parishioners. The sacrament also was to be carried in a properly closed ciborium.[101] The same statutes forbade carrying the sacrament to "individual parishioners or in other festivities than those on which it is usually carried by the universal Church." To display or carry the Eucharist outside these observances, for example by parading through the parish cemetery, was not to honor it but to cause it to be despised. No such display was to done, therefore, without "an authentic privilege."

96 *Repertorium Poenitentiariae Germanicum*, 7 no. 2282. Similarly see *Repertorium Poenitentiariae Germanicum*, 7 no. 2301.

97 Rob Dückers and Ruud Priem, *The Hours of Catherine of Cleves: Devotions, Demons and Daily Life in the Fifteenth Century* (New York, 2009), pl. 88. The gathering of manna in the desert appears as pl. 85 and the Last Supper as pl. 87.

98 *Repertorium Poenitentiariae Germanicum*, 8 no. 2994.

99 *Concilia Germaniae*, 5.153B–154A.

100 *Concilia Germaniae*, 5.408B, "Propter Divinissime Eucharistie Sacramento exhibendam, & ne populi fidelis devotio ex frequenti ejus visione tepescat, ordinat hec Sancta Synodus, quod deinceps ipsum Sacramentum visibiliter in Monasteriis, preterquam in festo Corporis Christi, & per ejus Octavas deferri, & tunc non nisi sub Divino Officio octave ejusdem ostendi debent, etiam occasione cujuscunque fraternitatis, aut institutionis desuper facte mandans Ordinarius locorum, ut contra Presbyteros, qui in premissis excederet per inflictionem gravium penarum procedant."

101 *Concilia Germaniae*, 5.646A.

Therefore, these practices were forbidden on the pain of a fine.[102] The papal curia, as will be noted below, was amenable to granting petitions for such privileges. This may be tied, in part, to its own ceremonial use of the Eucharist. For example, when Eugenius IV left Florence in 1443 to return to Rome, the solemn procession for his departure included "the holiest sacrament in a case covered in red taffeta." The case was carried on "a white horse with red covering."[103]

The requirement that parishes celebrate Corpus Christi added a new element to the discipline enforced by the local archdeacon. Thus the mid-fifteenth-century visitations of parishes in the archdeaconry of Josas often noted the presence of a vessel for carrying the host in procession "on the feast of the sacrament" (*in festo sacramenti*). This vessel (*jocale*) sometimes was described as a reliquary, reflecting the relationship of medieval monstrances to preexisting reliquaries displaying the remains of saints. Some of these vessels might have special artistic features, like angels supporting the consecrated host.[104] One *jocale* was described as "quite beautiful" (*valde pulchrum*).[105] One parish, however, was warned to have a lock on its vessel to prevent theft.[106] Some parishes were noted as having a vessel of special value, such as of gilded silver. In other cases, the visitors gave an estimate of the cash value of the *jocale*.[107] Many of the monstrances listed for the archdeaconry of Prague in the late fourteenth century show similar patterns of the use of silver, sometimes gilded. However, a few of these

[102] *Concilia Germaniae*, 5.646B, "Item consimili sub tenore districte prohibemus, ne rectores Ecclesiarum, Capellarum, aut aliorum piorum locorum, seu eorum vices gerentes de cetero illa levitate utantur, scilicet, ut in singulis patrociniis, aut aliis festivitatibus, quibus ab universali Ecclesia hoc non soleat observari, quovis modo publice per cimiterium deferant, aut in publico cum speciali ritui venerandum, exponant Sacrosanctum Corpus Dominicum adjunctis sibi vitricis, seu provisoribus Ecclesie laicis; cum in precipuo ipsius Sacramenti festo, & paucis festivitatibus aliis hoc specialiter indultum, aut fieri consuetum. Oppositum vero facere, non est Sacramentum honorare, sed in vilipendium ejus conari, propter assiduitatem, & nimiam laicorum ad ipsum familiaritatem. Nec non ex prohibitione Legatorum Sedis Apostolici, atque nostra, vobis inhibemus, quod Corpus Dominicum singulis diebus capsa publica, aut alio loco evidenti propter varia pericula non ponatis: nisi hoc Ecclesia vestra ex indulto, sive privilegio authentico habeat, quod Nobis infra unius mensis spatium mandamus exhiberi sub pena quatuor florenorum."

[103] Bartolomeo del Corazza, quoted in Elizabeth McCahill, *Reviving the Eternal City: Rome and the Papal Court, 1420–1447* (Cambridge, Mass., 2011), 143–144.

[104] *Visites archdidiaconales de Josas*, ed. J.-M. Alliot (Paris, 1902), 121 no. 370, 136 no. 424, 343 no. 1078, 396 no. 1290. For an example of a poor priest who stole a monstrance, see *Repertorium Poenitentiariae Germanicum*, 9 no. 1297.

[105] *Visites archdidiaconales de Josas*, 96 no. 290. See also *Visites Josas*, 66–67 no. 208, 97 no. 293.

[106] *Visites archdidiaconales de Josas*, 111 no. 348.

[107] *Visites archdidiaconales de Josas*, 110 no. 339 (gilded silver), 114 no. 351 (worth 25 francs), 396 no. 1290.

vessels are described as made of wood with gilding or only made from copper.[108]

The feast of Corpus Christi had additional impacts outside the liturgy. A house of a religious order, like the Carmelites of Straubing in the diocese of Ratisbon, asked to hold a procession on the anniversary of the dedication of their church.[109] Confraternities of the sacrament, intended for the devout laity, became common. Some were founded by diocesan statute, but some were begun on lay initiative. The guild of the sacrament at Lynn in the English county of Norfolk, for example, claimed to have been inspired by the sight of a priest carrying viaticum with only one candle carried before him during an outbreak of plague.[110] In Italy, following Trent and the Medici restoration (1530), sacrament confraternities were founded in Florentine parishes. Perhaps two dozen had been created or transformed from older associations by the eighteenth century. These were intended to provide an orderly expression of religion while excluding heresy. The company at Santa Maria Novella, like the one at Santa Maria sopra Minerva in Rome, was founded under Dominican auspices in 1539–1540. For all of these groups, the feast of Corpus Christi, with its orderly processions, was essential.[111] By 1559 the archdiocese of Santiago de Compostella in Spain had decided to create such a confraternity in every parish.[112] Some German confraternities had endowments supporting their Corpus Christi processions.[113] Atop Christian solidarity, confraternities, including those of the sacrament, could provide occasions for shared conviviality.[114]

These corporate bodies requested special privileges connected to the Eucharist. Thus a petition for use of a portable altar was made by one such guild during the reign of Paul II.[115] In the reign of Sixtus IV confraternities began requesting permission to hold processions with the host.[116] Petitions for the right hold processions around the parish cemetery also became common.[117] A confraternity from Kulm wanted to do

108 *Visitační protokol Pražského arcijáhna pavla z janovic z let 1379–1382*, 60, 62, 81.

109 *Repertorium Poenitentiariae Germanicum*, 9 no. 1601.

110 Brown, *Church and Society in England, 1000–1500*, 139.

111 Ronald F. E. Weissman, *Ritual Brotherhood in Renaissance Florence* (New York, 1982), 206–211.

112 *Synodicon Hispanum*, 1.334.

113 Zika, "Hosts, Processions and Pilgrimages: Controlling the Sacred in Fifteenth-Century Germany," 42 n. 53.

114 Dylan Reid, "Moderate Devotion, Mediocre Poetry and Magnificent Food: The Confraternity of the Immaculate Conception of Rouen," *Confraternitas* 10(1996), 3–10.

115 *Repertorium Poenitentiariae Germanicum*, 5 no. 1482.

116 *Repertorium Poenitentiariae Germanicum*, 6 no. 3415. For examples from the reign of Julius II see *Repertorium Poenitentiariae Germanicum* 9 no. 1479, 1563, 1594.

117 *Repertorium Poenitentiariae Germanicum*, 7 no. 1527.

this four times in a year.[118] A priest who moved from the diocese of Krakow, where he had held processions with a confraternity, asked to have the confraternity in his new parish in the diocese of Gnezno able to do the same thing.[119] A Corpus Christi guild in the diocese of Strasbourg wanted to carry the host around the parish boundaries, just as was done on the Eucharistic feast.[120] One confraternity from the diocese of Leslau used a host set in a cross as its monstrance in its Corpus Christi procession.[121]

Sacrament confraternities, in turn, commissioned works of art, including the picture of angels adoring the host in Gressenhall, Norfolk, defaced during the Reformation.[122] In Italy, these confraternities patronized not just individual works of art but entire decorated chapels.[123] Images of Man of Sorrows in a chalice, one of the many depictions of the altar cup in sacred art, may have originated at the Venetian Scuole del Sacramento.[124] The sacrament chapels in Brescia had their own interesting features. Most intriguing, atop the more usual biblical scenes of Melchisedek, the gathering of manna in the desert, and the Last Supper, one chapel included a picture of the Miracle of the Sacrament with a baby, the infant Jesus, standing on a paten upon an altar.[125] The most famous work commissioned by a Eucharistic confraternity was the altarpiece painted for the guild in Urbino. Its main painting was the Communion of the Apostles, an unusual theme in the West, by the artist Jos Van Ghent. More famous, however, is the

[118] *Repertorium Poenitentiariae Germanicum*, 7 no. 1587. See also *Repertorium Poenitentiariae Germanicum*, 7 no. 1588, 2419.

[119] *Repertorium Poenitentiariae Germanicum*, 7 no. 2918–2919.

[120] *Repertorium Poenitentiariae Germanicum*, 8 no. 2979.

[121] *Repertorium Poenitentiariae Germanicum*, 8 no. 2525.

[122] Eamon Duffy, "The Parish, Piety, and Patronage in Late Medieval East Anglia: The Evidence of Rood Screens," in *The Parish in English Life 1400–1600*, ed., Katherine L. French, Gary G. Gibbs, and Beat A. Kümin (Manchester, 1997), 133–162 at 152–153, pl. 8.7.

[123] Barbara Maria Savy, *"Manducatio per visum": temi eucaristici nella pittura di Romanino e Moretto* (Citadella, 2006).

[124] Dóra Sallay, "The Eucharistic Man of Sorrows in Late Medieval Art," *Annual of Medieval Studies at CEU* 6 (2000), 45–80 at 55.

[125] Savy, *"Manducatio per visum,"* 47–49, 53, 98–101, plates 4–7, 47–48, 60. A printed frontispiece for the Corpus Christi mass with a priest carrying chalice and host appears in plate 93. The interpretation of *exempla* recounting such appearances is discussed by Steven Justice, "Eucharistic Miracle and Eucharistic Doubt," *Journal of Medieval and Early Modern Studies* 42 (2012), 307–332. A murdered baby raised by Vincent Ferrer is presented as if on a paten; see Laura Ackerman Smoller, *The Saint and the Chopped-Up Baby: The Cult of Vincent Ferrer in Medieval and Early Modern Europe* (Ithaca, 2014), 155–157, esp. plate 1. Likewise, Birgitta of Sweden was depicted watching a priest elevate a baby instead of a host; see Wieck, *Illuminating Faith*, 70.

predella of this altarpiece by Paolo Uccello illustrating the story of the Paris bleeding host.[126]

A commercial or craft guild might also have commissioned a painting with Eucharistic significance. The powerful wool guild of Florence, the Arte de la Lana, paid to have a picture done of the institution of the Eucharist at the Last Supper (1423–1425). Sasseta depicted Christ holding a host with a cup in front of Him.[127] Many Last Supper paintings focused on Judas's betrayal, not the institution of the sacrament;[128] but all were tied to the drama of Christ's saving Passion, which every mass commemorated.

Cycles of mystery plays often were enacted on the feast of Corpus Christi beginning in the late fourteenth century. These plays were derived from festival processions and tableaux vivants,[129] but they were informed by the dramatic approach to the mass as reenacted sacrifice that was common in the later Middle Ages. The best-known mystery plays come from England, where pageant wagons rolled through the streets to repeat their actions at stational stops.[130] However, others can be found mentioned as far from England as Cividale, Riga, and Zerbst.[131] In addition, the Eucharist itself might be a theme for an individual drama, as in the *Croxton Play of the Sacrament*, which drew on stories of host desecration for its content.[132] One diocese in Spain, Toledo, imposed limits on performances in churches, saying that even those given on Corpus Christi had to be "honest and decent."[133]

Wonder hosts

Apart from the veneration of consecrated hosts at mass or when carried in processions, cults of "wonder hosts," frequently associated with supposed attacks by Jews, flourished in the later Middle Ages. Even where

[126] Marilyn Aronberg Lavin, "The Altar of Corpus Domini in Urbino: Paolo Uccello, Joos Van Ghent, Piero della Francesca," *The Art Bulletin* 49 (1967), 1–24; Bettina Bildhauer, *Medieval Blood* (Cardiff, 2006), 46–48, figure 3.

[127] Diana Hiller, *Gendered Perceptions of Florentine Last Supper Frescoes, c. 1350–1490* (Farnham, 2014), 9–10 with figure 1.2.

[128] Hiller, *Gendered Perceptions of Florentine Last Supper Frescoes*, 12.

[129] The procession at Yeovil in Dorset became a play, according to French, *People of the Parish*, 133–134, 192.

[130] Rosemary Woolf, *The English Mystery Plays* (Berkeley, 1980), 71–75. The Last Supper was not always enacted, thus leaving the Eucharist out of the "Towneley" mystery plays; see Woolf, *The English Mystery Plays*, 233.

[131] Woolf, *The English Mystery Plays*, 59, 69.

[132] John T. Sebastian, *The Croxton Play of the Sacrament* (Kalamazoo, 2012).

[133] *Synodicon Hispanum*, 10.772–773, "siendo honestas y decentes."

an attack had no named perpetrator, the Jews might be blamed.[134] Hosts thus attacked were reported to have bled, revealing divine presence and displeasure at these attacks. The first such story arose in Paris in the late thirteenth century, but they were most common in the German-speaking lands.[135] This type of miracle tale, arousing veneration of host relics, flourished parallel with older beliefs about holy blood left behind by Christ. Those relics were venerated in places as far apart as Mantua in Italy and Hailes and Westminster in England.[136] (In the fifteenth century, Pius II had to quash a debate between the Franciscans and Dominicans over the possibility that Christ had left some of the blood He shed on earth behind after the Ascension.[137]) This affirmation of miraculous interventions via matter was linked not just to a desire for wonders but, more widely, to the Passion-centered piety of the later Middle Ages, including the development of art motifs graphically representing the physical reality of the Crucifixion.[138] The extent of such beliefs in bleeding hosts is illustrated in Orvieto, where the cathedral displays the corporal onto which the host was believed to have bled when a German priest visiting nearby Bolsena had doubts about the Real Presence while celebrating mass.[139] The Miracle at Bolsena was illustrated in Raphael's Stanze in the Vatican Palace. The theology of the Real Presence was represented in the same rooms in Raphael's Disputation on the Sacrament, dominated by a

[134] Thomas M. Izbicki, "The Bleeding Host of Dijon: Its Place in the History of Eucharistic Devotion," in *Saluting Aron Gurevich: Essays in History, Literature and Other Related Subjects*, ed. Yelena Mazour-Matusevich and Alexandra Shecket Korros (Leiden, 2010), 227–246; Wieck, *Illuminating Faith*, 72–78.

[135] Caroline W. Bynum, *Wonderful Blood: Theology and Practice in Late Medieval Northern Germany and Beyond* (Philadelphia, 2007); Miri Rubin, *Gentile Tales: The Narrative Assault on Late Medieval Jews* (New Haven, Conn., 1999).

[136] Nicholas Vincent, *The Holy Blood: King Henry III and the Westminster Blood Relic* (Cambridge, 2001); *La reliquia del sangue di Cristo: Mantova, l'Italia e l'Europa al tempo di Leone IX*, ed. Glauco Maria Cantarella and Arturo Calzona (Verona, 2012). The Mantua relic was supposed to be the source of the Holy Blood of Weingarten in Germany; see Caroline W. Bynum, "The Blood of Christ in the Later Middle Ages," *Church History* 71 (2002), 685–714 at 692.

[137] Antonia Fitzpatrick, "Mendicant Order Politics and the Status of Christ's Shed Blood," *Historical Research* 85 (2012), 210–227.

[138] Ann W. Astell, *Eating Beauty: The Eucharist and the Spiritual Arts of the Middle Ages* (Ithaca, 2006), 52–53.

[139] Dominique Rigaux, "Miracle, reliques et images dans la chapelle du Corporal à Orvieto (1357–1364)," in *Pratiques de l'eucharistie dans les Eglises d'Orient et d'Occident (Antiquité et Moyen Age)*, 1: *L'institution: Actes du séminaire tenu à Paris, Institut catholique, 1997*, ed. Nicole Bérioux, Béatrice Caseau, and Rigaux (Paris, 2009), 201–245; Lucio Ricetti, "Dal concilio al miracolo, mistero del corporale," in *Spazi e imagini dell'eucharistia: il caso di Orvieto*, ed. Gianni Ciolli, Severino Dianich, and Valerio Mauro (Bologna, 2007), 171–227. Similarly see *Historia del sanct corpocrist de Luchent*, in facsimile Luch Chabàs, *El miracle de Llutxent* i*: Els corporals de Daroca: relacions i documents estudiats* (Valencia, 1981).

monstrance over which the Trinity hovers.[140] Illustrations of the Dijon bleeding host were less grand in choir books, books of hours, and posters. (Depiction of that host continued well into the eighteenth century, before the relic was destroyed during the French Revolution.)[141]

Cults of bleeding hosts were open to suspicion that the miracles were false, their stains made by greedy clerics to lure pilgrims with full purses. Theologians like Jan Hus and Heinrich Toke attacked these cults on theological grounds, and prelates like Nicholas of Cusa tried to discourage these devotions.[142] A worry about possibly reverencing unconsecrated hosts already has been noted in connection with the elevation at mass. Another concern arose especially from the cult of the bleeding hosts of Wilsnack. In 1383, a local knight burned down the local parish church during a quarrel with the bishop. Afterward three hosts were found in the rubble. Since they were tinged with red, the belief arose that these hosts were marked with the blood of Christ. There was doubt, however, not just about the supposed miraculous nature of the stains but about the original status of these hosts. It was not certain that they had been consecrated at all.[143] Early in the fifteenth century, Otto von Rohr, bishop of Havelberg, issued a letter complaining that the cult was promoted with "work, word and fallacious signs" (*opere, sermone & fallaciis signis*). The bishop said "incredible miracles" (*incredibilia miracula*) had been compiled in great volumes, which were supposed to confirm this erroneous cult.[144] The signs on the hosts were described as "similar to gore" (*simile cruori*). These relics were venerated, Otto wrote, without the permission of the Apostolic

[140] Dioclecio Redig de Campos, *The Stanze of Raphael* (Roma, 1968), 43–47. Sasseta's A Miracle of the Eucharist, painted for the Carmelites [http://en.wikipedia.org/wiki/Stefano_di_Giovanni#mediaviewer/File:Sassetta_-_Miracle_of_the_Eucharist_-_WGA20846.jpg], has been connected to that miracle.

[141] Roger S. Wieck, "The Sacred Bleeding Host of Dijon in Choir Books and on Posters," in *Manuscripten en miniaturen: Studies aangeboden aan Anne S. Korteweg bij haar afscheid van de Koninklikje Bibliotheek*, ed. Jos Biemans, Klaas van der Hoek, Kathryn M. Rudy, and Ed van der Vlist (Zutphen, 2007), 385–331; Wieck, "The Sacred Bleeding Host of Dijon in Books of Hours," in *Quand la peinture était dans les livres: Mélanges en l'honneur de François Avril*, ed. Mara Hodfmann and Carline Zöhl (Turnhout, 2007), 393–404.

[142] Morimichi Watanabe, "The German Church Shortly before the Reformation: Nicolaus Cusanus and the Veneration of the Bleeding Hosts at Wilsnack," in *Reform and Renewal in the Middle Ages and the Renaissance: Studies in Honor of Louis Pascoe, S.J.*, ed. Thomas M. Izbicki and Christopher M. Bellitto (Leiden, 2000), 208–223.

[143] Hus especially attacked the Wilsnack cult; see Bynum, *Wonderful Blood*, 26, 37, 108–109. Toke also denounced the cult at Wartenburg bei Wittenberg as fraudulent; see Bynum, *Wonderful Blood*, 32–33, 252.

[144] *Concilia Germaniae*, 5.35A, "In majorem confirmationem errorum, magna miraculorum volumina conscripta sunt." Bishop Otto described these wonders as *figmenta*, reported daily (*dietim*).

See. Furthermore, the priests of Wilsnack built sumptuously, absolved sins not under their jurisdiction, and made money selling badges (*signa*) to pilgrims.[145] Eventually, Pope Eugenius IV addressed the issue of the authenticity of the relics by issuing a letter endorsing them but requiring that a recently consecrated host be displayed with the relics as a precaution against involuntary idolatry.[146]

This type of authorization did not suffice for Cusanus, who saw possibilities of fraud and avarice in these miracle tales.[147] During his German legation, he issued a synodal decree at Salzburg in 1451 based on his legatine role as a guardian of the faith (*custos fidei*). He knew, he said, from reliable men that many flocked to certain places in the Germanic lands "to adore the precious blood of Christ our God, which species they think they have in no few reddened transformed hosts."[148] Concerned about people believing in these "wonder hosts" and adoring them, Nicholas ordered the clergy not to publicize them in the hope of receiving money. The legate wanted these hosts consumed by priests at mass so that their flocks might feed on the spiritual food (*spritualem refectionem*) given to them as a divine gift.[149] At Cologne in the following year, the legate ordered that, if a host transformed into bleeding flesh (*in cruentem carnem*) or yielded what apparently was blood, it should be hidden and not publicly displayed. Alms raisers were prohibited from telling the people about these "wonders."[150]

Even when Cusanus authorized the veneration of the "incorrupt" Andechs hosts, he urged caution in their veneration. These three hosts, two reputed to have been consecrated by Pope Gregory I and the third by Pope Leo IX, were kept as relics at the monastery on the Heiliger Berg.[151]

145 *Concilia Germaniae*, 5.36A–B.

146 Eugenius IV, *Decet Romanum* (1446) in Matthaeus Ludecus, *Historia von der Erfindung, Wunderwerken und Zerstörung des vermeinten heiligen Blutes zur Wilssnagk* (Wittenberg, 1586), no. XV. Eugenius IV also granted 100 days of indulgence for visiting the wonder host at Saint Gudele in Brussels; see *The Apostolic See and the Jews*, ed. Shlomo Simonshon, 3 vols. (Toronto, 1989) 2.828–830, no. 708.

147 Miracle tales about the sacrament also appeared in sermon *exempla*, e. g. *Friars' Tales: Thirteenth-Century exempla from the British Isles*, ed. David Jones (Manchester, 2011), 81.

148 *Acta Cusana: Quellen zur Lebensgeschichte des Nikolaus von Kues*, ed. Erich Meuthen and Hermann Hallauer, 3a (Hamburg, 1996), 980. Note that Cusanus, although advised by Heinrich Toke, a known foe of the cult, did not mention the Wilsnack cult by name; see Caroline W. Bynum, "A Matter of Matter: Two Cases of Blood Cult in the North in the Later Middle Ages," in *Medieval Paradigms: Essays in Honor of Jeremy DuQuesnay Adams*, ed. Stephanie Hayes-Healy, 2 (New York, 2005), 181–210 at 183–184.

149 *Acta Cusana*, 3a.980–981. 150 *Acta Cusana*, 3b.1504.

151 Mitchell B. Merback, *Pilgrimage and Pogrom: Violence, Memory and Visual Culture at the Host Miracle Shrines of Germany and Austria* (Chicago, 2012), 163–170. Caroline Bynum has suggested that politics lay behind Cusanus's decision; see *Wonderful Blood*, 147–148.

Cusanus said in a letter to the monks of Tegernsee that he regarded the documentation, a charter with seal, as reliable, allowing "a credible conjecture about the hosts." He even secured a papal grant of indulgences. Nonetheless, he tried to restrict their display to pilgrims once in a year: "I ordered them to be displayed once a year to a gathering of the people, and that they were to be kept locked up at other times."[152]

Previous investigations of wonder hosts already had included worries whether they had been consecrated. This certainly was true in the case of the Korneuburg host, which was of uncertain origin.[153] In 1338 the bishop of Passau, as Pope Eugenius would do later, ordered a consecrated host displayed with the wonder host of Pulkau to avoid the danger of idolatry.[154] This same caution may be behind a decree for the province of Reims saying a miracle could not be preached "without having consulted the ordinary" (*ordinario inconsulto*).[155]

Despite these worries, canon law had no universal strictures about these cults. The only text addressing such a relic was issued by Alexander III in the late twelfth century. A woman of the diocese of Arras had custody of a host "manifestly" changed to Christ's body. In it one could see flesh (*ut caro uideretur*). The host later passed from the parish, which was held by a cathedral canon, to bishop and chapter. A dispute arose focused on the revenues from visits to the relic, and the pope deputized two nearby bishops to see that the money went to repair of the parish church. The validity of the relic never seems to have been questioned. This text appeared in *Compilatio prima* in a title about tithes and offerings, but it was not included in the Gregorian Decretals.[156] Johannes Andreae warned against displaying relics outside their containers (*extra capsam*) out of avarice. The canonist also warned against alms seekers preaching errors and fables to raise money.[157]

A rare reflection in a canonistic context on the possibility of wonder hosts was offered by the Dominican cardinal Juan de Torquemada in his commentary on Gratian's *Decretum*. Torquemada discussed miraculous manifestations in the Eucharist at length. He said that the sacramental body was present "in a spiritual way, not a corporeal one" (*modo spirituali*

[152] Edmond Vansteenberghe, *Autour de la Docte Ignorance* (Münster, 1915), 150: Letter 26.

[153] Birgit Widel, "The Host on the Doorstep: Perpetrators, Victims, and Bystanders in an Alleged Host Desecration in Fourteenth Century Austria," in *Crime and Punishment in the Middle Ages: Mental-Historical Investigations of Basic Human Problems and Social Responses*, ed. Albrecht Classen and Connie L. Scarborough (Berlin, 2012), 299–345 at 303–317–318.

[154] Widel, "The Host on the Doorstep," 324 n. 84. [155] Mansi 26.10.

[156] *Quinque Compilationes Antiquae nec non Collectio canonum Lipsiensis*, ed. Emil Friedberg (Leipzig, 1882; Graz, 1956), 38: 1 Comp. 3.26.30.

[157] Johannes Andreae, *In quinque libros decretalium commentaria*, 3, fol. 231ra.

non corporali). Consequently the human eye could not see the body of Christ as it was present on the altar.[158] Adoration was acceptable only where it had to be held (*tenendum*) that the body of Christ remained under the miraculous appearances. Then the believer, he said, saw not Christ but "a species miraculously formed either in the eyes of the beholders or even in those sacramental dimensions."[159] There could be some changes in appearance, like the color of the host, without Christ departing and the worshiper being led into idolatry.[160] The flesh of Christ was not there bodily; but the appearance perceived was truthful, showing the body of Christ to be truly in the sacrament. This was not the same as "the tricks of mages" (*magorum praestigijs*).[161] Torquemada argued against locking up a transformed host in a pyx (*in pixide reseruatum*), not trying to enclose Christ "according to His proper species" (*secundum propriam species*). The point of the miracle was to show Christ was present in the sacrament itself.[162] Only if a wonder host retained the appearance of flesh (*sub specie carnis appareret*) was it to be placed among the relics (*cum reliquiis*) of that church.[163]

Prelates and writers on pastoral care, however, occasionally considered the possibility of a Eucharistic miracle. As early as Carolingian times, a lamb, the *Agnus Dei*, Christ, was reported to appear in the host.[164] This type of phenomenon was reported more often later. Thus John de Burough allowed for the possibility that a miracle might occur during mass. If the host manifested the appearance of an infant (*in forma pueri*)[165] after it had been consecrated, the priest was to rest content with spiritual

158 Juan de Torquemada *Commentaria super tertia parte decreti*, 121B: De cons. D. 2 c. 45.

159 Juan de Torquemada *Commentaria super tertia parte decreti*, 124A: De cons. D. 2 c. 45, "sed species miraculose formata vel in oculis videntium, vel etiam in ipsis sacramentalibus dimensionibus."

160 Juan de Torquemada *Commentaria super tertia parte decreti*, 124A: De cons. D. 2 c. 45, "vnde si hostia consecrata quocunque colore nigro vel rubeo tingeretur, adhuc remaneret ibi verum corpus Christ." Torquemada answered an argument of Durand de Saint-Pourçain saying that, with a change occurring in such an apparition, the body of Christ departed.

161 Juan de Torquemada *Commentaria super tertia parte decreti*, 124B: De cons. D. 2 c. 45.

162 Juan de Torquemada *Commentaria super tertia parte decreti*, 124B: De cons. D. 2 c. 45, "ad ostendenum per hanc miraculosam apparitionem, quòd in hoc sacramento est vere corpus Christi, & sanguis."

163 Juan de Torquemada *Commentaria super tertia parte decreti*, 124B: De cons. D. 2 c. 45.

164 Hans Geybels, *Adelman of Liège and the Eucharistic Controversy* (Louvain, 2013), 21. Writers like Berengar of Tours were not convinced by such stories, and even the theologians of Liège did not refer to them for support of the Real Presence; see Geybels, *Adelman of Liège*, 21–23.

165 The baby was the Christ Child understood as a sacrifice; see Leah Sinangalou Marcus, "The Christ Child as Sacrifice: A Medieval Tradition and the English Cycle Plays," *Speculum* 48 (1973), 491–509.

communion and place the miraculous host among the church's relics.[166] The Franciscan John of Erfurt said a host that transformed into flesh or a chalice that filled up with blood should be kept among a church's relics unless it reverted to the appearances of its species after mass.[167]

Nicholas of Ausimo, updating the *Summa Pisanella*, treated the same issue. He too said the host that appeared as a baby or bloody flesh was not to be consumed by the celebrant to whom it appeared. The bread no longer had the "nature of food" (*ratio cibi*). If the baby or flesh appeared to everyone, it was to be preserved as a relic. In support of this opinion, Nicholas appealed to the authority of Thomas Aquinas. He also discussed conflicting opinions about what the priest should do next. The priest might celebrate again, whether or not he consumed the "wonder host." The possibility of repeated manifestation in the host was considered. In that case, the priest might rest content with spiritual eating by sight, since the law could be flexible in such a case.[168] The *Supplementum Summae Pisanellae* also said that, in such a case, the eye might see "the accidents of flesh or a boy," but only the "sign" was seen. No human "bodily eye" beheld Christ Himself in the sacrament.[169]

The 1410 *Liber synodalis* of Salamanca too was concerned about miracles during mass, especially that Jesus might appear in a host on the altar as bloody flesh or a baby. The statute said the host was not to be

166 Johannes de Burough, *Pupilla oculi*, Cambridge, Corpus Christi College Manuscript 255, fol. xviii^{ra}, "Item si aliquando contingeret quod corpus Christi post consecrationem appareret sub alia specie quam panis: utputa in form pueri frustri carnis cruentute vel sanguinis: quia sic non haberet rationem cibi: non debet sumi ab eo cui sic apparet: se ab alio cui apparet in specie panis. Si autem ab omnibus in alia specie quam panis vel vini apparet: non deberet sumi sed cum reliquiis poni secundum Tho." On a child seen in the host, see Jody Enders, "Theatre Makes History: Ritual Murder by Proxy in the *Mistere de la Sainte Hostie*," *Speculum* 79 (2004), 991–1016.

167 Johannes de Erfordia, *Die Summa confessorum des Johannes von Erfurt*, ed. Norbert Brieskorn. 3 vols. (Frankfurt, 1980–1981), 3.869.

168 Nicholas of Ausimo, *Supplementum Summae Pisanellae* (Venezia, 1489), fol. I-2ra, "Quid agendum sit quando corpus Christi sic apparet in alia specie. Responsum Tho. vbi supra. cum usus huiusmodi sacramenti sit per manducationem: ideo quando apparet in specie pueri vel carnis cruentate uel simili non habet rationem cibi nec assumi debet ab eo cui sic apparet. Quid sit omnibus appararet. Debet cum reliquiis poni. A. Idem in suo cons. eo. ti. q. 87, vbi subditur. Idem dicit Albricus in scripto. Et sic appareret sacerdoti in altari in missa. dicunt quidam quod debet iterum celebrare et corpus Christi sumere. quidam secundum canones qui consecrat etiam sumere debet. de conse. di. 2. Relatum. Et si 2° hoc acciderit 3° Celebrare debet et sumere. Quidam autem dicunt quod in tali casu sufficit spiritualis manducatio: nec propter hoc efficitur transgressor constitutionis ecclesie. quia ad ea que frequentius accidunt leges aptantur."

169 Nicholas of Ausimo, *Supplementum Summae Pisanellae*, fol. I-2ra, "Utrum Christus in sacramento eucharistie aliquando uideatur oculo corporali sed tamen quandoque illa species panis circumsunditur quibusdam accidentibus carnis vel pueri que non sunt accidentia corporis Christi. vnde quamuis ibi expressiori signo uideatur: non tamen uidetur in specie propria."

consumed by a priest who saw these signs, but it could be eaten by anyone who saw the host as bread. If this sign appeared to all who were present, the host was to be reserved as a relic, according to the opinion of Thomas Aquinas. Then, the decree says, a second host could be consecrated, according to canon law and the opinions of some doctors.[170] Nicholas of Cusa, in his legatine constitutions of 1452 for the province of Cologne, was less accepting of such wonders appearing in the mass: "Similarly, if a host is transformed into bloody flesh or the appearance of blood, it should be hidden entirely and utterly according to the tradition of the law. Nor should it be displayed or shown to the people in any way lest they be seduced."[171]

Whatever the objections, these wonder cults flourished. Petitions to the Apostolic Penitentiary might request favors for such a site of pilgrimage. Thus the Holy Blood of Braunschweig was the subject of a spate of petitions. These asked for the ability to hold a procession "with the sacrosanct blood of Christ our lord and other relics" (*cum sacrosancto Cruore domini nostri et aliis reliquiis*) on major feasts, and a request to grant indulgences for the pilgrims followed. All this was supported by the local dukes.[172]

These cults were defended, not just attacked. The Holy Blood of Braunschweig was defended in writing by educated Benedictine monks Johannes Witten and Hermann Bansleben. They defended the relic as having been brought from the Holy Land by Henry the Lion, although it cannot be dated earlier than the thirteenth century.[173] This was a stronger pedigree than that of the Wilsnack hosts, but even this did not satisfy the Protestant Reformers. They treated such relics as idolatrous. Martin Luther attacked host cults, demanding the destruction of these relics. His wrath fell especially on Wilsnack. It is not surprising, therefore, to read that the Protestant pastor of Wilsnack burned the host relics in 1552.[174]

[170] *Synodicon Hispanum*, 4.139, 257–258. The Latin text cites De cons. D. 2 c. 11 in Gratian's *Decretum*. Similarly see Johannes de Friburgo, *Summa confessorum* (Paris, 1519), fol. cxxiii[va] (q. lxxxvi).

[171] Acta cusana, 3b.1496–1505 Nr. 2343 at 1504, "Similiter, si hostia transformatur in cruentem carnem seu in sanguinem apparentem, occultetur penitus et omnino iuxta tradicionem iuris nec populo quomodolibet publicetur seu ostendatur, ne seducatur."

[172] *Repertorium Poenitentiariae Germanicum*, 7 no. 2071–2076.

[173] These defenses of the relic were not universally accepted; see Bynum, *Wonderful Blood*, 38, 51–52, 64–66.

[174] Watanabe, "The German Church Shortly before the Reformation," 129.

Conclusion

Belief in the Real Presence, whether understood as transubstantiation or not, faced a more serious challenge in the Protestant Reformation than it had from Wyclif and the Lollards, Hus and Hussites. When the Dominican theologian Sylvester Prierias published his *Summa Silvestrina* in 1518, it included detailed recitation of traditional teachings about the Eucharist and the mass. Within two years, he was faced with defending the very theological foundations of these rites in his polemics against Martin Luther.[1] Luther and other Protestant reformers challenged many established beliefs and practices of the medieval Church Europe-wide, often successfully. Transubstantiation was among their targets; but they became divided over the doctrine to be put in its place, even while they were abolishing most medieval Eucharistic practices, including the adoration of the host.[2] Ironically, Luther, in an early work, accused the Unity of Czech Brethren, the heirs of the Utraquists, of idolatry for carrying the Eucharist in a monstrance during processions, even though he believed in that period that the sacrament should be adored during the liturgy.[3] Similarly, his first version of a reformed mass included the elevation, a concession to the past that some early supporters of the Reformation had difficulty with retaining. At first Andreas Bodenstein von Karlstadt accepted the practice, but eventually he criticized it. Karlstadt concluded that any adoration of the host was a

[1] Sylvester Mazzolini (Prierias), *Summa summarum quae Silvestrina dicitur* (Bologna, 1515), fol. 210vb–218vb, 467rb–472vb. It is worth noting that Prierias began his exposition of the sacrament with an emphasis on the Church's unity in the sacrament; see *Summa summarum quae Silvestrina dicitur*, fol. 210vb, "corpus Christi uerum et corpus Christi mysticum. id est. ecclesia uel unitas ecclesie." On Prierias, see Michael M. Tavuzzi, *Prierias: the Life and Works of Silvestro Mazzolini da Prierio, 1456–1527* (Durham, N.C., 1997).

[2] For reasons of brevity, no effort will be made to cite the full body of literature on sacramental issues in the Reformation and Counter Reformation; see, however, *A Companion to the Eucharist in the Reformation*, ed. Lee Palmer Wandel (Leiden, 2013).

[3] Zdeněk V. David, *Finding the Middle Way: The Utraquists' Liberal Challenge to Rome and Luther* (Baltimore, 2003), 67.

form of idolatry.[4] Even early on, while encouraging reception of communion under both species instead of spiritual communion by sight, in an early pamphlet he said of traditional priests: "What should be given to our mouths, they display over their heads."[5] Another of Karlstadt's criticisms of Luther's first reformed mass was that it was a version of what unreformed priests did. Karlstadt, like Luther in *The Babylonian Captivity of the Church*, described the elevation as deriving from Jewish rites that were not appropriate in a reformed liturgy.[6] Luther, late in life, claimed he was slow to abandon the elevation, which could be interpreted in a reformed manner, because of his argument with Karlstadt. He had by then (1540), however, come around to abandoning it since it had ceased being used in much of Germany.[7]

Luther and his followers were able to accept the Real Presence in some form,[8] but others were not. Reformed theology, evolved by Ulrich Zwingli and his successors, emphasized Christ's spiritual presence, commemoration of the Passion, and the corporate identity of the Church united in reception of the sacrament. Versions of this theology were embraced at Zurich, Strasbourg, and (eventually) Geneva.[9] Although they both rejected transubstantiation and the mass as a sacrifice, Luther and Zwingli so disagreed at the Colloquy of Marburg (1529) that the opponents of Rome remained divided thereafter.[10] Eventually a different terminology, that of the Lord's Supper, was developed in Reformed circles to replace the term "mass." Its celebration was intended to be plain, without the altar, lights, and vestments used by those loyal

[4] *The Eucharistic Pamphlets of Andreas Bodenstein von Karlstadt*, ed. Amy Nelson Burnett (Kirksville, Mo., 2011), 6–10.

[5] *The Eucharistic Pamphlets of Andreas Bodenstein von Karlstadt*, 51.

[6] *The Eucharistic Pamphlets of Andreas Bodenstein von Karlstadt*, 111–113; *Luther's Works*, 36.53. Luther said in the same work that the elevation could be used to provoke faith in the Christian, but he said it could be accompanied by words said aloud, even in German; see *Luther's Works*, 36.97–98. Luther did suggest the elevation might have led to the idea of the mass as a sacrifice; see *The Misuse of the Mass* (1521) in *Luther's Works*, 35.183–184.

[7] See Luther's *Brief Confession concerning the Sacrament* (1544); see *Luther's Works*, 38.313–317. In 1533, Luther said he had, while young, heard courtiers in Rome mock the consecration and the elevation; see *The Private Mass and the Consecration of Priests*, in *Luther's Works*, 38.166.

[8] Lee Palmer Wandel, *The Eucharist in the Reformation: Incarnation and Liturgy* (Cambridge, 2006), 94–138.

[9] These Reformers divided the medieval emphasis on the Real Presence (Lutherans) from the social aspects of communion (Reformed), according to Amy Nelson Burnett, "The Social History of Communion and the Reformation of the Eucharist," *Past and Present* (2011), 77–119.

[10] Both groups competed in the city of Augsburg, for example; see Joel Van Amberg, *A Real Presence: Religious and Social Dynamics of the Eucharistic Conflicts in Early Modern Augsburg* (Leiden, 2012), 203–249.

to Rome.[11] In his polemical exchange with John Calvin, Jacopo Sadoleto said that Catholics worshiped "the most true body of Christ." Dissidents used "dialectics and vain philosophy, to enclose the very Lord of the universe." In reply, John Calvin addressed the most metaphysical question of the Reformation debate over the Eucharist. He argued that "the glorious body of Christ must not be degraded to earthly elements," dismissing "your gross dogma of transubstantiation" as a fiction. The laity, the Reformer said, was encouraged to "gaze stupidly at the visible sign, without any understanding of the spiritual mystery."[12] (There is no room here to explore the Anabaptist or "Spiritualist" traditions, which can be described as focusing more on the Holy Spirit than on Christ.[13])

Liturgical change did not come easily; but it did occur eventually wherever the Reformation took root, as the English example shows. Luther expressed indifference to the use of bells, vestments, and other materials used in the past, that is, he did not believe their use was necessary for salvation.[14] Many reformers, however, would not tolerate any of these past usages. Thus the elevation of the host with the use of sacring bells was among the casualties of the English Reformation once its leaders were able to replicate the uses of reformed Zurich. This practice was forbidden under Edward VI in the 1549 *Book of Common Prayer*.[15] A prohibition of adoring, elevating, and carrying about the Eucharist was included in the 1552 Articles of Religion.[16] This eliminated not just the rite but the bells that accompanied it. Bells were confiscated for sale, and the proceeds went to support the Tudor court and its policies.[17] In 1553, the parish of St. Mary's at Hill in London surrendered its bell, among other things, to the Crown. This may be the same bell the churchwardens had paid for in 1504–1505

[11] Wandel, *The Eucharist in the Reformation*, 139–207. Martin Bucer retained some traditional elements in his sacramental theology; see Nicholas Thompson, *Eucharistic Sacrifice and Patristic Tradition in the Theology of Martin Bucer, 1534–1546* (Leiden, 2005).

[12] John Calvin and Jacopo Sadoleto, *A Reformation Debate*, trans. John C. Olin (New York, 1966), 41, 70–71.

[13] John D. Rempel, "Anabaptist Theologies of the Eucharist," in *A Companion to the Eucharist in the Reformation*, 115–137.

[14] *Confession concerning Christ's Supper* (1528) in *Luther's Works*, 35.370–371. Early on, Luther even thought a monstrance acceptable if it did not give the impression that the mass was a sacrifice; see *Treatise on the New Testament in Luther's Works*, 35.97.

[15] Caroline Litzenberger, *The English Reformation and the Laity: Gloucestershire, 1540–1580* (Cambridge, 1997), 64–65. John Hooper, bishop of Gloucester, forbade adoration of the consecrated host in his 1551 articles for visitations; see Litzenberger, *The English Reformation and the Laity*, 68.

[16] Edward Cardwell, *Synodalia: A Collection of Articles of Religion, Canons, and Proceedings of Convocations in the Province of Canterbury, from the Year 1547 to the Year 1717*, 1 (Oxford, 1842), 14.

[17] Eamon Duffy, *The Stripping of the Altars: Traditional Religion in England 1400–1580* (New Haven, Conn., 1992), 464.

and had given a new clapper, plus a new iron brace, in 1521–1522.[18] In the same period, most of the parishes subject to Saint Paul's reported hanging bells and hand bells that were surrendered to the Crown.[19] Morebath in Devon also admitted to having Sanctus and "lych" or funeral bells to surrender.[20] A leader of the Prayer Book Rebellion of 1549, the priest Robert Welsh, was hanged in irons clad in his vestments. Among the objects added to his chained body was a sacring bell.[21]

The elevation of the host, with the use of bells, was restored briefly in England under Mary; and prayers to be said upon seeing the consecrated bread were printed in new primers.[22] Marian visitation instructions also required kneeling before the Blessed Sacrament when it could be seen.[23] Failure to venerate the elevated host was regarded as a sign of heresy. The authorities were quick to note those who avoided seeing it by ducking their heads, hiding behind pillars, or even turning away.[24] The rite of elevation vanished from authorized church services once more under Elizabeth I. The 1552 prohibition of adoring the host reappeared verbatim in the Articles of Religion of 1562.[25] Another casualty of Elizabeth's ascension was the store of vessels, vestments, and bells added under Mary as replacements for objects confiscated under Edward VI.[26] The Elizabethan church added its own accessories, such as communion cups and a communion seat for those who were to receive the sacrament under both species.[27]

18 *The Medieval Records of a London City Church (St. Mary at Hill) A. D. 1420–1559*, ed. Henry Littlehales (London, 1904), 52, 255, 313.

19 *Visitations of Churches Belonging to St. Paul's Cathedral*, 115–122. On the Crown's financial gain from confiscations, see Duffy, *Stripping of the Altars*, 482–486.

20 Eamon Duffy, *The Voices of Morebath: Reformation and Rebellion in an English Village* (New Haven, Conn., 2001), 145. Morebath also had to pay to recover the clappers of the hanging bells after their removal was imposed by the Crown following the Prayer Book Rebellion; see Duffy, *The Voices of Morebath*, 145, 147–149.

21 Duffy, *Voices of Morebath*, 134.

22 Duffy, *The Stripping of the Altars*, 539; Duffy, *Marking the Hours: English People and Their Prayers 1240–1570* (New Haven, Conn., 2006), Plate 111, a printed copy of "O Jhesu Lorde, welcome thou be" in a primer produced under Mary and cancelled by an owner under Elizabeth.

23 Litzenberger, *The English Reformation and the Laity*, 101.

24 Eamon Duffy, *Fires of Faith: Catholic England under Mary Tudor* (New Haven, Conn., 2009), 131–133 notes other rites that also were used to detect heresy among those who failed to participate.

25 Cardwell, *Synodalia*, 1.47. See also Cardwell, *Synodalia*, 1.85 (1571).

26 Margaret Clark, "Northern Light? Parochial Life in a 'Dark' Corner of Tudor England," in *The Parish in English Life 1400–1600*, ed. Katherine L. French, Gary G. Gibbs, and Beat A. Kümin (Manchester, 1997), 56–73 at 64, 66.

27 Caroline Litzenberger, "St. Michael's, Gloucester, 1540–80: The Cost of Conformity in Sixteenth-Century England," in *The Parish in English Life 1400–1600*, 230–249 at 246–247. The parish might face contradictory instructions under Elizabeth. The Book of Common Prayer required using common bread in the Eucharist, but the Crown

The elevation also was a sore point wherever the Catholic and Reformed grudgingly coexisted, as they did in parts of continental Europe. Even near the end of the sixteenth century, an old woman in a parish of the German diocese of Bamberg cried out at the moment of the elevation against the Catholic priest imposed on the parish by the authorities.[28] The elevation was that controversial because it was a manifestation of belief that matter could be transformed into the body and blood of Christ. Faced with this form of idolatry, the Reformers had tried to take away not just belief in transubstantiation but its external manifestations. The Council of Trent replied by reaffirming the Roman theology of the Real Presence and the rite of the mass, together with decrees endorsing each of the seven sacraments.[29] Thus Session 13 issued a decree defending transubstantiation, the adoration of the Eucharist, Corpus Christi processions, and reservation of the sacrament, as well as addressing proper preparation for communion and the benefits of receiving the host. A list of errors about the Eucharist was issued, anathematizing those who denied transubstantiation.[30] The *Professio Fidei Tridentinae* issued by Pope Pius IV in 1564 reaffirmed the mass and transubstantiation. The text also affirmed that communion under one species sufficed for the faithful.[31] However, not all Catholic writings in this period were polemical. Thus the Theatine Lorenzo Scrupoli, in his *Spiritual Combat* (1589–1610), gave advice on both spiritual and sacramental communion, including preparation for receiving the Eucharist.[32]

Canon law was in decline as an intellectual pursuit by the late sixteenth century. Nonetheless, efforts to promote faith and discipline impacted the canonists. Gregory XIII (r. 1572–1585) commissioned a new edition of the Corpus Iuris Canonici (1687), entrusted to Pierre and François Pithou. In addition to the well-known medieval collections, the Pithou brothers added a *Liber septimus* containing newer texts, even those of

mandated using communion wafers instead; see Litzenberger, "St. Michael's, Gloucester," 247.

[28] Richard Ninness, "Protestants as Agents of the Counter-Reformation in the Prince-Bishopric of Bamburg," *The Sixteenth Century Journal* 40 (2009), 699–720 at 707.

[29] See, most recently, John O'Malley, *Trent: What Happened at the Council* (Cambridge, Mass., 2013), 120, 131, 189–193. Concessions of the chalice and mass in the vernacular for endangered regions north of the Alps were considered but not adopted; see O'Malley, *Trent*, 183–184, 186–190. These decrees eventually cut off French ideas of compromise with the Lutherans; see Luc Racaut, "The Sacrifice of the Mass and the Redefinition of Catholic Orthodoxy during the French Wars of Religion," *French History* 24 (2013), 20–39.

[30] *Decrees of the Ecumenical Councils*, 2.695–698.

[31] O'Malley, *Trent*, 284.

[32] *Theatine Spirituality: Selected Writings*, ed. William V. Hudon (New York, 1996), 191–199.

recent popes. This collection contained a statement of the Council of Florence on the Eucharist excerpted from the decree of union with the Greeks and a bull of Pius IV citing the Council of Trent in support of transubstantiation.[33] A short book of *Institutiones Iuris Canonici* also was included. It reaffirmed the mass as a sacrifice, the use of the traditional elements, wheat bread and watered wine, which were transformed by the priest's words in the sacrament of unity and charity.[34]

Tridentine Catholicism was planted in the New World, regularizing the practices of missionaries and newly created hierarchies. Thus the Third Mexican Council (1585) decreed that the faithful, including indigenous converts, must be taught the seven sacraments. It ordered use of the missal and breviary of Trent, but it also restated such practices as renewing the reserved sacrament every seventh day and keeping it in a locked tabernacle. The host was to be reverently carried to the sick, just as was required in Europe. Corpus Christi processions were to be held but with men and women kept apart.[35] The translation of Christian concepts into indigenous languages was not easy, and misunderstandings could easily arise. One need only understand that the host translated into Nahua as *iztac tlaxcaltzintli*, "the little white tortilla," to comprehend the pastoral difficulties faced by friars and secular clergy in the New World.[36]

Catholic apologists like Robert Bellarmine defended both transubstantiation and the mass as a sacrifice. Bellarmine described those who advocated abolition of the "Eucharistic sacrifice" as "precursors of the Antichrist."[37] Such apologetics did not undo the Reformation, but Counter Reformation Catholicism survived not just Protestant critiques but the dissident opinions of writers like Tommaso Campanella and Giordano Bruno.[38] The elevation continued to be in use in the Latin

[33] *Liber septimus* in *Corpus juris canonici Gregorii XIII pontificis maximi jussu editum a Petro Pithoeo, et Francisco fratre, jurisconsultis* ... (Leipzig, 1695), 1–2. Texts by Pius V on the mass appear at *Liber septimus*, 46.

[34] *Institutiones Iuris Canonici* in *Corpus juris canonici Gregorii XIII*, 104.

[35] Mansi 34B.1026–1028, 1093, 1127, 1131, 1133–1134. These decrees were reviewed and revised in Rome; see Ernest J. Burrus, "The Third Mexican Council (1585) in the Light of the Vatican Archives," *The Americas* 23 (1967), 390–407.

[36] Jaime Lara, "The Spanish New World," in *A Companion to the Eucharist in the Reformation*, 293–319.

[37] Bernard Bourdin, *The Theological-Political Origins of the Modern State: The Controversy Between James I of England & Cardinal Bellarmine*, trans. Susan Pickford (Washington, D.C., 2010), 212.

[38] Thomas F. Mayer, *The Roman Inquisition on the Stage of Italy, ca. 1590–1640* (Philadelphia, 2014), 53, 115. 117. Marcantonio De Dominis thought Protestants would come back to the fold if Catholicism abandoned transubstantiation; see Mayer, *The Roman Inquisition on the Stage of Italy*, 148.

mass worldwide. The Tridentine missal of 1570 provided detailed instructions for the elevation, including that the attending *minister* (acolyte) should help the priest by holding up the hem of the chasuble so that it did not impede the elevation.[39] Meanwhile paraliturgical rites like Benediction of the Blessed Sacrament and Forty Hours Devotion added dramatic manifestations of belief in the Real Presence outside the mass. These rites combined music, incense, and lights to make that affirmation more dramatic and banish doubt in the minds of the beholders of the host.[40] Affirmation of the Real Presence in the rites of the Church was so important that an artist as busy as Gian Lorenzo Bernini took time out in 1628 to provide spectacular lighting effects for Forty Hours at Carnival time.[41] Peter Paul Rubens provided a spectacular affirmation of the Real Presence in his *Triumph of the Eucharist*, a series of panels designed as patterns for tapestries. One, *Triumphus ecclesiae*, shows a monstrance being carried on a float by *ecclesia*, who is being crowned with the papal tiara. Other panels affirmed the triumph of the sacrament over idolatry and heresy. These pictures were turned into tapestries for Isabel Clara Eugenia, an *infanta* of Spain in Antwerp, in the religiously divided Low Countries.[42]

The belief in transubstantiation and its affirmation in the elevation of the host remained fixed in canon law despite the Protestant challenge, with texts like Honorius III's decretal *Sane* retaining their validity. Only in the 1917 *Codex Iuris Canonici* would the elevation vanish from canon law, its regulation left to the rubrics provided by liturgists, with approval given by the Roman curia for any changes in practice.[43] Only with the liturgical *aggiornamento* mandated by the Second Vatican Council (1962–1965) would the Tridentine mass undergo major changes, including widespread

[39] *Missale Romanum ex Decreto Sacrosancti Concilii Tridentini restitutum* (Antwerp, 1577), 23–24, cited from Google Books, accessed on April 22, 2011.

[40] *The Forms and Orders of Western Liturgy from the Tenth to the Eighteenth Century: A Historical Introduction and Guide for Students and Musicians* (Oxford, 1991), 163–164; James L. Connolly, "Benediction of the Blessed Sacrament: Its History and Present State," *The Ecclesiastical Review* 85 (1931), 449–463.

[41] Franco Mormando, *Bernini: His Life and His Rome* (Chicago, 2011), 167–168.

[42] Alejandro Vergara, *Spectacular Rubens: The Triumph of the Eucharist* (Malibu, 2014), 57, 68–75, 91–92, 95,102–103.

[43] See Book III title 3, De sanctissima Eucharistia, *Codex Iuris Canonici, 1917* [http://www.catho.org/9.php?d=fo] accessed on May 1, 2011. See especially Can. 818, "Reprobata quavis contraria consuetudine, sacerdos celebrans accurate ac devote servet rubricas suorum ritualium librorum, caveatque ne alias caeremonias aut preces proprio arbitrio adiungat." As James Brundage has noted, much needs to be done to track the decisions of curial congregations in the post-Tridentine period; see *Medieval Canon Law* (London, 1995), 183 no. 9. The decisions of the Congregation of Rites would be most relevant to this inquiry.

use of the vernacular and a revised missal. Communion with bread and wine was permitted. Liturgical practices like the elevation of the host and paraliturgical observances like adoration of the host displayed at Benediction were deemphasized. Despite conservative reactions, the Tridentine mass and other practices, tied to a strong emphasis on the Real Presence, have not been entirely restored.[44]

[44] Philip Kennedy, *Christianity: An Introduction* (New York, 2011), 242–248; Roger E. Reynolds, "Eucharistic Adoration in the Carolingian Era?: Exposition of Christ in the Host," *Peregrinations: Journal of Medieval Art & Architecture* 4/2 (2013), 70–153.

Select bibliography

Primary sources

Acta Cusana: Quellen zur Lebensgeschichte des Nikolaus von Kues, ed. Erich Meuthen and Hermann Hallauer, vol. 1, pt. 3 (Hamburg: Felix Meiner Verlag, 1996).

Akten zur Reform des Bistums Brixen, ed. Heinz Hürten, Cusanus-Texte 5, fasc. 1 (Heidelberg: Carl Winter Verlag, 1960).

Amalar of Metz, *On the Liturgy*, ed. Eric Knibbs, 2 vols. (Cambridge, Mass.: Harvard University Press, 2014).

Anselm of Lucca, *Collectio canonum una cum collectione minore*, ed. Friedrich Thaner (Innsbruck: Libraria Academica Wagneriana, 1906–1915; Aalen: Scientia Verlag, 1965).

Antoninus of Florence, *Confessionale "Defecerunt scrutantes scrutinio"* (Köln, 1470).

Antonius de Butrio, *Super [-sex] libris decretalium* . . . 6 vols. (Venezia, 1575–1578; Torino: Bottega d'Erasmo, 1967).

Bannister, A. T., "Visitation Returns of the Diocese of Hereford in 1397," *The English Historical Review* 44 (1929): 279–289, 444–453, 45 (1930): 92–101, 444–463.

Bodenstein von Karlstadt, Andreas, *The Eucharistic Pamphlets of Andreas Bodenstein von Karlstadt*, ed. and trans. Amy Nelson Burnett (Kirksville, Mo.: Truman State University Press, 2011).

Burchardus Worm, *Decretum*, PL 140.537–1057, accessed via the *Patrologia Latina Database*, August 5, 2012.

Catholic England: Faith, Religion and Observance before the Reformation, trans. R. N. Swanson (Manchester: Manchester University Press, 1993).

Concilia Germaniae, ed. Johann Friedrich Schannat and Joseph Hartzheim, vol. 5 (Köln, 1763), accessed via Google Books, February 13, 2014.

Constitutiones Concilii Quarti Lateranensis una cum commentariis glossatorum, ed. Antonio García García (Città del Vaticano: Biblioteca Apostolica Vaticana, 1981).

Corpus Iuris Canonici, ed. Emil Friedberg, 2 vols. (Leipzig: Tauchnitz, 1879; Graz: Akademische Druck- u. Verlagsanstalt, 1959).

Coulton, G. G., "A Visitation of the Archdeaconry of Totnes in 1342," *The English Historical Review* 26 (1911): 108–124.

Councils & Synods with Other Documents Relating to the English Church, 2 vols. in 4, vol. 1, ed. Dorothy Whitelock, Martin Brett, and Christopher N. L. Brooke

(Oxford: Clarendon Press, 1981); vol. 2, ed. F. M. Powicke and C. R. Cheney (Oxford: Clarendon Press, 1964).

Decrees of the Ecumenical Councils, ed. Norman P. Tanner, 2 vols. (Washington, D.C.: Georgetown University Press, 1990).

Decretales Gregorii noni pontificis ... (Lyon, 1556).

Decretales Pseudo-Isidorianae et capitula Angilramni, ed. Paul Hinschius (Leipzig: Tauchnitz, 1863; Aalen: Scientia Verlag, 1963).

Delisle, Léopold, "Visites pastorales de maître Henri de Vezelai, archidiacre d'Hiémois, en 1267 et 1268," *Bibliothèque de l'École des Chartes* 54 (1893), 457–467.

Denzinger, Heinrich, *The Sources of Catholic Dogma*, trans. Roy J. Deferrari (Fitzwilliam, New Hamp., 2002).

Devotio Moderna: Basic Writings, ed. John Van Engen (Mahwah: Paulist Press, 1988).

Franciscus de Zabarellis, *Lectura super clementinis* .... (Venezia, 1481), accessed on the website of the Bayerische Staatsbibliothek, Jan. 2, 2014.

Geoffrey of Trani, *Summa perutilis et valde necessaria do. Goffredi de Trano super titulis decretalium* ... (Lyon, 1519; Aalen: Scientia Verlag, 1968).

Gratian, *Decretum divi Gratiani* ... (Lyon, 1554).

Gui, Bernard, *The Inquisitor's Guide: A Medieval Manual on Heretics*, trans. Janet Shirley (Welwyn Garden City: Ravenhall Books, 2006).

Gui, Bernard, *Manuel de l'inquisietur*, ed. Guillaume Mollat, 2 vols. (Paris: Les Belles Lettres, 1964).

Guido de Monte Rocherii, *Handbook for Curates*, trans. Anne T. Thayer (Washington, D.C.: Catholic University of America Press, 2011).

Guido de Monte Rocherii, *Manipulus curatorum* (London, 1508), accessed via *Early English Books Online*, November 29, 2014.

Guillelmus de Monte Lauduno, *Apparatus* ... *super Clementinas* ... (Paris, 1517), accessed via Google Books, January 1, 2014.

Guillelmus Durantis senior. *Rationale divinorum officiorum*, ed. Anselm Davril and Timothy M. Thibodeau, 3 vols., Corpus Christianorum Continuatio Medievalis 140 (Turnhout: Brepols, 1995–2000).

Henricus de Segusio (Hostiensis), *Henrici de Segusio Cardinalis Hostiensis Decretalium commentaria*, 2 vols. (Venezia, 1581; Torino: Bottega d'Erasmo, 1965).

Henricus de Segusio (Hostiensis), *Summa domini Henrici cardinalis Hostiensis* ... (Lyon, 1537; Aalen: Scientia Verlag, 1962).

Huguccio, *Summa decretorum*, Admont Stiftsbibliothek MS 7.

Innocent IV, *Commentaria apparatus in V libros decretalium* (Frankfurt, 1570; Frankfurt: Minerva, 1968).

Inquisitors and Heretics in Thirteenth-Century Languedoc: Edition and Translation of Toulouse Inquisition Depositions, 1273–1282, ed. Peter Biller, Caterina Bruschi, and Shelagh Sneddon (Leiden: Brill, 2011).

Ivo Carnotensis, *Decretum*, PL 161.48–1022, accessed via the *Patrologia Latina Database*, September 7, 2012.

Ivo Carnotensis, *Epistola 63*, PL 162.77–81, accessed via the *Patrologia Latina Database*, September 7, 2012.

Johannes Andreae, *In primum [-sextum] decretalium librum novella commentaria* ... (Venezia, 1581; Torino: Bottega d'Erasmo, 1966).

Johannes de Erfordia, *Die Summa confessorum des Johannes von Erfurt*, ed. Norbert Brieskorn, 3 vols. (Frankfurt: Lang, 1980–1981).

Johannes de Friburgo, *Summa confessorum* (Paris, 1519), accessed via Google Books, January 4, 2014.

Johannes de Imola, *Super clementinis* (Lyon, 1525), accessed via Google Books, December 23, 2013.

Lanfranc of Canterbury and Guitmund of Aversa, *On the Body and Blood of the Lord*, trans. Mark G. Vaillancourt (Washington, D.C.: Catholic University of America Press, 2009).

Lothar of Segni [Innocent III], *De sacro altaris mysterio libri sex*, PL 217.763–916, accessed via the *Patrologia Latina Database*, January 2, 2012.

Lothar of Segni [Innocent III], *Liber de quadrapartita specie nuptiarum*, PL 217.921–968, accessed via the *Patrologia Latina Database*, January 2, 2012.

Lyndwood, William, *Lyndwood's Provinciale: The Text of the Canons Therein Contained, Reprinted from the Translation Made in 1534*, ed. J. V. Bullard and H. Chalmer Bell (London: Faith Press, 1929).

Lyndwood, William, *Provinciale, (seu Constitvtiones Angliæ,) continens constitutiones provinciales quatuordecim archiepiscoporum Cantuariensium, viz. á Stephano Langtono ad Henricum Chichleium* (Oxford, 1679; Farnborough: Gregg, 1968).

Manuale et processionale ad usum insignis ecclesiae Eboracensus (Durham: Andrews & Co., 1975).

Medieval Handbooks of Penance: A Translation of the Principal "libri poenitentiales" and Selections from Related Documents, ed. John T. McNeill and Helena M. Gamer (New York: Columbia University Press, 1938).

Mirk, John, *Instructions for Parish Priests*, ed. Edward Peacock, 2nd ed. (London Early English Text Society, 1902; Woodbridge: Boydell & Brewer, 1996).

Nicholas de Tudeschis (Panormitanus), *Apparatus solemnis ... in Clementinas de nuovo correctus cum additionibus* ... (Lyon, 1513), accessed via Google Books, January 4, 2014.

Nicholas Eimeric, *Directorium inquisitorum*, ed. Francisco Peña (Rome, 1587).

The Occult in Medieval Europe, ed. P. G. Maxwell-Stuart (Basingstoke, Palgrave Macmillan, 2005).

Panormia Project, www.documentacatholicaomnia.eu/03d/1040–1116,_Ivo_Carno tensis,_Panormia,_LT.pdf, accessed on September 15, 2012.

Pastors and the Care of Souls in Medieval England, ed. John Shinners and William J. Dohar (Notre Dame, Ind.: University of Notre Dame Press, 1998).

Paucapalea, *Die Summa des Paucapalea über das Decretum Gratiani*, ed. Johann Friedrich von Schulte (Giessen: Roth, 1890; Aalen: Scientia Verlag, 1965).

Paulus de Liazariis, *Super clementinis*, University of Notre Dame MS Latin e.3.

Peter Lombard, *The Sentences*, trans. Giulio Silano, 4 vols. (Toronto, 2010).

Pontal, Odette, *Les statuts synodaux français du XIIIe siècle*, 5 vols. (Paris: Bibliothèque Nationale, 1971–2001).

Quinque compilationes antiquae nec non Collectio canonum Lipsiensis, ed. Emil Friedberg (Leipzig: Tauchnitz, 1882; Graz: Akademische Druck- und Verlagsanstalt, 1956).

Regestre d'inquisition de Jacques Fournier (éveque de Pamiers) 1318–1325, ed. Jean Duvernay, 3 vols. (Paris: Mouton, 1978).

Regino of Prüm, *Das Sendhandbuch des Regino von Prüm*, ed. F. W. H. Wasserschleben and Wilfried Hartmann (Darmstadt: Wissenschaftliche Buchgesellschaft, 2004).

The Register of John Chandler Dean of Salisbury 1404–1417, ed. T. C. B. Timmins (Devizes: Wiltshire Record Society, 1984).

Repertorium poenitentiariae Germanicum: Verzeichnis der in den Supplikenregistern der Pönitentiarie Kirchen, und Orte des Deutschen Reiches, 9 vols. (Tübingen: Niemeyer, 1996–2014).

Rufinus, *Summa decretorum*, ed. Heinrich Singer (Paderborn: Schöningh, 1902; Aalen: Scientia Verlag, 1963).

Sacrorum Conciliorum nova et amplissima collectio, ed. Giovan Domenico Mansi et al., 53 vols. (Paris: H. Welter, 1901–1927; Graz: Akademische Druck- u. Verlangsanstalt, 1961).

Sicardi Cremonensis episcopi Mitralis de officiis, ed. Gábor Sarbak and Lorenz Weinrich, Corpus Christianorum Continuatio Medievalis 228 (Turnhout: Brepols, 2008).

Sicardus Cremonensis, *Summa decretorum*, Bamberg Staatsbibliothek Can. MS 38, fol. 56ra-116ra.

Simon de Bisignano, *Summa decretorum*, Augsburg Staats- und Stadtbibliothek MS 1, fol. 1ra–72vb.

Simon de Bisignano, *Summa in Decretum Simonis Bisiniansis*, ed. Petrus V. Aimone Braida (Città del Vaticano: Biblioteca Apostolica Vaticana, 2014).

Stephen of Tournai, *Die Summa über das Decretum Gratiani*, ed. Johann Friedrich von Schulte (Giessen: Roth, 1891; Aalen: Scientia Verlag, 1965).

Synodicon Hispanum, ed. Antonio Garcia y Garcia and Francisco Cantelar Rodriguez, 11 vols. (Madrid: Biblioteca de Autores Cristianos, 1981–2013).

The Synodicum Nicosiense and Other Documents of the Latin Church of Cyprus, 1196–1373, ed. Christopher David Schabel (Nicosia: Cyprus Research Center, 2001).

Synody a statuta Olomoucké diecéze období středověku, ed. Pavel Krafl (Praha: Historický ústav, 2003).

Thomae de Chobham summa confessorum, ed. F. Broomfield (Louvain: Éditions Nauwelaerts, 1968).

Tracts on the Mass, ed. J. Wickham Legg (London: Henry Bradshaw Society, 1904).

Visconti, Federico, *Les sermons et la visite pastorale de Federico Visconti archevêque de Pise (1253–1277)*, ed. Nicole Bériou, Isabelle le Masne de Chermont, Pascale Bourgain, and Marina Innocenti (Roma: École Française de Rome, 2001).

Visitační protokol Pražského arcijáhna pavla z janovic z let 1379–1382, ed. Iavan Hlaváček and Zdeňka Hledíková (Praha: Akademia, Nakladatelství Česklovenské akademie věd, 1973).

Visitations in the Diocese of Lincoln 1517–1531, ed. A. Hamilton Thompson, 3 vols. (Hereford: Lincoln Record Society, 1940).

Visitations of Churches belonging to St. Paul's Cathedral, in 1297 and in 1458, ed. W. Sparrow Simpson (Westminster: Printed for the Camden Society, 1895; New York: Johnson Reprint Corporation).

Visites archdidiaconales de Josas, ed. J.-M. Alliot (Paris: Picard, 1902).

William Durand, *On the Clergy and Their Vestments: A New Translation of Books 2 – 3 of the Rationale divinorum officiorum*, trans. Timothy M. Thibodeau (Scranton: University of Scranton Press, 2010).

William Durand, *Rationale IV: On the Mass and Each Action Pertaining to It*, trans. Timothy M. Thibodeau (Turnhout: Brepols, 2013).

William of Pagula, *Oculus sacerdotis*, University of Pennsylvania MS Codex 721.

Witch Beliefs and Witch Trials in the Middle Ages: Documents and Readings, ed. P. G. Maxwell-Stuart (London: Continuum, 2011).

Secondary Sources

Adams, Marilyn McCord, *Some Later Medieval Theologies of the Eucharist: Thomas Aquinas, Giles of Rome, Duns Scotus and William of Ockham* (Oxford: Oxford University Press, 2012).

Beckwith, Sarah, *Christ's Body: Identity, Culture and Society in Late Medieval Writings* (London: Routledge, 1993).

Browe, Peter, "Die Eucharistie als Zaubermittel im Mittelalter," *Archiv für Kulturgeschichte* 20 (1930), 134–154.

Browe, Peter, *Die Verehrung der Eucharistie im Mittelalter* (Roma: Herder, 1967)

Brundage, James A., *Medieval Canon Law* (London: Longman, 1995).

Bynum, Caroline Walker, *Christian Materiality: An Essay on Religion in Late Medieval Europe* (Boston: Zone Books, 2011).

Bynum, Caroline Walker, *Holy Feast and Holy Fast: The Religious Significance of Food to Medieval Women* (Berkeley: University of California Press, 1987).

Bynum, Caroline Walker, *Wonderful Blood: Theology and Practice in Late Medieval Northern Germany and Beyond* (Philadelphia: University of Pennsylvania Press, 2007).

Cheney, C. R., *English Synodalia* (London: Oxford University Press, 1968).

A Companion to the Eucharist in the Middle Ages, ed. Ian Christopher Levy, Gary Macy, and Kristen Van Ausdall (Leiden: Brill, 2012).

Coulet, Noël, *Les visites pastorals* (Turnhout: Brepols, 1977).

Cushing, Kathleen G., *Papacy and Law in the Gregorian Revolution: The Canonistic Work of Anselm of Lucca* (Oxford: Oxford University Press, 1998).

Duffy, Eamon, *Marking the Hours: English People and Their Prayers 1240–1570* (New Haven, Conn.: Yale University Press, 2006).

Duffy, Eamon, *The Stripping of the Altars: Traditional Religion in England 1400–1580* (New Haven: Yale University Press, 1992).

Duffy, Eamon, *The Voices of Morebath: Reformation and Rebellion in an English Village* (New Haven: Yale University Press, 2001).

French, Katherine L., *The Good Women of the Parish: Gender and Religion after the Black Death* (Philadelphia: University of Pennsylvania Press, 2008).

French, Katherine L., *The People of the Parish: Community Life in a Late Medieval English Diocese* (Philadelphia: University of Pennsylvania Press, 2001).

Geybels, Hans, *Adelman of Liège and the Eucharistic Controversy* (Louvain: Peeters, 2013).

Goering, Joseph, "The Invention of Transubstantiation," *Traditio* (1991), 147–170.

The History of Medieval Canon Law in the Classical Period, 1140–1234: From Gratian to the Decretals of Pope Gregory IX, ed. Wilfried Hartmann and Kenneth Pennington (Washington, D.C.: Catholic University of America Press, 2008).

Izbicki, Thomas M., "Baptism, Confirmation and the Eucharist," in *The Cambridge Companion to Medieval Canon Law*, ed. Anders Winroth and John Wei (forthcoming).

Izbicki, Thomas M., "The Bleeding Host of Dijon: Its Place in the History of Eucharistic Devotion," in *Saluting Aron Gurevich: Essays in History, Literature and Other Related Subjects*, ed. Yelena Mazour-Matusevich and Alexandra Shecket Korros (Leiden: Brill, 2010), 227-246.

Izbicki, Thomas M., "How the Language of Transubstantiation Entered Medieval Canon Law," in *Proceedings of the Thirteenth International Congress of Medieval Canon Law* (forthcoming).

Izbicki, Thomas M., "*Manus temeraria*: Custody of the Eucharist in Medieval Canon Law," in *Proceedings of the Thirteenth International Congress of Medieval Canon Law: Esztergom*, 3–8 August 2008, ed. Peter Erdö and Szabolcs Anzelm Szuromi (Città del Vaticano: Biblioteca Apostolica Vaticana, 2010), 539–532.

King, Archdale, *Eucharistic Reservation in the Western Church* (London: Mowbray, 1965).

Kumler, Aden, "The Multiplicity of the Species: Eucharistic Morphology in the Middle Ages," *Res: Anthropology and Aesthetics* 59/60 (2011), 179–191.

Landau, Peter, "Die Dekretsumme *Fecit Moyses tabernaculum* – ein weiteres Werk der Kölner Kanonistik," *Zeitschrift der Savigny-Stiftung für Rechtsgeschichte, Kanonistische Abteilung* 127 (2010), 602–608.

Macy, Gary, *The Banquet's Wisdom: A Short History of the Theologies of the Lord's Supper* (New York: Paulist Press, 1992).

Macy, Gary, "The Dogma of Transubstantiation in the Middle Ages," *Journal of Ecclesiastical History* 45 (1994), 11–41.

Macy, Gary, "Nicolas Eymeric and the Condemnation of Orthodoxy," in *The Devil, Heresy and Witchcraft in the Middle Ages: Essays in Honor of Jeffrey B. Russell*, ed. Alberto Ferreiro (Leiden: Brill, 1998), 369–381.

Macy, Gary, *Theologies of the Eucharist in the Early Scholastic Period* (Cambridge: Cambridge University Press, 1984).

Macy, Gary, *Treasures from the Storehouse: Medieval Religion and the Eucharist* (Collegeville, Minn.: Liturgical Press, 1999).

Merback, Mitchell B., *Pilgrimage and Pogrom: Violence, Memory and Visual Culture at the Host-Miracle Shrines of Germany and Austria* (Chicago: University of Chicago Press, 2012).

Miramon, Charles de, "Innocent III, Huguccio de Ferrare et Hubert de Pirovano: Droit canonique, théologie et philosophie à Bologne dans les années 1180," in *Medieval Church Law and the Origins of the Western Legal Tradition. A Tribute to Kenneth Pennington*, ed. Wolfgang P. Müller and Mary

E. Sommar (Washington, D.C.: Catholic University of America Press, 2006), 320–346.

Pixton, Paul B., *The German Episcopacy and the Implementation of the Decrees of the Fourth Lateran Council, 1216–1245: Watchmen on the Tower* (Leiden: Brill, 1995).

Pontal, Odette, *Les statuts synodaux* (Turnhout: Brepols, 1975).

Reynolds, Roger E., "Christ's Money: Eucharistic Azyme Hosts in the Ninth Century According to Bishop Eldefonsus of Spain: Observations on the Origin, Meaning, and Context of a Mysterious Revelation," *Peregrinations: Journal of Medieval Art & Architecture* 4/2 (2013), 1–69.

Rolker, Christof, *Canon Law and the Letters of Ivo of Chartres* (Cambridge: Cambridge University Press, 2010).

Rolker, Christof, "The Earliest Work of Ivo of Chartres: The Case of Ivo's Eucharist Florilegium and the Canon Law Collections Attributed to Him," *Zeitschrift der Savigny-Stiftung für Rechtsgeschichte, Kanonistische Abteilung* 124 (2007), 109–127.

Rubin, Miri, *Corpus Christi: The Eucharist in Late Medieval Culture* (Cambridge: Cambridge University Press, 1991).

Rubin, Miri, *Gentile Tales: The Narrative Assault on Late Medieval Jews* (New Haven, Conn.: Yale University Press, 1999).

Schabel, Christopher, "Martyrs and Heretics, Intolerance of Intolerance: The Execution of Thirteen Greek Monks in Cyprus in 1231," in Schabel, *Greeks, Latins, and the Church in Early Frankish Cyprus*, Variorum Reprints (Farnham: Ashgate, 2010), III, 1–33.

Schabel, Christopher, "The Quarrel over Unleavened Bread in Western Theology, 1234–1439," in *Greeks, Latins, and Intellectual History 1204–1500*, ed. Martin Hinterberger and Schabel (Leuven: Peeters, 2011), 85–127.

Snoek, G. J. C., *Medieval Piety from Relics to the Eucharist: A Process of Mutual Interaction* (Leiden: Brill, 1995).

Swanson, R. N., *Religion and Devotion in Europe, c. 1215–c. 1515* (Cambridge: Cambridge University Press, 1995).

Tabacco, Giovanni, *Le metamorfosi della potenza sacerdotale nell'alto Medioevo*, ed. Grado Giovanni Merlo (Brescia: Morcellina, 2012).

Thibodeau, Timothy M., "The Doctrine of Transubstantiation in Durand's *Rationale*," *Traditio* 51 (1996), 308–317.

Thibodeau, Timothy M., "The Influence of Canon Law on Liturgical Exposition c.1100–1300," *Sacris erudiri* 37 (1997), 185–202.

Trexler, Richard, *Synodal Law in Florence and Fiesole, 1306–1518* (Città del Vaticano: Biblioteca Apostolica Vaticana, 1971), 57.

Van Engen, John, "Observations on *De consecratione*," in *Proceedings of the Sixth International Congress of Medieval Canon Law, Berkeley, California, 28 July–2 August 1980*, ed. Stephan Kuttner and Kenneth Pennington (Città del Vaticano: Biblioteca Apostolica Vaticana, 1985), 309–320.

Vodola, Elisabeth, "Legal Precision in the Decretist Period: A Note on the Development of the Glosses on *De consecratione* with Reference to the Meaning of *cautio sufficiens*," *Bulletin of Medieval Canon Law, n.s.* 6 (1976), 55–63.

Walters, Barbara R., Vincent J. Corrigan, and Peter T. Ricketts, *The Feast of Corpus Christi* (University Park, Pa.: Pennsylvania State University Press, 2006).

Watanabe, Morimichi, "The German Church Shortly before the Reformation: Nicolaus Cusanus and the Veneration of the Bleeding Hosts at Wilsnack," in *Reform and Renewal in the Middle Ages and the Renaissance: Studies in Honor of Louis Pascoe, S.J.*, ed. Thomas M. Izbicki and Christopher M. Bellitto (Leiden: Brill, 2000), 208–223.

Wieck, Rogers S., *Illuminating Faith: The Eucharist in Medieval Life and Art* (New York: The Morgan Museum and Library, 2014).

Winroth, Anders. *The Making of Gratian's Decretum* (Cambridge: Cambridge University Press, 2000).

Index